MW00579473

AGENTS OF SUBVERSION

AGENTS OF SUBVERSION

The Fate of John T. Downey and the CIA's Covert War in China

John Delury

CORNELL UNIVERSITY PRESS   ITHACA AND LONDON

Cornell University Press gratefully acknowledges receipt of a publication grant from the Chiang Ching-kuo Foundation for International Scholarly Exchange.

First published 2022 by Cornell University Press

Printed in the United States of America

Library of Congress Cataloging-in-Publication Data

Names: Delury, John, author.
Title: Agents of subversion : the fate of John T. Downey and the CIA's covert war in China / John Delury.
Description: Ithaca [New York] : Cornell University Press, 2022. | Includes bibliographical references and index.
Identifiers: LCCN 2021057492 (print) | LCCN 2021057493 (ebook) | ISBN 9781501765971 (hardcover) | ISBN 9781501765995 (epub) | ISBN 9781501765988 (pdf)
Subjects: LCSH: Downey, John T., 1930–2014. | United States. Central Intelligence Agency—History—20th century. | Espionage, American—China—History—20th century. | Intelligence officers—United States—Biography. | Spies—United States—Biography. | Intelligence service—United States—History—20th century. | Cold War. | United States—Foreign relations—China. | China—Foreign relations—United States. | China—Politics and government—1949-1976.
Classification: LCC JK468.I6 D454 2022 (print) | LCC JK468.I6 (ebook) | DDC 327.1273—dc23/eng/20220322
LC record available at https://lccn.loc.gov/2021057492
LC ebook record available at https://lccn.loc.gov/2021057493

For Jeong-eun

Contents

AGENTS OF SUBVERSION

PROLOGUE

Hong Kong was already a spy's paradise when war between American and Chinese forces in Korea gave added impetus to covert activity in the British colony. Under the anxious eye of the colonial police, CIA officers, Communist underground, and Nationalist sympathizers scrambled for intel on the enemy and recruits for their cause. It didn't take long before someone spotted Li Junying, a forty-four-year-old junior officer in the National Army who chose not to follow his commander in chief, Generalissimo Chiang Kai-shek, into exile in Taiwan. Instead, Li slipped over the porous border into the Crown Colony of Hong Kong sometime in 1949, joining half a million refugees eking out a meager existence in the shadow of the Communist-controlled mainland. Li was the ideal recruit for a clandestine project, sponsored by the CIA, to recruit agents of subversion from the so-called Third Force—patriotic Chinese like him who rejected Mao Zedong's Communist Party yet despised Chiang Kai-shek's Nationalists almost as much.

The CIA arranged for Li's surreptitious transport to a secret base on the Western Pacific island of Saipan for paramilitary training, and then moved him onward to another CIA facility near the US Navy airfield outside Tokyo. In September 1952, with fighting in Korea locked in a bloody stalemate, an unmarked American plane dropped Li into the forbidding wilderness of China's Changbai mountain region straddling the border with North Korea. His assignment was to link up with a pair of five-man teams who had parachuted in the months prior. Collectively, their mission was to foment counterrevolution against Mao's young nation, the People's Republic of China, in the name of the Third Force.

A couple months later, during Thanksgiving week, Connecticut-born John Thomas Downey, only a year out of Yale College, was far from home. He was enjoying a convivial dinner in Tokyo with his fellow CIA officers in the Far East outfit, and spirits were high. Downey's unit had been running Li Junying and the other Third Force agent teams in Manchuria, maintaining radio communications and keeping them resupplied by airdrop. Some very good news had come from Li that the alpha team, dropped in July, established contact with a disaffected ex–National Army general. Li requested exfiltration as soon as possible so that he could report to headquarters in person. Downey's dinner companions in Japan felt pangs of envy for Jack and his partner Dick, twenty-seven-year-old Boston University graduate Richard George Fecteau, who were headed from Tokyo to Seoul, where they would continue into Communist China to pick up Agent Li.

The unmarked C-47 made an uneventful flight from South Korea to Sandao Gully—the rendezvous point in a remote location on the China side of the Yalu River. The pilot and co-pilot were employees of CAT (Civil Air Transport), a Taiwan-based commercial airline secretly owned by the CIA and chartered when needed for covert missions across Asia. Jack Downey had been on one of these flights before, in August, when he rode along for a resupply drop. But this time around he had a most unusual assignment. As the plane came in low and slow, Downey and Fecteau were supposed to lower a hook that would latch onto a wire strung between goalposts on the ground. The wire was fastened to a backpack to be worn by the intrepid Li Junying, who would be lofted in the air without the plane having to land. Once snatched off the ground, Li was to be reeled in like a fish by Downey and Fecteau. The CAT pilots would speed back to safety, and debriefing, in Japan.

As the plane approached Sandao Gully the men could make out Li's ground signal for the go-ahead, a triangle of small fires. But it was not Li Junying lying on the snow-packed ground—he was in the custody of Chinese public security officers. And there would be no pickup without landing. As the C-47 coasted in on the third pass to drop the hook, guns opened fire from both sides of the ravine. The plane careened down to the hard earth, crashing into a bank of trees. The two CAT pilots were dead on impact, but Downey and Fecteau survived the crash. A grainy photograph captures the moment when two CIA spies were caught red-handed, hands behind their backs, in the winter wilderness of Red China, day one of the longest-known imprisonment of American intelligence officers by a foreign government. It would take over two decades before Downey was able to walk back to freedom across Lo Wu Bridge into Hong Kong, where the Third Force project had begun.

Hero with a Thousand Faces

The seed of this book was planted one day in November 2014 as I learned about the events of November 1952 in Jack Downey's obituary in the *New York Times*. I was teaching Chinese history and international affairs at Yonsei University in Seoul, South Korea, having returned to academia from a stint working on US-China relations at a nongovernment organization in New York, the Asia Society. Before that, I had spent a dozen years studying at Yale, with extended periods of language training and historical research in Beijing, Nanjing, and Taipei. Given my background, I wondered how I could never have heard of Jack Downey, Yale class of 1951, sent by the CIA to fight in the Korean War, imprisoned in Beijing for over twenty years. How could our paths not have crossed when I was at Yale for undergrad or when I returned to New Haven for graduate school, with Downey living nearby as a retired judge? Why wasn't his story, which intersected with so many pivotal events in US-China relations in the early Cold War, better known, and could it serve as the basis for a book? My friend Evan Osnos told me he was intrigued by the same obituary, but whereas he regretted it was too late to talk to Downey and profile him for the *New Yorker*, I had just the opposite reaction. As I tell my students, the simplest definition of history is the study of the dead.

Soon I was immersing myself in the worlds that created the failed covert mission of Jack Downey and the counterespionage coup of the fake Li Junying. I read widely and scoured for sources on US-China relations in the early Cold War, the overheated debates over China policy and profound reflections on America's place in the postwar order, the murky history of intelligence and rocky rise of the CIA, the role of counterrevolutionary subversion in US foreign policy and perceived threat of subversion at home. I delved into the civil/international wars in China, Korea, and Vietnam that reshaped East Asia, and tracked covert activities along an archipelago of subversion radiating out from the islands of Hong Kong, Taiwan, Saipan, and Okinawa, with targets reaching all the way to the Manchurian mountaintops and Tibetan plateau. I pulled the thread of the Third Force, studying writings by its philosophers like Carsun Chang, generals like Zhang Fakui, and admirers like George Marshall. The research allowed me to reexamine aspects in the construction of the early Maoist state, from the deft diplomacy of Zhou Enlai to the thick security apparatus overseen by Luo Ruiqing. The histories of early Cold War America and high socialist China presented unexpected and unnerving parallels, despite their obvious and profound differences.

As happens when inspiration meets with reality, the nature of my project shifted along the path of research. My attempt to reach out to the Downey family went unanswered; I learned of book projects in the works that would tell the story of his life; and—above all—the more research, reading, and drafting I did, the less my manuscript had to do with the person Jack Downey. Historians stress the importance of agency—a choice, made by the historian, about *who* or *what* functions as the primary actor in a narrative or analysis. As I dove deeper in this project, Downey was turning out not to have much agency in the story I was telling. Instead, he functioned like a cipher whose decryption unlocked insights into the individuals, organizations, and forces operating around him: his professors at Yale and their peers in the world of ideas; his employers at the CIA and their colleagues in the circles of government and intelligence; his agents in Hong Kong and across the archipelago of subversion; his enemies on the ground in Manchuria and party headquarters in Beijing.

And so, Downey's journey from Connecticut to China and back provides a narrative arc, akin to the archetypal hero in the monomyth identified by Joseph Campbell in *The Hero with a Thousand Faces* (1949), to which this book's section titles owe their names. But while Downey's experience provides an almost mythic journey structure, he is not in fact the hero or central subject of this book. He is more like the White Rabbit in *Alice in Wonderland*. He calls us to adventure, then vanishes from sight for long stretches of time, and finding him is the key to getting back home.

The hero—in the historiographical sense of agency—of this book is not any single person, but rather the relationship between two countries and peoples, the United States and China, during an extended period of profound hostility, suspicion, and ignorance captured by the term "Cold War." The principal theme is how unreasonable hopes and irrational fears of subversion aggravated destructive tendencies toward political repression—in both nations, albeit to differing degrees. The forces of subversion and repression link US and Chinese political, intelligence, and diplomatic history during the 1950s and 1960s in complex and disturbing ways and are documented here in depth.

There were voices speaking out against subversion, repression, and secrecy, and these counterforces, too, have agency in this book—in particular, an extraordinary quartet of thinkers active in the early Cold War, in the years Jack Downey was studying at Yale and working for the CIA, whom I call simply the "realists." Midwestern WASPs George Kennan and Reinhold Niebuhr and German Jewish refugees Hans Morgenthau and Hannah Arendt wrote seminal works in the late 1940s and early 1950s that, in different ways, warned of the perilous linkage between subversion abroad and repression at home. Decrying McCarthyism, the realists worried more about the threat of repression—even totalitarianism—emerging from within the United States than the risk of communism conquering the world in the name of Moscow or Beijing.

Applying the philosophical insights of the realists to the narrower field of Far Eastern policy were another counterforce, referred to as the "China Hands," epitomized by John King Fairbank of Harvard University. Liberal China Hands in government and out bore the brunt of McCarthyism, starting with Joe McCarthy's attack on Owen Lattimore of Johns Hopkins University. Reactionary defenders of the Nationalist regime on Taiwan, supported by scholars like David Nelson Rowe at Yale, won the policy argument in the Eisenhower era. Lattimore ended up in England and Fairbank retreated into scholarship. The realists, too, faded somewhat from public prominence, overshadowed by the powerful consensus around hawkish liberal internationalism.

It took the nightmare of the war in Vietnam to bring Kennan, Morgenthau, and Fairbank back to the public stage, as the realists renewed their arguments against hubris and China Hands called for détente with Beijing. The realists' call for self-reflection and restraint may have seemed off-key during that golden decade of American power, virtue, and covert action running from the Korean armistice to the Kennedy assassination. But the tragic prescience of realist prudence is painfully evident by the end of our story—the dark age of Watergate.

I researched and wrote the manuscript while living in South Korea, making regular trips to China, frequent visits to my native United States, and an extended stay in Vietnam. Even if much of the story ended up being about America's approach to China and the US role in Asia, I have done my best to tell it with a rich and nuanced sense of the Chinese/Asian context and significance. Historians are forever looking for ways to escape our modern discipline's original sin as a handmaiden to the birth of the nation-state. I do not claim to have escaped the prison. But in exposing the covert underbelly of US-China relations and probing the tensions between grand strategy, government policy, and individual experience, I hope that my telling of the tale at least rattles the bars of the self-satisfied patriotic narratives common in historical discourse on both sides of the Pacific. If Chinese and Americans are going to work out their future, they had better take a hard look at their past. My book is offered in that spirit of gazing unflinchingly into the mirror of history.

Map of the Journey Ahead

The first section of the book, Axis Mundi, tells the backstory of US-China relations coming out of World War II and through the Chinese Civil War, combining diplomatic, intelligence, and intellectual history to reconstruct the early Cold War conditions of possibility for the covert initiative that would ultimately put Jack Downey on a plane into Manchuria.

The story begins with a jarring experience that Americans came to describe as "The Loss of China" (chapter 1). From the high point of signing an alliance days after Pearl Harbor, the relationship sank to a nadir of mutual disillusionment as Chiang Kai-shek's large but demoralized National Army was challenged by Mao Zedong's disciplined People's Liberation Army (PLA). Many American observers were rooting for the unarmed underdog—a moderate option known as the Third Force. After the failure of a year-long mediation by an American envoy, George Marshall, Mao took the mainland, Chiang fled to Taiwan, and the Third Force regrouped in Hong Kong. The blame game in Washington over who had lost China was only getting started.

With the Chinese Civil War and loss of China as background, "Realism and Restraint" (chapter 2) widens the lens to look at the dilemmas posed by America's postwar determination to defend the Free World. The writings of a strategist (Kennan), theologian (Niebuhr), academic (Morgenthau), and philosopher (Arendt) articulate a philosophical dissent from the emerging Cold War consensus.

From the writings of the realists, we turn to the China Hands, reconstructing the argument between three of the country's leading experts—Owen Lattimore, John King Fairbank, and David Nelson Rowe. "Subversion and Repression" (chapter 3) explores how their policy debates became wrapped up in toxic political struggles with the rise of anti-communist politicians like Representative Richard Nixon and Senator Joe McCarthy, and the toll that McCarthyite repression took on the China field in particular.

In "Intelligence or Psywar" (chapter 4), we shift frames again to look at the emergence of covert foreign policy and the birth of the CIA. The WWII experiment in civilian intelligence and guerrilla warfare—glamorized by the Jedburgh teams operating behind Nazi lines—was dismantled by President Truman, anxious about the risk of an American gestapo. But Truman changed his mind amid Cold War fears of communist subversion and hopes in political warfare and psywar, duties that fell to the CIA. From its founding in 1947, the Agency carried out separate functions embodied in two men profiled in this chapter—the analytical project of strategic intelligence pioneered by Sherman Kent and the spying and subversive activities beloved by Allen Dulles.

Readers will notice throughout the Axis Mundi chapters that Yale University functions as a window onto US-China relations in early Cold War America. An exclusive, elite institution of about ten thousand faculty, students, and administrators, Yale was an important center for China studies, with a program led by the political scientist David Nelson Rowe—an obscure figure now who was in his day an influential scholar in the pro-Chiang camp, taking on Harvard's Fairbank and Hopkins's Lattimore. In chapter 2, Yale offers a twist on the story of realism, as the university housed an influential school of geostrategists at the Yale Institute of International Studies. The Yale realists argued for restraint based strictly on power politics and national security, dispensing with the ethical dimension found in Niebuhr's Christian realism or Morgenthau's principled realism. In chapter 3, the Yale campus is presented as a local battleground in the surge of subversion and repression unleashed by McCarthyism, pitting the right-wing student activist William F. Buckley Jr.—who rocketed to fame with the publication of *God and Man at Yale* (1950)—against the liberal university president Whitney Griswold, and reconstructing Professor Rowe's efforts to assist the prosecution of Owen Lattimore. Finally, chapter 4 considers the leading role that Yalies played in the early days of the CIA, which had a field day recruiting on campus, especially during the Korean War years. The Yale of Jack Downey's college years (1947–51), in other words, provides an illuminating microcosm of the main themes of the section—the loss of China, the philosophy of realism, the fear of subversion and tendency toward repression, and the rise of intelligence.

The second part of the book, "Call to Adventure," moves the locus of the action across the Pacific Ocean, showing how the US government, spurred by frustration over the Korean War and fear of Communist influence, launched a covert campaign to subvert the People's Republic of China. Jack Downey recedes even further from view as we survey decisions, events, and forces operating well above his pay grade.

Just as "Axis Mundi" provides the backstory of the Chinese Civil War, "Call to Adventure" starts with a conflict that casts a long shadow. The focus is on the failures in intelligence by the United States and China that led them to be "At War in Korea" (chapter 5) and the American reliance on covert paramilitary methods as conventional fighting failed to yield victory. For Mao Zedong, the so-called War to Resist America and Defend Korea created ideal conditions to launch his first nationwide mass movement, the Campaign to Suppress Counterrevolutionaries, sweeping up a handful of American residents in the PRC along with millions of politically suspect Chinese.

The Korean War strengthened American resolve to resist Mao Zedong, but reservations about Chiang Kai-shek were not easily shed—in the space created by that contradiction, renewed attention fell on "The Third Force" (chapter 6). Variations on the idea of a Third Force were in the air during the early years of the Cold War, found in the speeches of the French socialist Léon Blum, the novels of the British espionage writer Graham Greene, and the books of the American historian Arthur Schlesinger Jr. It was an idea with a long history in twentieth-century Chinese politics as well, best exemplified by the trials and tribulations of Carsun Chang, a philosopher-politician whom George Marshall probably had in mind when he pined for a "splendid group of men" from the Third Force to take power, rather than the Communists or Nationalists. Carsun

Chang made a big pitch for US support in his book *Third Force in China*, published in New York just months before Downey and Fecteau set off on their secret mission.

"Making Counterrevolution" (chapter 7) continues the story of the Third Force, focusing on the evolution of America's covert, military interest in anti-Mao, anti-Chiang elements. Early contacts were established by the US wartime intelligence service OSS, and during the Chinese Civil War, bold plans for arming anyone opposing the Communists were floating around Washington. In the context of the Korean War, Truman's National Security Council secretly approved aiding anti-Communist forces, and the senior intelligence official at Far East Command in Tokyo encouraged the CIA to operationalize the Third Force idea as an armed group. The Third Force mission targeting Manchuria was just one of the CIA's counterrevolutionary projects, which ranged from China's frontier with Burma in the remote southwest to the southeastern coastal provinces in easy reach of Chiang Kai-shek's island fortress of Taiwan.

Ground zero for weaponizing the Third Force was the British colony of Hong Kong, where our story moves next. "Hong Kong Fight League" (chapter 8) reconstructs CIA outreach to Third Force intellectuals, generals, and agents, drawing on the memoirs of a key intermediary, Zhang Fakui, who along with Carsun Chang founded the Fight League for a Free and Democratic China. Zhang doubted the efficacy of the Jedburgh model as applied to Mao's China, but he worked with his nameless American contacts to weaponize the Third Force. CCP counterintelligence watched the covert involvement of the United States in Hong Kong and Taiwan warily, while back at CIA headquarters, Director Beetle Smith worried that covert ops were distracting the Agency from its primary mission of providing policymakers with strategic intelligence.

Having established a recruitment node in Hong Kong, the Third Force operation transported volunteer agents to America's archipelago of subversion in the Western Pacific, with intensive training in Saipan. The initial infiltration of counterrevolutionary teams escaped detection, but discovery of the liaison Li Junying triggered a "Manchurian Manhunt" (chapter 9) by the public security and counterespionage authorities. PRC sources allow in-depth reconstruction of the capture of CIA-backed Third Force guerillas, shedding light on the workings of the internal security apparatus in the early Mao years. As the agents of subversion were being captured and killed in Manchuria, US military leaders continued to be stymied by Chinese defenses in Korea as the American public, unhappy with the war effort, elected the WWII hero, former general Dwight Eisenhower, as president.

The third section, "Road of Trials," opens with "Exfiltration" (chapter 10), which narrates the action-adventure story of Downey and Fecteau's mission into

Manchuria in November 1952. PRC sources reveal Mao Zedong's personal comment on their capture and need to enhance antisubversion efforts. The vicissitudes in US-China relations during the first two years that Downey and Fecteau were held incognito, assumed dead by the CIA, is the subject of "Quiet Americans" (chapter 11), including the Eisenhower administration's recalibration after the Korean War of support for Chiang Kai-shek and defunding of the Third Force.

When Beijing shocked the CIA by announcing Downey and Fecteau were alive and imprisoned, a drawn-out diplomatic struggle commenced in which Eisenhower and his secretary of state, John Foster Dulles, denied all charges of espionage and subversion, while Chairman Mao and Premier Zhou Enlai used the case to denounce American imperialist aggression—the topic of "Subversion on Trial" (chapter 12).

"Implausible Denial" (chapter 13) traces the diplomatic standoff through the mid-1950s, with the two countries mired in a hostility epitomized by the American captives, despite a high-profile intervention by the United Nations secretary-general and initiation of direct US-China talks in Geneva. Even as the furies of McCarthyism subsided and the CIA shifted focus away from sponsoring subversion to technologies of surveillance, Mao Zedong unleashed brutal grassroots campaigns to eliminate counterrevolutionaries and oppose rightists.

The final section, "Rescue from Without," returns to the individual plane of history, looking at how private citizens resisted the US government ban on traveling to China—from journalists like William Worthy Jr. to the spy moms, including Mary Downey, who visited their imprisoned sons in 1958. "Prisoners of the Past" (chapter 14) uses their journeys to chart Sino-US relations into the Kennedy years, an era of public apathy and policy inertia toward China despite a second flare-up in the Taiwan Strait and uprisings across Tibet (assisted covertly by the CIA). By the early 1960s, the cultural significance of the Anglo-American secret agent was being reimagined and contested—from James Bond films and John le Carré novels to lesser-known academic works like Paul Blackstock's *The Strategy of Subversion*—even as Downey and Fecteau had become forgotten spies rotting in their cells.

"War and Revolution" (chapter 15) covers the tumultuous years when Mao's Great Proletarian Cultural Revolution turned China upside down and LBJ's war in Vietnam tore America apart. A pivotal Senate hearing called by William Fulbright in 1966 ties together strands running from the beginning of the book, as the realists and China Hands made a triumphant return to the public stage to challenge the conventional wisdom on Vietnam and China.

Ironically, their theories were put into action through the complicated figure of Henry Kissinger, who negotiated an end to the era of hostility with China and the war in Vietnam, but who also, as consigliere to Richard Nixon, gutted realism of its moral compass—the subject of "Release" (chapter 16). Kissinger included the two spies on the agenda for US-China détente, and freedom for Dick Fecteau came in the lead-up to Nixon's visit to Beijing in February 1972. It took another year, and a mother's love, to liberate the last prisoner of the era of enmity, Jack Downey.

The time traveled in our journey extends from the Chinese Civil War (1945–49) until US-China rapprochement (1971–73), denoted as the Cold War between the United States and China. The standard meaning of "Cold War" refers, appropriately, to the geopolitical and ideological competition between the United States and the Soviet Union. But in Asia, the Cold War took the form of a secondary competition between Washington and Beijing, who positioned themselves precariously amid the explosive nationalist leaders, movements, and peoples of postcolonial Asia. This Sino-American Cold War was hotter than the Soviet-American one, constrained as Washington and Moscow were by the logic of mutually assured destruction based on massive nuclear arsenals pointed at each other's heartland. Americans and Russians studiously avoided direct military altercations, and their Cold War worked in that sense. Americans and Chinese, by contrast, participated on either side of fratricidal conflicts in China, Korea, and Vietnam. These civil wars of international proportions defined the two-plus decades of enmity, and they cast their shadows over all four sections of this book. It is with the end of US-China hostility, embodied in the release of Jack Downey, that the book concludes. The fears of subversion and tendencies toward repression in late Maoist China and in Nixonian America, alas, would not be extinguished, despite the breakthrough in bilateral relations.

The seven years devoted to this book were happy ones for the author, anchored in the hard work of teaching and buoyed by the boundless joy of family. But they were increasingly unhappy times in the ties between two countries I happen to care about deeply, as the unsteady superpower and surging great power fell under the sway of hypernationalistic leaders who promised to "rejuvenate China" and "make America great again." As the book went to press, trends in bilateral relations were ominous, with seasoned China Hands in Washington and America experts in Beijing struggling to find areas of meaningful cooperation, questioning the premise of engagement, and embracing a brave new world of rivalry. Think pieces on a new cold war littered the op-ed pages as America's newly elected leader, Joe Biden, promised to rally the world's democracies against an "alliance of autocracies," as the *New York Times* put it. The Chinese leader Xi Jinping celebrated the centenary of the CCP by invoking the memory of how "in the process of socialist construction, we overcame subversion, sabotage, and armed provocation by imperialist and hegemonic powers." Xi warned darkly that "the Chinese people will never allow foreign forces to bully, oppress or enslave us. . . . Whoever nurses delusions of doing that will crack their heads and spill blood on the Great Wall of steel built from the flesh and blood of 1.4 billion Chinese people."[1]

Consciously or not, the historian's present shapes her understanding of the past. In my case, the steep and steady deterioration of US-China relations, aggravated even further by distrust over the origins of the COVID-19 pandemic and divergence in responding to Russia's invasion of Ukraine, added a sobering relevance to my study of the era before normalization, when the two governments were openly hostile and two societies deeply alienated from one another.

Part I
AXIS MUNDI

1 THE LOSS OF CHINA

Two devastating military contests, the Second World War and the Chinese Civil War, defined the contours of US-China relations heading into the Cold War period. Although WWII brought Americans and Chinese together as allies in the fight against Imperial Japan, it was a fraught and uncertain partnership at best. The alliance was unraveling by the time Chiang Kai-shek's Nationalist Party–controlled regime faced a postwar challenge from Mao Zedong's Communist movement. The failure of US intervention, sending General George Marshall to head off the brewing civil war between the National Army and the People's Liberation Army, was an early blow to Washington's confidence. When China fell to the Communists, it came as a shock to the American people—despite efforts by Truman's secretary of state Dean Acheson to prepare them by releasing the China White Paper. The impact of the loss of China can be seen through the prism of Yale College, an institution with deep missionary ties to China and a strong sense of mission as a bulwark of liberal values in Cold War America.

Between Chiang and Mao

Just days after Japan's surprise attack on Pearl Harbor on December 7, 1941, US president Franklin Delano Roosevelt signed a treaty of alliance with the president of the Republic of China and generalissimo of the National Army, Chiang Kai-shek. FDR would try hard in the months and years to come to convince the American people that Chiang's Free China could emerge as a great power on par with the US, UK, and USSR in the fight against fascism. Nicknamed "the G-mo" by American officials, Chiang and his Nationalist Party ruled a shrinking corner of Chinese territory with an iron fist as they tried to fend off an Imperial Japanese invasion and fretted over an indigenous Communist insurgency. But American readers of *Time* and *Life* magazines, run by the Chiang admirer Henry Luce, were offered a lionized portrait of the G-mo as the Churchill of the East—ironic, given that Churchill thought little of Chiang and saw Roosevelt as "sadly distracted by the Chinese story, which was lengthy, complicated and minor."[1] Another key ally in Roosevelt's project of promoting the Sino-American alliance was Chiang Kai-shek's Wellesley-educated wife Soong Mei-ling, who made a celebrated visit to the United States in early 1943, addressing a joint session of Congress in elegant English and filling the stands at Madison Square Garden. That year, Congress replaced an outdated, unequal treaty with the Republic of China and rolled back racist "exclusion laws" barring Chinese immigration to the United States.

Even facing the common enemy of Imperial Japan, however, it was not easy to convince the American public to embrace the idea of Chinese as allies and equals. The social foundations of the ties between the Middle Kingdom and the American heartland were thin, and anti-Asian prejudices ran thick among the white majority population. There were only about one hundred thousand ethnic Chinese living in the continental United States, mostly cloistered in Chinatowns in the West and subjected to a century of marginalization and violence. On the other side of the Pacific, only a small number of American missionaries and merchants were based in China, and while close to one hundred thousand GIs saw fighting there during WWII, many returned with the same prejudices toward "yellow" people they had held before deployment.[2] Coordinating military strategy in the China Burma India Theater paradoxically generated distrust between the allies, as Chiang felt the Americans and British were making Chinese do the fighting against Japan for them, and Roosevelt came to doubt Chiang's will to fight.

The top brass in the War Department and Joint Chiefs, like their civilian counterparts in the East Coast foreign policy establishment, agreed with General of the Army George Marshall that Asia was a secondary theater in the fighting of the war, just as it would be in the geopolitics of the peace to follow. Asia-First generals like Douglas MacArthur and Claire Chennault were the outliers. When leading China Hand (as Americans with expertise and experience in China were known) Owen Lattimore argued in his book *Solution in Asia* (1945) that WWII had thrust Asia into the center of US grand strategy, he was arguing against conventional wisdom, and he knew it.

By the time victory in Europe was in sight in early 1945, even FDR had lost faith in China's potential as a great power.[3] The Big Three—Roosevelt, Churchill, and Stalin—met at the Yalta Conference in February 1945 to plan the rest of the war and sketch the contours of a postwar order, but Chiang Kai-shek was conspicuously absent as FDR secured Stalin's commitment to join the war against Japan in return for concessions to a range of Soviet demands in Asia. Roosevelt acceded to Russian demands for special privileges in Manchuria, Chinese territory that had been invaded by Japan in 1931 and carved out as a Japanese puppet state called Manchukuo. Stalin also wanted to ensure independence for Mongolia, meaning a loss of territory claimed by China. Roosevelt and Stalin left the future status of Korea, then under Japanese colonial occupation, ambiguous.

As FDR worked out a separate peace with Stalin, reports from US officials based in Chiang Kai-shek's wartime capital Chongqing grew increasingly dour. American observers bemoaned the incompetence of Chiang's Nationalist Party officials in economic affairs, the corruption of his general staff, and the repressiveness of his security apparatus. Three of the government's most knowledgeable China Hands—John Paton Davies, John Stewart Service, and John Carter Vincent—worried the Sino-American alliance was built on quicksand.[4] Roosevelt's envoy to Chongqing, Ambassador Patrick Hurley, remained sanguine about Chiang's prospects. But just weeks after the Yalta Conference, the Chongqing embassy's political officers took advantage of Hurley's absence to send a damning telegram to State Department headquarters laying out the case against Chiang.[5] Ambassador Hurley was outraged at the insubordination, blaming a sinister force at work—Communist sympathizers who had infiltrated the State Department.

Roosevelt's death in April 1945 created a vacuum in American planning for a postwar order in the Far East, including, crucially, the place of Free China. US foreign policy had been determined for over a decade by "the improvisations of President Roosevelt alone, guided by an intuitive grasp of the international realities," as University of Chicago professor Hans Morgenthau put it, and his sudden loss was disorienting.[6] It didn't help that his replacement, Harry S. Truman, a farmer's son from the heartland state of Missouri, seemed an unlikely figure to lead the country out of world war and into a new era of world history. Although Truman had served with distinction in France during World War I, he was not known for foreign policy acumen during his years in the Senate, and he was vice president for only a couple months before Roosevelt died in office. Truman and his advisers also miscalculated the amount of preparation time they would have to plan the postwar order, anticipating at least another full year of bloody fighting to defeat Japan.

When Japanese emperor Hirohito abruptly announced surrender after the atomic bombing of Hiroshima and Nagasaki in August 1945, Stalin did not miss a beat. Soviet troops moved deep into Manchuria to secure the port at Dalian. Mongolian independence was ensured. Soviet Red Army soldier Kim Il Sung arrived on a Soviet ship in his native North Korea to set up a communist regime. Stalin cannily signed a Friendship and Alliance Treaty with Chiang Kai-shek that locked in the Yalta concessions, manipulating Chiang's hopes of keeping Moscow at bay in the coming confrontation with Mao. The Americans at least seized the biggest prize in Northeast Asia by occupying Japan's main islands along with Okinawa, an island kingdom known as the Ryukyus that had been annexed by Japan in 1879. The United States also helped install a friendly regime in the southern half of Korea, led by Syngman Rhee, who returned from decades-long exile in the United States to Seoul on board a plane chartered by General MacArthur.

China remained the big question mark in postwar Asia, yet the American public did not appear to be terribly interested in the answer to the question, even after years of wartime propaganda promoting a Sino-American alliance. Rather than vie with Stalin in the race to occupy squares on the Far Eastern chessboard, Americans' all-consuming desire was to collect their pieces and go home. After victory, even Europe felt far away again, as GIs flooded back from across the world. General Marshall complained, "For the moment, in a wide-spread emotional crisis of the American people, demobilization has become, in effect, disintegration, not only of the armed forces but apparently of all conception of world responsibility and what it demands of us."[7] But as Mao's Communist movement surged and Chiang's Nationalist regime faltered, the Truman administration hoped that political measures, rather than military commitments, would be sufficient to steer events in China toward the preferred outcome of a stable, non-Communist government that could rebuild the war-torn country into a strong, prosperous, democratic American ally. To that end, Truman instructed Ambassador Patrick Hurley to mediate between the Nationalists and Communists and prevent civil war.

Hurley had been to the Communist base camp at Yan'an in northwest China once before, in November 1944, as part of the so-called Dixie Mission sending Americans to get to know Mao and his comrades. The lanky, mustachioed ambassador, who grew up in Indian Territory in Oklahoma, made a splash on arrival by belting out a Choctaw war cry. His second mission in August 1945 was for the purpose of escorting Mao back to Chongqing, giving the Communist guerrilla his first experience flying in a plane.[8] After six weeks of negotiations, Chiang and Mao agreed to set up a power-sharing mechanism called the Political Consultative Conference, with representatives drawn from the Nationalists, Communists, and a scattering of small and unarmed third parties known collectively as the Third Force. But squabbling among politicians and skirmishes between Communist and Nationalist troops broke out almost as soon as the agreement was announced. A frustrated Hurley resigned in protest, openly blaming the "un-American" tendencies of China experts in the government as the root of the problem—a harbinger of the Red Scare on the horizon of US politics.

Truman turned in desperation to the greatest American hero around, General George Marshall, persuading him to take on the China portfolio.[9] As the general set off in December 1945 for what would be known as the Marshall Mission, debate over China policy split into two opposing theories of the case. Dominant voices in the White House and War Department, preoccupied by the Soviet threat, viewed Mao as a pawn in Stalin's game. By their logic, Marshall's goal should be ensuring the victory of Chiang Kai-shek.[10] On the other side of the argument, China Hands in the State Department and outside government largely considered Chiang and his Nationalist Party a lost cause. They harbored hopes that Mao—more nationalist than Bolshevik—could be deflected away from Moscow. The objective of the Marshall Mission from this view should be wooing Mao away from Stalin in anticipation of Chiang's inevitable, probably imminent, demise.[11]

As Marshall's year-long intervention unfolded, the general came around to the view that fascistic elements to Chiang's right had taken hold within the Nationalist Party and were provoking a civil war that, ironically, Mao's Communists were likely to win. Marshall pushed Chiang to move in a liberal direction and wanted to make US aid contingent on political reform. But the military cease-fire that Marshall brokered in January 1946 broke down within a matter of months, and the political framework of the Political Consultative Conference was unraveling by the summer. On the pivotal issue of the two major parties merging their rival military forces, there was no progress whatsoever. Marshall's professions of neutrality as mediator were fatally undermined by Truman's announcement of $50 million in aid to the Nationalists, coming just as Chiang defiantly promised to resolve the Communist threat militarily within a year. Chiang's statement outraged Marshall, but the damage was done. Mao Zedong logically concluded that US strategy was to feign impartiality while covertly assisting Chiang in destroying the Communist movement.[12]

America's leading China Hands watched in dismay as developments spiraled out of Marshall's control and China plunged into civil war. The Yale Divinity School professor Kenneth Scott Latourette published a book for the moment, *The United States Moves across the Pacific* (1946), which transmuted the missionary spirit into the language of geopolitics. Latourette maintained that Asia was America's twentieth-century destiny, foreordained just as the westward frontier expansion had been in the nineteenth century. Echoing Owen Lattimore's *Situation in Asia*, Latourette worried that "few Americans are even dimly aware of the implications of the trans-Pacific trend of their history." The paradox of Asia's centrality to America's destiny, he argued further, would be the lack of control by the United States—over China in particular. "Chinese nationalism will resent any attempt at dictation or patronage by the United States. . . . Strain between the two peoples will, accordingly, arise," Latourette predicted.[13]

Midway through the Marshall Mission, Latourette conveyed a prescient warning about the limits of American influence: "The United States government cannot call forth the moral or spiritual forces essential to the creation of a stable government in China. . . . At most it can only give an opportunity for constructive forces and by its example and self-restraint create an international atmosphere congenial to them." Instead of accepting this limited role, the United States was getting "still more deeply mired down in that bog" of Chinese domestic politics. Latourette worried about backing any horse, let alone the wrong one. "In no case should it [American aid] be with the express purpose of supporting one faction as against another. . . . Ultimately the Chinese will succeed in establishing such a government, but foreign intervention, no matter how well intentioned, may delay the attainment of that goal."[14]

Further north in New England, the historian John King Fairbank at Harvard University concurred with Latourette. Born in South Dakota in 1907, Fairbank began studying the diplomatic history of Qing dynasty China as a Harvard undergraduate, went to Oxford for his doctorate, spent four years in China, and joined the Harvard faculty in 1936. During WWII, Fairbank did a stint in Chongqing and then returned to the city in the first half of 1946, enjoying a front-row seat on the Marshall Mission. He added a visit to the Communist's temporary base at Kalgan en route back to the United States. In an essay published on his return to Cambridge for the fall semester, Fairbank put his finger on the general dilemma at work in the specific challenge posed by China policy. "In the postwar period, we face in China the dilemma that confronts us elsewhere: how to foster stability without backing reaction; how to choose between authoritarian extremes of Communism and incipient Fascism . . . how to reconcile socialism and liberalism."[15]

Looking back on Marshall's mediation in hindsight a couple years later, Fairbank would fault the inability to resolve "our divided objective." "We wanted to press the Kuomintang leaders into democratic reforms which would diminish their autocratic power and facilitate internal peace; at the same time, we wanted to strengthen the Kuomintang-controlled regime as a step toward political stability in East Asia. We became involved in continuing to build the Kuomintang dictatorship up materially at the same time that we tried to get it to tear itself down politically. We did neither." The Marshall Mission was sustained on "a forlorn hope" that civil war was avoidable and coalition government was feasible. "Neither Chinese party trusted the other, nor was ready to give up its hope of eventual, country-wide control. They had antithetical class bases, rival armies

FIGURE 1. Man in the middle: Chiang Kai-shek, George Marshall, and Zhou Enlai (1946). Wikimedia Commons.

and organizations, bitter memories of two decades of killing and being killed, incompatible ideologies."[16] Chiang and Mao were destined for civil war, and George Marshall was simply standing, unarmed, in the way.

By the end of Marshall's mediation in the last months of 1946, the general had lost all faith in Chiang and Mao. The architect of victory over the Nazis threw up his hands at the intractable nature of the Chinese conflict and eagerly accepted a reassignment from President Truman in early 1947 to craft a plan that would protect Western Europe from Soviet influence. China might be sliding into civil war, but Europe—the true hinge point of world order, after all—was at risk of being swallowed whole by Moscow, and something had to be done to stop it.

Plan for Europe, Strategy for Asia

Not long after the Marshall mediation officially ended in failure, President Truman stood before a joint session of the newly elected Eightieth Congress, making an appeal for aid to Greece and Turkey and painting an expansive picture of the postwar role that America would have to play in world affairs. Retreating back into splendid isolation was simply not an option. "I believe we must assist free peoples to work out their own destinies in their own way," Truman declared, asserting that "it must be the policy of the United States to support free peoples who are resisting attempted subjugation by armed minorities or by outside pressures."[17] Although Republicans held the majority in Congress for the first time since 1932, freshmen lawmakers like Wisconsin senator Joseph R. McCarthy and California representative Richard M. Nixon were hard-pressed to refuse the president's request for hundreds of millions of dollars to defend Greece and Turkey against "aggressive movements that seek to impose upon them totalitarian regimes." The Senate and House would pass the aid bill by sizeable margins, and the press hailed the president's speech to Congress that day in March 1947 as the articulation of a Truman Doctrine. Truman avoided calling out the Soviet Union by name, but his speech was the closest thing to a declaration of cold war against Moscow and allied forces of totalitarianism worldwide.

With Marshall going to work on a plan to save Europe from communism, Truman tapped a China Hand, John Leighton Stuart, born in Hangzhou to missionary parents and fluent in Mandarin, as his new ambassador. Even Stuart would concede the fact, as he put it in his 1954 memoirs, that "in a global strategy for peace it was inevitable, and to the ultimate advantage even of China, that America consider Europe first."[18] Ambassador Stuart meekly took up the mantle from Marshall to encourage coalition government, but facts on the ground made a mockery of calls for peaceful sharing of power as Chiang's Nationalists and Mao's Communists engaged in full-scale civil war. For a fleeting moment in the spring of 1947, it seemed that Chiang Kai-shek might actually deliver on his promise to eliminate the Communist "bandits," when his troops captured the abandoned Chinese Communist Party (CCP) base of Yan'an. But it proved a Pyrrhic victory, Chiang's final battlefield triumph. By May, Communist forces scored their first major victories in Manchuria and the Shandong Peninsula, followed by a summertime march across China's Central Plain that convinced Mao victory was inevitable.[19]

In his new capacity as Truman's secretary of state, Marshall wanted a strategic review of the whole China question. He turned to an in-house strategic planner, George Kennan, head of a brand-new office in the State Department called Policy Planning Staff. Kennan was an expert on Russia and Europe, so for an understanding of China, he relied heavily on his adviser John Paton Davies, who was born and raised in Sichuan Province to Baptist missionary parents. Davies had spent much of his government career in China since being posted to Kunming in 1933, and he began working under Kennan when he was sent to the US embassy in Moscow in 1945.[20] The bad news in the initial analysis by Kennan and Davies was that the Nationalists were beyond America's capacity to salvage. The good news was that the Communists' victory did not necessarily spell "catastrophe."[21] What was truly disconcerting to Kennan was the lack of a general strategic framework for American objectives by which to evaluate Mao's impending victory in China. As Kennan wrote to Marshall in early 1948, "Today, so far as I can learn, we are operating without any over-all strategic concept for the entire western Pacific area."[22] So that is what Kennan and Davies set out to provide.

As Kennan and Davies worked on a strategy for Asia, the Chinese Communists' Winter Offensive delivered more victories in Manchuria. By April 1948, Mao's troops had also retaken Chiang's trophy of Yan'an. The US Congress approved more guns and money for the Nationalists' imploding regime and evaporating troops in the China Aid Act, a sop by Truman and Marshall to ensure votes from pro-Chiang senators for the European Recovery Program (aka the Marshall Plan). Congress allocated hundreds of millions of dollars in economic aid and $125 million in military assistance to the Republic of China, as what would amount to billions in aid to Western Europe began to flow. The rationale for transatlantic aid got a boost when Stalin cut off rail and road access to West Berlin in June, sending the United States and its allies scurrying to organize an airlift to supply their zones of the city. The airlift saved West Berlin, while Manchuria was soon lost to a decisive Communist offensive known as the Liao-Shen Campaign.[23]

As Mao took Manchuria, George Kennan presented his China strategy to the National Security Council.[24] Banking on Davies's assessment that the Chinese could be pried loose from the Russians, Kennan counseled restraint, leaving Chiang to his fate and looking for openings with the CCP.[25] A dramatic turn of events in Yugoslavia, where Communist leader Josip Broz Tito was openly resisting Moscow's influence, endowed the China strategy with a name: Titoism. Heeding Kennan and Davies's counsel, Truman and Marshall did not flinch as Mao's massive army took the Manchurian city of Mukden (Shenyang) in October. It was campaign season in the US, and the Republican Party challenger, New York governor Thomas E. Dewey, tried to make hay of the deteriorating situation in the Far East. Dewey warned in his campaign kick-off speech, "If China falls we may reasonably assume that all Asia is gone, and Western Europe and the Americas will stand alone—very much alone in a hostile world."[26] But Dewey's rhetoric, an early iteration of the so-called domino theory, fell on deaf ears. The electorate gave Truman four more years in the White House.

By the time of Truman's inauguration, Mao's million-man army was sweeping south across the Great Wall to seize "Peiping"—as Beijing was then known—and the Yellow Sea port city of Tianjin. In January 1949, the PLA wiped out a half million of Chiang's besieged Nationalist forces at the junction city of Xuzhou. Truman's second term secretary of state, Dean Acheson, rued that "I arrived just in time to have him [Chiang Kai-shek] collapse on me."[27] As if to drive home the point, Chiang Kai-shek resigned as president of the Republic of China on Truman's inauguration day, leaving one of his rivals within the Nationalist Party, Vice President Li Zongren, to try to hold a line of defense at the Yangtze River. With Chiang sidelined, acting president Li sought US support in a last-ditch bid to cobble together what he called a "third force"—politicians and generals who were opposed to Mao but independent of Chiang.[28]

Truman and Acheson stuck to the Kennan/Davies strategy, and Li Zongren's men could not hold the line.[29] The Nationalists' postwar capital city of Nanjing as well as the commercial metropolis of Shanghai fell into Communist hands in the spring of 1949. Up to this point, the US Navy had kept a toehold at the port of Qingdao (a former German concession on the Shandong Peninsula), mirroring the Soviet presence on the Liaodong Peninsula. But in May the Joint Chiefs ordered the evacuation of military personnel.[30] Mao celebrated with a major speech on the anniversary of the founding of the CCP in July, declaring a new party line of "leaning to one side"—aligning with Moscow and people's democracies—dashing cold water on the Titoist hopes of Acheson, Kennan, and Davies. The PLA pressed their zone of control northwest, as Communist troops took Lanzhou, gateway to the Silk Road, by the fall.

What Americans christened the "loss of China" was ratified on October 1, 1949, when CCP chairman Mao Zedong declared the founding of the People's Republic of China (PRC). Senate Republicans wielded the loss of China as a club with which to batter the Truman administration as it charted the course for a second term. Even a few Democrats indulged, like freshman congressman John F. Kennedy, who lamented to his constituents in Salem, Massachusetts, "Our policy in China has reaped the whirlwind. . . . So concerned were our diplomats and their advisors, the Lattimores and the Fairbanks, with the imperfections of the diplomatic system in China after twenty years of war, and the tales of corruption in high places, that they lost sight of our tremendous stake in a non-communist China."[31]

Hoping to drown the criticism in documents, Secretary Acheson compiled a tome of internal government deliberations on China policy and released them to the public in a two-volume anthology, *United States Relations with China* (August 1949)—what came to be known as the China White Paper. Acheson's preface put blame for the loss of China squarely on the shoulders of one man: Chiang Kai-shek. The Truman administration had done all it could, but the decision was always for the Chinese themselves to make, even "if only a decision by default," and it was Chiang who failed to win his people's support. "The unfortunate but inescapable fact is that the ominous result of the civil war in China was beyond the control of the government of the United States. Nothing that this country did or could have done within the reasonable limits of its capabilities could have changed the result; nothing that was left undone by this country contributed to it. It was the product of internal Chinese forces, forces which this country tried to influence but could not."[32]

Acknowledging the reality of events beyond a superpower's control did not turn out to be a very winning argument, politically at least. Apart from a few fans (like Fairbank), the China White Paper served mostly as a lightning rod for more attacks against the administration.[33] Even Owen Lattimore was unimpressed, observing that the publication only demonstrated how Americans still didn't get the lesson that meddling in Chinese affairs was precisely the problem, and the reason the Soviets were more influential was owing to their ability to maintain a façade of noninterference.[34] For influential liberal columnist Walter Lippmann, the China White Paper exposed the Truman administration's failure to "bargain with Chiang" and refusal to consider alternatives.[35] Republican congressmen in the pro-Chiang China bloc used the anthology as ammunition in their ongoing assault against the Democrats for botching China policy, as did prominent figures in the China lobby, spearheaded by conservative businessman Alfred Kohlberg and publisher William Loeb.[36]

The most outraged reader of the China White Paper may have been Mao Zedong. In a series of published commentaries, Mao mocked the arrogance of Acheson for warning him that the new line of "leaning to one side" would lead to another era of foreign imperialism. Mao noted the irony that the China White Paper documented how the United States had been fighting a neo-imperialist war, "a war in which the United States of America supplies the money and guns and Chiang Kai-shek the men to fight for the United States and slaughter the Chinese people."[37] Mao sarcastically expressed gratitude to Washington's factional bickering for forcing Acheson to do something imperialists rarely did: "reveal publicly some (but not all) of their counter-revolutionary doings."[38] Mao also warned Chinese liberals against falling for this latest imperialist ploy. There were many intellectuals who were on the fence, pretending in words to support the CCP, but in their hearts they were "easily duped by the honeyed words of the U.S. imperialists. . . . They are the supporters of what Acheson calls 'democratic individualism.'"[39] Mao called on "progressives"—including non-CCP members—to criticize, educate, and win over these passive liberals, to dispel their illusions about the United States and hesitation toward joining the peoples' revolution. The China White Paper should be a "bucket of cold water" for liberal intellectuals who could not decide between the Nationalists and Communists.[40]

Even after Mao officially declared the establishment of a new state on October 1, pockets of organized resistance to CCP rule remained in the far south. The region's largest city, Guangzhou (Canton), fell to PLA troops in mid-October. It took another six weeks before the Red Army finally marched into the Nationalist wartime capital of Chongqing in the southwest. By then, Chiang Kai-shek and two million of his followers had decamped to the island of Taiwan, where they braced for the final battle of the civil war.

Truman adjusted to the reality of Mao's triumph by signing off on a National Security Council report, "The Position of the United States with Respect to Asia" (NSC 48/2), cutting the cord to Chiang Kai-shek while seeking covert means to split Mao away from Stalin. "The United States should exploit, through appropriate political, psychological and economic means, any rifts between the Chinese Communists and the USSR and between the Stalinists and other elements in China, while scrupulously avoiding the appearance of intervention. Where appropriate, covert as well as overt means should be utilized to achieve these objectives."[41] Owen Lattimore, it seemed, may have been wrong. The Americans were learning the lesson of *appearing* not to intervene, after all.

President Truman unveiled the essence of the new China policy in a "Statement on Formosa" (using the old Portuguese name for Taiwan) that he read to the press on January 5, 1950. Without taking questions, Truman stated bluntly that "the United States government will not pursue a course which will lead to involvement in the civil conflict in China. Similarly, the United States government will not provide military aid or advice to Chinese forces on Formosa."[42] Secretary Acheson elaborated the following week in a speech to the National Press Club, where he offered an analysis of the civil war and strategy for the future that had its "roots in realism." The bottom line was that Chiang lost the people's mandate while Mao harnessed the "great force" of nationalism that was ascendant across Asia as a whole. Acheson promised that the United States would respect the territorial integrity of China but evaded the question of whether the United States would follow the recent lead of the United Kingdom and recognize the People's Republic of China. He drew a line connecting Japan, Okinawa, and the Philippines, defining it as the US "defense perimeter." Acheson's line left the status of Taiwan, and South Korea for that matter, in doubt as to the strength of US commitment.[43]

Truman and Acheson put on a stoical face, but the loss of China cut deep into the national psyche, at least among observers of international affairs. Yale's Latourette described it as "the major reverse in all the history of its dealings with foreign nations."[44] The Republican Party's foreign affairs guru John Foster Dulles was so dumbfounded at the prospect of a Communist China that he simply wished it away, writing in his book *War or Peace* (1950) that "it would be a miracle" if the Communists were able to mobilize the people and "maintain order where disorder has been chronic."[45] Left-leaning journalist Harold Isaacs would describe Mao's victory as the catalyst of an unnerving sense of impotence on the part of the American public: "The 'loss' of China was part of a larger loss so many

Americans suffered at this time, a loss of self-confidence, a loss of assurance about security and power, especially atom power, a loss of certainty about the shape of the world and America's place in it—most of all, perhaps, the loss of hope and expectation that they could return to their private American world, the best of all possible worlds, and be free without fear or concern to enjoy it. The China 'loss' was all these losses."[46] The Princeton University historian Eric Goldman agreed with Isaacs, seeing the loss of China, together with the Soviet atomic bomb test, as triggering a disorientation of the American sense of the world and itself. Goldman would write in *The Crucial Decade: America, 1945–1955* (1956): "1949 was a year of shocks, shocks with enormous catalytic force. The shocks were hurtling a good deal of the nation into a new mood. . . . The shocks of 1949 loosed within American life a vast impatience, a turbulent bitterness, a rancor akin to revolt. It was a strange rebelliousness, quite without parallel in the history of the United States."[47]

Cold War College

The shock of losing China hit hard on the campus of Yale University, an institution with deep historical ties to China. Yalies had long stood at the forefront of American involvement with China, and faculty members were pioneers of sinology and China studies. These linkages grew out of the school's missionary drive to convert the population to Christianity, stretching back to the efforts of early nineteenth-century missionaries like the physician and medical educator Peter Parker. Yale became the first US university to confer a degree on a Chinese student, Yung Wing, in 1854, and it appointed the country's first professor of Chinese, missionary linguist, publisher, and diplomat Samuel Wells Williams, in 1877. The tragic killing of a Yale alumni, missionary Horace Tracy Pitkin, during the anti-foreign, anti-Christian Boxer Rebellion in 1900 inspired his classmates to set up the Yale Foreign Missionary Society, which led in turn to the establishment of a school, Yali College, in the city of Changsha, and a teaching program for graduates known as Yale-in-China. It was Yali that brought Latourette to China and set him on the path of China studies to supplement his career at Yale as the nation's leading historian of Christianity.[48]

World War II channeled Yale's missionary tradition as a center of sinology to meet the needs of geopolitics. Yale's president Charles Seymour promised that the university would fulfill "whatever demands the necessities of national defense lay upon us," putting the school on year-round operations and shortening the bachelor's degree to three years.[49] A crash course in Oriental Studies was specifically designed to churn out intelligence officers and military advisers for deployment in the China Burma India Theater.[50] To support the alliance with Chiang's Free China, the US Army urgently needed enlisted men with Chinese language skills, and producing them was a job that fell to Yale's brilliant sinologist George Kennedy.[51]

A child of missionaries, Kennedy was born in the idyllic hill station of Moganshan, where foreigners built stone cottages to escape Shanghai's insufferable summers. Kennedy ended up in Berlin to do his doctorate on Chinese medieval law; as he pored over the medieval Tang dynasty legal code, Adolf Hitler and the Nazi Party came to power around him. Kennedy made it back to New Haven in 1936 and joined the university faculty. In 1942, he took charge of the Military Intelligence School and Army Specialized Training Program in Chinese at Yale. After the war, Professor Kennedy continued to teach with the immersion techniques designed under wartime conditions for practical use rather than scholarly research. He would miss the good old days, before the war, of pure scholarly inquiry. "For one head that is curious about Wang Mang's socialism of the first century," he later complained, "there are ten whose excitement is over Mao Tse-tung's latest speech."[52]

Professor Latourette meanwhile made the case for a special relationship between the United States and China in *The Development of China*, published in its sixth edition in 1946. Explaining China's modern transformation as the by-product of "the growing pressure upon her of Western peoples and culture," Latourette argued that European imperialism had destroyed the old China and now Americans bore a special duty to "know her better" in order to help the "new China" put herself back together again. If not, a broken and weak China would end up a "menace" to herself and the world.[53]

To help Americans "know China better" in the postwar era, Yale built up a program in Far Eastern Studies that would "provide the student with the means for understanding the complex life and civilization of a modern country in its totality," as the coursebook explained. The lead faculty member was the China expert and political scientist David Nelson Rowe, who taught the East Asia survey, co-taught a year-long history course, and directed seniors through a seminar, Government and Politics of Eastern Asia, and thesis writing. A legacy of wartime mobilization, Far Eastern Studies fit neatly into the emerging priorities of the "Cold War university" and the rage for foreign area studies, ways of understanding the communist and postcolonial Other.[54] Postwar Yale also offered new programs to teach students about their American/Western Self, like Directed Studies, a freshman-year immersion in the great books of Western civilization, and American Studies, a new undergraduate major that implicitly treated the United States as the culmination of the West.[55]

Overseeing the rough passage from WWII to Cold War was President Charles Seymour, a historian who boasted numerous Yale presidents in his family tree and liked to pepper speeches with quotations from *Tom Brown's School Days* and *The Pilgrim's Progress*. Despite his Victorian airs, Seymour knew something of the weight of the modern world. His academic career was put on pause in 1919 when he was appointed by President Woodrow Wilson to join the American Commission to Negotiate Peace in Paris after World War I. Seymour was in charge of analyzing political intelligence on Central Europe, managing a team that included a young Princeton graduate by the name of Allen Dulles.[56] Seymour was tapped as president in 1937 and guided Yale through WWII, and his presidential addresses in the postwar years reflected the warring impulses of liberal intellectuals during the onset of the Cold War.

Addressing graduates at the 1947 commencement ceremony, Seymour sounded the alarm on the threat posed by the Soviet Union and fretted that the brutal lesson of Munich on the perils of appeasement was already being forgotten. Seymour warned that "the furnace of adversity is all about us," yet one heard "certain political figures today, who tell us that if we will honestly trust Russia, all will be well" (likely an allusion to former vice president Henry Wallace, a progressive critic of the emerging Truman Doctrine).[57] But after a year of escalating tensions with Moscow, President Seymour was worried that a different German lesson was being forgotten: that of Weimar democracy's descent into Nazi totalitarianism. Speaking at the 1948 commencement, Seymour was more concerned about the "tendency toward repression" in America than the threat posed by Russia:

> As one would expect in a time of ferment, the tendency toward repression is today becoming dangerously apparent. . . . We know where that tendency ends. Once controls are established over sociological or economic inquiry we are on the path to the kind of state which Hitler set up and which we fought to the death in the cause of freedom. . . . It is with such an assurance of the right of question, the right of criticism, the right of opinion that we in this country must meet the threat of communism. . . . Repression is never a remedy.[58]

Behind Seymour's shift in concern from appeasement to repression lurked a third specter—the mushroom cloud. Even before the Soviets tested the bomb, Seymour somberly posed the existential question of the atomic age: "It is yet to be decided whether mankind, for the first time in history disposing of adequate means for the purpose, will or will not commit mass suicide."[59] By June 1949, delivering what would be his last baccalaureate address, Seymour's jitters over a second Munich had evaporated entirely in dread over the prospect of World War III. America must find a means of "antagonistic cooperation" with the Soviets, he now insisted, invoking a concept from the Yale sociologist William Graham Sumner. If Cold War passions were not somehow "tempered with a spirit of generosity," the world would find itself on the brink of Armageddon.[60]

Seymour found hope in one thing at least: his students, especially the class of 1951, which he considered "the finest to enter Yale."[61] They were the second-largest cohort in college history and boasted the best high school transcripts on record. They were older than average, with veterans bringing a worldliness from the battlefields of Europe and the Pacific into the classroom.[62] The GI Bill enabled a wider swath of young men to afford the Ivy League—farmers' kids, like James Lilley, who would go on from Yale to become one of the leading China Hands of his generation . . . and children of German Jewish refugees, like Henry Kissinger, who transferred into Harvard College in 1947.[63] But most came straight from high school, like Jack Downey, in many ways a prototypical member of the group who arrived on campus in the fall of 1947.

Downey was male, like all his classmates, and white, like the vast majority of them.[64] A Depression baby born in the wake of the 1929 stock market crash, he hailed from a prominent family in Wallingford, Connecticut, that had the means to weather hard times. Jack's uncle Morton Downey was a celebrity tenor known to a national radio audience as the "Irish Nightingale," and his father was a probate judge. Tragically, the elder Downey died in a car accident in 1938, leaving Jack and his younger siblings, William and Joan, to be raised by their mother, Mary, who would take a job as an elementary schoolteacher in New Britain.

Neither Downey's father nor his uncle had been Yale men, placing Jack in a slightly lower caste than about a third of his classmates, called "legacies," whose parents or relatives were alumni.[65] Like about two-thirds of the class, Downey did come from a prestigious college prep academy (Choate), where he excelled not just in academics but also athletics.[66] Sports remained central to life at Yale—as the *Yale Banner* put it, "What interfered most with scholarly pursuits, besides best girls, next-best girls, and any girls, was sports."[67] Downey was captain of the freshman wrestling team and would play left guard on the varsity football team as he grew into a six-foot, two-hundred-pound senior. He majored in one of the most popular subjects, English, and was chosen for one of the finals societies, St. Anthony Hall (Delta Psi).[68] About the only notable way in which Downey did not quite fit the postwar Yale profile was religion: barely more than a tenth of his classmates were Roman Catholic (a strict cap of 10 percent was applied to the Jewish student population).[69] Other than that, Downey was pretty much the perfect Yalie, an all-American product of the first class of the Cold War, ready for duty.

2

REALISM AND RESTRAINT

As Yale students tried to focus on books, girls, and sports, four of the country's foremost public intellectuals were wrestling with the sobering realities and moral dilemmas posed by America's role in the Cold War and whether the United States could defend liberal democracy against communist totalitarianism on a global scale. Although they were Europeanists by background and training, their writings were shaped profoundly by events in the Far East, including the shocks of the loss of China and war in Korea. Writing in the distinct languages of diplomacy, theology, international relations, and political philosophy, George Kennan, Reinhold Niebuhr, Hans Morgenthau, and Hannah Arendt grappled with the contradiction between the idealism of America's liberal vision on the one hand, and the realities of geopolitics, risk of hubris, and danger of repression on the other. They ultimately arrived at a philosophy of international affairs and strategy for the United States that can best be described as realism.

Despite their different disciplines, the realists shared an important touchstone in their reflections on the emerging Cold War. Each of them was haunted by the ghosts of fascism in its Germanic guise, which they knew intimately: Morgenthau and Arendt were born to comfortable German Jewish families shattered by the rise of Nazism, Niebuhr was born to German immigrants who spoke their native tongue around the house in Wisconsin, and Kennan's first trip abroad as a boy was to Germany, where he learned the language and would return for graduate studies. After World War II, each was quick to recognize Stalin's totalitarian aspirations as a force of evil. And yet, what all four thinkers feared most—even more deeply than the Soviet menace—was what fighting the Cold War could do to the soul of the United States.

None of the realists was expert on the Far East, but their ideas shaped the debate on China policy and national security strategy in Asia. Reconstructing their brand of Cold War realism illuminates the larger philosophical debate over American foreign policy, in the context of which the US government decided to launch a covert war against Communist China that would send college graduates into Manchuria to pick up agents of subversion.

The Irony of American Diplomacy

George Kennan was deputy chief of mission at the US embassy in Moscow when he transmitted the best-known cable in American diplomatic history—the storied Long Telegram, sent February 22, 1946. Kennan's memo on Soviet intentions and the appropriate strategic response electrified the upper echelons of the US government. A year and a half later, Kennan's assessment of Stalin and proposed counterstrategy of "containment" were featured in *Foreign Affairs*, the unofficial organ of the foreign policy establishment. Though the article was published under the pseudonym "X," the article's authorship was the worst-kept secret in Washington.[1]

Kennan was a subtle, if not conflicted, strategic thinker, and dueling impulses could be felt in his prescriptions. On the one hand, Stalin's messianic ambitions demanded of the United States a proactive role in applying "a policy of firm containment, designed to confront the Russians with unalterable counter-force at every point where they show signs of encroaching upon the interests of a peaceful and stable world." Eventually, the Soviet regime would collapse under the weight of its own contradictions. On the other hand, Kennan feared that the United States was just as susceptible to the peril of imperial overstretch. His counsel of "a long-term, patient but firm and vigilant containment of Russian expansive tendencies" contained within it a call for American *self*-restraint. The measure of ultimate success would be "the degree to which the United States can create among the peoples of the world generally the impression of a country which knows what it wants, which is coping successfully with the problems of its internal life and with the responsibilities of a world power, and which has a spiritual vitality capable of holding its own among the major ideological currents of the time."[2]

In Kennan's *Foreign Affairs* article, published in July 1947 as he took up duties advising Secretary of State George Marshall, Kennan urged his countrymen to stick to their national traditions. "To avoid destruction the United States need only measure up to its own best traditions and prove itself worthy of preservation as a great nation."[3] In lectures at the National War College in March 1947, Kennan was blunter in stating his conviction that the United States had no magical immunity to totalitarianism. "The fact of the matter is that there is a little bit of the totalitarian buried somewhere, way down deep, in each and every one of us. It is only the cheerful light of confidence and security which keeps this evil genius down at the usual helpless and invisible depth. If confidence and security were to disappear, don't think that the totalitarian impulse would not be waiting to take their place."[4]

Between the Long Telegram and the "containment" article, Kennan established his reputation as the most influential foreign policy strategist of the emerging Cold War. But not everyone liked what they read. The columnist Walter Lippmann was appalled at Kennan's containment doctrine, labeling it a "strategic monstrosity."[5] Lippman devoted a series of articles in the fall of 1947 to a refutation of Kennan, gathered together as *Cold War: A Study in U.S. Foreign Policy*, one of the first uses of the term "cold war" in a book title. He faulted Kennan for placing the United States in the untenable position of marshaling "counter-force" wherever Moscow chose to give a push, demanding a level of "vigilance" that endangered the capitalist, democratic soul of America. Lippman argued that containment would be impossible given the rapid postwar demobilization. "The policy can be implemented only by recruiting, subsidizing and supporting a heterogeneous array of satellites, clients, dependents and puppets," he warned (presciently). A diehard Europe-firster, Lippmann was content to allow the Yalta Conference concessions in Asia, while negotiating mutual withdrawal of US and Soviet troops from Europe. He, too, invoked the idea of a return to "tradition," but with a different heritage in mind: "We shall be acting once more in the great American tradition which is to foster the independence of other countries, not to use other countries as the satellites of our own power, however beneficent, and as the instruments of our own policy, however well meant." Lippmann even defended the failed Marshall Mission. Marshall in China may not have succeeded in preventing civil war, but he demonstrated the courage "to disentangle the United States, to reduce, not to extend, our commitments in Asia, to give up the attempt to control events which we do not have the power, the influence, the means, and the knowledge to control."[6]

Lippmann's rebuke of containment stung because Kennan largely agreed with it. While enjoying the sudden fame brought by the Long Telegram, Kennan insisted that his idea was misconstrued as the theoretical basis for the Truman Doctrine, when in fact he blushed at the sweeping nature of Truman's oath before Congress to support the fight against totalitarianism everywhere and anywhere.[7] Kennan would be lukewarm on the idea of a military alliance for Europe, formalized in 1949 as the North Atlantic Treaty Organization (NATO). He preferred to focus on economic rebuilding through the Marshall Plan as a step toward the optimal long-term solution of a unified Europe. Stepping down as director of policy planning, to be succeeded by the more hawkish Paul Nitze in early 1950, Kennan felt increasingly out of step with the drift of the foreign policy establishment. The Korean War in particular alienated Kennan from the world of Washington. "The Korean attack had stirred us all up like a stone thrown into a beehive," Kennan later recalled. "People went buzzing and milling around, each with his own idea of what we were trying to do."[8]

When Kennan received an invitation from the University of Chicago to deliver a lecture series on the history of US foreign policy, he decided to use it as a platform to rebut critics like Lippmann, who misconstrued him as a hawkish Cold Warrior. The invitation came at the recommendation of Professor Hans Morgenthau, whom Kennan had invited to the Department of State in 1949 for an exchange with the Policy Planning staff.[9] Kennan's lectures served as the basis for his first book, *American Diplomacy 1900–1950*. He framed America's changed role in world affairs as a puzzle: "How did a country so secure become so insecure?"[10] The short answer was the rise of what he termed a "legalistic-moralistic" paradigm for international relations. That quintessentially American theory assumed everyone else in the world enjoyed comparable conditions of territorial security as the United States and shared the same aspiration to the same liberal values. This projection became the root cause of American insecurity and overreach. Kennan urged his audience to let go of the compulsion to fashion the world in their nation's image. In a critical passage, Kennan sought to temper the ardor of legalistic-moralism by advancing the concept of "national interest." Realism was not a rejection of liberalism, but a humble and restrained version of it.

> We will have the modesty to admit that our own national interest is all that we are really capable of knowing and understanding—and the courage to recognize that if our own purposes and undertakings here at home are decent ones, unsullied by arrogance or hostility toward other people or delusions of superiority, then the pursuit of our national interest can never fail to be conducive to a better world. This concept is less ambitious and less inviting in its immediate prospects than those to which we have so often inclined, and less pleasing to our image of ourselves. To many it may seem to smack of cynicism and reaction. I cannot share these doubts. Whatever is realistic in concept, and founded in an endeavor to see both ourselves and others as we really are, cannot be illiberal.[11]

For Kennan, the loss of China stood as a testament to the limits of American understanding of and influence on foreign realities. It was an irony rather than a tragedy that the long-standing US goal of a strong and independent China was at long last being achieved . . . under Communist rule![12]

The unknowability of international politics defied legalistic-moralistic self-righteousness. Kennan detected a karmic law underlying the vagaries of foreign affairs, but one whose pattern was too complex for human understanding: "Every mistake is in a sense the product of all the mistakes that have gone before it, from which fact it derives a sort of cosmic forgiveness; and at the same time every mistake is in a sense the determinant of all the mistakes of the future, from which it derives a sort of cosmic unforgivableness. Our action in the field of foreign policy is cumulative; it merges with a swelling stream of other human happenings; and we cannot trace its effects with any exactness once it has entered the fluid substance of history."[13]

Such complexity should engender humility. But American diplomacy, enthralled by legalistic-moralistic confidence, acted with self-righteous abandon. This was especially the case in Asia, where a patronizing sentimentality rooted in missionary instincts to save heathen souls removed inhibitions to imperialist behavior. In order to check this imprudent tendency, Kennan advised that the United States should hew to the narrow demands of "national self-interest," rather than pretend to act for the benefit of "the peoples of the East." "If . . . instead of making ourselves slaves of the concepts of international law and morality, we would confine these concepts to the unobtrusive, almost feminine, function of the gentle civilizer of national self-interest in which they find their true value—if we were able to do these things in our dealings with the peoples of the East, then, I think, posterity might look back upon our efforts with fewer and less troubled questions."[14]

Kennan's thoughts on *American Diplomacy* got the attention of the great American theologian Reinhold Niebuhr as he worked on his masterpiece, published the following year as *The Irony of American History.* The Missouri-born son of a German Evangelical pastor, Niebuhr studied at Yale Divinity School, began his ministry in Detroit, and then settled in New York City to join the Union Theological Seminary in 1928. A gifted writer, Niebuhr gained national prominence in the 1930s for promoting "Christian realism," rebutting Christian pacifism and mainstream isolationism by arguing that a world threatened by Nazism demanded America's entry into the war. Kennan invited Niebuhr, like Morgenthau, to consult with the Policy Planning staff in June 1949, by which time Niebuhr was among the most influential religious thinkers in the country and a theologian of foreign policy.[15]

The Irony of American History constituted Niebuhr's attempt to apply his philosophy of Christian realism to the moral dilemmas posed by the Cold War. As indicated by the title, irony was the essential teaching of the book. Kennan was an ironic thinker too, drawing deep inspiration from Edward Gibbon, whose *The History of the Decline and Fall of the Roman Empire* was described by Hayden White as "the greatest achievement of sustained irony in the history of historical literature."[16] For Niebuhr, the ironic muse was Cervantes. Niebuhr likened the Cold War to a battle between vainglorious knights: a demonic Quixote armed in Soviet collectivism versus an angelic Quixote clothed in American materialism. To "win" the Cold War in a moral sense, Americans would have to resolve the irony inherent in their angelic self-conception: "If virtue becomes vice through some hidden defect in the virtue; if strength becomes weakness because of the vanity to which strength may prompt the mighty man or nation; if security is transmuted into insecurity because too much reliance is placed upon it; if wisdom becomes folly because it does not know its own limits—in all such cases the situation is ironic."[17]

The irony of American virtue was compounded by American ignorance of the wider world. Echoing Kennan's critique of how the "legalistic-moralistic" worldview projected an illusion of a planet populated by Americans-in-waiting, Niebuhr insisted that his readers recognize the limits of their understanding of foreign nations and peoples. "We can understand the neat logic of either economic reciprocity or the show of pure power. But we are mystified by the endless complexities of human motives and the varied compounds of ethnic loyalties, cultural traditions, social hopes, envies and fears which enter into the policies of nations, and which lie at the foundation of their political cohesion." Blithe to the messy realities of other countries, intoxicated by a self-image of unsurpassed virtue and unlimited power, America risked falling victim to hubris. For Niebuhr, the fact that the loss of China came as a devastating surprise was yet another proof of Americans' ignorance and vanity.[18]

With the acquisition of the atomic bomb, Niebuhr thought America may have reached "the ironic climax of its history." There were only two ways for the irony to end: contrition or evil: "An ironic situation must dissolve, if men or nations are made aware of their complicity in it. Such awareness involves some realization of the hidden vanity or pretension by which comedy is turned into irony. This realization either must lead to an abatement of the pretension, which means contrition; or it leads to a desperate accentuation of the vanities to the point where irony turns into pure evil." Niebuhr's purpose in writing *The Irony of American History* was to lead his readers to self-consciousness of the irony in the American predicament, in hopes of catalyzing dissolution in an "abatement of pretensions."

Niebuhr was asking his fellow citizens, as they set off on the American Century, to realize the limits of their liberal idealism: "The ironic elements in American history can be overcome, in short, only if American idealism comes to terms with the limits of all human striving, the fragmentariness of all human wisdom, the precariousness of all historic configurations of power, and the mixture of good and evil in all human virtue." As a theologian, Niebuhr naturally cast the abatement of pretensions in a religious light. It was by seeing themselves in the eyes of their Creator that Americans could leap from irony to contrition. "The whole drama of human history is under the scrutiny of a divine judge who laughs at human pretensions without being hostile to human aspirations. The laughter at the pretensions is the divine judgment. The judgment is transmuted into mercy if it results in abating the pretensions and in prompting men to a contrite recognition of the vanity of their imagination."[19]

Niebuhr was pessimistic about the prospects of the escape from irony coming soon. He cautioned against "the temptation to become impatient and defiant of the slow and sometimes contradictory process of history. We may be too secure in both our sense of power and our sense of virtue to be ready to engage in a patient chess game with the recalcitrant forces of historic destiny."[20] Here he sounded like Kennan the grand strategist, who warned that containment would be a long, complex affair and that the Soviets would be defeated not by sudden clash of arms, but by the glacial conquest of economic superiority.

Niebuhr's and Kennan's general admonitions against American impatience echoed specific arguments on the question of China policy made by the likes of Fairbank and Latourette. Back in 1946, Fairbank had insisted that the best policy "in the long run" was for the United States to promote "freedom of contact" so as to nurture China's liberal tradition. "If our liberal political principles are as universally valid as we believe, we must wait for modern China, Communist or otherwise, to realize it. We cannot compel her to do so."[21] Latourette similarly concluded *American Record in the Far East* (published the same year as Niebuhr's *Irony*) by chiding Americans for their tendency "to be dogmatic and to demand quick returns."[22] But as Eric Goldman would observe, the Cold War realists' call for gradualism ran against powerful currents in American society, with newfound expectations of a "swift, total solution, brought about by ourselves alone."[23]

For all the consonance between their forms of ironic realism, Niebuhr departed from Kennan on one critical issue. Toward the end of *The Irony of American History*, Niebuhr praised *American Diplomacy* as "the most rigorous and searching criticism of the weaknesses in our foreign policy."[24] But he categorically rejected Kennan's suggestion that Americans cleave to the concept of "national interest" and content themselves with the "modesty to admit that our own national interest is all that we are really capable of knowing," as Kennan put it.[25] Kennan correctly diagnosed the problem, but "his solution is wrong. For egotism is not the proper cure for an abstract and pretentious idealism."[26] The cure, according to Niebuhr, was not self-interest, but love. Only "a concern for both the self and the other," bounded by respect for the limits of one's ability to understand the other, and humility in one's use of power, could guide American foreign policy. In the essay "Augustine's Political Realism," Niebuhr expanded on the requirement that "the love of the other and the love of the community"—concepts he derived from St. Augustine—anchor a realist philosophy of international relations.[27]

Defense against Totalitarianism

As Niebuhr the theologian and Kennan the strategist sparred over the proper place of "national interest" in a realist's approach to the world, Professor Hans Morgenthau was busy writing a book of his own on the subject. Morgenthau was born in 1904 (one day after Kennan) to a well-off Jewish family in Coburg, German. As a boy, Hans experienced the cruelties of rising anti-Semitism—in 1929, Coburg became the first town where the Nazi Party won local elections. By then, Morgenthau was in Frankfurt finishing his doctorate on how the realities of international power politics limited the influence of international law.[28] Pursing postgraduate studies in Geneva, Morgenthau could no longer return to Nazi Germany, and after drifting around Europe, he finally secured a visa to enter the United States in 1937. Joining the faculty at the University of Chicago in 1943, Morgenthau heard Niebuhr deliver a visiting lecture in 1944, which was the beginning of a lifelong mutual admiration and influence.[29] Morgenthau's first English-language book, *Scientific Man versus Power Politics* (1946), was followed by an academic sensation, *Politics among Nations: The Struggle for Power and Peace* (1948), which quickly became a required text in the study of international relations.[30]

Morgenthau framed *Politics among Nations* around the same puzzle that Kennan would later use in *American Diplomacy*—the paradox of America's postwar insecurity. For the first time in its history, the United States "stands outside the enclosures of its continental citadel, taking on the whole of the political world as friend or foe. It has become dangerous and vulnerable, feared and afraid." Morgenthau was unafraid to write about his adopted country as a proto-imperialist power. With clinical detachment, he described the hypnotic spell of nationalism at work in America society, enthralling individuals into identification with the power of the nation—something he glimpsed in demonic form with the rise of Nazism. "When we are conscious of being members of the most powerful nation on earth, the nation with the greatest industrial capacity and the monopoly of the atomic bomb, we flatter ourselves and feel a great pride. It is as though we all, not as individuals but collectively, as members of the same nation, owned and controlled so magnificent a power."[31]

This intoxication with power was particularly dangerous in the hands of idealistic Americans. In a lyrical passage of *Politics among Nations*, Morgenthau wrote about how the perils of the postwar era exceeded even the world wars, since the two principal antagonists in the Cold War each claimed "to possess the whole truth of morality and politics." There was no limit to the cause on either side of the superpower divide, with American and Russian nationalisms asserting competing universal forms: "The morality of the particular group, far from limiting the struggle for power on the international scene, gives that struggle a ferociousness and intensity not known to other ages. For the claim to universality which inspires the moral code of one particular group is incompatible with the identical claim of another group; the world has room for only one, and the other must yield or be destroyed."

It was a bleak vision. Niebuhr at least offered the consolation of his faith that a "divine judge" was out there in the cosmos laughing at the irony of human pretensions, and hope that the good Quixote might awaken to the irony of his quest. For Morgenthau, no divinity was there to laugh or cry, and the faith of "nationalistic masses" only made them more dangerous. "Carrying their idols before them, the nationalistic masses of our time meet in the international arena, each group convinced that it executes the mandate of history, that it does for humanity what it seems to do for itself, and that it fulfills a sacred mission ordained by providence, however defined. Little do they know that they meet under an empty sky from which the gods have departed."[32]

Morgenthau saw the loss of China as an epochal event. "In the short run, our failure in China constitutes one of the most resounding defeats our foreign policy has ever sustained. In the long run, it threatens to become a disaster of unprecedented magnitude for the Western world as a whole, an event from which future historians may well date the ultimate decline of the West in its relations with the colored races."[33] In the spring of 1950—as Mao's victory and Stalin's bomb sunk into the American psyche—Morgenthau gave a lecture course, out of which emerged his book *In Defense of the National Interest*. He presented himself as reviving a lost tradition of American foreign policy realism, a strain of thought originating with Alexander Hamilton and Thomas Jefferson that had been buried under the rubble of Woodrow Wilson's idealistic liberalism. In geopolitical terms, Morgenthau's realism limited US national interest to a prudential grand strategy of defending hegemony in the Western hemisphere. Eurasian entanglements were to be avoided, except insofar as necessary to right the balance of power and prevent the emergence of a great power that could challenge stability.

Morgenthau understood World War II as a rupture in history, "the definite and radical end of the political, technological, and moral conditions under which the Western world lived for centuries."[34] The new postwar—even postmodern—age demanded humility on the part of the superpowers. Merely to survive, the US and USSR would have to refrain from nuclear holocaust, making war unwinnable in military terms. "Today war has become an instrument of universal destruction, an instrument that destroys the victor with the vanquished."[35] In the Cold War struggle for hearts and minds, victory would go to the superpower with the lightest footprint. Morgenthau used Asia as the prime example of a place where Moscow had positioned itself as champion of national self-determination and social justice, while the West seemed more intent on asserting dominion. He affirmed the need for the territorial integrity of China, not for sentimental reasons, but rather because "the domination of China by another nation would lead to so great an accumulation of power as to threaten the security of the United States."[36]

Like Niebuhr and Kennan, Morgenthau worried about "panic and oppression at home" as a natural tendency within American universalism. Growing up in a German-Jewish family destroyed by the failure of Weimar democracy and rise of Nazi fascism, Morgenthau knew the damage that universalist regimes could unleash in their host societies. Fighting for "universal counter-revolution abroad" went hand in hand with asserting "conformity in thought and action at home." The danger in fighting totalitarianism was the temptation to become it, and the risk to the United States was real.

> If instead we conceive of the American mission in some abstract, universal, and emotional terms, we may well be induced, against our better knowledge and intent, yet by the very logic of the task in hand, to raise the banner of universal counter-revolution abroad and of conformity in thought and action at home. In that manner we shall jeopardize our external security, promote the world revolution we are trying to suppress, and at home make ourselves distinguishable perhaps in degree, but not in kind, from those with which we are locked in ideological combat.[37]

As evidence of this dangerous tendency in American life, Morgenthau pointed to the hunt for subversives triggered by the loss of China. The Chinese chose a revolution that America tried and failed to stop. "And as a result of these failures abroad, we hunt at home as spies and traitors innocent dissenters whom we can hold responsible for those failures, as though their roots were to be looked for anywhere but in the confusion of our own thoughts and actions. We thus silence thinking and informed counsel or force it into the mold of conformity." The frustrations of American power turned inward and undermined American virtue:

> When political failure and military defeat ought to show us the limits of our power, we still cling to the delusion of our omnipotence. The only way to explain failures and defeats when we assume ourselves to be omnipotent is to look for some devilish machinations depriving us of the successes and victories that are rightfully ours. So it becomes plausible that we are unable to stop the revolutions in Asia by military means, not because they cannot be stopped that way, but because the State Department is full of Communists.

Instead of facing up to the unpalatable reality that power had shifted from Nationalists to Communists, the United States made itself into the enemy of the vast majority of the Chinese people. "In spite of the better knowledge of some of our wisest and best-informed officials, we drifted into opposing Chinese Communism as such, regardless of the benefits and disadvantages to American interest which would result from that opposition." It was time for Americans to temper their universalism and restore the modest tradition of the Founders, by narrowing the focus of foreign policy to national interests. "The vital objective of our foreign policy in Europe and Asia is the restoration of the balance of power by means short of war."[38] And nothing more.

The same year that Hans Morgenthau completed his Frankfurt dissertation on the limits of international law, a brilliant philosophy student not far away at the University of Heidelberg, Hannah Arendt, submitted her doctorate, "On the Concept of Love in the Thought of Augustine." Like Morgenthau's, Arendt's early career was upended by the rise of Nazism and the tumult of Europe in the 1930s—she was briefly arrested by Gestapo agents before fleeing Germany, and detained in Vichy France before escaping to the United States in the spring of 1941. A decade later, Arendt produced her first major work, a breathtaking treatise of intellectual history and political philosophy titled *The Origins of Totalitarianism* (1951).

Arendt dissected totalitarian theory and practice as embodied in the Nazi and Bolshevik regimes and extracted from within them an imperialist heart and antisemitic soul. Totalitarianism was not an invention of Hitler or Stalin, but rather, the logical extension of Cecil Rhodes and the Dreyfus affair. Like Niebuhr trying to make his readers conscious of irony, Arendt explained her purpose as instilling in her readers a stoical "comprehension" of the grim reality in which the world found itself. Like her fellow early Cold War realists, Arendt wanted the reader of *The Origins of Totalitarianism* to face up to "the irritating incompatibility between the actual power of modern man (greater than ever before, great to the point where he might challenge the very existence of his own universe) and the impotence of modern men to live in, and understand the sense of, a world which their own strength has established."[39]

It was in Cold War America where that incompatibility could be felt most intensely. Arendt concurred with Morgenthau that modernity had reached an impasse where "the essential structure of all civilizations is at the breaking point." The spirit of totalitarianism survived Hitler's suicide and Nazi defeat, only to be given new life by Stalin, through whom it continued to threaten "the destruction of humanity." She hardly downplayed the existential threat posed by Soviet totalitarianism. Arendt placed less emphasis on national interest in her analysis of the drivers of Moscow's behavior. "The struggle for total domination of the total population of the earth, the elimination of every competing nontotalitarian reality, is inherent in the totalitarian regimes themselves." Yet she arrived at conclusions similar to those of the statecraft thinkers Kennan and Morgenthau. For the United States to risk military struggle against the Soviets would only ensure the destruction of human existence. Arendt likened the year 1950 to "the calm that settles after all hopes have died," in anticipation of World War III.[40]

What role, then, should Arendt's adopted country of the United States, with its unrealistic optimism and "legalistic-moralistic" self-confidence, play in the world? How could the radical evil of totalitarianism be fought, if nuclear weapons paradoxically eliminated a military option? Conventional political life would not suffice. Neither the liberal nor the conservative answer went deep enough. It would not suffice to "escape the grimness of the present into nostalgia for a still intact past," as conservatives yearned to do, nor would it suffice to grasp at the "anticipated oblivion of a better future," as liberals imagined. Kennan counseled a grand strategy of patient containment and self-restraint, Morgenthau advanced a similarly restrained doctrine of national interest, Niebuhr offered of politics of contrition and love. Arendt's answer was probably closest to Niebuhr's—she had written a dissertation on Christian love and ended *The Origins of Totalitarianism* by citing scripture, a message of solidarity from the Gospels. In the years to come, Arendt would develop a positive philosophy around the core concept of *amor mundi*, "love of the world." But as of the time of writing *The Origins of Totalitarianism*, with vivid memories of narrowly escaping the death camps, Arendt's realism was closer to the existentialism of Albert Camus's *The Rebel* (1951). All there was to do, Arendt admonished, was to face things as they are. "This is the reality in which we live."[41]

Yale School of Realism

As Arendt, Morgenthau, Niebuhr, and Kennan argued before a national audience in defense of realism as a political philosophy and guide to American statecraft, international relations scholars in New Haven were propagating an academic school of realism that similarly counseled restraint, if without the moral reflection on the dangers to democracy in America. Housed in the Yale Institute of International Studies (YIIS), the Yale realists' publications neither rose to the strategic heights of Kennan and Morgenthau nor plumbed the philosophical depths like Niebuhr and Arendt. Yale colleagues at the law school and affiliated with YIIS raised pointed critiques of the lack of moral consideration. In that way, the Yale debates offer a microcosm in which to examine the postwar clash between the legalistic-moralistic paradigm and a variety of realist alternatives.

When George Kennan, freshly returned from Moscow, set off on a nationwide lecture tour in the fall of 1946 to educate Americans about the true nature of the Soviet challenge, his first stop was the Yale Institute of International Studies.[42] The institute had been founded in 1935 to deepen linkages between scholarship and foreign policy. Funded by private foundations like Rockefeller and Carnegie as well as the State Department, the institute's first director was Nicholas Spykman, a Dutch immigrant who joined the Yale faculty in 1925 and pioneered the modern study of "geostrategy."[43] Spykman was a fish out of water during the interwar years, rejecting both the internationalism of Wilsonian liberals at the Yale Law School—where international relations was mostly taught—and the isolationism of the America First Committee, which was founded in New Haven in September 1940.

Spykman saw the world in terms of power and geography rather than law and principle, but that did not mean global order could be simply ignored. He fashioned YIIS into a home for thinking about American grand strategy. As the country belatedly entered WWII, Spykman published *America's Strategy in World Politics*, a geopolitical handbook in the mold of Alfred Thayer Mahan and Halford Mackinder, in which he argued the United States was no longer safe in its own hemisphere. The country had no choice but join the war—not on the liberal internationalist rationale of combating the evil of fascism, but rather to avert being caught between German hegemony over Europe and Japanese hegemony over Asia. Splendid isolation was an outdated myth. "Oceans are no barriers; they are routes for the thrusts of sea power as well as highways of commerce."[44]

Spykman tried to sugarcoat the harshness of "balance of power" theory for American readers by likening it to the Founding Fathers' notion of checks and balances—like Morgenthau, he endeavored to root realism in American traditions.[45] Even though the United States had just joined WWII, he was already thinking about the peace, anticipating Washington's challenges in constructing a postwar order. "The end of a war is not the end of the power struggle," he wrote prophetically. In Europe, Russia was the natural candidate to fill the void left by Germany. In Asia, China threatened to fill the vacuum left by Japan. Neither option was good for the United States.[46] Spykman had a strong Eurocentric bias—he thought the Atlantic, as the source of American culture and center of gravity for Great Powers, would always overshadow the Pacific.[47] Yet he worried about the postwar threat of a strong China, able to dominate the "Asiatic Mediterranean" just like the United States dominates the "American Mediterranean." He predicted that the United States would have to revert to a pro-Japan policy after the war in order to guard against the rise of a hemispheric power in China.[48]

Spykman died of cancer at the peak of his intellectual powers in June 1943. He was succeeded as director of the institute by Frederick Dunn, who saw through the posthumous publication of Spykman's unfinished manuscript *The Geography of the Peace* (1944). In it, Spykman attempted an integrated strategic analysis of the European and Asian theaters. "Global war, as well as global peace, means that all fronts and all areas are interrelated. . . . The grand strategy of the war must thus be seen in terms of the intimate relationship between these [European and Far Eastern] centers of power."[49] Written at the high-water mark of the Soviet-American alliance, Spykman's book envisioned a postwar order in which the three "super-powers" (a word he is sometimes credited with coining) of the US, the USSR, and Great Britain could work together as "the only effective guarantors of the European situation."[50]

Dunn's associate director was William T. R. Fox, who had completed his doctoral work at the University of Chicago just before Morgenthau's arrival and joined Yale the year Spykman died. Fox popularized Spykman's term by making it the title of his own book, *The Super-Powers: The United States, Britain, and the Soviet Union—Their Responsibility for Peace* (1944). Following Spykman's lead, Fox sketched out an anticipatory analysis of the postwar order based on the relative power of states, divided into elephants and squirrels. Fox rejected the tradition of Wilsonian liberal internationalism, which he derided as a uniquely American delusion. "It is a peculiarly American notion to assume that problems in a world of power politics can be solved by creating a world of no-power politics. . . . In the world we are going to have to live in, differences in power do and will exist. Our problem is to discover the conditions of security in that world." Fox also scorned the vogue for ideas about a postwar world government, mocking the concept of a "supra-national police force." On the contrary, the key to postwar stability would be "to seek a definition of the national interest of each [surviving great power] in such terms that each will find it possible to collaborate with the others to maintain a stable and just postwar order." Fox hoped the three superpowers, the US, the UK, and the USSR, could settle for security rather than strive for domination—"then there is at least a possibility that in our time the great powers can collaborate in a system of general security."[51]

Fox notably excluded China from the short list of world powers. Deferring to his YIIS colleague David Nelson Rowe, Fox contended that while China (along with France) might be granted pro forma great power status in what became the United Nations, it was in reality a regional power at best. "China is exclusively an Asiatic power; no one would expect her to assume responsibilities for the enforcement of security in Europe." In the end, the key to postwar stability was the US-USSR relationship. Taking a coldly realist view and ignoring ideological incompatibility, Fox was optimistic that Russian interests could be harmonized with Anglo-American ones. "A Soviet-Anglo-American coalition for prolonging peace is not sufficient to guarantee permanent peace. It does offer real promise that the next twenty years will be a transition to something other than a third world war."[52]

Perhaps the most influential book published by the Yale Institute of International Studies in the postwar years was the edited volume *The Absolute Weapon: Atomic Power and World Order* (1946). The lead author was Bernard Brodie, who was born in Chicago to Russian Jewish immigrant parents, received his doctorate at the University of Chicago, and served in the Navy during the war. The central question of *The Absolute Weapon* was whether atomic bombs made the world more or less safe. Conventional wisdom might say the latter, but Brodie argued that the threat of nuclear attack would turn out to be the most effective means ever devised to avert actual war. Brodie disagreed with Robert Oppenheimer's self-criticism that he had helped to invent "an aggressor's weapon." Oppenheimer overlooked the likelihood that the Soviets would get the bomb too, which, Brodie asserted, would put both nuclear powers on the defensive given the prospect of retaliation. Frederick Dunn's chapter echoed Brodie, arguing that the only way to "safeguard" the use of atomic power was the threat of nuclear retaliation: "The prize for his violation of his agreement would be ashes!"[53] Nuclear deterrence theory, predicated on a logic of mutually assured destruction, was born. *The Absolute Weapon* implied that the real danger would be a world in which a single state maintained a monopoly on a power so singular—even if that country were the United States. Correctly anticipating that the Soviets would get the bomb relatively soon, the YIIS scholars implicitly made the claim that it would be a good thing for world peace.

One prominent political scientist associated with the Yale Institute of International Studies tried to defend the legalist-moralist tradition against these geostrategic arguments. Arnold Wolfers was born and educated in Switzerland and spent a decade at the University of Berlin, helping to set up the international relations program there. He left Germany as Hitler took power in 1933, joining Yale and helping Spykman with the founding of YIIS. In the first years of the Cold War, Wolfers wrote a series of articles pushing back against the excesses of realism, with some appearing in the institute's quarterly journal, *World Politics*, launched in the fall of 1948. He worried that the realist approach at YIIS, even if intended to induce restraint, could instead invite an endless game of power politics.

Although Wolfers conceded that the United States had no choice but to play the game of geostrategy to protect the "rimland" and "offshore islands" of Eurasia from Soviet aggression, he defended the American public's distaste for it. "Nothing has been more characteristic of American public opinion in respect of international affairs than the hatred of the struggle for power and security called 'power politics,' cause of the ever recurring evil of war."[54] In the essay "Statesmanship and Moral Choice," Wolfers rejected Kennan and Morgenthau's doctrine of national interest, labeling their approach the unrealistic one. "Under the circumstances usually prevailing in a multi-state system, painful limitations are set on policies of self-negation, generosity or restraint of power. It would be utopian to expect drastic changes in this respect. But to say that the field of international politics is reserved for selfishness, brutality, self-righteousness or unrestrained ambition for power is not only cynical but manifestly unrealistic."[55] Wolfers also thought deeply about the role of intelligence in foreign affairs, although it was a subject reserved for his teaching rather than published writings.[56]

Like Wolfers, the Yale Law School professor Harold Lasswell recoiled at the cult of power politics and national interest forming around him on campus in the early days of the Cold War. A pioneering figure in political psychology as well as the study of propaganda, Lasswell raised doubts about the deeper implications of the new "national security" architecture for the health of liberal democracy. In *National Security and Individual Freedom* (1950), Lasswell warned that the quest for national security threatened to turn the United States into a police state.[57] Like Kennan, Lippmann, and Morgenthau, Lasswell appealed to what he thought of as America's best traditions. "The United States has recently engaged in measures out of key with the basic traditions of the nation. The holding of wholesale loyalty investigations is an example. There is no need to terrorize the population by mass surveillance."[58] The obsession with national security, stoked by fears of foreign subversion, unleashed dangerous forces of internal repression, leaving 1950s America vulnerable to the same disease that had ravaged Weimar Germany. Lasswell's book went into print in June 1950, the same month that North Korea's Soviet tanks rolled across the thirty-eighth parallel in a surprise invasion of South Korea. His critique of the emerging national security complex was drowned out in the mobilization for war, which was a blank check for precisely the kind of national security apparatus he warned against.

Lasswell's publication timing may have been unfortunate, but his thinking was in line with that of Yale's new president, tapped at the same critical moment in the summer of 1950. A. Whitney "Whit" Griswold was, like Charles Seymour, a descendent of presidents past, hailing from a patrician family related to Eli Whitney on one side and six Connecticut governors on the other. Twenty years Seymour's junior, Whit was also a historian, and author of the well-regarded *Far Eastern Policy of the United States* (1938). In his view, the university, like the rest of the country, needed to heal from the scars of the Second World War: "War with its passions, its aftermath of fear and hate, its crushing debt, has shaken our whole society to its foundations, and our colleges and universities have not escaped this cosmic disturbance."[59]

Before Whit knew what was coming, another "cosmic disturbance" hit campus. As Griswold reported to alumni, "On June 25, just five days before I assumed office, the North Koreans launched what then seemed—and yet might prove—the opening encounter of the third World War. The effects of this aggressive action, which forced us back into large-scale mobilization for an unpredictable period, were immediately felt by our colleges and universities." Korea forced Yale to answer a "vital, all-embracing question" for liberal institutions under the conditions imposed by the Cold War: "How can we fulfill our responsibilities and realize our objectives as a private university in an age of steadily expanding public enterprise and protracted war?"[60]

Griswold answered the question in his inaugural presidential address delivered on the afternoon of October 6, 1950—which unknown to him or his audience, took place just days after Mao Zedong's fateful decision to send Chinese troops to fight in Korea. Whit appealed to three traditions—higher learning, university life, and American democracy—that together defined the soul of Yale. These were "things to cherish and defend in times of war; to fight for, when there is fighting; and to return to when the fighting is over." After five fleeting years of postwar peace, the United States found itself back on the battlefield, intervening in an obscure civil war that felt like prelude to a third "total war." As during WWII, mobilization threatened the core of Yale's mission. "The times are not auspicious for learning. They are times of war, and war imposes a terrible burden of proof on everything that does not directly serve its ends. Just and noble as we believe those ends to be in our own case, war and the preparation for war are not conducive to the reflective life that produces great teaching and great scholarship."[61]

In the wake of the Soviets' atomic test, the specter of nuclear holocaust loomed large, something almost too terrifying to name outright. Griswold mused how "the Promethean secret of the atom breeds fear and suspicion in all our hearts, inclining us to dismiss the past, to dread the future, and to live in the present." Measured by the instrumentalities of war, learning and scholarship seemed to lose their value: "What price the scholar's life in times like these, or the university's, whose purpose is to foster that life?" But the university had to preserve and pass down its traditions. "If the scholars of the past had waited for auspicious times to do their work, I doubt that we should be assembled here today. If they should now wait for total war to produce total peace, I doubt that our successors will be assembled here to mark Yale's three hundredth anniversary."[62]

Most dangerous of all, the traditions of American democracy, undergirded by freedom of inquiry and sacred to university life, were under threat from within. Just as in other eras Athens forced Socrates to drink the hemlock, the Vatican censured Galileo, the Nazis exiled Germany's best scholars, and the Soviets terrorized the intelligentsia, so now in the United States the "tendency toward repression" (as Seymour called it) could be felt on campuses. Alluding to loyalty oaths foreswearing communism that were being demanded of employees at the University of California, Griswold lamented, "Even British and American scholars have suffered from test oaths—as they once did in the early days of both Oxford and Yale and do now in California."[63]

A year into the war, Arnold Wolfers took up the argument being made by Griswold and Lasswell, publishing a forceful assault on the false idol of national security and the limits of realism. Deconstructing the term "national interest," Wolfers showed how the phrase's original emphasis on prosperity, found in the seminal writings of the economic historian Charles Beard, had been securitized, such that national interest was now conflated with national *security* interest. Wolfers feared that the American public had lost their sense of moderation and moral compass—after "a new relapse into wishful thinking in 1945," Americans seemed to be "swinging toward excessive security apprehensions."[64] The United States, like all countries, would have to plot a course between two extremes, "the pole of complete indifference to security" and "the pole of insistence on absolute security or of complete reliance on coercive power."[65] Each step toward absolute security required sacrificing public goods, whether economic growth or civil liberties.[66]

Wolfers aimed above his colleagues in the Yale Institute of International Studies, taking on the nation's two most influential foreign policy thinkers, Morgenthau and Kennan. "It is not without irony that of the two authors who have recently come out for a policy of the national interest, the one, George F. Kennan, who calls for a policy of national self-restraint and humility, usually identified with morality, should deny 'that state behavior is a fit subject for moral judgment,' while the other, Hans Morgenthau, calling for a policy of unadulterated national egotism, claims to speak in the name of morality."[67] Ironically, Kennan and Morgenthau agreed with their legalist-moralist critics at Yale on the dilemma posed by the Cold War, a danger graver even than Soviet totalitarianism, the one that could come from within.

The tendency toward repression, fueled by the fear of subversion, was coursing through American society and politics. It was also running amok in Communist China.

3

SUBVERSION AND REPRESSION

America's second Red Scare was quietly underway by the day in February 1950 when Joe McCarthy gave his now infamous speech, "Enemies from Within," to a polite audience at the Ohio County Republican Women's Club in Wheeling, West Virginia. Cribbing material from Congressman Richard Nixon, McCarthy's allegations that the Department of State was a hotbed of subversion, crawling with communists and traitors, at first generated only modest headlines.[1] So a couple weeks later, McCarthy slipped the national press a name, letting it be known that the top Soviet agent of subversion at work in the United States of America was none other than one of the country's leading China Hands, Professor Owen Lattimore.

Lattimore was a fifty-year-old ethnographer, historian, and geostrategist, a polyglot who felt perfectly at home wandering the vast Inner Asian frontier, an occasional diplomat who served as personal liaison between President Franklin Roosevelt and Generalissimo Chiang Kai-shek during WWII. In his current iteration, Lattimore was director of the nation's first school of international relations, the Walter Hines Page School of International Relations (established in 1925) at Johns Hopkins University. The accusation against him sent shockwaves through the small world of China studies, pitting his staunchest defender—Harvard's John King Fairbank—against his persistent accuser—Yale's David Nelson Rowe.

The public clash and private maneuvering of three of the country's leading China scholars reveals the force of the wave of repression generated by McCarthyite fears of subversion, as well as countervailing efforts to defend liberal values of academic freedom and political dissent. This tension between repression and openness played out on campuses around the country, including at Yale—not only in the person of Professor Rowe, but also in the fight between a new-style conservative firebrand in the class of 1950, William F. Buckley Jr., and the old-school liberal president, Whit Griswold. A struggle for the soul of America was bound up in the fierce debate over who was to blame for the loss of China, whether restraint was a realistic foreign policy for Cold War America, and whether subversion could be resisted without empowering the forces of repression.

Tale of Three China Hands

When Owen Lattimore arrived in Chongqing in the sweltering summer of 1941, it was a kind of homecoming. Raised in the northern port city of Tianjin, where his American parents worked as English teachers, Owen went off to Europe for schooling from age twelve, but returned to China after college to work as an insurance salesman. He married the equally adventurous Eleanor Holgate, and their honeymoon road trip served as the basis for a pair of books—his *Desert Road to Turkestan* (1928) and her *Turkestan Reunion* (1934). Spending a year at Harvard and then based out of Beijing, Lattimore turned from travelogue to geopolitics in a succession of books on the borderland where China and Russia meet: *High Tartary* (1930), *Manchuria: Cradle of Conflict* (1932), and *The Mongols of Manchuria* (1934). A job as editor of the new journal *Pacific Affairs*, published by the Institute of Pacific Relations (IPR) with funding from the Rockefeller Foundation, allowed Lattimore to wander the Far East. But Japan's full-scale invasion of China in 1937 made the wandering life impossible, and Lattimore accepted an offer by the university president Isaiah Bowman to join the faculty at Johns Hopkins. Lattimore published a more academic book, *Inner Asian Frontiers of China* (1940), a kind of mid-career summa that fused geography and history in a manner akin to the French historian Fernand Braudel, who was in a German POW camp writing his historical masterpiece on the inner sea frontier of Europe, the Mediterranean.

When FDR's economic adviser Lauchlin Currie returned from a visit to Chongqing in early 1941 with the recommendation to send a trusted figure to embed with Chiang Kai-shek, Lattimore was chosen for the mission.[2] One of Owen's traveling companions on the Pan American Airways Clipper flying out of San Francisco in July was Lieutenant General Claire Chennault, who was preparing his American Volunteer Group, affectionately known as the Flying Tigers, for deployment to help encourage the unofficial alliance forming with Chiang Kai-shek's Nationalist regime.[3] For a tumultuous year, Lattimore worked closely with Generalissimo Chiang and Madame Soong Mei-ling, even if his advice was often ignored.[4] In the critical month of the Pearl Harbor attack, Lattimore held daily sessions with the ruling couple, his special place in their inner sanctum symbolized by his presence as the only foreigner at the family Christmas dinner.[5]

The Lattimore mission overlapped only briefly with the arrival of a fellow China Hand in Chongqing, David Nelson Rowe.[6] For Rowe, too, it was a homecoming—he was born to Methodist missionary parents in Nanjing in 1905 and grew up speaking Chinese and English before he left for Princeton. In 1935, Rowe completed his doctoral thesis at the University of Chicago comparing the history of US foreign policy in the Americas (the Monroe Doctrine) versus in China (the so-called Open Door policy). Following in Lattimore's wake, Rowe spent two years at Harvard studying Chinese and Japanese, and then received a Rockefeller Foundation grant to head to Beijing, where he amassed a large collection of Japanese propaganda materials. After a year, Rowe took a job at Princeton lecturing on Far Eastern affairs, at around the same time that Lattimore assumed the directorship at Johns Hopkins.

In the lead-up to America's entry into WWII, Rowe was a natural recruit for the brand-new intelligence service, the Office of Strategic Services (OSS). After a brief stint at the Experimental Center for the Study of Wartime Communication at the Library of Congress, Rowe was dispatched to Chongqing under diplomatic cover. His assignment was to use his knowledge of Japanese propaganda to create effective counterpropaganda and to acquire materials for classification and analysis by the OSS Research and Analysis Branch.[7] Rowe enthusiastically subjected Chinese press reports to "content analysis," a cutting-edge social science research method of counting keywords to quantify textual meaning, which Rowe had learned from its progenitor, Harold Lasswell, who had been Rowe's boss at the Library of Congress's Experimental Center (before Lasswell joined the faculty at Yale Law School).[8] In Chongqing, Rowe watched in consternation as other American observers' assessments of the Nationalist regime grew increasingly pessimistic. The "open cynicism and disillusion" with Chiang among US embassy officials led, in Rowe's view, to a naïve willingness to let Communists share "a measure of governmental power."[9]

Like Rowe, John King Fairbank was an early recruit for the OSS, and he took a leave from Harvard in 1941 to head the China/Japan shop in the Research and Analysis Branch.[10] Fairbank was a great admirer of Lattimore, having read *Manchuria: Cradle of Conflict* on his maiden voyage to Peking in 1932. As he put it later, "Owen's imagination fused his field observations with the known facts to build castles of historical theory."[11] Whereas Lattimore embodied the virtues of a worldly humanism, Rowe represented the worst of social science. Fairbank sneered at Rowe's faith in content analysis to provide "an objective procedure that would make the cacophony of political discussion into a science happily based on numbers." Reading Rowe's reports sent back to OSS headquarters, Fairbank wondered if their man in Chongqing had lost his mind. "He felt he was being followed and indeed conspired against and endangered. We feared he had gone bonkers and brought him back to see doctors."[12] Fairbank himself headed to Chongqing in August 1942 to clean up Rowe's mess and get the intelligence effort going again. By the following spring, liaison with Nationalist military intelligence officers started to yield worthwhile documents to microfilm and send back to Washington.[13] Fairbank completed his tour at the end of 1943, flying home in the company of the legendary OSS chief, "Wild Bill" Donovan.[14]

As for Rowe, after leaving the OSS in mid-1942, he linked up with the Yale Institute of International Studies, which commissioned a policy memo from him, "China's Military Potential and the Enforcement of Peace," and then published an expanded version as Rowe's first book, *China among the Powers* (1945). Rowe was trying to resolve the contradiction between the American desire for China to play the role of a great power in the postwar era with the reality that China lacked the capacity to do so. He insisted that China should make the shortlist of Fox's "superpowers," asserting that "today China stands with Britain, the Soviet Union, and the United States as one of the great powers, and few would question her right to such a position in world affairs." And yet, he had to acknowledge that "although politically China is one of the 'Big Four,' militarily she cannot at present by any definition be termed a great power, nor will she be a military power of the first rank at the end of the war, no matter what elements of military strength are contributed to her by others." Rather than idealize Chiang Kai-shek, Rowe fell back on the contention that the leader China needed at the moment was not necessarily the one America wanted for her. China was in a life-and-death struggle for its very existence and could not afford the luxury of a liberal, democratic leader. "It is not necessary to admire Chiang Kai-shek or always to agree on the ethics of his use of power in specific instances to recognize that without him China might not exist as an entity today. . . . Those who urge the Chinese to lift the level of their political morality should remember that without survival there could be no morality."[15]

Rowe insisted that the national interest of the United States was a strong China, one that could stand as the fourth pillar of the world order; and for that, China needed development before democracy. "The improbability of the development in China within the next generation of anything like what Americans think of as working democracy should not be allowed to obscure the chief issues, which concern the content of socio-economic policy. For these are the issues which will determine how soon and to what extent China can strengthen herself in order to participate in the maintenance of peace and security in the postwar world." Presciently, Rowe identified the key to China's modernization as being the transformation of rural life ("the enterprise of creating out of China a state in the modern sense of the word cannot succeed without wiping out the sources of political disunity and civic weakness inherent in the present-day life of the Chinese countryside").[16] But he either failed or refused to recognize that the Communists, not the Nationalists, were the ones focused on political mobilization and "socialist transformation" of the rural areas.

In Rowe's view, the role of the United States was to bridge the gap between the current reality of China's economic-military weakness and the future requirement for China to stand as a great power. China needed massive aid in order to develop industrial might, and until then, the United States would have to shoulder much of the load. Acquiring territory would help—Rowe insisted that all territory acquired by Japan since 1868 should revert to the "original owners." He specifically included the Ryukyu Islands, an autonomous kingdom absorbed by the Japanese empire and renamed Okinawa in the later nineteenth century. Rowe argued that Okinawa should be "returned" to the Republic of China, on the condition that US military forces were assured access for a period of twenty-five years. Korea should be made into an "Allied tutelage" until ready for self-government, while "wealth created by the Japanese in Korea" should be "finally given to the Korean people as a small recompense for what they have suffered at the hands of the Japanese." As for Japan itself, the United States would have to enforce the peace after victory. "For the policing of Japan after the war, it will be impossible to place primary reliance on China."[17]

At the time Rowe's *China among the Powers* came out in 1945, Fairbank was headed back to China to set up operations for the State Department's overseas propaganda arm, the United States Information Service (USIS). He came away utterly disgusted with the brutality of Chiang Kai-shek's men and impressed by the "imagination and vitality" of Zhou Enlai's group in Chongqing.[18] After returning to Harvard in mid-1946, Fairbank began to weigh in on the national debate over China policy with a flurry of publications laying out a framework of analysis and set of prescriptions entirely different from Rowe's. Fairbank's first book, *The United States and China* (1948), argued that China, and Asia generally, remained a blank space in the emerging polarity of West (the US and Western Europe) and East (the USSR and Eastern Europe). Asia represented a third pole, defined by nationalism rather than the struggle between liberalism and communism. Cautioning about the limits of American understanding and influence, Fairbank asserted that "the Asiatic half of mankind is entering upon an era of change which the West has precipitated but which we cannot control."[19] Nationalism, not Marxism, was the proper metric by which to understand Mao Zedong's success.

> Like all Communist movements the Chinese Party stood to rise or fall by its relationship to the spirit of nationalism. If it represented a foreign influence infiltrating Chinese society and subverting the national culture and independence, its progress would be slow and its social revolution might be thwarted by Nationalist aspirations. If, on the other hand, the Chinese Communist movement could establish a claim to true patriotism and become a vehicle for Chinese nationalistic sentiment, its revolutionary task would be much easier. From this point of view, one key to the increase of Communist power in China has been its championing of national resistance to Japan.[20]

The Chinese Communists were sincere in their Marxist-Leninist beliefs—it was naïve to consider them mere "agrarian reformers." But they were at the same time independent of the USSR—it was equally naïve to think of them as mere "puppets of Moscow."[21]

The key, therefore, to a successful China policy was for the United States to stay on the good side of Chinese nationalism. Backing Chiang and the Nationalist Party made that impossible. In the wake of the ill-fated Marshall Mission, Fairbank wrote, "We are cast in the role of imperialists intervening in Chinese affairs to prop up a reactionary Kuomintang. Every help we give to our ally the National Government of China therefore seems to Chinese Communists to prove the correctness of their ideology."[22] As a short-term policy, Fairbank opposed pouring more aid into the Nationalist sinkhole, and instead called for preparing for official dealings with the CCP. In the long run, however, Fairbank held out hope in a liberal alternative to the Chiang's Nationalists and Mao's Communists—the small parties and independent moderates known as the Third Force. Supporting liberals added another reason to break from Chiang.

> We cannot expect to find in the near future a Chinese liberal movement on which we can base a policy. Yet liberalism, in its peculiar Chinese form, will be an important and continuing factor in Chinese politics. We have nurtured it in the past. But recently we have been losing its allegiance. American aid to the National Government is widely regarded in China as a chief factor permitting the Kuomintang right wing to terrorize and stultify those Chinese liberals who have heretofore looked upon us as their natural allies.[23]

Owen Lattimore returned to Washington in early 1942 and spent half a year promoting Chiang's cause, a thankless task that left him eager to take a job offer from the Office of War Information (OWI) doing propaganda work out of San Francisco. He schlepped all the way back to Chongqing to ask Chiang's permission before moving to the new role. Chiang gave him leave and flew him home in style, putting Lattimore on the plane with Madame Soong as she set off on her famous American tour and speech to Congress.[24] Lattimore spent the next two years as deputy director of Pacific Operations for OWI, during which time he produced a pair of ardently pro-Chiang books, *America and Asia* (1943) and *Making of Modern China* (1944), expressing a view closer to Rowe than to Fairbank. In May 1944, he was conscripted once again for semi-official governmental service, accompanying Vice President Henry Wallace and John Paton Davies on a fact-finding trip through Siberia, Mongolia, and ultimately Chongqing.

By V-J Day in August 1945, Lattimore had turned decisively against Chiang Kai-shek and the Nationalist Party, writing a personal letter to President Truman warning that continued aid to the generalissimo ran counter to the will of the Chinese people and would only end up giving Moscow the upper hand.[25] Lattimore's columns and essays during the Chinese Civil War tracked the sentiments of Fairbank, and he put them together in a hastily assembled book, *The Situation in Asia*, published in April 1949.[26] The United States was not only about to lose China—Asia as a whole was "out of control" and would expose the impotence of the American military colossus, whose costly war machine was no match for guerillas enjoying popular support.[27] "The grandiose and disastrous American attempt to determine the character and outcome of the Chinese civil war then proved that America does not have the kind of power that can settle Chinese issues."[28] Lattimore predicted that Asia's postcolonial leaders would resist both American and Soviet efforts to establish hegemony. Asia was skidding on two rails, nationalism and revolution, and United States had to match the Russians' "professional skill in the art of influencing revolutions which we cannot control."[29]

Like the realists, Lattimore agonized over the painful contradiction between the limits of American power and boundlessness of American responsibility. The United States could not choose to deal with Europe first and then turn to Asia—she would have to act on both stages simultaneously. "There are limits to our power. When power is limited, successful policy consists in doing what you can do in each situation, not in trying to do exactly what you would like to do, when you do not have what it takes."[30] In such a situation, the United States could not afford to pour aid into a broken vessel like Chiang Kai-shek.[31]

Ironically, Lattimore, who worked up close with Chiang, expressed higher praise for the generalissimo than did Rowe. He described the G-mo as "a great and farsighted world statesman . . . never a dictator," who maneuvered as best he could. Lattimore argued that unconditional US aid, perversely, only undermined Chiang by emboldening the despotic elements within the Nationalist camp, denying Chiang leverage he needed to move in a more liberal direction.[32] Despite this lingering loyalty to Chiang, Lattimore was unequivocal that supporting the Nationalists was a mistake. He agreed with Fairbank that in the near term Beijing could be lured away from Moscow, and over the long run liberal elements could be encouraged. Writing in 1950, Lattimore also pushed the idea of supporting the Third Force.

> It is possible that a middle-of-the-road or democratic group in China not necessarily part of the Nationalist Government—those whom General Marshall rightly called "a splendid group of men"—can still maintain their strong position in the confidence of the Chinese people unless we drive them completely into the hands of the Communists. . . . To encourage in every possible way the conditions that will make possible the survival of a so-called third force, a democratic group within China, that can change the character of the government . . . our long-term objective should clearly be . . . to build up conditions that favor a democratic group, including such elements of the Kuomintang as may be available and suitable.[33]

There was one key element in providing effective support to China's non-Communist left: it should be invisible. Foreign ties would compromise its legitimacy and only justify repression by the CCP. "The danger of malignant secret police development begins when, after victory, a revolutionary government feels that it has to keep watch on all kinds of people who have foreign sympathies or may be receiving foreign support," he wrote in 1949.[34] Lattimore apparently was unaware that his own government had been keeping watch on him, for years, by the time *Situation in Asia* came out.

With Mao's victory in the Chinese Civil War and the outbreak of the Korean War, Fairbank stepped up his efforts to educate Americans, publishing a book on the nineteenth-century treaty port system and co-editing a pair of seminal reference works.[35] Inspired by the Institute of Pacific Relations with funding from the Rockefeller Foundation, Fairbank and Têng Ssu-yü's anthology, *China's Response to the West: A Documentary Survey, 1839–1923* (1954), insisted that Americans needed a better understanding of the world. "Perhaps the moral is that we cannot really help another society unless we first understand it ourselves," Fairbank and Têng wrote.[36] They explicitly linked modern Chinese leaders' response to the challenge of the West to the current China policy conundrum: "Does the Chinese communist victory constitute, as it seems to some, a rejection of the West? Or is it, in a sense, a final step in accepting certain aspects of the West? Or again, is it merely the latest phase of a continuing process within the body of

Chinese society?" The educator in Fairbank refused to give a straightforward answer, instead, he made a homework assignment of it. "Since this event [the rise of the CCP] is certainly the most portentous in the whole history of American foreign policy in Asia, every intelligent American must strive to understand its significance."[37] But a discerning reader could appreciate how the main theme of the book, the "ethnocentric and China-centered" nature of Chinese leaders' efforts to adapt to the challenge of the West, implied that Chairman Mao probably fit the same mold.[38]

As a companion volume to *China's Response to the West*, Fairbank and two graduate students, Conrad Brandt and Benjamin Schwartz, produced another foundational anthology for Chinese studies, *A Documentary History of Chinese Communism* (1952). Fairbank argued that US policy would succeed or fail based on the depth of historical understanding on the part of the American public. "No aspect of Modern China is more important for Americans to comprehend if they would attempt to gauge the strength of the ideological bond which now links the Chinese and Russian Communist states. . . . [Is] Peking a puppet of Moscow . . . or is Chairman Mao Tse-tung a potential Chinese Tito, biding his time until he can escape the Russian embrace?"[39] Once again, rather than answer his own question outright, Fairbank let the documents do the talking.

David Nelson Rowe, the workhorse of Yale's Far Eastern Studies program and active in the Yale Institute of International Studies, could not compete with Fairbank's burst of scholarly productivity. But he tried his best to countereducate the public by giving lectures at Yale and talking to the press. "I take an opposite view on almost everything Prof. Fairbank says," Rowe told one newsman.[40] Then-student James Lilley recalled that Rowe "attacked" Fairbank and others "for their positive view of the Communists as a force that China needed."[41] Rowe also found covert means to advance the cause of anti-communism. A lieutenant colonel in the Army Reserve, Rowe set up an on-campus unit of the Military Intelligence Reserve in the summer of 1949, called the 463rd Strategic Intelligence Research and Analysis Unit on the Far East at Yale.[42] He was confirmed in July 1951 as a specialist in strategic intelligence in charge of a "cell" of three faculty members and three students.[43]

Un-American Activities

The policy disagreements tinged with professional rivalry between Professors Lattimore, Fairbank, and Rowe took on a new gravity and viciousness when Senator Joe McCarthy had Lattimore's name leaked to the press as the "top ranking Soviet spy in this country," an allegation that made the front page of the *New*

York Times on March 27, 1950.[44] McCarthy's case against Lattimore could be traced back to a friendly picnic held in the final months of the Second World War. Owen and Eleanor Lattimore hosted the party, inviting an acquaintance from their visit to Mao's base in Yan'an in the summer of 1937, Philip Jaffe. Jaffe was the editor of the left-leaning journal *Amerasia* and under secret surveillance by J. Edgar Hoover for publishing confidential OSS reports.[45] FBI agents were tailing Jaffe when he attended the picnic, which also included the suspected source of the leaked documents—State Department foreign service officer and China Hand John Stewart Service.[46] Although the *Amerasia* case would have to be scuttled due to inadmissible evidence, Lattimore was now on the FBI's counterespionage radar. He became a public target of the China lobby, accused of Soviet sympathies in *Reader's Digest* and subjected to a scathing profile, "Owen Lattimore: Expert's Expert," written by proto-McCarthyite businessman Alfred Kohlberg.[47]

As Cold War tensions intensified in Europe and General Marshall headed off on his mediation mission to China, the hunt for subversives at home brought China Hands under increasing scrutiny. The campaign came into public view the month that Marshall declared his mission over, when senators in the China bloc held up the nomination of another China Hand, John Carter Vincent, as career minister due to suspicions, based on "evidence" procured by Kohlberg, that Vincent was a leftist.[48] Looming ominously in the background was J. Edgar Hoover, the powerful security czar who rose to prominence chasing subversives during America's first Red Scare after WWI and would hang onto the position of FBI director from 1924 until his death almost a half-century later. Hoover's files gave him extraordinary leverage over the nation's power elite, and he was a master of leaks to the press and information sharing with whoever occupied the White House and key members of Congress. Hoover embraced the mission of finding and neutralizing subversive forces. "A good citizen must be on guard against subversion in all its forms. Call it Communism, Fascism, or what you will—it is un-American," Hoover declared in 1939, as the House Committee on Un-American Activities (HUAC) was born as a Congressional tool to heighten public awareness of the dangers of subversion.[49]

Wary of an American gestapo, Truman kept Hoover at arm's length and disdained the work of HUAC. But in the same week that the president gave his so-called Truman Doctrine speech to Congress, he also signed Executive Order 9835 (the Loyalty Order) that established the Federal Employee Loyalty Board and the Attorney General's List of Subversive Organizations. If these were flanking moves to pre-empt Republican attacks on his administration as soft, they backfired, engendering a culture of suspicion inside the federal government and generating a paper trail for more Republican-led investigations in Congress.[50]

As HUAC went after prominent film industry figures known as the Hollywood Ten, China bloc stalwart Congressman Walter Judd (R-Minnesota) railed against the conspiracy of "a handful of Communists, fellow-travellers, and misguided liberals" in speeches demanding aid to Chiang Kai-shek. Judd, who had spent a decade in China as a missionary, denounced "what has become widely known as the 'Red cell' in the State Department, the Far Eastern Office."[51]

One of the most prominent anti-communist voices in the Eightieth Congress was the young Republican Richard Nixon, a war vet from Southern California who championed draft legislation called the Subversive Activities Control Act (also known as the Mundt-Nixon Bill) that would require Communist Party members to register with the attorney general. Passing the House in the spring of 1948, the bill did not make it out of the Senate Judiciary Committee. Representative Nixon kept up the fight, leading the charge from his perch on the House Un-American Activities Committee during the sensational spy trial of senior US diplomat Alger Hiss in August.[52] Nixon's persistence in questioning Hiss brought about the first televised hearings in congressional history. A former Communist named Whittaker Chambers gave sensational testimony confessing that he and Hiss were part of a Soviet spy ring. Adding to the drama (or absurdity) of the case, Chambers led HUAC investigators to his Maryland farm and produced microfilmed documents hidden in a pumpkin patch that Hiss allegedly gave him for their intelligence value, dubbed the "Pumpkin Papers."

Hiss's grand jury trials dragged on for a year, fanning fears of domestic subversion. The public naturally wondered, as Eric Goldman put it, "If a man of Hiss's background, achievements, and reputation for character had spied for Communism, who could be trusted?"[53] Meanwhile, J. Edgar Hoover ordered FBI surveillance on Lattimore based on the accusation of a Russian defector. Agents were tailing Lattimore, in fact, when he visited John King Fairbank for his annual appearance at the Harvard China seminar.[54] Now Fairbank's name was added to the FBI list. Hoover's paranoia over a communist conspiracy was fed by his access to decrypted Soviet communications known to only a handful of US government analysts and officials. Counterintelligence cryptographers working for the Venona Project began deciphering wartime Soviet cables, exposing extensive spying operations that employed US citizens as agents. One of the spies implicated by the decryptions was a Department of Justice employee, Judith Coplon, who was arrested in New York in March 1949. An even bigger bombshell spy revelation hit early in 1950 when the public was told that a German-born British physicist, Klaus Fuchs, had passed atomic secrets to the Soviets during the time he worked at Los Alamos National Laboratory in New Mexico. Fuchs's trial in the UK, coming on the heels of the perjury conviction of Alger Hiss, created the unnerving impression of a global conspiracy to subvert the West from within.[55] This was the context in which Senator McCarthy gave his Enemies Within speech in Wheeling, West Virginia.

Senate Democrats went on the offensive in the spring of 1950, hoping to nip the Red Scare in the bud and outflank McCarthy, just as Truman had tried to do with the Loyalty Order three years earlier.[56] The Senate Subcommittee on the Investigation of Loyalty of State Department Employees, or Tydings Committee, after chair Millard Tydings (D-Maryland), convened special hearings from March 8 to July 17, 1950. The Democrats' strategy was to put Joe McCarthy, not the State Department, on trial. There were elements of a culture war at play in the contest pitting "Fighting Joe" McCarthy, a working-class hero to many for his patriotic crusade, against the Alger Hisses and Dean Achesons, "bright young men who are born with silver spoons in their mouths."[57] As the historian Christopher Elias has shown, the battle between McCarthy and his critics was also bound up in Cold War notions of masculinity that conflated communism and homosexuality, linking subversion of national security to perversion of sexual mores.[58] After stumbling through the early hearings with vague allegations, McCarthy finally created the sensation he needed by publicly denouncing Owen Lattimore as "the top Russian espionage agent" in the United States.[59]

If McCarthy thought he had a soft target in Lattimore as a genteel scholar who would crack under pressure, it was a miscalculation. Lattimore was in Afghanistan on a United Nations mission when he received a telegram from the Associated Press—McCarthy "says off record you top Russian espionage agent in United States and that his whole case rests on you."[60] He hurried back to Washington to face his accuser. Fairbank swung into action the same day Lattimore's name appeared in the *New York Times*, circulating a letter to many of the country's leading Asia experts, assuming that they, too, were "naturally appalled at McCarthy's reckless and irresponsible name-calling." Fairbank appealed to their sense of solidarity not only because Lattimore was innocent, but also because "the taint could easily spread."[61] Paul Linebarger, professor of Asiatic politics at the Johns Hopkins School of Advanced International Studies, wrote drolly that "if Lattimore is a master spy, the *Saturday Evening Post* is a voice of Moscow, General Marshall is a traitor, and Elmer Davis a rascal."[62]

All but one of the recipients of Fairbank's letter signed. The lone refusal came from David Nelson Rowe. "I am certainly not qualified to state anything, either pro or con, on the question of whether Owen is a Communist agent or not," Rowe replied. "Any such letter might lay me open to a charge of participating in an attempt to establish 'innocence by association.'"[63]

Lattimore began his testimony before the Tydings Committee on April 6. He did not see himself as the real target of McCarthy's campaign: "He was using me as an excuse to attack the China policy of the State Department; through the State Department, evidently, he was hoping to throw the Administration off balance in an election year." Lattimore viewed McCarthy as a pawn in the battle over China policy and whether to support Chiang Kai-shek's regime in Taiwan. McCarthy was "the dupe of a bitter and implacable and fanatical group of people who will not tolerate any discussion of China which is not based upon absolute, total, and complete support of the Nationalist Government in Formosa. . . . Their methods are to intimidate persons like me and even officials of the United States Government from expressing views that are contrary to their own." McCarthy exploited pre-existing fears—"For a long time now fear of spies had been feeding

FIGURE 2. The professor and the senator: Owen Lattimore and Joe McCarthy (1950). AP Photos.

fear of Communist subversion, and fear of Communism had been building up fear of espionage." The "McCarthy method" of accusing experts of being agents as a means to silence them was dangerously effective.[64]

Lattimore and the Democrats won round one. The Tydings Committee chastised McCarthy for making groundless accusations of infiltration in the State Department, which were characterized as "a fraud and a hoax perpetrated on the Senate of the United States and the American people." Senator Tydings exonerated Lattimore by revealing that the subcommittee members had read his "file" in the presence of J. Edgar Hoover, who personally compiled the dossier ("it was quite lengthy"), and "there was nothing in that file to show that you were a Communist, or that you were in any way connected with any espionage information or charges."[65] To Lattimore it was an unnerving exculpation. His innocence was defended, but on the basis of a secret police file that seemed like something out of George Orwell's recently published *Nineteen Eighty-Four.*

Lattimore was right to worry that the forces of repression were not done trying to make a lesson of him. In the fevered atmosphere of the Korean War, the senatorial inquisition into subversion spearheaded by McCarthy and supported by the China bloc gained a new lease on life.[66] A week after General MacArthur's Incheon landing, Congress passed the Internal Security Act of 1950 over President Truman's veto, establishing a special government agency, the Subversive Activities Control Board, to investigate organizations working to advance "totalitarian dictatorship" in the United States, in connection with either the Communist Party or its front organizations. Also known as the McCarran Act, after Nevada senator Pat McCarran, the lone Democrat in the China bloc, the law was based on the anti-subversion legislation championed back in 1948 by Nixon. McCarran headed the special Senate Subcommittee on Internal Security, the McCarran Committee, whose first target in the hunt for "subversive forces" was the independent research network the Institute of Pacific Relations (IPR).

Hearings commenced in July 1951 and would drag on for almost a year, putting China policy and China experts on trial for treason, investigating, in the committee's own words, "whether and to what extent these agents and their dupes . . . exerted an influence on United States far eastern policy."[67] As with Whittaker Chambers and his Pumpkin Papers, the McCarran Committee investigators built their case on a cache of documents, the IPR files, discovered in a barn in Massachusetts. The star witness for the prosecution was another ex-Communist, Louis Budenz, who accused Lattimore, Fairbank, and John Carter Vincent of being closet members of the Communist Party.[68] Lattimore was called back before Congress, where he defended himself with the fury of an innocent man, driving the committee members mad with his defiant tone.

Harvard versus Yale

John King Fairbank testified to the committee in March 1952, following Lattimore's combative appearance.[69] Though less confrontational, Fairbank was just as unflappable. He coolly went on the offensive, chiding the committee for using methods of inquiry that "turned our traditional American freedom of contact into totalitarian 'guilt by association.'"[70]

Two weeks later, David Nelson Rowe appeared before the committee to do just the opposite, denouncing many of his fellow China experts. Rowe's views had hardened since the outbreak of the war in Korea, and he was eager to join the Cold War fight. In December 1950 he told the *New Haven Register* that the United States should mobilize an "Asiatic force" of 1.5 to 2 million soldiers (half of them Japanese) to prepare for the defense of Asia against Communism. If the Communist forces did not accept unconditional surrender in Korea, the US should take the war to China with a complete blockade and selective bombing of infrastructure, in addition to subsidizing a Taiwan-based airlift to supply anti-Communist guerillas in mainland China. Americans "who know or want to learn guerilla warfare" should be sent to assist the anti-Communist insurgency.[71]

Rowe was also probing for opportunities to return to the world of intelligence. After failing to get a job with the CIA, Rowe wrote to a contact at the State Department's Office of Intelligence Research hoping to secure a "consultancy" status with the CIA, and he enclosed his rebuttal of Fairbank's request to sign the letter in solidarity with Lattimore.[72] Rowe worked closely with the US Army's Operations Research Office, affiliated with Johns Hopkins University, which sponsored a wide range of research projects—sending ambitious graduate students like Henry Kissinger, for example, to Korea in mid-1951 to do an external review of the US military's handling of civil affairs in wartime South Korea.[73] Rowe joined his CIA-connected Yale colleague, Willmoore Kendall, in editing *China: An Area Manual* ("a compendium of general information for use by military personnel") and contributing to *China: A Handbook for Psywar Operators*.[74]

Rowe's appearance before the McCarran Committee happened to take place exactly two years to the day since McCarthy had accused Lattimore of being a Soviet spy. Rowe stated categorically, "Within the field of far eastern studies, Asiatic studies, and particularly Chinese studies . . . I consider him principal agent for the advocacy of Stalinist ideas."[75] Unsatisfied with leaving it at Lattimore and the IPR, Rowe went out of his way to also denounce Fairbank. "Could I say one more word on Fairbank?" he requested of the counsel. "There is unquestioned sympathy on the part of Fairbank for the Chinese Communists," Rowe stated for the record.[76]

Fairbank hit back against Rowe's accusations, releasing a statement, picked up by the *Boston Herald* and *Harvard Crimson*, that "judging by press reports,

Professor Rowe has now been infected with the denunciatory virus which is epidemic this year along the Potomac. I am sorry to hear it and hope he gets over it."[77] Rowe wrote privately to Fairbank, whose conciliatory reply stressed their shared goal of an effective China policy. Fairbank was never a supporter of the CCP; his position had been that "instead of backing the revolution under Communist control we have to compete with the Communist leadership of this revolution and wrest it away from them so that we can back a non-Communist leadership of the revolution in our own interests."[78] The letter echoed Fairbank's 1946 article, where he wrote, "Our problem is how to influence the Chinese revolutionary movement in our proper interest."[79] Fairbank asked Rowe to write back to his lawyer clarifying his accusations; in his response, Rowe made it clear that he would refuse to alter, clarify, or retract anything in his testimony.[80]

The Internal Security Subcommittee concluded its investigation in July 1952. Chairman McCarran made the stunning claim that the loss of China was the fault of the Institute of Pacific Relations. "I am convinced, from the evidence developed in this inquiry, that but for the machinations of the small group that controlled and activated the Institute of Pacific Relations, China today would be free and a bulwark against a further advance of the Red hordes into the Far East. . . . Our Government agencies have been infiltrated by persons whose allegiance is with Communist Russia."[81] Citing Rowe's testimony, McCarran made a damning judgment on Lattimore: "Lattimore was for some time, beginning in the middle 1930's, a conscious, articulate instrument of the Soviet conspiracy."[82]

The political pressure on China policy generated by the IPR hearings and relentless media speculation on the existence of a "Red cell" in the State Department contributed to the downfall of three of the government's best China experts. John Stewart Service, John Carter Vincent, and John Paton Davies would all be forced out of the State Department.[83] Fairbank remained influential in scholarly circles, but government agencies kept a distance.[84] As for Owen Lattimore, his persecution moved into the endgame of trial on perjury charges. In December 1952 a grand jury indicted him on seven counts of lying under oath, starting with the allegation "that he had been a promoter of communism or Communist interests."[85] Behind the scenes, Rowe volunteered his services in the effort to convict Lattimore. Hunting for a government job after Eisenhower's election in November 1952, Rowe approached Representative Judd, who offered to introduce him to incoming secretary of state John Foster Dulles. Judd assured Rowe that "the Lattimores, Fairbanks, Schlesingers, Peffers, and IPR and FPA associates" would have "absolutely no influence" in the new Republican era.[86] Rowe told Judd he was eager to help "clean-out" every trace of the old China Hands, starting with Lattimore. Judd assured Rowe that "all the top brass in the Department are determined to make the strongest possible case," and introduced Rowe to the prosecutor, Leo Rover.[87] Judd wrote to Rover:

> Now that he [Lattimore] has been indicted, unless we get a conviction, particularly on the first count, our whole case against the Far Eastern Policy of the former State Department may be gravely weakened, and the Pro-Communist forces be given a new lease on life in this country. One of the men who knows most about this whole situation and the infiltration of the academic world by Lattimore and his ideas, is Dr. David N. Rowe. He occupies the same position at Yale University, as Lattimore occupies at Hopkins and Fairbanks [*sic*] at Harvard.[88]

The legal problem was that Rover needed a way to *prove* that Lattimore's writings really did "promote communism or Communist interests." He got the green light from J. Edgar Hoover to hire a team of outside experts from American University to analyze Lattimore's collected writings using Harold Lasswell's content analysis method. Ironically, Lattimore's lawyers were being advised by a team from Yale Law School, where Lasswell was on the faculty, and the defense team won a major victory against the government prosecutors when the judge threw out the key counts of the perjury case in May 1953.[89] Rover asked for Rowe's help in proving "'parallelism' between the position of the Soviet Union and the Chinese Communist Party and the 'line' forwarded by Owen Lattimore."[90] Rowe applied the Lasswell method, while at the same time warning Rover against contacting Lasswell, who was presumably unsympathetic to their inquisition.[91] The American University team meanwhile submitted its report in October 1953, but they concluded that the charges against Lattimore could not be proven using content analysis.[92] Rover came under massive pressure to win an appeal—at one point, it was suggested that he call Chiang Kai-shek himself to testify. Even Director Hoover thought that was a bridge too far. In January 1954, the Washington, D.C., Court of Appeals upheld the ruling in favor of Lattimore.[93]

A few months after Lattimore's acquittal, Joe McCarthy finally overplayed his hand. First, he tried to direct his hunt for subversives against the CIA, but was outmaneuvered by the Agency and had to backtrack. More fatefully, McCarthy and his investigative team, led by Roy Cohn, went after the US Army. Already unpopular with his Senate colleagues and despised by the White House, McCarthy now lost his ace in the hole—public support. Americans were repelled by what they saw during the televised Army-McCarthy hearings as the senator showed off his bullying methods of interrogation and dubious arguments by insinuation.

David Nelson Rowe was not among those Americans turned off by McCarthyism in the spring of 1954. He continued to do what he could, in public and private, to support the McCarthyite inquiries through to the bitter end. In

June, Rowe testified to the Reece Committee to Investigate Tax-Exempt Foundations that the Institute of Pacific Relations funded Communist subversion. In his testimony, Rowe launched a broader critique of social and political science for having become "infected" with Marxist and other un-American ideas. Rowe also volunteered to testify against John Paton Davies at a "private session" of the State Department's security board held on June 24.[94] He worried about being sued for libel, but elicited reassurance from State Department counsel that neither Davies nor any other "unauthorized person" would see the testimony, and thus the odds of a suit were "unlikely."[95]

Leo Rover could not let go of the Lattimore case, and he announced a new indictment in August that claimed new material evidence in the form of "content analysis" proved that Lattimore's writings converged with the Communist line.[96] A four-man team working under Rover's direction since January 1954 produced a five-hundred-page report in September that concluded with 97 percent certainty that Lattimore's writings were faithful to the Communist line.[97] The trials went on for another year, until the case against Lattimore was finally dropped. In the meantime, John Paton Davies was recalled from his posting in Peru to be fired in person by Secretary of State John Foster Dulles.[98]

Students of McCarthy

If Professor Rowe quietly embodied the McCarthyite spirit on the faculty at Yale, a strident, vocal champion of repressing subversion could be found amid the student body in the person of William F. Buckley Jr., class of 1950. For Buckley, the Wisconsin senator was a hero of the "American Resistance" against subversion. In *McCarthy and His Enemies* (1954), co-authored with his Yale classmate and brother-in-law, Buckley wrote:

> For nearly three decades a handful of prophets—an American Resistance—tried to alert the nation to the Communist threat; and fought a lonely and costly fight. After the Second World War, in the dawn of a new realism about international affairs, these prophets began to get a hearing; for it had become apparent that nothing but the integrity of the United States stood between the Soviet Union and world domination. But it was only when one spy scandal after another rocked the nation that the American Resistance enlisted recruits in sizable numbers and fixed our attention on the problem of Communist infiltration. By 1950, a genuine mobilization was under way. And Senator McCarthy—having fairly recently been mobilized himself—became one of its leaders.[99]

Buckley credited McCarthyism with stiffening America's back in the fight to isolate the enemies within. As a result, the country was "rallying around an orthodoxy whose characteristic is that *it excludes Communism*; and adherents of Communism are, therefore, excluded from positions of public trust and popular esteem."[100] One of those to be excluded was of course Owen Lattimore, whom Buckley blamed for single-handedly bringing down a Bamboo Curtain over Asia:

> Owen Lattimore's skills, energies, and single-mindedness enabled him to play a dominant role in a movement that dispossessed our allies in the Far East of their homeland, enslaved four hundred million people, and doubled the perimeter of the Iron Curtain. Owen Lattimore moved discreetly throughout the period. His name was not known—except in academia and Far Eastern circles—until McCarthy attacked him. But in his unobtrusive way, Lattimore was serving the Roosevelt and Truman Administrations as the oracle on all matters Asiatic.[101]

Disguising himself behind "pretensions to being a disinterested and sedentary expert on the Far East," Lattimore "now succeeded Alger Hiss as the First Lady among American witches."[102] It was probably the first time in his peripatetic life that Owen Lattimore had ever been accused of being sedentary.

In his years at Yale, Buckley was a force of nature, using his platform as editor of the *Yale Daily News* to draw the attention of his classmates and drive the administration to distraction. Soon after graduation, he catapulted to national fame with the publication of his first book, *God and Man at Yale* (1951), a blistering screed against the college's godless, collectivist mentality, and destined to become a classic text in the American conservative movement. Polemical and self-righteous, Buckley contrasted his blend of patriotic, Christian, anti-subversive libertarianism to the permissive and unpatriotic liberalism of his successor as editor of the *Yale Daily News*: "Where he sympathized with Truman, Acheson, Hiss, Humphrey, and Bowles, I contemned them. Where I back the McCarran Act, the Taft-Hartley Law, the Committee on Un-American Activities, the autonomy of private clubs and associations, and restriction of government activity, he deplored them."[103]

Buckley denounced classmates, professors, and administrators for promoting secularism and socialism. The Department of Religion rejected God and the Department of Economics rejected capitalism. The spirit of liberalism at post-war Yale was simply equivocation in the crusade against Communism, at a moment in history when America needed zealots. "A responsible, reflective man must, soon in life, cast his lot with the Communists or against them. He may change, to be sure; but at any given moment, if he and others like him embrace certain values, as civilized men who recognize that they are 'involved in mankind,' they must cherish and advance them with fervor."[104]

Buckley's list of targets included the new American Studies program, which he accused of betraying the original promise to donor William Robertson Coe that the major would celebrate "the preservation of our System of Free Enterprise and is opposed to a system of State Socialism, Communism and Totalitarianism."[105] Ironically, American Studies was staying all too faithful to the purpose articulated by President Seymour in February 1949 "to solidify faith in the American philosophy and devotion to its maintenance."[106] American Studies not only explicitly inculcated nationalism, but under the leadership of director Norman Holmes Pearson, it assisted in recruiting efforts by the CIA.[107]

God and Man at Yale was a public relations nightmare for Yale's historian-turned-president Whit Griswold. Buckley's book captured the McCarthyite zeitgeist, putting Griswold on the defensive in alumni relations and the national debate between defending free inquiry and ferreting out subversion. In a preemptive move on campus similar to Truman's creation of the Loyalty Board and Senate Democrats' establishment of the Tydings Committee, Griswold appointed a President's Advisory Committee to investigate students' "intellectual and spiritual welfare," including the charges that they were "being indoctrinated or unduly influenced by teaching of a Communistic or subversive character."[108]

Griswold also drew upon university traditions to push back against Buckley and McCarthyism, borrowing a technique from his predecessor, President Seymour. At the 1950 commencement ceremony, Seymour had awarded an honorary degree to George Kennan as a symbol of solidarity with the State Department "in the face of MacCarthy's [*sic*] attacks."[109] To mark Yale's 250th anniversary commencement in 1951, Griswold conferred a degree on Edward Tolman, the controversial psychology professor at UC Berkeley who refused to sign the University of California's anti-Communist loyalty oath and would fight the legality of the oath all the way to the California Supreme Court.[110] In his Alumni Day address of 1952, Griswold took the opportunity to remind the sons of Yale that bowing to "people who would combat the menace of communism by limiting the freedom of our universities and prescribing through outside political or other nonprofessional authority what they shall teach . . . would mean a renunciation of our educational philosophy."[111]

As Griswold defended the autonomy of the university from the political pressures of McCarthyism, he became increasingly disconcerted by the Yale Institute of International Studies. Griswold disapproved of how, under the directorship of Frederick Dunn, the institute blurred the distinction between scholarly inquiry and government intelligence, producing "topical, ad hoc information service and analysis now being offered by other agencies." In keeping with the university's true mission, the institute should instead encourage "fundamental inquiries into first principles," undertaken by independent scholars, not group research projects on "peripheral activities."[112] Griswold was in effect defending the prewar tradition of liberal education against the rise of the "Cold War University," described by the historian Jeremy Suri as blurring the line between scholarship on the one hand and policy analysis and national defense on the other.[113]

Fox left YIIS in 1950 for Columbia, where the university's president Dwight Eisenhower tasked him with setting up the Institute of War and Peace Studies. In April 1951, the core of the YIIS fellows, led by Director Dunn, defected to Princeton, taking the journal *World Politics* with them and founding Princeton's Center of International Studies. The exodus was welcomed by Griswold, who raised half a million dollars from the Henry L. Stimson Fund to rebuild and reorient YIIS. As most of his colleagues fled, Rowe managed to stay on as research associate at the institute, which now found itself in a crowded field—in addition to the institutes at Columbia and Princeton, Johns Hopkins incorporated the experimental graduate program set up by Paul Nitze and Christian Herter as the School of Advanced International Studies (SAIS) in 1950, and MIT established the Center for International Studies in 1951.

But graduating seniors in the class of 1951 like Jack Downey had more urgent matters to worry about than the institutional fate of the Yale Institute of International Studies. As they prepared to march for commencement in June, Mao's million-man army in Korea had been attacking US troops for months as part of the Chinese Spring Offensive.[114] To their class, the Korean War felt like a prelude to something even worse—87 percent of graduates expected WWIII to break out with the Soviet Union within five years.[115] The *Class Banner* voiced the sense of uncertainty: "Would we crush the North Koreans? was question number one. . . . Would we pull out against the Chinese Communists? was question number two. . . . Would eighteen-year-olds be drafted, and would the new draft law include veterans? . . . Would we ever see complete peace instead of total or partial war? . . . Questions for which we had no answer, for which there might be none."[116] Uncertainty reinforced a palpable ambivalence over the war. In James Lilley's recollection, "most of my colleagues didn't want to countenance another war so soon after the last one had ended and preferred to concentrate on enjoying their final year at college."[117]

President Griswold shared his students' sense of ambivalence, decrying the forces of militarization and repression emboldened by Cold War with the Soviets and hot war in Korea. "Communist aggression in Asia has scored one tactical success not commonly recognized as such. It has struck a body blow at American higher education. Barely recovered from the disruptions of the Second World War, our colleges and universities are once more called upon to sacrifice their students, faculties, and curricula to military necessity," he lamented.[118] Griswold took a stand for the life of the mind against the demands for bodies for the generals. "While we lavish our ingenuity and resources on the weapons of war, we neglect and even handicap the men who will use them. This is a high price to pay for survival. And what price survival if we become a headless monster?"[119] Griswold's solution to the Cold War dilemma had less to do with power politics and international diplomacy than with knowledge and education, the "wisdom for defense."

> This civilization is now beset by powerful enemies who would destroy it. They outnumber us. They are unremitting in their efforts to foment local wars they hope will exhaust us. They are willing to gamble on global war. Their pressure puts every basic institution in our society under strain, not only for weapons for defense but for the wisdom for defense. There is, I submit, no such contradiction between the needs of higher education and the needs of national defense. . . . On the contrary, I think there never was a time when higher education had so much to offer in a national emergency.[120]

Griswold choreographed the Yale commencement ceremony on June 10, 1951, as a statement of defiance against the repressive tenor of wartime America. Not only did Yale confer an honorary degree on Berkeley's dissident Professor Tolman, but Griswold's guest of honor was John Dewey, the doyen of American liberalism who at ninety-one years of age was speaking out against loyalty oaths.[121] As Griswold took the lectern at Woolsey Hall to deliver his first baccalaureate address, also marking the 250th anniversary of Yale's founding, his oratory rose to the occasion (the *New York Herald Tribune* ran the speech in full).[122] Playing off Henry David Thoreau, Griswold described the mood of "cheerful resignation" among the 960 men who would soon face the Selective Service lottery. He insisted that America's liberal individualist ethos could overcome the faceless forces of war, technology, and bureaucracy. "We are not mere sponges or plankton afloat on a tide of causation over which we have no control. We are rational beings, capable of charting the tide, and navigating it, and even diverting and directing it."[123] Dark clouds hovered over his words—the atom bomb, the malevolence of the Kremlin, the age of machines. "We have beguiled ourselves with gadgets, with machines that work for us, and think for us, and entertain us, and (as we believe in our folly) educate us, until our God-given individual powers have become atrophied through disuse."[124] Griswold defended the sanctity of the thinking individual against the totalitarian logic of Soviet aggression and American scientism. He quoted the 1946 Nobel Prize winner Percy Bridgman (receiving an honorary degree): "Intelligence is based on the individual. An authoritarian society in which the individual is suppressed cannot, by the nature of intelligence, be characterized by *general* intelligence."[125]

To a considerable number of seniors, the word intelligence would soon take on a very different meaning than the definition elucidated by President Griswold on graduation day. They were leaving Yale and the hallowed world of the Ivy League, colleges whose histories stretched back to colonial times—"not only the preservers of our European inheritance but the makers of much that we value most in American civilization," as George Pierson, historian of Yale, put it.[126] Many of them, like Jack Downey, were joining the nation's newborn intelligence organization, the CIA.

4

INTELLIGENCE OR PSYWAR

As fate would have it, the Agency that gave Jack Downey and many of his classmates their first job out of college was founded on the very day they assembled for freshman orientation: September 18, 1947. Until that point, the United States' lack of a civilian intelligence organization was something of a distinctive national tradition, a badge of honor. Although the OSS, an innovative intelligence and paramilitary organization created by FDR, had proved its mettle during World War II, Truman dismantled it in the postwar demobilization. To fight the Cold War, however, the need for strategic intelligence as well as covert instruments of subversion came back into fashion. The CIA was born out of the marriage—not always a happy one—of those two missions, analytical and operational, and the Agency had to grow up quickly, finding its place in the national security state being built to fight the Cold War.

The American Way to Spy

Before World War II, there was something almost un-American about the figure of the spy. To be sure, tales of patriotic cunning could be traced back to the American Revolution, like the semi-fictional hero in James Fenimore Cooper's hit novel *The Spy: A Tale of the Neutral Ground* (1821), Henry Wadsworth Longfellow's antebellum paean to signals intelligence, "Paul Revere's Ride" (1860), and the many statues of George Washington's famous scout Nathan Hale, including the bronze sculpture erected at Yale in 1914 to honor the martyred graduate of the class of 1773. But while these Revolutionary War legends contributed to the national mythology, they did not coalesce into an American archetype of the spy as hero. On the contrary, the idea of espionage ran counter to the country's ethos of authenticity, embodied in ideal types like "Honest Abe" Lincoln, as well as the championing of individualism, expressed in verse in Walt Whitman's epic "Song of Myself" (1855). Even the great American trickster Huckleberry Finn, while talented at disguise and deceit, was the antithesis of a foreign agent. Huck worked for no one and was more likely to be running from the law than serving the state.

Of course, even in the days of Whitman and Twain there was such a thing as foreign intelligence reporting, a job that fell mostly to a hodgepodge of embassies and consulates run by the Department of State on a modest budget. As the United States military expanded its role in the Western Hemisphere and extended its reach across the Pacific Ocean by the 1880s, the Army set up the Military Intelligence Division and the Navy created the Office of Intelligence. The perceived need for overseas intelligence intensified with victory in the Spanish-American War in 1898, when the US seized a sprawling far-off colony, the Philippines, and consolidated control over small, strategically located islands from Hawai'i to Guam. American imperialism managed to steer clear of land wars in Asia, although US Marines did march into Beijing in 1900 as part of the Eight Nation Alliance to quell the Boxer Rebellion. In 1917, millions of doughboys flooded the trenches of France to fight the Central Powers in WWI, with a small contingent of US troops lingering in the Russian Far East to help White Russians in their doomed civil war against the Bolsheviks. Despite the steady expansion of foreign entanglements, Americans maintained a self-conception of New World purity and isolationist virtue that entailed a certain disdain for the spy trade, which was associated with scheming European royal courts and agents of the British Empire. As Secretary of State Henry Stimson purportedly said when shutting down a pioneering cryptography program in 1929, "Gentlemen do not open one another's mail."[1]

The rise of expansionist fascist regimes in Italy, Germany, and Japan and the outbreak of war at both ends of the Eurasian Rimland, as Spykman called it, finally rendered the traditional aversion to espionage untenable in the eyes of America's leaders. Henry Stimson, now serving as secretary of war in the Roosevelt cabinet, came to appreciate the code-breaking skills of the Army's Signal Intelligence Service. FDR, a former assistant secretary of the Navy, was gung-ho about old-fashioned "human intelligence."[2] With a nudge from Churchill, Roosevelt tasked Colonel William J. "Wild Bill" Donovan, a lawyer and decorated war hero from WWI, with cobbling together a civilian intelligence arm of the government in anticipation of entering the war. On July 11, 1941, the president named

Donovan his "coordinator of information" by signing a one-page military order, with a vague writ typical of Roosevelt's mercurial style of making foreign policy. Receiving generous help from the Brits, Donovan began laying the groundwork for an outfit that would combine intelligence collection, research, and analysis, along with something he genteelly called "unorthodox warfare."[3] Donovan's first priority was building up human capital by recruiting talented, worldly Americans, men (and women) like John King Fairbank and David Nelson Rowe.

Then came December 7, 1941, a day that would "live in infamy" as the most spectacular intelligence failure in American history.[4] The day of the attack, Donovan arrived at the White House at midnight and did not leave until 2 a.m., conferring with President Roosevelt on what war would mean for their budding intelligence initiative.[5] It would take six months before Donovan's band received proper resources, authority, and a name—the Office of Strategic Services (OSS), so christened on June 13, 1942. Under Wild Bill's dynamic, if disorganized, leadership, the OSS carved out a niche in the war effort by marrying two "cardinal purposes, secret collection abroad and expert appraisal at home," in the words of the intelligence historian (and former Yale professor) Arthur B. Darling.[6] The OSS appealed to well-educated Americans, offering them entry into a derring-do organization that valued elitist egalitarianism over military seniority and put their brains to work in the service of the nation's brawn. OSS analysts pored over materials at the Library of Congress while field units carried out clandestine paramilitary operations in regions from the snowy fjords of Norway to the steaming jungles of Burma, helping the War Department fight the covert side of total war.

The quintessential OSS guerrilla infiltration was Operation Jedburgh, training American, British, and French commandos in the Scottish Highlands and equipping them with guns, funds, and wireless radios ("Jed sets"). Small teams of Jedburghs, as they became known, parachuted behind Nazi lines into occupied France and the Netherlands, to reconnoiter with local resistance and radio back to headquarters with intelligence. Of the eighty-four American Jedburghs, only six were killed, two captured, and seven wounded—according to OSS veterans Stewart Alsop and Thomas Braden, who brought their exploits to life for postwar readers in *Sub Rosa: The O.S.S. and American Espionage* (1946). Alsop and Braden painted the portrait of a pseudonymous agent, "William Wheeler," to show how three technological breakthroughs—planes, parachutes, and radios—made modern subversive warfare possible.[7] Hollywood released the feature film *O.S.S.* that same year, starring Alan Ladd as a Jedburgh on a sabotage mission into wartime France.

Despite the romantic image of the OSS, Donovan's lobbying for a peacetime civilian intelligence organization ran up against lingering public discomfort with espionage and revulsion at the idea of a secret police. Ironically, J. Edgar Hoover was also hostile to the OSS, but for different reasons. For one thing, Hoover despised Donovan since working under him when Wild Bill was an assistant attorney general in the 1920s. On top of that, Hoover wanted to monopolize intelligence and security functions for himself and the FBI, which claimed jurisdiction over intelligence related to Latin America.[8]

As Allied victory came within sight in early 1945, Donovan sent a memo to FDR urging that the OSS be put on a permanent footing, to ensure continuity of intelligence gathering and analysis during the "tumult of rehabilitation" that would come after the war.[9] FDR demurred, leaving the status of the OSS cloudy at the time of his death in April 1945. Donovan asked President Truman to allow the experiment in civilian intelligence to carry on after V-J Day, but the OSS was vulnerable to public euphoria over demobilization and a return to prewar practices.[10] The rapid, global drawdown included the return home of seventy thousand US military personnel, many involved in intelligence work, stationed in China.[11] Donovan argued that China in particular required the presence of a "strategic intelligence agency," but interagency rivalry also worked against the OSS.[12] From his perch in Tokyo as supreme commander for the allied powers, General Douglas MacArthur dismissed the idea of civilian intelligence in postwar Asia, just as he had tried to keep the OSS out of his theater during the war.[13] Truman himself was skeptical of covert activity and suspicious of Donovan. Explaining that he did not want to sign off on an American gestapo, Truman relieved Donovan and disestablished the OSS in October 1945.

The intelligence collection assets built up by the OSS migrated into the War Department as a semiautonomous construct called the Strategic Services Unit (SSU). Initially led by an officer with extensive China experience, Brigadier General John Magruder, the SSU launched a smattering of espionage operations across Europe and Asia. The SSU set up a special unit to focus on the Soviet Union, but unit chief Harry Rositzke lacked clear instructions on exactly what it was he should do.[14] The lack of clarity at the SSU reflected the tug of war between warring impulses in the immediate wake of WWII—between the yearning to return to prewar normalcy and mounting anxiety over the challenge posed by Soviet communism.[15]

It wasn't long before a frustrated Truman realized that, at a minimum, he needed some mechanism to coordinate the flow of foreign intelligence pouring in via military analysis and embassy reporting. In January 1946, he picked a Missouri businessman and naval intelligence officer, Rear Admiral Sidney Souers, to serve as the inaugural director of central intelligence (DCI). Truman gave Souers a small organization, the Central Intelligence Group (CIG), with the mission of "centralizing" the flow of intelligence into a daily report to the president—a newspaper for one. The director was a czar without a kingdom, and Souers moved on, as planned, after six months, to be replaced by Air Force Lieutenant General Hoyt Vandenberg.

The CIG was a bare-bones operation of about a hundred men and women under Vandenberg, whose attempts to get more authority and resources were blocked by the Departments of State and War.[16] The second director did achieve at least one bureaucratic victory in extracting the SSU from the War Department, absorbing its assets and mission in a new unit called the Office of Special Operations (OSO) under the CIG.[17] The OSO Far East unit chief visited the US Navy base at Qingdao, China, in the summer of 1946 to arrange the transfer of the rump OSS operation in China, known as External Survey Detachment #44. However, the distractingly handsome Vandenberg (nephew of the influential senator Arthur Vandenberg) was no match for General MacArthur in a Northeast Asian turf war. MacArthur claimed jurisdiction over all intelligence matters in the theater, including China, as the head of what would soon be known as Far East Command (FEC), limiting the scope of OSO activity.[18]

Vandenberg had a bit more success in expanding the analytical wing of the CIG, growing the staff at the Office of Research and Estimates (ORE) to three hundred by the end of 1946.[19] But the bureaucratic battles were a slog. It took four months for the Intelligence Advisory Board, composed of intelligence chiefs across the government, to approve the ORE's "National Intelligence Requirement–China."[20] Like Souers, Vandenberg lasted less than a year as intelligence director, eagerly returning to the Air Force.

Political Warfare

Truman was getting ready for his third director of central intelligence, Rear Admiral Roscoe Hillenkoetter (another Navy man from Missouri), at the time he declared the Cold War in his speech to Congress in March 1947. To make good on the Truman Doctrine, the administration sent Congress draft legislation for a fundamental restructuring of the military, foreign policy, and intelligence apparatus of government. The most sensitive issue was not intelligence but the armed services, which were wracked by intense rivalries. Once the reorganization of the military was settled, Congress passed and Truman signed the National Security Act into law in July.

The National Security Act was a watershed moment in the history of US foreign policy, establishing a new administrative machinery and conceptual vocabulary for the conduct of foreign affairs. The president was given the National Security Council (NSC), housed in the White House, to quarterback the process of making foreign policy. The jealous armed services were merged under the newly christened Department of Defense (DOD) where a civilian secretary of defense was to resolve differences, or at least mute the squabbling, between the Army, Navy, Air Force, and Marines (an independent service under the Navy). Last but not least, the National Security Act added one more instrument to the exercise of foreign policy, subordinating the intelligence units sprinkled across government and military to the newly established Central Intelligence Agency (CIA), responsible for advising the president on intelligence matters under the authority of the National Security Council.

The CIA opened for business in September, working out of the former OSS headquarters at 2340 E Street in Washington, D.C. Congress approved a secret budget to fund three overt missions: foreign intelligence collection (espionage), overseas counterintelligence, and strategic intelligence analysis.[21] But there was a fourth mandate as well, inscribed with artful ambiguity in the language of the National Security Act, which authorized the CIA "to perform, for the benefit of the existing intelligence agencies, such additional services of common concern as the NSC determines can be more efficiently accomplished centrally" and "such other functions and duties related to intelligence affecting the national security as the National Security Council may from time to time direct." These clauses were the Pandora's box that, once opened, gave the CIA authority to carry out "subversive operations."[22]

If fear over the fall of Greece to communism was the casus belli for the public launch of America's Cold War, it was anxiety over the fate of Italian democracy that drew the newborn CIA onto its first battlefield in the covert struggle against Soviet influence. Dread was mounting in Washington in the autumn of 1947 that the Communist Party of Italy, with aid from Moscow, might actually win the parliamentary elections scheduled for April 1948. George Kennan, riding high from the publication of his article in *Foreign Affairs* and entrusted by Secretary Marshall to be the master strategist of the State Department, thought he might have the answer to the Italy dilemma.

Kennan's proposal was to try out "political warfare": covert intervention in the domestic politics of a sovereign country, just as Britain's Political Warfare Executive had done against Axis countries during WWII.[23] Kennan himself had dabbled in covert waters during the war on a posting to Lisbon, a "seething cauldron of espionage and counterespionage."[24] After the war, Truman's first intelligence director (Souers) appointed Kennan a special adviser on the USSR in early 1946.[25] With Cold War architecture based on the blueprint of the National Security Act building up around him, Kennan counseled outstretching an unseen hand into Western Europe to counter Moscow's efforts to tilt the board. The first match would be the parliamentary elections of the Italian Republic, and the winner would be invisible by design.

Political warfare dominated the agenda at the inaugural sessions of the National Security Council in September 1947 led by the formidable duo of Secretary of Defense James Forrestal and Secretary of State George Marshall. The NSC in effect agreed to extend a covert Monroe Doctrine across all hemispheres, interpreting the National Security Act to give themselves authority to undertake clandestine actions worldwide so long as "the national security" was at stake.[26] The concept of "national interest," codified as "national security," was invoked internally by the NSC to justify covert intervention around the world. At its third meeting (in December), the NSC reviewed a secret annex, designated NSC 4-A, giving the CIA responsibility for what the Agency historian Arthur Darling described as "the use of 'black' propaganda, and the related arts of political interference, economic intrusion, and physical subversion."[27] NSC 4-A was another step down the slippery slope Niebuhr had warned against, of becoming like the enemy in the fight to defeat it. Due to the "vicious psychological efforts of the USSR," the National Security Council advised President Truman that "in the interest of world peace and national security, the foreign information activities of the U.S. Government must be supplemented by covert psychological operations."[28] Subversion was justified as antisubversion.

Although there was consensus that the black arts had to be used, no one wanted to be directly responsible for practicing them. Director Hillenkoetter resisted the push to make his Agency carry the burden of "psychological warfare," but he was outranked by Secretary Marshall, who, nervous that covert ops would undermine his overt plan for European recovery, wanted the job parked at the CIA. Yet Marshall wanted to retain a guiding hand for the Department of State, exerted through his intelligence liaison George Kennan.[29] Precisely how the approval and funding for covert action would work also remained unresolved. Kennan tinkered with the idea of forming some kind of group—to be headed by the OSS veteran Allen Dulles—that could align clandestine work with official foreign policy.[30]

Events in Europe would not wait on organizational clarity in Washington. A Communist Party takeover in Czechoslovakia in February 1948, followed by the shocking suicide—presumed to be murder—of its non-Communist foreign minister Jan Masaryk, accelerated covert planning to defend Italy against being next to slip under the Iron Curtain.[31] With the Italian elections months away, Hillenkoetter ordered the OSO to create the Special Procedures Group to carry out psychological warfare operations.[32] The CIA's man in Rome was James Jesus Angleton, a protégé of Yale English literature professor Norman Holmes

Pearson and former OSS agent in Italy. Angleton took up the call with gusto to save Italian democracy by subverting it.[33]

When Italy's Christian Democratic Party triumphed over the Communists in the 1948 election, the National Security Council scored it as America's first victory in the covert Cold War.[34] Subversion worked! George Kennan was strengthened in his conviction that the United States would have to dabble in the dark arts, and he oversaw the writing of a concept paper at Policy Planning, "The Inauguration of Organized Political Warfare," soon after the Italian elections.[35] Kennan acknowledged up front that this was uncharted waters for the United States, but the "realities of international relations" left no choice but to follow in the footsteps of the secret agents of the British Empire and keep up with the Kremlin's men: "Covert operations are traditional in many European chancelleries but are relatively unfamiliar to this Government. Having assumed greater international responsibilities than ever before in our history and having been engaged by the full might of the Kremlin's political warfare, we cannot afford to leave unmobilized our resources for covert political warfare. We cannot afford in the future, in perhaps more serious political crises, to scramble into impromptu covert operations."[36] Kennan's suggestion to create a political warfare directorate faced opposition from the CIA's Hillenkoetter, who objected to having "responsibility without authority" over covert action, while State and Defense wrangled over where to sheathe this new double-edged sword.

As the Soviets imposed a blockade on West Berlin in June, triggering a crisis in the heart of Europe, the National Security Council approved NSC 10/2, a landmark document in the history of US intelligence that created an instrument of subversion, initially called the Office of Special Projects but renamed the Office of Policy Coordination (OPC). Echoing the logic of NSC 4-A, NSC 10/2 argued that evil had to be met in kind—the "vicious covert activities" of the Soviet bloc required countermeasures in the form of "covert operations" by the US.[37] The OPC was given a colorful mandate to conduct "any covert activities related to: propaganda, economic warfare; preventive direct action, including sabotage, anti-sabotage, demolition and evacuation measures; subversion against hostile states, including assistance to underground resistance movements, guerrillas and refugee liberation groups, and support of indigenous anti-communist elements in threatened countries of the free world."[38] Crucially, NSC 10/2 established a principle for hiding covert foreign policy from the American public, what came to be known as "plausible deniability." Covert actions were not only to be done in secrecy, but they were also to be planned and implemented in such a way that "if uncovered the US Government can plausibly disclaim any responsibility for them."[39] Kennan, a driving force behind political warfare, would come to rue the day that the doctrine of plausible deniability was born.[40]

NSC 10/2 completed the CIA's trifecta of functional bureaus dealing in covert activity: the Office of Special Operations (OSO) collected raw foreign intelligence; the Office of Research and Estimates (ORE) cooked it into analyses and estimates; the Office of Policy Coördination (OPC) plotted covert means to intervene overseas. Allen Dulles was asked but turned down the offer to head the OPC, so the job went to another OSS veteran, Frank G. Wisner, chief of Southeast European covert operations during WWII. Appointed assistant director for policy coordination, Wisner quickly took advantage of the gap created by reporting relationships to two bosses—Kennan at State and Hillenkoetter in the CIA, neither of whom could exercise complete control.[41] Tensions surfaced with OSO veterans, who resented that OPC newbies were better paid and worried that their cloak-and-dagger antics could jeopardize painstaking collection work that relied on vulnerable networks of human assets. The OPC and OSO formed distrustful parallel worlds within the CIA, even sitting at separate tables in the cafeteria at headquarters.[42] Meanwhile Congress provided the Agency with a stronger legal footing in the summer of 1949 by passing the Central Intelligence Act, clarifying responsibilities and authorities, endowing generous, secret funding, and shielding personnel from normal transparency requirements.[43]

Wisner's OPC wasted no time reviving the Jedburgh model, fighting Soviet influence and Communist elements across the European periphery by inaugurating a new mode of political warfare in the form of paramilitary subversive operations. The Baltic region was an early target for paramilitary activity by Wisner's men. Working with Britain's Secret Intelligence Service, the OPC aided Baltic partisans starting in late 1948.[44] Another covert battlefield was Albania, where Operation Valuable, devised jointly with the British and launched in October 1949, sought to topple the Communist government of Enver Hoxha. Hundreds of Albanians living in exile in Europe as well as Albanian Americans would be infiltrated over the next few years, most of them swiftly captured or killed.[45] The British pulled out of Albanian ops within a year, but the CIA carried on with what they called Operation Fiend, using C-47 transport planes to parachute ill-trained operatives into the small, rugged country.[46] As agents of subversion landed on the coasts and in the hinterland of Southeast Europe, the OPC also launched covert operations into the Soviet republic of Ukraine, where the OSO was already busy with espionage activities.[47] The CIA's first airborne infiltration inside the borders of the USSR took place on September 5, 1949, when Czech pilots flew Ukrainian partisans to their base in the Carpathian Mountains. C-47s would make covert trips in and out of the Ukraine for the next four years; they were regularly shot at but never downed.[48]

As the covert Cold War simmered in Europe in 1948 and 1949, Communist insurgencies were heating up across Asia. Ho Chi Minh was rallying resistance to French colonial rule in Indochina. The Huk insurgency was surging in the Philippines. Kim Il Sung was building an army to unify Korea by force. Even Japan looked vulnerable, as US occupation authorities fearing communist influence launched the "reverse course" policy of rehabilitating elites in the wartime fascist regime. Most importantly, Mao appeared to be on the path to victory in the Chinese Civil War. At this pivotal moment, the United States lost its eyes and ears in China.

John K. Singlaub, a young US Army intelligence officer, was sent to Shenyang in March 1946 to manage intelligence activities, recruiting White Russians and Koreans under the cover of the US Army Liaison Group.[49] His deputies, working out of the border town of Antung on the Yalu River, recruited and trained Korean agents and infiltrated them into Pyongyang.[50] Like almost all American intelligence officers in China, Singlaub had to pack up by the end of 1949.[51] The CIA Shanghai Station (formerly known as External Survey Detachment #44) folded up shop, as did the Office of Naval Intelligence unit attached to the Navy presence in Qingdao.[52] There were flailing efforts to plant stay-behind networks, like a proposal to train Mongol agents "to establish a permanent base for collecting intelligence" (according to Harry Rositzke).[53] Douglas MacKiernan, a CIA officer posted to the US consulate in Tihwa (Urumqi), Xinjiang, was the last US government official to heed the State Department's evacuation order, fleeing overland via Tibet. He was shot dead by a Tibetan patrol in April 1950.[54]

Strategic Intelligence

The dearth of solid intelligence from Asia and the snowballing of subversive activities in Europe troubled the new director of central intelligence, General Walter Bedell Smith, better known as "Beetle," who took over the CIA from Admiral Hillenkoetter in the fall of 1950—Truman's fourth intelligence director in four years. Beetle was a career soldier and George Marshall protégé. He served in military intelligence early in his career, as Eisenhower's chief of staff during WWII, and as Truman's ambassador to the Soviet Union from 1946 to 1948. When Beetle arrived for ambassadorial duties in Moscow, George Kennan had just fired off the Long Telegram. Beetle described Kennan as "my mentor and principal adviser during my first months in Moscow."[55]

True to President Truman's initial conception of central intelligence, Director Smith did not want the CIA to become a "covert War Department." He argued that covert action, and paramilitary warfare in particular, was "contrary to its own interest as an intelligence organization" and violated the Agency's original mandate from the NSC to carry out only such activities that were related to the production of intelligence.[56] Beetle wanted to focus on the "primary mission" of intelligence—obtaining raw information, from open sources and secret collection, and analyzing it for strategic insights for use to policy makers. To accomplish this, Beetle brought in a pair of historians, both OSS veterans: William Langer of Harvard and Sherman Kent of Yale. Langer spent only a year at CIA, as planned, to get the ball rolling. Kent took a leave from Yale and never returned, guiding the Agency's analytical work for the next seventeen years.

Born to an elite California family at the turn of the century, Sherm was a Yale man through and through—he followed in his father's footsteps by taking his BA in 1926, stayed on for a PhD in modern French political history (1933), and joined the faculty two years later. Yale University Press even published his revised dissertation, *Electoral Procedures under Louis Philippe* (1937). But the war interrupted Kent's academic career, when like many other historians, including John King Fairbank and David Nelson Rowe, he was recruited for the OSS Research and Analysis branch. Kent started off running the Mediterranean section and ended up in charge of the Europe-Africa division.

When Truman disbanded the OSS in October 1945, analysts like Kent were merged into the State Department's Office of Research and Intelligence, while spies and operatives went to the War Department's new Strategic Services Unit. Kent, as acting director of the Interim Research and Intelligence Service, oversaw the OSS migration to State, where his staff were decidedly unwelcome.[57] The situation became so dire, with the OSS transfers barely receiving pay, that Kent was pushed to the brink of a nervous breakdown and chose to step down.[58]

Rather than return to his position at Yale, Kent accepted an offer in June 1946 to teach at the newly founded National War College, joining a small powerhouse faculty of military and civilian thinkers.[59] Bernard Brodie was there, having just finished *The Absolute Weapon* with his Yale Institute for International Studies colleagues. So was George Kennan, enjoying what he recalled as "a veritable outpouring of literary and forensic effort on my part," including the drafting of his seminal *Foreign Affairs* article.[60] Kennan invited Kent to guest lecture on French politics and Indochina in his class on current political affairs in January 1947.[61] The War College had that kind of collegial atmosphere conducive to reflection and cross-fertilization of ideas. Kent gave a lecture on his pet topic, "strategic intelligence," and lingered on for a semester to expand the paper into a book-length manuscript.[62]

Kent finally returned to Yale for the fall term of 1947, having been promoted and tenured in absentia. He tried to stay engaged off campus, making a series of trips to New York, for example, to attend a discussion series hosted by the Union Theological Seminary on the hot topic of human rights, as United Nations member states reviewed the draft Universal Declaration of Human Rights (approved by the UN General Assembly in December 1948). Reverend Reinhold Niebuhr was at his peak of national prominence, his tormented visage gracing the cover of *Time* magazine, with an admiring profile written by, of all people, Whittaker Chambers.[63] Kent also kept the door open to the world of intelligence by agreeing when Director Hillenkoetter asked him to do a crash survey of the Office of Research and Estimates in February 1948. The gist of Kent's critique was that the CIA needed a stronger mandate to extract intelligence from State and Defense, along with a larger staff dedicated to analysis. Kent was on the draft list to be part of another external review, known as the Intelligence Survey Group, but in the end he did not participate.[64]

Kent's opus, *Strategic Intelligence for American World Policy*, was published by Princeton University Press in 1949. The book was immediately hailed as a breakthrough in the study of international relations by no less an authority than Hans Morgenthau, riding high from the success of *Politics among Nations*. Morgenthau anticipated that Kent's theory of intelligence would serve as an "indispensable guide for the understanding of a vital and neglected branch of governmental activity."[65]

The essence of Kent's vision of intelligence was indicated in the title: the word "strategic" carried special connotations in the national security discourse of early Cold War America. The concept of strategic intelligence subordinated various kinds of information, and the units that produced them, to a higher cause. Tactical, military intelligence picked up by the Army and Navy and political information (including gossip) gathered by the State Department through its embassies—these were the proverbial blind men clinging to the trunk, legs, or tail. Strategic intelligence claimed to see the whole elephant. *Strategic* intelligence also implied taking the long-term view, as distinct from "current intelligence," the urgency of which perennially threatened to overwhelm analysis. It was for these reasons that back in 1941, Wild Bill Donovan had asked President Roosevelt to appoint him coordinator of strategic information, but the War Department demanded that the word "strategic" be dropped (leaving Donovan with the prosaic title "coordinator of information"). Donovan got the last word when his organization was named the Office of Strategic Services (OSS). Director Vandenberg captured the transcendent meaning of strategic intelligence: "Strategic and national policy intelligence is that composite intelligence, interdepartmental in character, which is required by the President and other high officers and staffs to assist them in determining policies with respect to national planning and security in peace and in war and for the advancement of broad national policy. It is in that political-economic-military area of concern to more than one agency, must be objective, and must transcend the exclusive competence of any one department."[66]

Kent explained his theory of strategic intelligence by borrowing a metaphor from the world of business, reflecting a quintessentially American cast of mind. Intelligence "production" should be structured around the relationship between analytical "producers" and policy "consumers." In this specialty trade in intelligence "products," consumers had to ask for the right kind of products, and producers had to ensure quality control based on three measures: timeliness, completeness, and actionability. In an interview at Yale, Kent explained that the good analyst combined the skills of "a student, a statesman, and a newsman."[67] He compared intelligence to "the protective shield of our national security"—what one state needs to know about other states.[68]

Consumers (policymakers and government officials) would have to include things in their "information requirements" that they might rather not know; otherwise, "when intelligence producers realize that there is no sense in forwarding to a consumer knowledge which does not correspond to his preconceptions, then intelligence is through."[69] Kent agreed with Walter Lippmann that the proper place of "intelligence officers" was standing behind policymakers "with the book open to the proper page, to call their attention to the stubborn fact they may neglect."[70] Producer and consumer should maintain an optimal equidistance, neither too far apart nor too close. "Intelligence must be close enough to policy, plans, and operations to have the greatest amount of guidance, and must not be so close that it loses its objectivity and integrity of judgment."[71]

The central task of strategic intelligence was the production of "estimates," which Kent explained in terms of a formula to measure oneself against an adversary. There were three basic steps: add up another nation's strengths and capabilities in order to determine its strategic stature; subtract its specific vulnerabilities; and infer its probable course of action. Repeat the assessment for one's own nation. Combining the two resulted in a *net estimate*. Estimates required the language of probability, so Kent invented a lexicon to make terms more precise: "almost certain" meant 90 percent likely to occur; "probable" meant 75 percent; "about even" translated into 50 percent; and "improbable" meant almost certainly not.[72] In producing estimates, the secrecy and intrigue commonly associated with espionage played a trivial role. "Some of this knowledge may be acquired through clandestine means, but the bulk of it must be had through unromantic open-and-above-board observation and research," Kent explained.[73] As Allen Dulles (of all people) confessed in a memorandum to the Senate in 1947, most intelligence—he estimated 80 percent—was gleaned from open sources.[74]

Not everyone agreed with Kent's way of doing intelligence. His colleague at Yale, the political scientist Willmoore Kendall, argued that Kent's characterization of the apolitical nature of intelligence work was unrealistic and his old-fashioned empiricism failed to take into account advances in social science theory and method.[75] In a critical review of *Strategic Intelligence*, Kendall quipped that Kent's bureaucratized intelligence experts would be "mere research assistants to the George Kennans."[76] Kendall would later co-author a manual on China with David Nelson Rowe for the Johns Hopkins Operations Research Office, whose chief of psychological warfare studies, George Pettee, also criticized Kent's empiricism, albeit from a different angle.[77] The author of *Future of American Secret Intelligence* (1946), Pettee argued that strategic intelligence in the Cold War would be less about empirical research into facts than about countering the Marxist narrative.[78]

Kent had been back at Yale for three years teaching European history and was summering in Kentfield, his family's town north of San Francisco, when the news of North Korea's invasion hit in June 1950. He returned to New Haven for the fall term as normal. "I must confess that I had been a bit disappointed with not having been invited to go back into government service to assist with this latest problem area," he recalled.[79] In fact, the new director, Beetle Smith, had Kent high on his list for a reorganized CIA. Beetle and his top deputy, William Jackson, wanted the Yale historian to implement his vision of "strategic intelligence" production. Beetle called Kent in for an interview and essentially ordered him to take the job. President Griswold gave his senior colleague in the History Department another leave in light of the mobilization for Korea.[80]

Kent finished up his fall course on modern world history (with two hundred students enrolled) and left Yale for the CIA.[81] By the end of November 1950, he was ensconsed at the Agency as a founding member of the eight-man Board of National Estimates (five of whom had doctorates in history) and deputy chief of the newly created Office of National Estimates (ONE).[82] His boss for the first year was Harvard's legendary European historian Bill Langer, a friend and former superior at the OSS. Langer could dominate a room and fight the necessary battles to get the ONE off the ground, with the blessing of the obstreperous Beetle. Kent was heir apparent from the get-go, slotted to take Langer's place. The ONE, after all, was built according to the specifications Kent had laid out in his book.

Instruments of Subversion

As Sherman Kent implemented his vision of strategic intelligence, Beetle brought in another deputy, Allen Dulles, to elevate the tradecraft of spies in the OSO and agents in the OPC. Born a decade earlier than Kent, Dulles grew up around statesmen—his uncle served as Woodrow Wilson's secretary of state during WWI, as his grandfather had done under President Benjamin Harrison. Young Allen got his first taste of espionage on the slow boat to India in 1914 when he became enraptured by Rudyard Kipling's classic tale of British imperial intrigue, the novel *Kim* (1901).[83] After recovering from the Spanish flu, Dulles enjoyed a front-row seat at the 1919 Paris Peace Conference, where he analyzed Central European issues under the guidance of the future Yale president Charles Seymour.[84] Allen pursued a career in the foreign service and launched a profitable career in law at his elder brother's firm, Sullivan and Cromwell.

When the United States belatedly entered WWII, Dulles sprung to action, heading to Europe for the OSS. While Kent was at his desk in Washington poring over maps of the Mediterranean on the eve of the North Africa campaign, Dulles slipped onto the last train through Vichy France into neutral Switzerland. He set up the OSS station in Bern, a capital of espionage, pumping a network of agents, assets, and associates for intelligence on Hitler's next moves and ways to weaken the Nazis from within. Dulles cast his net wide, consulting, among others, the famed psychoanalyst Carl Gustav Jung.[85]

After the war, Dulles returned to his law firm while keeping up his profile in the world of intelligence. In his spare time, he tracked down survivors of a failed assassination plot against Hitler and wrote the story up in his first book, *Germany's Underground* (1947). The notion of a noble resistance in the top echelons of the Third Reich aligned nicely with America's postwar rehabilitation of West Germany, not to mention the covert reliance on former Nazi intelligence officers like Reinhard Gehlen. *Germany's Underground* also served to justify subversive efforts to foment anti-Communist rebellion across the Soviet sphere of influence. For Dulles, totalitarianism had to be fought in the shadows. "It is not merely a story of a plot," Allen wrote of the attempt to assassinate Hitler. "It is, indeed, incontrovertible proof that even in a totalitarian state the struggle for individual liberty does not cease. The knowledge that this was so in Nazi Germany can inspire all those who hope and work to build something better in the Germany of tomorrow."[86]

When the National Security Council commissioned an external review for reorganizing the fledgling CIA, Allen Dulles chaired the group, whose findings, released in January 1949, were known simply as the Dulles Report. According to the report, the CIA was failing to realize the mandate of centrality given it by the National Security Act; instead, it was just another cog in the chaotic machinery of intelligence. The Dulles Report called for strengthening the Agency's role in producing *national* intelligence estimates—that is, transcending department-level estimating. Crucially, Dulles and his co-authors also stressed the need to marry the "static" analytical function with covert operational activities. Clandestine operations in turn should be integrated seamlessly, rather than divided into different offices. "The collection of secret intelligence is closely related to the conduct of secret operations in support of national policy. These operations, including covert psychological warfare, clandestine political activity, sabotage, and guerilla activity, have always been the companions of secret intelligence. The two activities support each other and can be disassociated only to the detriment of both."[87]

Whereas Kent's *Strategic Intelligence* de-emphasized the value of secret material, the Dulles Report argued that the "abnormal" information blockade presented by the Iron Curtain required unprecedented powers of secret intelligence gathering. To penetrate a totalitarian adversary, the traditional methods of open-source analysis would no longer suffice.[88] For Kent, intelligence was a form of knowing ("knowledge indispensable to our welfare and security"), whereas for Dulles, intelligence was a form of action.[89] An intelligence organization used secret information as a guide to covert activity. Spies see without being seen, acquiring information to help operatives intervene without being observed, employing agents who act without being aware of the true significance of their action. Kent's goal was to estimate probabilities of future developments so as to inform policymaking. Dulles wanted to change the future, to alter its course in line with policy objectives. Just as Kent's book provided the blueprint for the ONE, so Dulles's report led to the creation of the Department of Plans, overseeing both clandestine collection (OSO) and subversion (OPC). Brought on (like Kent) as a consultant in November 1950, Dulles was formally named deputy director for plans on January 2, 1951.[90]

With his bushy mustache, rimless spectacles, rumpled suits, and pipe in hand, Allen Dulles could have been mistaken for a professor at Yale—Alfred Hitchcock playfully named the Dulles character in *North by Northwest* (1959) "the Professor." But his theory of intelligence was the antithesis of professorial, having little to do with knowledge and everything to do with action. Although Kent got along well with Dulles, there was an obvious chasm dividing their respective notions of what intelligence was and why it mattered. "However polite, intelligent and understanding of our work on the overt side of things, I have a strong suspicion that Allen's heart was truly with the clandestine operations. . . . There was something of the little boy in Allen with respect to the various clandestine activities that went on," Kent recalled.[91] The British intelligence liaison and infamous double agent Kim Philby, who had close contact with Dulles when he was posted to Washington, deemed Allen's boyishness a mark of superficiality: "AD was an active man, in the sense that he would talk shop late into the night, jump into aeroplanes, rush around sophisticated capitals and exotic landscapes. But did he ever apply his mind *hard* to a problem that did not engage his personal interest and inclination; or was he basically a line-of-least-resistance man?"[92]

As much as Beetle Smith may have wanted to advance Sherm Kent's vision of strategic intelligence as the CIA's "primary mission," he found himself saddled with expectations to realize Allen Dulles's dreams of covert action. After the National Security Council reaffirmed the OPC's lead role in guerrilla warfare in January 1951, Beetle determined that at the very least, if his agency were going to be stuck with "monkey business," he would run the zoo. Smith complained that "the covert activities of CIA have been stepped up considerably, even though the policies established by NSC 68 have never been spelled out in terms of a specific covert program directive to CIA."[93] He was successful in forcing the OPC chief, Wisner, who was accustomed to autonomy, to report solely to him, severing the tie established by Marshall and Kennan to the State Department. Beetle left Wisner some latitude to determine what was "worthy" of reporting, which he would probably later regret.[94]

With the war dragging on in Korea, the scale of covert subversive operations continued to expand across Europe. In the Baltics, an agent team air-dropped into Lithuania in April 1951 sent encouraging word via wireless in September that, although the team leader had been killed, they were ready for a resupply of what Kent elegantly referred to as "the instrumentalities of total war": a radio operator, a propaganda specialist, a portable printing press, and rubles.[95] Promising messages continued to arrive on Beetle's desk, assuring HQ that an "organized resistance movement exists and that, while a certain number or its members live surreptitiously in the forests, the majority work at regular jobs." The infiltration team was preparing "drop zones and a reception committee for future air support operations."[96] At their peak, the Lithuanian partisans may have numbered up to thirty thousand. But by the end of 1952, the Lithuanian resistance would be almost entirely annihilated.[97]

Southeastern European operations were faltering badly by late 1951. After apparent success in resupplying a two-man team in Albania's northernmost region, devastating news came via Albanian national radio.[98] The CIA director was briefed:

> Radio Tirana reported on 24 October the liquidation of 13 U.S. espionage agents who had been dropped into Albania. Of the 8 men mentioned by name, 6 were members of CIA teams. This announcement, coupled with testimony at the Tirana spy trials, indicates that the Communists may know of the covert training school for Albanian and Bulgarian agents at the Hambuchen Estate near Munich. It also raises the possibility that Communist agents have penetrated the National Committee for a Free Albania as well as the possibility that a 2-man team which parachuted into Albania last May is under Albanian control.[99]

The failure of Operation Valuable would later be pinned on the double cross of Kim Philby, the British intelligence liaison in Washington secretly working for the Soviets. In his memoirs, Philby took no credit for leaking secrets; instead, he faulted the operation's flawed assumption that rural Albanians would help partisan strangers and that guerillas could enter the cities without being identified.

> We did finally succeed in landing a small party on the Albanian coast with instructions to work their way inland, spy out the land, and then move southwards into Greece. . . . Our infiltrators could achieve something only by penetrating the towns, which were firmly under Communist control. For bare survival, they had to hide in mountains, where their presence would have been useful only if the country was seething with revolt. That, perhaps, was the unspoken assumption of the whole venture. . . . In due course, the operation was quietly dropped without having made any noticeable dent on the regime in Tiranë.[100]

Harry Rositzke, head of the Soviet Division, recalled how hard it was to extract credible intelligence from within the enemy's borders. Even when there were successful penetrations, like the agent parachuted into western Byelorussia in September 1951, the problem was getting them out.[101] In May 1952, penetration agents made radio contact from within the USSR, but Rositzke heard nothing until four months later . . . when Moscow Radio reported on the capture of two "imperialist" agents who both confessed to being on a sabotage mission.[102] Rositzke concluded dryly: "It was clear at the time that the Soviet security services were genuinely convinced that their country was riddled with large numbers of Allied spies. Their concern was unjustified, perhaps even more so than the spy mania in Washington during the same years."[103] The most embarrassing example of a foiled subversive plot had to do with a Free Poland resistance group known as Freedom and Independence, which received extensive aid from the CIA and SIS based on information provided by a Polish émigré contact in London. Days after Christmas in 1952, a Polish state radio broadcast revealed that the whole enterprise was a fraud put in play by their counterintelligence.[104]

Declassified CIA meeting transcripts, known as Director's Logs, from 1951 testify to how much of Beetle Smith's time was consumed with keeping track of spying and subversion operations.[105] CIA stations worldwide were on the lookout for targets of interest or opportunity that might be induced into defection: one Polish diplomat in Geneva looked promising, as did the Czech delegation head to the San Francisco Peace Conference (were it not for the "insufficient time to mount a sound operation").[106] In Finland, operatives were trying to build a network of stay-behind agents who could be activated after the feared Soviet invasion. Reports trickled in on partisan groups directed or funded by the Agency—Albanians, Ukrainians, Taiwanese. The dizzying entry for one day in September reads like the fragment of a John le Carré plotline: "Successful W/T playback of a Bulgarian agent in Greece during the past year seems confirmed by interrogation of another agent recently arrived from the same headquarters. Continued operation with 2 double agents offers improved prospects of controlling Bulgarian intelligence activities in Northern Greece and a channel for eventual deception. Joint U.S.-Greek playback of a Communist guerrilla agent based in Rumania will reinforce this operation."[107]

Subversive operations and political warfare spread beyond the primary theater of geopolitical contestation, Europe. CIA stations across Asia, for example, endeavored to purchase the loyalty of men close to the center of power. In the space of two days in September, Beetle received updates on operations to woo the sultan of Jogjakarta, the chief of police in Thailand, and the minister of defense in the Philippines (the much-touted Ramon Magsaysay, who would be coached by his case officer, Edward Lansdale, all the way into the presidency).[108] In Indonesia, a group of intelligence officers were brought for covert training in the United States as a means of "establishing control" over the service.[109] The news from Seoul was especially encouraging: "A covert CIA agent has been appointed Special Assistant to Republic of Korea President Rhee. This agent has been instrumental in the change of attitude of the ROK Government toward the US Government. It is anticipated that with careful control this agent will develop into an outstanding deepcover agent in the Far East."[110]

Rather than becoming entranced by the global breadth of covert influence, Beetle was frustrated by the scattershot nature of these sundry subversive activities. He saw how clandestine services gobbled up an increasing proportion of Agency bandwidth. As of mid-1949, the OPC's 302 employees, working out of seven stations, got by on a mere $4.7 million.[111] OPC personnel nearly tripled from 584 in 1950 to 1,531 in 1951.[112] By 1952, OPC was operating on a budget of $82 million supporting 6,000 personnel (2,812 employees plus 3,142 contractors) working out of forty-seven stations around the world.[113] The following year, the Agency spent $100 million on Eastern Europe operations alone, half of which went to paramilitary activities.[114] Beetle took some of his frustration out on his deputies in charge of monkey business. A truculent boss, the director did not hide his dissatisfaction with Dulles and Wisner, who pushed "plausible deniability" to its outer limits. Beetle's second-in-command later recalled how the director "came to suspect that Dulles and Wisner were actually pursuing a policy contrary to his own. In exasperation, he visited upon them more violent manifestations of his wrath than he did upon anyone else."[115]

Truman and his second-term cabinet, led by Secretary of State Dean Acheson and Secretary of Defense Marshall, were by no means opposed to subversive options in principle. But they approached them with a measure of caution. Truman set up something called the Psychological Strategy Board in 1951, tasked with drafting a blueprint for how "psychological operations" should fit into the broader Cold War struggle. But the board never reached a definite consensus.[116] Truman entertained a number of covert proposals that would have amounted to coups, like the time Frank Wisner floated a plan in the summer of 1952 to destabilize Guatemala. Truman approved further exploration until Acheson convinced him to kill off the project a few months later.[117] British intelligence proposed a joint covert action against the government of Iranian prime minister Mohammad Mossadegh, but Truman and Acheson held off.[118]

With the White House demurring on political warfare in the Middle East and Latin America, the CIA pushed hard across Europe and right up to the Soviet Union's doorstep. The intelligence historian Richard Aldrich suggests that the ultimate purpose of subversive activities in Eastern bloc countries was to provoke repressive measures by communist authorities, thereby generating antipathy toward Moscow. The trials and executions of traitors and subversives across Eastern Europe in the late 1940s and early 1950s could thus be seen as perverse evidence of success.[119] Whereas Aldrich sees a method in the madness, the historian Sarah-Jane Corke has characterized the CIA's early years as "fragmented, inconsistent and chaotic." In Corke's judgment, the "unprecedented degree of autonomy" enabled "psychological warriors" to persist in covert operations despite consistent failure to achieve objectives.[120]

Whether judged a failure or a success, one thing that is clear is that the unseen hand of the CIA was acting at the behest of elected leaders and not in some rogue capacity. Political warfare and psychological operations were conducted at the instruction of the White House, without objection from Congress. Indeed, Beetle Smith *complained* to the National Security Council in April 1952 of the "three-fold increase in the clandestine operations of this Agency," as he braced for another threefold increase in the year to come.[121] Congress funded exponential growth of the CIA while accepting limited oversight—that is, occasional reporting to the Armed Services and Appropriations Committees and an "ad hoc" group of senior legislators informed as a matter of "courtesy."[122]

From Old Campus to "The Farm"

It was not easy attracting and retaining the right kind of recruits to staff the rapidly expanding Agency. From senior intelligence officers like Kent, Dulles, and Wisner down to entry-level analysts and operatives, the CIA drew heavily from alumni of Ivy League universities, and in particular, Yale. Kent described universities as the ideal training ground for intelligence and lauded the emergence of area studies, especially on Russia and China, as the most significant development taking place in American higher education.[123] A friendly exposé on the

Agency in the *Saturday Evening Post* made no bones about the extent of on-campus recruiting:

> CIA recruits many employees from our colleges and universities through a process beginning even before individual students realize that they are being singled out as possible CIA timber. Former G-2 and OSS officers, now members of the faculties of some eighty of our top institutions of higher learning, look over members of their junior-year classes with an eye for prospective CIA material. Not until the youths become seniors and are thinking about postgraduate appointment does the CIA conduct interviews.[124]

Yale served as the coordinating point for the CIA's nationwide recruitment effort in 1951—the classics professor Alfred Bellinger took on "the position of establishing college contacts in 50 or more American colleges and universities primarily for the purpose of recruiting high-level basic trainees."[125] Student athletes came in for special attention—the historian Robin Winks described how Agency recruiters like Yale's crew coach looked out for "young men with an ease with themselves that athletic success can often bring, with a wise awareness of the nuance of patriotism, and with an unfettered sense of curiosity."[126]

FIGURE 3. Agents in the making: the Yale Bulldogs (1950). From *The Yale Banner 1951*.

Yale's English Department boasted a number of OSS veterans who promoted careers in the CIA—most notably Norman Holmes Pearson, the Nathaniel Hawthorne scholar–turned-counterintelligence guru who headed Yale's American Studies program.[127] James Lilley was recruited in the fall term of 1950 by an "eminent professor" during office hours, surrounded by weighty tomes, with smoke curling up from the professor's pipe. "The State Department, he told me, was stuck in cement. 'Look at what you are interested in and consider intelligence. It's a growth industry.'"[128] Lilley took the bait, as did William F. Buckley Jr., who worked for the Agency under embassy cover in Mexico in 1951.

Yalies flocked to the CIA during the Korean War years. Lilley estimated that about one hundred classmates signed up in 1951—some looking for better odds to survive the war than as infantrymen.[129] But others were drawn in by the growing allure of the secret agent in the popular culture of Cold War America, modeled by the Hollywood icon Gary Cooper's scientist-turned-spy in the Fritz Lang film *Cloak and Dagger* (1946).[130] Yale student William Sloane Coffin Jr. had planned after graduation to devote himself to God and join the Union Theological Seminary in New York. But he changed his mind, abandoning Reinhold Niebuhr for Allen Dulles and signing up for the CIA. Seeing the secret service as a noble calling at the time, Coffin later reflected that his urge to join the CIA in 1950 was rooted in a flight from selfhood. "How could I better avoid myself than to live under another name, in countries other than my own, speaking for the most part a language not my own, living a life of high adventure—praiseworthy to boot—about which I was pledged to secrecy?"[131]

The philosophical significance of the spy as a modern mode of selfhood by negation was the subject of a section of Hannah Arendt's *Origins of Totalitarianism*. Arendt deconstructed the archetype found in British spy literature, a genre that boasted contributions from Rudyard Kipling, Joseph Conrad, W. Somerset Maugham, and Graham Greene (Ian Fleming was just around the corner). In Arendt's reading, secret agents of the British Empire embodied a distinctively modern form of *purposelessness*—they played the game of espionage for the game's sake. Perpetually manipulated by imperial masters, the agent of subversion did not care, because all that interested him was the invisible action itself. The ultimate agent-hero, T. E. Lawrence, wrote in his autobiography *Seven Pillars of Wisdom* (1922) of his desire to annihilate his "English self" and replace it with . . . nothing. Lawrence of Arabia resigned himself to an existence as "a functionary or agent of the secret forces which rule the world," embracing life as an empty self.[132] The spy ideal represented a modern form of nihilism, taking on larger significance in Arendt's argument as a bridge between British imperialism and the rise of totalitarianism in Europe. "When the British Intelligence Services (especially after the first World War) began to attract England's best sons, who preferred serving mysterious forces all over the world to serving the common good of their country, the stage seemed to be set for all possible horrors."[133]

Whether they aspired to become an American Lawrence of Arabia or just wanted to avoid dying on some hill in Korea, Yalie recruits, just like all the other volunteers for the CIA, soon found themselves in summer training camp—six weeks of general infantry training by Army instructors combined with six weeks of instruction in paramilitary warfare and covert tradecraft. Beetle's deputy, William Jackson, brought in a Princeton pal, Colonel Matt Baird, in the spring of 1951 to reorganize the training program.[134] Recruits learned "street surveillance, dead drops, safety and danger signals, the fundamentals of compartmentation, and the 'need to know' principle."[135] The *Basic Tradecraft Manual* taught what trainee Joseph Smith described as the "vocabulary of espionage."[136] One cardinal principle was drilled into all the cadets: "The key to operations is communications."[137] Williams College graduate Don Gregg recalled numerous Yale grads in his training cohort of forty, a fair portion of whom dropped out under the strain of infantry training at Fort Bragg, Georgia, in August and September 1951.[138] The Agency soon acquired its own training camp at Camp Peary outside Williamsburg, Virginia, a site that would become affectionately known as "The Farm." Gregg remembered fondly, "One young man who impressed me a great deal was Jack Downey. He was right at the top of the group, as I think I was, too. But Jack was very smart, likeable, and he had a record that I couldn't touch as a collegiate athlete."[139]

The training included ideology, with recruits watching patriotic (McCarthyite) films like *I Was a Communist for the FBI* (1951) and sitting through lectures on the "international virus" of communism.[140] A training manual, *The Nature of Psychological Warfare*, put together in 1952 by the Johns Hopkins Operations Research Office, dismissed the anxiety of Cold War realists like Arendt who worried that engaging in psywar threatened to undermine America's moral underpinnings. The authors of the manual insisted that the country had no choice:

> Like Nazi Germany, Communist Russia and her allies use psywar with skill and put very large resources in money and manpower into it. Even in "cold" war we are placed in the position of having to defend ourselves against psychological attack in many parts of the world. Whenever the cold war has turned hot, psywar has been used by both sides as one weapon in the power arsenal. Therefore, no matter what our wishes and feelings about psywar may be, we are in the position of having to use it. If we Americans use such a weapon, it behooves us to know how it works and how to use it as well as possible. The purpose of this volume is to help us along toward such knowledge.[141]

Recruits sometimes sat in on classes by Professor Paul Linebarger, who taught a psychological warfare seminar at Johns Hopkins SAIS. Joseph Smith audited the class in 1952, eagerly learning from the man who had literally written the book on the subject, *Psychological Warfare* (1948). Linebarger happened to be a leading China expert—his father was a legal adviser to Chiang Kai-shek's mentor and Nationalist Party founder, Sun Yat-sen (who was godfather to young Paul). Linebarger's students at Hopkins discussed key questions in the emerging field of psywar: how to manipulate people without them knowing it; how to weaken the enemy's will to fight without actually fighting him; how to differentiate propaganda into white (open attribution), gray (hidden source), and black (faked as enemy source).[142] Smith remembered how Linebarger would use students' confessionals to elicit their natural propensity toward deceit, assigning David Maurer's classic *The Big Con: The Story of the Confidence Man* (1940). Linebarger also encouraged students to make a case study of Edward Lansdale, adviser to the government of the Philippines in winning hearts and minds against the Huk insurgency.[143] The admiration was mutual—Lansdale took a copy of *Psychological Warfare* with him to South Vietnam when the CIA sent him there as adviser in 1954 and assigned it as on-the-job training to his staff.[144]

Psywar was indeed a growth industry, as the Yale recruiter had put it to James Lilley. By the end of the Korean War, the CIA would be running upwards of fifty "covert propaganda and political action operations" globally.[145] In the second edition of *Psychological Warfare*, Linebarger would lament the lack of propaganda effort in Korea, responding to legalistic-moralistic critics of psywar. "Even at the time of writing [1954] there is still some doubt as to whether the United States needs propaganda facilities. The William Jackson report of July 1953 indicated that the terms *propaganda* and *psychological warfare* were unsatisfactory. Of course they were. They still are. The world itself is unsatisfactory—in terms of the traditional, humane, rational U.S. point of view."[146] Linebarger insisted the United States had no choice but to engage in foreign propaganda and psychological warfare. At the same time, he maintained a faith in American virtue that would make it qualitatively different. "U.S. propagandists sometimes forget that they are not speaking for a mere nation, but are the representatives of something which is far bigger than any single nationality—they are the spokesmen, whether they like it or not, for a way of life which is new in the world, for a kind of freedom which, though coarse, is real."[147]

Part II

CALL TO ADVENTURE

5

AT WAR IN KOREA

Forces shaping American foreign policy and domestic politics at the dawn of the Cold War—the loss of China and containment of the Soviet Union, tradition of liberalism and philosophy of realism, fear of subversion and tendency toward repression, need for intelligence and temptation of psywar—coalesced in the first major military conflict of the new era: Korea. Erupting in an unexpected corner of the geostrategic map, the Korean War unfolded in a series of intelligence failures that brought Truman's America and Mao's China to blows. The Korean War incited the CIA, still in its infancy, to ramp up covert subversive warfare, and it galvanized forces of repression in the United States and China.

Intelligence Failures

The original estimating blunder of the Korean War was the US failure to anticipate the North Korean invasion in June 1950 across the established line of division at the thirty-eighth parallel. The US Army's official history would find a litany of reasons to explain away the failure to hear the signal in the noise at a time when "situations similar to that in Korea existed in virtually every other land area around the periphery of the USSR," and Korea was near the bottom of the list of strategic priorities.[1] The Truman administration was flying blind when it came to dynamics between Stalin, Mao and Kim Il Sung, and discounted the possibility that the young North Korean leader would have the temerity to initiate a full-scale war of reunification. The Americans were blindsided.

Facing a still war-weary public, and having publicly downgraded the strategic value of the Korean Peninsula in major speeches at the beginning of the year, Truman and Acheson did not dare go to Congress for a declaration of war. Instead, the administration went to the United Nations Security Council—an institution not much older than the CIA—for an authorization to use force. Harkening back to his 1947 speech to Congress, Truman tried to rally world opinion, declaring that "Korea is the Greece of the Far East."[2] Unlike the political methods used by communist parties in Europe, however, communist movements in Asia relied on military means to seize power and territory, fighting three wars of unification simultaneously in China, Korea, and Vietnam. Truman said, "The attack upon Korea makes it plain beyond all doubt that communism has passed beyond the use of subversion to conquer independent nations and will now use armed invasion and war."[3] Force would have to be met by counterforce.

North Korean's invasion initially went well, and Kim Il Sung nearly triumphed in his bold gambit. As of late summer, US and South Korean forces were hanging on tenaciously to a foothold in the southeast known as the Pusan Perimeter. Now it was Kim's turn to commit a colossal intelligence failure by ignoring warnings—including specific alerts from Mao and Zhou—that US forces were likely to stage a rear-guard amphibious landing on Korea's west coast.[4] General Douglas MacArthur's surprise landing at Incheon in mid-September 1950 was a masterstroke that reversed the course of the war. Unloading a huge force virtually unopposed, he marched easily to recapture the South Korean capital of Seoul and severed the supply lines of Communist forces. As North Korean soldiers scattered in a pell-mell retreat back up either side of the peninsula, the once-besieged US Eighth Army smashed through the Pusan Perimeter and marched northward.

The intoxicating success of Incheon set Americans up for the third intelligence disaster of the Korean conflict—the failure to anticipate China's entry into the war. In the early stages of the conflict, the Truman administration carefully avoided giving Beijing an excuse to intervene, for fear of getting drawn into the tail end of the Chinese Civil War. Chiang Kai-shek offered to send troops from Taiwan to help defend South Korea immediately after North Korea's invasion, but Acheson talked Truman out of the temptation lest Mao be provoked into the fray.[5] After Incheon, the lure of pushing north all the way to the Yalu River and reunifying Korea for the South was irresistible. The question was, how would Beijing respond?

In the absence of formal diplomatic relations or a reliable back channel to Chairman Mao and Premier Zhou, US intelligence analysts and decision makers had to rely on inferences from the deployment of Chinese capabilities, like troop movements to the northeast, and the nuances in official statements, supplemented by private messages passed through third parties. Anticipating China's response was a critical test of the CIA's ability to do current intelligence and near-term estimating. Looking back a decade later, Allen Dulles tried to excuse the Agency for its failure to see the Chinese coming:

> We had to estimate the intentions of Moscow and Peking. We were not in on their secret councils and decisions. In such cases, it is arrogant, as well as dangerous, for the intelligence officer to venture a firm opinion in the absence of telltale information on the positioning and moving of troops, the bringing up of strategic supplies and the like. I can speak with detachment about the 1950 Yalu estimates, for they were made just before I joined the CIA. The conclusions of the estimators were that it was a toss-up, but they leaned to the side that under certain circumstances the Chinese probably would not intervene. In fact, we just did not know what the Chinese Communists would do, and we did not know how far the Soviet Union would press them or agree to support them if they moved.[6]

In fact, US intelligence analysts had access to fairly reliable information about Chinese troop movements, at least until the highly secretive buildup within North Korean territory proper. In late 1949, Mao repatriated about three divisions worth of ethnic Korean soldiers to join the Korean People's Army.[7] Despite ongoing PLA operations to quell anti-Communist resistance in the far west (Xinjiang and Tibet) and deep south (Guangdong and Guangxi Provinces) as well as planning for amphibious assaults on the islands of Hainan and Taiwan, Mao kept shuffling troops to Manchuria and the Shandong Peninsula throughout early 1950.[8] By the time of the Incheon landing, MacArthur's intelligence chief, or G-2, Major General Charles A. Willoughby, was aware that at least a quarter of a million troops were mustered in Manchuria.[9]

Chinese capabilities for intervention were ready, and the Americans knew it. The difficult question remained how to gauge the intention behind the capability. Were these merely reserve forces marshaled to prevent US troops from spilling over into Manchuria? Or were they the makings of an expeditionary force to intervene across the Yalu River? Truman and Acheson wanted to believe they could have it both ways—conquering North Korea and avoiding Sino-Soviet intervention. Even more, they wanted to maintain an international mandate by fighting on the authority of a UN Security Council resolution, at the head of "United Nations Command" (UNC) troops, even flying the UN flag. Strictly speaking, the UN Security Council mandate only justified re-establishing the status quo antebellum of division at the thirty-eighth parallel. But the National

Security Council instructed MacArthur to continue north of the parallel, provided that no Soviet or Chinese troops joined the fight and neither Moscow nor Beijing were making a credible threat to do so.[10]

But how to judge a threat as credible or not? Beijing had been strengthening the rhetoric around its commitment to stand by their Korean comrades ever since Kim Il Sung's invasion began to stall in the late summer. In the weeks after MacArthur's Incheon landing, British and Dutch diplomats in Beijing warned of indications that the PRC would enter the war if US forces breached the thirty-eighth parallel.[11] Perhaps Washington might have trusted a telegram sent from one of their own, a George Kennan in Peking. It was hard to trust the Brits, after all, as they were pursuing a very different China policy, having offered to normalize relations with the PRC in January and hoping for an accommodation that would leave them in possession of their valuable colony in Hong Kong.

The Joint Chiefs asked for assurance from MacArthur, who confirmed there was no sign of China entering the war even if the parallel were transgressed.[12] As the historian Masuda Hajimu points out, the final decision to move north of the thirty-eighth parallel came on the same day that President Truman signed off on NSC-68, a grand strategy of containment on steroids drafted that spring by Kennan's hawkish successor as director of policy planning, Paul Nitze.[13] George Marshall, recently appointed secretary of defense, sent a separate message to MacArthur with direct authorization to move above the parallel as necessary and defining the mission as the "destruction of North Korean forces."[14] But Marshall added a note of caution, advising MacArthur to rely on South Korean troops and avoid dispatching American soldiers into northern territory.[15]

In Beijing, Premier Zhou Enlai delivered his most credible threat yet, in a speech marking the one-year anniversary of founding the PRC. Zhou declared that the Chinese people "will not stand aside if the imperialists wantonly invade the territory of their neighbor."[16] George Kennan, one of the few dissenters in Washington to the idea of pushing north of the thirty-eighth parallel, floated an alternative idea of offering a grand bargain to Mao and Zhou: the United States would recognize the PRC at the United Nations so long as China stayed clear of Korea. But Kennan had become too cautious for the hardening Cold Warrior consensus. Kennan's idea was shot down by John Foster Dulles, whom Truman had appointed as a special adviser to the State Department in a fit of bipartisanship in April 1950. MacArthur sent South Korean troops across the thirty-eighth parallel the day after Zhou's statement and moved ahead with his plan to land Marines at Wonsan, on North Korea's east coast.[17]

Mao Zedong convened the senior party and military leadership in the first days of October for secret councils, as Allen Dulles called them, to decide whether or not to intervene in Korea.[18] There were compelling arguments against taking on the Americans, a list that started with Taiwan. Chiang Kai-shek's exile government still enjoyed support in Washington and held the coveted permanent seat on the United Nations Security Council. An argument could be made that the PLA should concentrate its resources on an amphibious invasion of Taiwan, along with finishing the job of pacification in restive border areas in the far west and deep south where support for Communist rule was still tepid. With one last push, the PLA might be able to unite the motherland and deliver the first real peace dividend in a century to a populace tired of war and chaos. Korea threatened to bog China down in a fight on foreign territory against the world's economic and military superpower. It seemed to PLA leaders such as General Lin Biao like a fool's errand.

Chairman Mao disagreed, seeing incentives where others saw objections. If the masses were weary of struggle, all the more reason to re-energize them with a just war, as motivation for advancing down the next stretch of the revolutionary road. As for the need to secure borders, no region was more essential to economic progress than Manchuria, an industrial engine built up (and exploited) by Japanese colonial overseers and the portal to Soviet aid and investment. Without a buffer in the northern part of the Korean Peninsula, Manchuria would be vulnerable to economic pressure and military threat.[19] On the issue of Taiwan, the PLA lacked the naval and air power necessary for the invasion and a buildup would require Soviet assistance, which Stalin might refuse if Mao failed to help Kim. It was a false choice between Korea or Taiwan.

Finally, as far as daring to take on the Americans, imperialist GIs fighting far from home were exactly the kind of enemy that a people's army should want to fight, to strike a blow for nationalist liberation movements across Asia and prove to the Chinese people that their nation could no longer be bullied. More cynically, one resource China had in excess was soldiers—including Nationalist Army veterans of dubious loyalty to the party and revolution. Cannon fodder. General Peng Dehuai—a kind of Chinese Marshall—came around to Mao's position, and the Politburo followed suit. Peng later explained his logic: "The tiger always eats people and the time when it wants to eat depends on its appetite. It is impossible to make any concessions to a tiger. Since America came to invade us, we had to resist its invasion."[20]

At the pitch of Politburo deliberations, Zhou Enlai made one final effort to pass a warning along to Washington. On the night that Chairman Mao named General Peng Dehuai commander of Chinese "volunteer" forces in Korea, Zhou summoned the senior non-Communist diplomat in Beijing, the Indian ambassador Kavalam M. Panikkar, to his residence for a midnight conference. Panikkar had already passed on a warning delivered at a recent dinner with the PLA acting chief of staff General Nie Rongzhen, whose portfolio included closely monitoring intelligence coming out of Korea. On that prior occasion, General Nie had, "in a quiet and unexcited manner," informed Ambassador Panikkar "that the Chinese did not intend to sit back with folded hands and let the Americans come up to their border."[21] Now, it was Premier Zhou's turn to talk to the Indian go-between. Zhou apologized for waking Panikkar in the wee hours of the morning, expressed his appreciation for Prime Minister Jawaharlal Nehru's efforts to mediate Sino-US relations, and then came to the point, stating bluntly: "If the Americans crossed the thirty-eighth parallel China would be forced to intervene in Korea."[22]

Panikkar immediately sent an encrypted cable to New Delhi and informed his British and Burmese ambassadorial counterparts in Beijing the next day, while a CIA asset in the Indian embassy reported Zhou's message to Washington.[23] "We were inclined to write off most of this belligerency as bluff, but was any of it real?" wondered U. Alexis Johnson, a leading Korea Hand in the State Department at the time.[24] Nehru's government, with its philosophy of neutralism, was viewed by US officials as "naïve if not malicious," and not a trusted intermediary.[25] Zhou's warning to Panikkar—the signal in the noise—fell on deaf ears.

A few days after the party Central Committee agreed on forming a Chinese People's Volunteers (CPV) army to fight in Korea, MacArthur sent US soldiers across the thirty-eighth parallel. This was, in the words of the historian Allen Whiting, "the final contingency" that ensured Chinese involvement in the Korean War.[26] CPV troops began crossing the Yalu River in the stealth of night, in the beginning of a masterful deception campaign. Mao and Peng worked quietly and patiently, employing the trusted guerrilla stratagem of "drawing the enemy deep" before springing the trap. The tiger's hunger made him dangerous, but easier to lure in.

To Americans, the Korean situation as of October 1950 looked bright. The president naturally wished to bask in the glory of what appeared to be imminent victory. He also worried about the independent streak of his ambitious field commander, General MacArthur. So Truman made a long flight out to Wake Island, about halfway between Honolulu and Tokyo, for a tête-à-tête with MacArthur. For his in-flight reading, Truman asked the CIA to prepare a binder of intelligence estimates on the probabilities of Chinese intervention in Korea, Taiwan, Indochina, and the Philippines, and Soviet intervention in Korea.[27] Agency analysts estimated that Beijing would not intervene overtly in any of the four theaters.[28] Although China had the capability to intervene "effectively, but not necessarily decisively" in Korea, there were "no convincing indications" of the intention to do so. "Despite statement by Chou En-lai, troop movements to Manchuria, and propaganda charges of atrocities and border violations," analysts did not see a "credible" threat.[29] Ironically, the Wake Conference took place on the same day that Chinese troops crossed into North Korean territory.

The meeting between Truman and MacArthur was as awkward as it was brief. Truman asked for MacArthur's assessment of Beijing's intentions. The general assured the president, "We are no longer fearful of their intervention. We no longer stand hat in hand. The Chinese have 300,000 men in Manchuria. Of these probably not more than 100/125,000 are distributed along the Yalu River. They have no air force. Now that we have bases for our Air Force in Korea, if the Chinese tried to get down to Pyongyang there would be the greatest slaughter."[30]

The Wake Conference was a debacle. MacArthur resented being pulled away from the war room for a photo op with a civilian—even if it was the president—trying to ride the coattails of *his* triumph. Truman flew home disconcerted at the utter lack of respect for the commander-in-chief displayed by the elderly, vainglorious commander, who was out of touch after fourteen years without having set foot on the continental US.

As American egos clashed in the middle of the Pacific, Chinese forces were slipping undetected onto the battlefield. Lieutenant Commander Eugene Clark, famous for his scouting mission in advance of the Incheon landing, led a reconnaissance team along the far northwestern coast of Korea and warned of signs the Chinese were crossing the Yalu border.[31] But the CIA confidently reported to Secretary Acheson that "the Soviet Korean venture . . . has ended in failure," and dismissed the prospect of Chinese intervention ("The Chinese Communists are unlikely to be willing to come to the assistance of the North Koreans at the risk of becoming involved in open hostilities with the US and its UN allies").[32] Riding the wave of victory, MacArthur pressed beyond his orders by sending American troops toward the banks of the Yalu River.

Chinese soldiers first engaged South Korean troops on October 25. As Chinese-speaking POWs landed in interrogation rooms, MacArthur's G-2 Charles Willoughby flew from Tokyo to Korea to see the captives in person. He refused to believe the evidence before his eyes and reported to Washington that the Chinese would not send a significant force to Korea.[33] The public back home was primed from victory day, with the *New York Times* editorializing in late October that "except for unexpected developments along the frontiers of the peninsula, we can now be easy in our minds as to the military outcome."[34]

Even as the presence of Chinese forces became impossible to deny, CIA estimates insisted that Beijing's interest was limited to establishing a "cordon sanitaire" along their border, with a narrow objective of protecting China's share of the Suiho hydroelectric dam.[35] On the collective intelligence failure in the autumn of 1950, the military historian Max Hastings judged the negligence of MacArthur and Willoughby especially harshly. "The conduct of the drive to the Yalu reflected a contempt for intelligence, for the cardinal principles of military prudence, seldom matched in twentieth-century warfare," Hastings concluded.[36]

Chinese and American soldiers first exchanged fire in early November. CPV maneuvers pushed the US Eighth Army back to Chongchon River and the Marines X Corps toward Changjin Lake (known to Americans as Chosin Reservoir). Still, the United States clung to its preconceived notion that Beijing, lacking the resources and stomach for a real fight, was merely trying to protect the dam on the border.[37] The CCP, joined by "minor parties," released a statement making it clear that national security was at stake, invoking the proverb that "if you lose your lips then your teeth will freeze, and if the door is broken then the whole house is in danger."[38]

Belatedly and abruptly, MacArthur changed his tune. Acknowledging the Chinese intervention, he now fretted that hordes could be en route from Manchuria and asked permission to bomb the bridges across the Yalu River. Permission was granted, but prohibitions against entering Chinese airspace constricted bombing operations.[39] The CIA also dramatically revised previous estimates. Analysts now wrote that within thirty to sixty days, the Chinese could mobilize enough troops (350,000) to stabilize North Korea's position. At the United Nations, the US and its allies floated a resolution calling on Chinese troops to withdraw that included a promise to leave PRC territory untouched. Moscow vetoed the resolution, but Truman tried to underscore the point at his weekly press conference. "Speaking for the United States Government and people," the president affirmed, "I can give assurance that we support and are acting within the limits of United Nations policy in Korea, and that we have never at any time entertained any intention to carry hostilities into China."[40]

The battlefield fell eerily quiet as General Peng massed troops at night, drawing MacArthur's UNC forces closer to the border and deeper into the Chinese trap. Sherman Kent took over the new Office of National Estimates (ONE) on November 15 with what he later recalled as "a feeling of tragedy and despair" over the situation unfolding in Korea.[41] Yet MacArthur kept up the veneer of victory, promising on a visit to the western front that the impending Thanksgiving offensive would ensure US troops could be home by Christmas. Instead, a CPV assault hit overstretched, unsuspecting UNC troops at Thanksgiving like a cement truck. Steeled by decades of guerrilla and civil war experience, fighting on their country's doorstep, and incited by revolutionary indoctrination, lightly armed Chinese units shredded the South Korean II Corps, opening up the US Eighth Army's flank and severing the supply line to the First Marine Division. Racist condescension undermined American preparedness down to the last moment: as the X Corps commander General Ned Almond's men were about to be mowed down, his St. Crispin's Day speech was, "Don't let a bunch of Chinese laundrymen stop you."[42] General Peng Dehuai's "laundrymen" sent the GIs scrambling from Chosin Reservoir to evacuation from the port at Hamhung, one of worst routs and largest evacuations in recent US military history.

"We face an entirely new war," MacArthur telegrammed grandly from Tokyo to the Joint Chiefs.[43] He submitted a list of two dozen targets in North Korea and China for atomic bombing. MacArthur's Christmas list was denied and the gap between the general and the president widened into a chasm.[44] Chairman Mao was ecstatic, but General Peng, with a field commander's prudence, tried to lower expectations. Victory was coming at a steep price, and each step south created vulnerabilities for CPV logistics and supply lines. Chinese casualties in the Winter Offensive were more than twice that of UNC forces.[45] The CPV succeeded in pushing back UNC forces below the thirty-eighth parallel, recapturing Seoul in the first days of 1951. But that would be as far as the Chinese tide of victory would take the Communist side. UNC soldiers took Seoul back a couple months later, and the fighting bogged down in a bloody "limited war" of attrition along roughly the same line of division, the thirty-eighth parallel, where it had all begun.

The failure to anticipate North Korea's invasion and China's intervention exposed the CIA's desperate need for better intelligence estimating and new leadership to make it happen. Beetle Smith took the reins at the CIA on October 7, 1950, as the die was being cast in Beijing to intervene, and he would rely on Sherman Kent to fashion the ONE into the kind of analytical community envisioned in *Strategic Intelligence for American World Policy* of "a strange and wonderful collection of devoted specialists molded into a vigorous production unit."[46] Estimating "requires of its producers that they be masters of the subject matter, impartial in the presence of new evidence, ingenious in the development of research techniques, imaginative in their hypotheses, sharp in the analysis of their own predilections or prejudices, and skillful in the presentation of their conclusions."[47] Kent's research support staff at the ONE increased to 461 personnel by July 1951 and up to 766 as of February 1953.[48]

The CIA at War

While the estimating failures in Korea energized Sherman Kent's efforts to improve strategic intelligence work, the military and diplomatic characteristics of the conflict encouraged experiments with covert warfare. As William Colby recalled, "The paramilitary and political-action 'culture' had unquestionably become the dominant one in the CIA, much to the chagrin of its bureaucratic bedfellows. . . . Under the impetus of the Korean War, in a time of fierce anti-Communist and anti-Soviet sentiment and rhetoric, covert paramilitary and political action was the name of the intelligence game."[49]

In pure military terms, as the war settled into a grinding stasis along the thirty-eighth parallel, the US military cast about for alternate ways to punish the enemy. UNC forces exploited air and sea power to the hilt in a relentless campaign to bomb North Koreans and their Chinese allies into submission, which included the widespread use of napalm incendiaries. In mid-1952, Truman authorized a massive bombing campaign against vital hydroelectric dams, designed to shut off power to the entire country, and Pyongyang was ravaged by over 1,200 USAF sorties in Operation Pressure Pump on July 11.[50] US Navy ships sat offshore, pounding away at coastal targets.[51] Yet, total war from the skies above and seas around North Korea brought no tangible results in what remained a frustratingly limited war on land. If conventional tactics were insufficient, perhaps unconventional warfare could make the difference?

The geopolitical imperative to avoid escalation beyond the peninsula and minimize risks of triggering World War III required staying clear of PRC territory—officially at least. Omar Bradley explained the reasoning behind *not* taking the war to China, in testimony to Congress:

> Under present circumstances, we have recommended against enlarging the war from Korea to also include Red China. The course of action often described as a "limited war" with Red China would increase the risk we are taking by engaging too much of our power in an area that is not the critical strategic prize. Red China is not the powerful nation seeking to dominate the world. Frankly, in the opinion of the Joint Chiefs of Staff, this strategy would involve us in the wrong war, at the wrong place, at the wrong time, and with the wrong enemy.[52]

How, then, to defeat Chinese forces in Korea, supplied and reinforced across their land border, without giving the appearance of "enlarging the war"? Ironically, the geopolitical constraints, like the military frustrations, served as a rationale for covert war in and around Korea.

Unfortunately for the advocates of unorthodox warfare, North Korea proved to be a hard target for covert action. As the intelligence historian Matthew Aid pointed out, prior to invading the south, Kim Il Sung ordered the evacuation of civilians in a band above the thirty-eighth parallel, creating a cordon sanitaire to defend against infiltration. Soon after North Korea's invasion, the US Army—pinned inside the Pusan Perimeter in the southeast corner of Korea—scrambled to parachute spies behind enemy lines. Few returned to safety. Army Signal Corps cryptographers struggled to tap Korean communications because the enemy avoided wireless radio.[53]

Covert efforts were further hamstrung by discoordination among intelligence services. The Far East Command (FEC), Eighth Army, Air Force, and CIA tripped over one another running parallel paramilitary operations. The Army set up a small unit in February 1951 to run Operation Leopard, training "Donkey teams" on Baengnyong Island in the Yellow Sea and infiltrating them onto the North Korean coast. Army irregular warfare units also ran thousands of partisans on the west coast.[54] At the same time, the Eighth Army's Miscellaneous Division in Daegu, set up by a veteran of guerrilla fighting in the Philippines during WWII, looked for ways to incite resistance in the North, parachuting agents of subversion into the mountainous middle of the peninsula.[55]

A trial mission involving two dozen commandos air-dropped north of the thirty-eighth parallel in mid-March 1951 was a disaster.[56] Team members landed in scattered positions outside the drop zone and their radios froze when a snowstorm hit. After almost a fortnight they made radio contact requesting extraction. When Navy helicopters arrived at the pickup site on the east coast, they came under ground fire. These were early days for combat helicopters—Captain John Thornton was one of only three hundred trained chopper pilots and his bird could carry only three passengers. Thornton's helicopter crash-landed. After a bloody and chaotic flight from the pickup spot, Thornton, the American team leader, and a few South Korean agents attempted to make their way by foot back south. Thornton was captured and spent the next two years in a POW camp.[57]

The Army would not give up on guerrilla warfare, and it tried to air-drop Korean Jedburghs into the central region of the Peninsula three months later. The infiltration team successfully called in an air strike on a nearby Chinese position, only to be exposed by a US Air Force resupply flight that violated a cardinal rule of covert operations by making a drop in broad daylight directly over the team's hideout. Flushed out by security forces, two team members reached a helicopter for evacuation, others escaped on foot across the thirty-eighth parallel, and two more were never heard from again.

The Fifth Air Force created a special missions squadron in order to improve future performance, and Americans and Brits were no longer allowed to lead Korean teams on long-term infiltrations.[58] Far East Command's Aviary Section made fifty flights in the fall of 1951 and reported no losses.[59] Meanwhile, a new covert mission was devised to send boys and elderly men on jumps twenty to thirty miles beyond the front, to wander back disguised as refugees for intelligence debriefings on what they saw walking south. A preliminary review of the program revealed inadequate training for the agents and carelessness by flyers. After implementing improvement measures, the program resumed in the fall of 1951, making seventy-eight flights into enemy territory.[60]

Not all the recruits chose their missions freely. The historian David Cheng Chang documented the activities of Military Intelligence Unit 8240's coercive use of Chinese POWs as "prisoner-agents." The most spectacular case was the double-cross of Zhang Wenrong, a Chinese POW who tossed a grenade back into the C-46 as he jumped out with his parachute.[61]

The CIA naturally joined the Army and Air Force in playing the covert action game in Korea.[62] The puppet master was Hans V. Tofte, a Dutch American OSS veteran tapped by Frank Wisner soon after the outbreak of the Korean War to build a platform for operations out of Japan. "Basically I was told to choose a site and build an operations base outside Tokyo, big enough to handle one thousand people, with our own communications," Tofte recalled. "Whatever else happened, I was on my own."[63] He set up a training area in Chigasaki, conveniently located near Atsugi Air Force Base. By the end of 1950, Chigasaki was buzzing with a thousand men and a modest fleet of transport planes.[64]

On the Korean Peninsula proper, the CIA hub was called the Joint Advisory Commission, Korea (JACK), and was set up in Pusan in November 1950. With the CIA swamped by "consumer demands" for targets and tactical intelligence, JACK ran its own guerrilla teams in the North. Over a thousand Koreans, including POWs, went through training on Yong Island in the Bay of Pusan, with select graduates going on to Chigasaki. Tofte shuttled between a half dozen CIA facilities in Japan and Korea overseeing espionage and paramilitary operations that stretched from the Russian Far East to the Shandong Peninsula. He sent "general resistance warfare groups" into North Korea throughout the course of 1951.[65]

The success rate was abysmal, but Washington asked for more. In the fall of 1951, the National Security Council called for "intensification" of covert action behind enemy lines, with a mandate to "develop underground resistance and facilitate covert and guerrilla operations in strategic areas to the maximum practicable extent."[66] According to a transcript examined by the historian Sarah-Jane Corke, Allen Dulles told an advisory group in a meeting at his alma mater, Princeton University, that subversion would not work without "martyrs": "You have got to have a few martyrs. Some people have got to get killed. I don't want to start a bloody battle, but I would like to see things started. I think we have to take a few risks."[67] By the second half of 1951, the covert war in Korea included offshore infiltration on the west and east coasts and paratrooper drops in the hinterland; exfiltration of escaped POWs and downed pilots; sabotage and demolition of supply lines, transportation corridors, and critical infrastructure; and an array of espionage efforts, focusing on targeting intelligence.[68]

The meeting logs of the CIA director, Beetle Smith, convey a vivid sense of the scope of covert activity, with reports streaming in of CIA-backed guerrilla warfare teams and raiding parties that claimed to have blown up mines and bridges, destroyed manufacturing plants, and slaughtered enemy livestock; ambushed North Korean troops; rescued downed American pilots and South Korean soldiers; and called in air strikes on North Korean military encampments and Soviet liaison offices.[69] Occasionally the CIA would ask the Air Force to verify these claims, but there were limited means to judge how many partisan success stories were true.[70]

The transcripts of the Director's Log also reflect the depth of bureaucratic rivalry among civilian and military intelligence officers. Having resisted a CIA presence in their theater, MacArthur and Willoughby finally allowed a small OPC team, headed by George Aurell, to use an office in Far Eastern Command (FEC) headquarters, Tokyo's Dai Ichi Building, in May 1950.[71] Even after Truman removed MacArthur from command, FEC-CIA ties were strained. The new head of the Far East Command, General Mark Ridgway, established a unit in Korea called CCRAK with authority to direct all covert operations by civilian and military intelligence.[72] CCRAK (Covert, Clandestine, and Related Activities in Korea—not much of a cover name) and JACK operated out of the Traymore Hotel in Seoul, with the Agency men resenting Army oversight.[73] From the CIA perspective, military intelligence demands "inevitably diverted the small CIA Mission from its primary job of getting high-level strategic information [*censored line*] and from making a concentrated effort to establish viable covert action cells in [*censored words*] North Korea. The diversion of long-range assets to tactical operations exposed agents and operations not only to the enemy but to the local population and to many United Nations agencies as well."[74]

It didn't help civ-mil cooperation when the CIA mission chief in Korea, D-Day hero Colonel "Vandy" Vandervoort, had to be recalled from Seoul for alienating the UN forces commander's staff.[75] Anxious to get out from under G-2's strictures, the CIA's ranking officer in Tokyo, George Aurell, asked for assurance that as soon as a Korean armistice was signed, the Agency would be unfettered. The answer was no. According to Ridgway's G-2, "armistice or no armistice, there would be no immediate peace in the Far East . . . Far East Command control and coordination of clandestine intelligence and covert operations was essential to intelligent planning and efficient operation and . . . present command channels should remain unchanged at least until such time as peace is insured in Korea."[76] CIA Tokyo complained bitterly in March 1952, "G-2 officers have clearly indicated their desire to take over CIA and its mission."[77]

Despite tensions with the military, the Agency continued to run guerrilla teams hassling the enemy in the northwest corner of the peninsula near the China border. OPC also thought there might be recruits in mountainous terrain to the east, where locals purportedly resented the dominance of cadres from the western provinces. Ex-Nationalist soldiers in the CPV were another logical target group.[78] After a hiatus, Tofte's infiltration missions (known as Operation

Blossom) resumed in April 1952. Hundreds of C-47s lumbered over the thirty-eighth parallel under cover of nightfall, dropping agents of subversion to their targets.[79] Many of those lucky enough to establish radio contact or return to South Korea had been turned and were acting as double agents.[80] The historian Michael Haas concluded that parachute operations during the second half of 1952 were "100 percent losses."[81]

Army efforts didn't fare much better, as the military intelligence veteran-turned-historian Ed Evanhoe documented. Irregulars led by a British commando provided support to a partisan group based on Taehwa Island off the northwest coast of Korea, near the mouth of the Yalu River. Chinese troops assaulted the island and crushed the guerrilla unit, taking the Brit prisoner. He was shot trying to escape a POW camp just prior to a prisoner release. An operation on the east coast to extract a downed Navy pilot in February 1952 turned out to be a trap: the exfiltration chopper was shot down and operations in the area had to be shut down. On the southwest coast, Donkey team units expanded beyond stealth commando strikes, staging larger operations in the summer of 1952 and suffering major losses. Airdrops and pickups by the so-called Mustang Raiders resulted in one team after another disappeared, killed, or turned. In the largest airborne covert op of the war, nearly a hundred partisans were parachuted into the mountains west of Pyongyang in January 1953 and reinforced with over fifty more men in May, yielding nothing—radio silence. After receiving a sketchy message that the group had located five downed American pilots, a plan to test an experimental snatch method of fixed-wing aerial pickup was aborted at the last minute when the rescue mission ran into anti-aircraft fire. The enemy, yet again, seemed to be aware help was on the way.[82]

A study by the Johns Hopkins Operations Research Office deemed the partisan warfare effort in Korea to be "futile and callous."[83] The vast majority of Allen Dulles's "martyrs" sent north were Koreans or Chinese, including POWs conscripted into covert activities in violation of the Geneva Convention, signed by the US government in 1949. Americans joined airborne covert missions only in exceptional cases, especially after the summer of 1951. John Singlaub complained that the Pentagon forbade Americans, even elite Army Rangers of the kind he had been training at Fort Benning, from embedding with Korean units, out of fear they would be captured and "brainwashed."[84]

Suppressing Counterrevolutionaries

Belying the Truman administration's promise to fight a limited war that would steer clear of Chinese and Soviet territory, covert warfare against North Korea occasionally spilled across the sea and land border into the PRC. In the late spring of 1951, Truman authorized aid to Chiang Kai-shek in support of covert ops against the mainland that might divert Beijing's resources away from Korea. Turf wars extended into China as well, with the CIA complaining that the FEC chief claimed "authority to carry out long-range missions beyond the Yalu and into China . . . in flat contradiction to the CCRAK Charter."[85] PRC state media complained in late July 1952 about naval provocations in the Taiwan Strait as well as "alleged violations of the Manchurian frontier by American war planes," as the *New York Times* put it.[86] The official PRC military history of the Korean War records an uptick in enemy use of commandos and covert operations in 1952, with 340 spies captured in the first part of the year and a special counterespionage campaign in September eliminating an additional 272 infiltrators.[87]

Mao Zedong had worried since the Chinese Civil War about American covert activities. The first "spy incident" involving the United States took place after the Communist capture of Shenyang in November 1948, when the US consul Angus Ward refused an order to turn over communications equipment. Mao warned the Politburo in December that "the main point of the current policy of the American State Department is how to prop up an effective opposition in China to resist the CCP" and feared the US would seek to retain naval bases in Shanghai and Qingdao as centers of resistance. He wrote to Stalin that same month describing the American plot against Chinese Communist rule:

> Americans intend to proceed from active support for the Guomindang to, on the one hand, support for local Guomindang [groups] and local southern Chinese warlords, so that their military forces will resist the People's Liberation Army; and, on the other hand, organize and send their lackeys so that they can infiltrate the Political Consultative Conference and the democratic coalition government and set up an opposition bloc there and undermine the people's liberation front from within, so that the revolution can not be carried out consistently.[88]

After the US Navy pulled out of Qingdao in June 1949, Mao ordered Shenyang consular officials barred from leaving the country and publicized espionage allegations against Consul Ward.[89] With the Civil War racing toward denouement, the CCP boasted of arresting tens of thousands of "spies and saboteurs" in urban areas and eliminating a million "armed bandits" in the countryside.[90] When the Communists took over Shanghai, long a spy haven, they moved quickly to round up suspected agents.[91] Ward was expelled in December and the State Department withdrew all personnel from the mainland.

Mao lowered the temperature of the anti-spy campaign, instructing local cadres to exercise restraint. While the campaign had targeted foreign missionaries and Christian followers, the new instructions advised localities that "the anti-spy campaign is not equivalent to opposition to freedom of religion."[92] Reviewing the internal security situation just prior to the outbreak of the Korean War, Mao reported that "the people's public security organs have uncovered large numbers of reactionary secret service groups and agents," but warned that more than four hundred thousand "bandits" remained at large.[93] He focused attention on the threat of US and Nationalist-backed subversion by "bandit guerrilla warfare" and "backward elements." The People's Republic was still infested with "bandits, secret agents, and spies":

> They have organized many secret agents and spies to oppose our government and spread rumours among the people . . . [and] these secret agents and spies are also engaged in sabotaging the people's economic undertakings, assassinating the personnel of the Party government organizations and collective intelligence for the imperialists and the Kuomintang reactionaries. All these counter-revolutionary activities are directed from behind the scenes by imperialism, and particularly by U.S. imperialism. All these bandits, secret agents and spies are imperialist lackeys. . . . In the newly liberated areas, the present task of the People's Liberation Army is to continue to wipe out the remnant bandits and that of the people's public service organs is to continue to strike at the enemy's secret service groups.[94]

Mao called for a divide-and-conquer counterespionage policy of "combining suppression with leniency . . . [with] certain punishment for the main culprits, no punishment for those accomplices who act under duress and rewards for those who render positive services. The whole Party and nation must heighten their vigilance against the conspiratorial activities of counter-revolutionaries."[95] The need to rally the people against covert threats foreign and domestic gave Mao a perfect excuse to practice what the political scientist Julia Strauss labels "paternalist terror" by ramping up pressure and then showing leniency.[96]

The war in Korea reinvigorated Mao's hunt for agents of subversion. Days after the secret decision to send Chinese troops to Korea, Mao officially launched the Campaign to Suppress Counterrevolutionaries, announced on October 10, 1950, in what was known as the Double Ten Directive. The chairman ordered party cadres to "strike surely, accurately and relentlessly in suppressing counter-revolutionaries."[97] While rooting out subversives, the masses were subjected to parallel indoctrination through the Campaign to Resist America, Aid Korea, Protect Our Homes, Defend the Nation. As suggested by the unofficial name of the Hate America Campaign, state propaganda ramped up the level of vitriol against US imperialism, playing on traumas of Japanese occupation by presenting Americans as the new "foreign devils."[98] Legal mechanisms for the trial and punishment of counterrevolutionaries were promulgated in February 1951, by which point the violence unleashed by the Campaign to Suppress Counterrevolutionaries seemed to be spiraling out of control as local cadres competed to fill execution quotas.[99]

Chairman Mao showed his paternalistic side in June by calling on cadres to restrain excessive "'Left' deviations" (in other words, carrying out the bloodletting he had originally commanded).[100] Mao told the Third National Conference on Public Security in May that "the number of counter-revolutionaries to be killed must be kept within certain proportions." Those who "owe blood debts," had committed "extremely serious crimes" that incurred hatred of people, or did "extremely serious harm to the national interest" were to be "executed without delay."[101] The rest should be sent to labor camps for observation and re-education. He estimated the capital cases would represent "roughly 10 to 20 percent." Even "certain secret agents who have done extremely serious harm to the national interest" but did not shed blood or incur "deep hatred of the masses" should be spared execution. Mao did not want to waste productive labor—unless the people's anger demanded death, counterrevolutionaries should be put to work for economic construction.[102]

Although Mao and party leaders exploited the Campaign to Suppress Counterrevolutionaries in order to tighten their grip on power, the threat of counterrevolution was real. Insurrection surged in the border regions, where discontent was deep and hope in resistance was lifted by the presence of American soldiers in Korea. Conditions were hard in Manchuria, which was strained by wartime mobilization, with starvation conditions in Jilin Province.[103] Internal party reports from Shenyang documented by the historian Masuda Hajimu warned that anti-Communist forces were taking advantage of the war in Korea to regroup and resist: "Reactionary groups—remnants of Chiang Kai-shek's troops and landlords—recognize that now is the time to change the government, and they are feeling extremely excited, becoming active, and spreading rumors and making trouble."[104] Emboldened landowners and disgruntled farmers struck out at party rule, and Chiang Kai-shek did what he could to fan the flames of insurgency, if only by dropping a lot of leaflets.[105] In the southwest, the CCP regional head Deng Xiaoping eased tax collection, increased "bandit suppression" operations, and shipped off disaffected men to fight as "people's volunteers" in Korea. Large-scale rebellion had erupted in the spring of 1950 in Guizhou Province, where 130,000 rebels seized control of nearly half of the province.[106] "Unpacified" areas of Guangxi Province also witnessed large-scale insurrection in 1950 and 1951.[107]

Mao Zedong would later state that during the Campaign to Suppress Counterrevolutionaries 1.2 million people were imprisoned and an equal number

FIGURE 4. Special agents and bandits: Mao's Campaign to Suppress Counterrevolutionaries (early 1950s). Everyday Life in Maoist China. https://everydaylifeinmaoistchina.org/.

detained, on top of the seven hundred thousand people killed outright.[108] Documents viewed by the historian Michael Dutton gave an even higher number of arrests (over 3.2 million) and incarcerations (1 million).[109] The exponential increase in arrests and detentions put a massive strain on the penal system, and the Ministry of Public Security had to scramble to find places to incarcerate so many counterrevolutionaries. As the historian Jan Kiely explained, "In the wartime guerilla manner, this could only be carried out with the stretching of minimal resources, extreme frugality, the intensive working of prisoners, the expropriation of local resources, and pragmatic adaptation to local conditions. This was how China's 'gulag archipelago'—a massive, widely dispersed prison labor-camp system commonly known as *laogai* (reform-through-labor) system took shape."[110]

The Indian intellectual Raja Hutheesing visited China during the high tide of the counterrevolutionary suppression campaign and left a vivid record of his observations in *The Great Peace: An Asian's Candid Report on Red China* (1953). The brother-in-law of Prime Minister Nehru, Hutheesing was jailed for independence activism, became a well-known writer, and, after a stint in government, dedicated himself to journalism. Hutheesing's friendship tour of China in October 1951 and return visit as an accredited journalist in May 1952 were part of Zhou Enlai's effort to cultivate ties to Nehru's neutralist India.

Hutheesing acknowledged the successes of the CCP. But he could also pick up on hints of darker sides to the revolution. He jotted down a news report on the Ching Ha Farm for Counterrevolutionaries, where political criminals were subjected to thought reform.

> They showed great resistance against the idea—many cried, many went on hunger strikes, many wrote their last letters, and some even tried to commit suicide and to escape. . . . Even after they started participating in labor, their thoughts were not immediately reformed and "stabilized," and were often influenced by outside situation—e.g., when American imperialists landed in Korea and the Korean People's Army retreated temporarily, many of the criminals were talking among themselves, expecting American victory and the return of Chiang Kai-shek.[111]

The state media report acknowledged recalcitrance. "Those who do not do their work, refuse to be reformed through labor, or try to commit sabotage or to escape are duly punished for their criminal acts. Tu Shih-chin, a secret agent of the KMT who led six criminals in their escape and was arrested along with them, was brought back to the farm and shot before a gathering of all inmates."[112]

While VIPs from India like Hutheesing could travel around the PRC, the few Americans left in China during the Korean War years were finding themselves targets of Mao's Campaign against Counterrevolutionaries. Many had missionary ties, like the group of Catholic priests persecuted in 1951 on charges of espionage.[113] Then there was the unusual young couple Allyn and Adele Rickett, who traveled to Beijing on Fulbright grants in late 1948 as graduate students from the University of Pennsylvania. As most of the city's expat community fled civil war and communist victory, the Ricketts settled into their university teaching jobs. The liberal-minded academics they met were disillusioned with the Nationalist regime of Chiang Kai-shek, telling the Ricketts "stories of how they had been beaten or threatened by the secret police."[114] Allyn became a low-grade source, passing on his observations to a US consulate officer whom he knew from his days in naval intelligence during WWII.[115] After State Department personnel were evacuated in January 1950, Allyn started meeting with a contact in the British legation in Beijing.

As a US citizen in regular, unmonitored contact with faculty and students at one of China's top universities, Allyn was uniquely placed to observe elite attitudes toward the Korean War mobilization. Initial euphoria over fighting in a just war against imperialism faded, followed by a "brief period of uncertainty and depression." Rickett even detected "signs of wavering" among some liberal faculty. But students remained enthusiastic, organizing propaganda teams to do "thought work" in factories and villages. "Thousands of groups of students, office clerks, politically advanced workers, peasants, and housewives spread into every factory, shop, and village to make speeches, display posters, sing improvised songs, and put on skits. . . . As these amateur propaganda teams reached everywhere, they aroused the whole population to form a mighty patriotic movement." It could be a tough sell to Chinese farmers, who thought of Koreans in Manchuria as "either opium peddlers or secret agents for the Japanese." Propaganda teams struck a chord by portraying US troops as following the same invasion path charted by the Japanese.[116]

In Rickett's estimation, the Korean War brought about a "final and complete break with the West" among most Chinese intellectuals.[117] He was astonished at the intensity of feeling that accompanied this shift when Mao ramped up the Campaign to Suppress Counterrevolutionaries in early 1951.

> It was with loathing that I watched the long series of public self-criticism meetings held by the students and teachers at Yenching. In both departmental and schoolwide meetings, before small groups of close friends and large crowds, they decried their former intellectual servility toward the West as manifested in everything from a love of American detective stories to helping American imperialism by working in the United States Information Service. Many had become so emotionally worked up in their self-criticism that they had broken down and sobbed. What had made all this even more incomprehensible to me was the fact that no force appeared to have been used other than the dynamic pressure of a group experience and the emotional patriotic upsurge produced by the Korean war.[118]

Rickett presumably attracted the Ministry of Public Security's attention in mid-1950, when he received a written order to report for duty mailed by the US Marines to his address on campus (he was active reserve).[119] He was not arrested until July 25, 1951, and was incarcerated in Caolanzi Hutong Prison in downtown Beijing. Built to detain political prisoners by the Nationalist government in the 1930s, the small complex was located not far from Zhongnanhai, CCP headquarters and Mao's official residence.

Rickett went through formal examination by counterintelligence officers and informal interrogation by his cellmates. A fellow prisoner, surnamed Liao, introduced himself as a former Nationalist intelligence officer who had benefited from the CCP's leniency policy, but then, inspired by MacArthur's Incheon landing, formed a sabotage squad with ex-Nationalist associates. They had guns and a radio set, and hearing rumors that the US would give money to resistance groups, they sent a team member to Taiwan "to procure funds and establish the right connections." Their man in Taiwan was never heard from again. After carrying out one attempted arson, the group disbanded as the tide turned against the Americans in Korea. According to Rickett, anti-CCP dissenters like Liao lost hope over the course of 1952. "The progress of the war in Korea had exploded the myth of American invincibility and the dreams that a Nationalist-American landing might bring about their release. The anticipated internal revolt and economic collapse had failed to materialize."[120]

Another American who, along with Catholic priests and Fulbright scholars, stayed in China through the Korean War, only to be swept up in the Campaign to Suppress Counterrevolutionaries, was Robert McCann, arrested in Tianjin in June 1951. Unlike the Ricketts, McCann was the real deal: an operative working for the OSO under the cover of being a foreign businessman. When the State Department learned of McCann's arrest, they passed the bad news on to the CIA that he was "undergoing severe and intensive interrogation aimed at establishing his involvement in espionage in addition to their clear case against him on a charge of unauthorized export of capital. McCann, a covert 00 agent who was involved in certain Tientsin operations, is resisting interrogation, but the informant believes he may crack under the pressure." The report added, ominously, "He knows the identities of three CIA officers."[121]

6

THE THIRD FORCE

As Mao campaigned against counterrevolutionary agents at home and imperialist soldiers next door, Truman sought means to put pressure on Beijing and break the impasse in Korea without expanding the war. The ideal solution, of course, would be if those subversive, counterrevolutionary forces Mao feared could actually succeed. If the Communists started losing control in China, they could hardly continue to fight a war in Korea. And if the real reason for the loss of China was Chiang Kai-shek and the Nationalist Party, then what if other non-Communist alternatives led the new counterrevolution? Could the Third Force, with effective aid from the United States, overthrow Mao—or at least help win the war in Korea?

The Third Force solution to the loss of China and war in Korea needs to be understood in a global context, as an extension of American efforts to promote a non-Communist Left in postwar Europe, in postcolonial Asia, and even in the United States itself. The idea of a Third Force was the inspiration behind books like Arthur Schlesinger Jr.'s *Vital Center*, written in a spirit of postwar liberal idealism that would be satirized by the British novelist Graham Greene in *The Quiet American*.

But the idea of a Third Force in China was not simply a Western projection or liberal fantasy. The search for a centrist, third way, in fact, was deeply rooted in twentieth-century Chinese politics, traceable back to the pre-eminent public intellectual Liang Qichao. Liang's heirs, most notably a philosopher-politician named Carsun Chang, carried on the quest for a third way in the shadows of the struggle between the two armed parties, Chiang's Nationalists and Mao's

Communists. America's finest China Hands—both government officials and scholars like John King Fairbank and Owen Lattimore—paid close attention to the Third Force as a proxy for the fate of Chinese liberalism. For a fleeting moment during the Chinese Civil War, and once again during the Korean War, the Third Force surged to the surface, carried by a wave of fear of Communist subversion, disillusionment with the Nationalist alternative, and hope in a vital center to world politics.

La Troisième Force Internationale

It was a conversation about the Third Force on a road trip in Indochina in 1951 that inspired one of the greatest spy novels of the Cold War. Graham Greene was on a reporting trip in Indochina and found himself sharing a ride with a US embassy attaché—typical cover for a CIA officer. "He lectured me all the long drive back to Saigon on the necessity of finding a 'third force in Vietnam,'" Greene recalled, "so the subject of *The Quiet American* came to me during that talk of a 'third force' on the road through the delta, and my characters quickly followed."[1]

Greene's novel (published in 1955) is narrated by Thomas Fowler, a cynical British correspondent bearing witness to the tragicomedy of exhausted French colonial authorities handing their debacle in Vietnam over to eager American liberators. The eponymous quiet American is Alden Pyle, a young idealist working (quietly) for the CIA who ends up being silenced by Vietnamese nationalists with a bullet to his head. Pyle is no James Bond, the tough, sexy British agent introduced to readers for the first time in Ian Fleming's *Casino Royale* (1953). Fleming's Bond, in fact, is jaded about the business of intelligence and closer to the nihilistic secret agent examined by Hannah Arendt. If Bond embodied the stoical hero of an empire in decline, Pyle symbolized the idealistic hero of an empire ascendant.

Pyle's missionary zeal for saving Asia from Communism is inspired by a fictitious scholar named York Harding, author of *The Dangers of Democracy*, *The Advance of Red China*, and *The Role of the West*.[2] It was Harding who planted the idea in Pyle's impressionable mind of the need for a Third Force as a centrist alternative to Viet Minh communists on the left and Bao Dai royalists on the right. The narrator, Fowler, caustically describes the fanaticism in Agent Pyle's idealized concept of moderates: "'York,' Pyle said, 'wrote that what the East needed was a Third Force.' Perhaps I should have seen that fanatic gleam, the quick response to a phrase, the magic sound of figures: Fifth Column, Third Force, Seventh Day. I might have saved all of us a lot of trouble, even Pyle, if I had realized the direction of that indefatigable young brain."[3] The narratorial voice of Fowler, with a reporter's eye for detail, demolishes the Third Force fantasy of Professor Harding and his undercover acolyte:

> [Pyle] would have to learn for himself the real background that held you as a smell does: the gold of the rice-fields under a flat late sun; the fishers' fragile cranes hovering over the fields like mosquitoes; the cups of tea on an old abbot's platform, with his bed and his commercial calendars, his buckets and broken cups and the junk of a lifetime washed up around his chair; the mollusk hats of the girls repairing the road where a mine had burst; the gold and the young green and the bright dresses of the south, and in the north the deep browns and the black clothes and the circle of enemy mountains and the drone of planes.[4]

Fowler returns to this meditation on the "junk of a lifetime" toward the end of the novel, after Pyle has been shot dead. Pyle's cover was blown due partly to Fowler's betrayal, which is symbolic of the jealousies and tensions lurking beneath the surface of Anglo-American friendship. Facts on the ground in Asia, like the corpse of a quiet American, defied the theorizing of Ivy League scholars a world away; the raw material out of which a Third Force might be fashioned bore little resemblance to the "graphic abstractions" in their books. Fowler observes: "I went back into the garage and entered a small office at the back. There was the usual Chinese commercial calendar, a littered desk—price-lists and a bottle of gum and an adding-machine, some paper-clips, a teapot and three cups and a lot of unsharpened pencils, and for some reason an unwritten picture-postcard of the Eiffel Tower. York Harding might write in graphic abstractions about the Third Force, but this was what it came down to—this was It."[5]

As Greene wrote his novel, the United States was sinking deeper and deeper into the quagmire in Vietnam, including in its support for the Third Force. The most promising candidate was Colonel Trinh Minh The, leader of a sect known as Cao Dai, who in mid-1951 denounced both the Viet Minh insurgents and the royalist regime. The CIA was closely monitoring the colonel and his seven thousand followers at their "'third force' headquarters" near the border with Cambodia. Analysts in Washington assessed that they held "enormous emotional appeal for the Vietnamese," and liberal journals like the *New Republic* promoted a Third Force solution to the Vietnam conundrum.[6]

It is telling that Greene first heard about the Third Force while visiting a colony of the French empire, since the phrase first came to prominence thanks to the Frenchman Léon Blum. As the leader of the Socialist Party, Blum became France's first Jewish prime minister in 1936, and he bravely opposed the Vichy collaborationist government, for which he was imprisoned and then turned over to the Nazis.[7] After the war, he tried to engineer a centrist bloc, led by the Socialists, to run the French republic from the space between Communists to the left and Gaullists to the right.

Blum imagined that if democratic socialist parties took power across the continent, Europe as a whole could emerge as "la troisième Force Internationale" in between the extremes of US individualist capitalism and Soviet collectivist communism. Coming just at the moment of Kennan's political warfare campaign in the Italian parliamentary elections of 1948, Italy's foreign minister picked up the baton from Blum, declaring in the pages of *Foreign Affairs* that "the democratic government of Italy, like that of France, is an example of the 'Third Force' in European parties."[8] Blum's speeches and writings on the Third Force resonated across the Atlantic among American liberals. At a minimum, moderate social democrats would siphon votes away from the French Communist Party, which held the largest number of seats of any one party in parliament throughout 1949.[9]

The most prominent American to pick up Blum's idea was the young Harvard historian Arthur Schlesinger Jr. Born in the year of the Russian Revolution, having served in the OSS during WWII, Schlesinger defended New Deal liberalism in the postwar years, joining Reinhold Niebuhr, Eleanor Roosevelt, and liberal luminaries in establishing a prominent political group called Americans for Democratic Action (ADA) in 1947. Just as Blum was trying to hold together a center-left coalition in France, Schlesinger and the ADA were fending off the leftist splintering led by former Vice President Henry Wallace, who challenged Truman in 1948 as a third-party candidate for the newly formed Progressive Party.[10] In the year that brought the loss of China and the Soviet atomic bomb test, Schlesinger published a moderate liberal's cri de coeur, *The Vital Center* (1949).

Vital Center charted a middle course for American politics between the conservative road to fascism and progressive path to communism. In a book bearing heavy intellectual debts to Niebuhr, Schlesinger credited Blum with coining the term "Third Force," more familiar to American readers as the "non-Communist left," which Schlesinger wanted to rebrand as the "vital center." Writing in a style one might imagine typical of York Harding, Schlesinger rhapsodized about the Third Force:

> Last fall the Socialist Government of France was struggling for its life, with de Gaulle to the right, Thorez to the left, volleying and thundering. In a courageous speech Léon Blum, the veteran Socialist leader, pointed to the twin dangers of communism and reaction. What we need in France, he cried, is a Third Force, committed against both totalitarian extremes and in favor of affirmative programs for political freedom

> and economic stability. The Third Force!—the idea caught the imagination of people across the continent fighting to escape being crushed between the millstones. The only hope lay in the revival of democracy as a fighting faith.

As Schlesinger had explained in an earlier op-ed version of his book, America's liberal capitalists needed to see that "democratic Socialists are our best allies against communism" in Europe.[11] Writing in the wake of Congressman Richard Nixon's attacks on Alger Hiss and the State Department, Schlesinger credited FDR's controversial foreign policy adviser Sumner Welles with forging a Third Force foreign policy: "A new breed of American foreign servant had been in the making—the modern professional diplomat, a close student of history and politics, convinced that the desire of men for freedom and economic security may be as legitimate a factor in foreign affairs as strategic bases or the investments of Standard Oil. The leader of this group was [Secretary of State Cordell] Hull's highly able undersecretary, Sumner Welles . . . who was to be in private life an influential supporter of the conception of the Third Force."[12] Welles's prescient advocacy of a European Third Force was carried forward by Truman's secretaries of state, James F. Byrnes and George Marshall. "Under Byrnes and Marshall the State Department began to understand the significance of the non-Communist left. The very phrase, indeed, was reduced in the Washington manner to its initials; and the cryptic designation 'NCL' was constantly to be heard in Georgetown drawing rooms. . . . By 1948 the State Department could tell Congress that the socialists were 'among the strongest bulwarks in Europe against Communism.'"[13]

One additional figure alongside Blum and Welles whom Schlesinger hailed as a pioneer of Third Force theory was DeWitt C. Poole, who headed the OSS branch in charge of intelligence collection from foreign residents in the US during WWII. By the time *Vital Center* went to print, Poole was helping set up CIA-funded groups like the National Committee for a Free Europe (in June 1949) and the American Committee for Freedom for the Peoples of the USSR.[14]

Although focused on Europe and the transatlantic context, Schlesinger did pause to contemplate the relevance of the Third Force for the Far East. Sharing the Truman administration's Titoist premise—the belief that Chinese nationalism would override communist solidarity with Moscow—Schlesinger thought China showed potential to join the global Third Force. "The bold and confident nationalism of the Chinese Communist movement, geographically isolated, economically independent, militarily strong, will put an even greater strain on Soviet uniformity. How will Vishinsky take to the emergence of 'the Mao Tse-tung road?'"[15] Schlesinger's sensitivity to the tension between Mao and Stalin probably owed a debt to John King Fairbank, who was not only Schlesinger's colleague at Harvard but also his brother-in-law. Schlesinger argued in *Vital Center* that America's priority should be to stay on the good side of anti-imperialist movements in Asia and Africa, luring them away from Moscow and nurturing a postcolonial Third Force to complement the *Troisième Force* envisioned by Blum.

Schlesinger proposed that the Third Force concept, rebranded as the vital center, should serve as the basis for the Democratic Party's foreign policy platform for the 1950s. He attacked Republicans for blindly promoting anti-communism and in the process emboldening illiberal autocrats in France and Spain, and from Argentina to Formosa. "A Republican victory in 1948 would almost certainly have altered the political and economic direction of United States policy—away from support of the Third Force, toward support of de Gaulle, Franco, Peron and Chiang Kai-shek."[16] Schlesinger wanted Americans to embrace Third Force allies abroad and vital center politics at home. He described his political association, Americans for Democratic Action, to *New York Times* readers as having "laid the foundations for a Third Force in this country."[17]

The Making of Carsun Chang

As American liberals and European socialists lofted the banner of an international Third Force, a hardened band of public figures in China was entering a new stage in the decades-long struggle to bring centrism to their country. China's best answer to Léon Blum and Arthur Schlesinger Jr. was Zhang Junmai, who went by the English name Carsun Chang.

Chang's biography encapsulated the agony and tragedy of modern Chinese liberalism. Born in 1886, Chang received a rudimentary Western education in Shanghai and, like many bright minds of his generation, came under the spell of the political activist and public intellectual Liang Qichao, who had to flee to Japan in 1898 for his reformist efforts at the Qing court. Carsun finally met his hero when he went to Japan to study at Waseda University, and Liang became a lifelong mentor. When Chang returned to China shortly before the fall of the Qing dynasty in 1911, his intellectual project was to develop a synthesis of Chinese and European philosophy, while his political energy was devoted to Liang Qichao's centrist efforts in the early years of the Republic of China.

Chang spent two years studying in Berlin and London as World War I erupted, and then returned to Europe accompanying Liang Qichao as an unofficial member in the Chinese delegation to the Paris Peace Conference in 1919 (perhaps bumping into Allen Dulles and Charles Seymour). Carsun lingered for a couple of years in Germany before returning to China, full of renewed energy to advance

FIGURE 5. Third Force in China: Carsun Chang in Paris with Liang Qichao (1919). Wikimedia Commons.

the causes of constitutionalism and democratic socialism amid the darkening atmosphere of warlordism and militancy.[18] In the 1920s, independent political thinkers like Chang could not do much more than publish journals, and even those often fell afoul of censors. So, Chang threw himself into educational reform. In 1929, he was kidnapped and held incognito in Shanghai, where torture, blackmail, and assassination were rites of passage for left-leaning liberals. Released on ransom after a month of beatings, he fled to Germany, where the University of Jena gave him a position teaching philosophy.[19]

Chang returned from Germany to take up a teaching post at Yenching University, arriving in Beijing just as Japanese troops launched a full-scale invasion of Manchuria in 1931. His outspoken criticism of the Nationalist Party made him too controversial for campus, and Carsun dedicated himself to a new political organization, the National Socialist Party (NSP), founded with philosopher Zhang Dongsun.[20] With a core group of Liang Qichao protégés, NSP's main activity was publishing the journal *Renaissance*, which spoke to the concerns of middle-class professionals and urbanites.[21] The NSP had to operate underground for years due to the authoritarian strictures of Chiang's Nationalist Party monopoly on power.

As the Anti-Japanese War intensified and pressure grew on Chiang Kai-shek to cooperate with rivals within the Chinese political sphere, Chiang invited Carsun and the NSP in the summer of 1938 to join the People's Political Council, a national political platform designed to include (and co-opt) smaller parties. When the Second United Front between the Nationalists and Communists collapsed in January 1941, CCP representatives pulled out of the People's Political Council. Third-party leaders asked Chiang's permission to organize a federation among themselves, but the generalissimo refused. In a moment of spine, the third parties went ahead anyway and, in March 1941, founded the League of Chinese Democratic Political Groups, better known (from 1944 on) as the China Democratic League (CDL).

The China Democratic League was an umbrella coalition rather than a party—not entirely unlike Schlesinger's Americans for Democratic Action. CDL brought together leading liberal figures like Carsun Chang, the educational reformer Huang Yanpei, the philosopher-activist Liang Shuming, and the political journalist Wu Xianzi. Carsun later described the China Democratic League as "the only organization based on liberal and democratic principles of any importance in the last thirty years of totalitarian rule in China," and would credit it as "the vanguard of the Third Force."[22]

Based out of Hong Kong, the China Democratic League released a manifesto and established a journal called *Enlightenment* (*Kwang Ming Pao*) in October 1941.[23] Within months, the CDL lost its safe haven when the British colony fell to Japanese occupiers. WWII forced many Third Force figures to seek sanctuary in the major cities of unoccupied China like Kunming and Chongqing, where they had chances to interact with Americans, who were duly impressed. The journalists Annalee Jacoby and Teddy White recounted the emergence of this "middle group" in glowing terms:

> A middle group did break through the ice blanket of political suppression—the Democratic League. It described itself as "standing midway between the Kuomintang on the right, and the Chinese Communist party on the left—unreservedly opposed to dictatorship of any shape, and believing implicitly in national unity as a prerequisite to victory" . . . . [The League] claimed professors, writers, scholars, some bankers and industrialists, and a few military men. It admitted its weakness among the peasants; organization was risky, with the Kuomingtang secret police working to suppress political action. Leaders of the League were rarely allowed to travel from city to city; they conducted meetings and issued statements with the greatest caution.[24]

John King Fairbank knew League members well. He recalled the irony of 1943 watching Soong Mei-ling wow Congress with talk of Free China on her visit to the United States, while his liberal Chinese friends suffered under her husband's dictatorial regime.[25]

As Chiang Kai-shek cracked down on liberal voices, Mao wooed Third Force leaders to his side. Addressing the Seventh Party Congress in April 1945, Mao went out of his way to invite the Third Force to be partners in a multiparty power-sharing arrangement, espousing a gradualist vision of socialist transformation that seemed to leave room for urban professionals and foreign capital. The historian Lyman Van Slyke described Mao's maneuvering as "an almost classic example of successful united-front work."[26] By offering financial assistance to third parties and adding liberal touches to his New Democracy platform, Mao appealed to intellectuals suffering under the iron fist of Chiang's Nationalist regime in Chongqing. Carsun Chang was convinced that China's best hope would have been if Chiang had accepted Mao's proposal for coalition government. "For the first time, a communist party would have been responsibly sharing power with democratic elements in the same state. But with skill, patience, and forbearance, something along those lines might have been worked out."[27] A Third Force delegation led by Huang Yanpei was sent to the CCP base at Yan'an in the summer of 1945, and, like most US observers, came back impressed by the economic reforms and democratic spirit.

By the tail end of WWII, Chiang Kai-shek had started playing nice with the third parties as well, seeking allies in preparation for postwar rule. Carsun accepted Chiang's invitation to join a multiparty delegation to the San Francisco Conference for the signing of the United Nations Charter in June 1945. Early the following year, Carsun was inducted into the Political Consultative Conference, where he drafted the new Constitution of the Republic of China. But unanimity within the Third Force bloc broke down over whether to join the first National Assembly, which was boycotted by the CCP in protest against Chiang's stratagems to ensure Nationalist Party dominance. Carsun tried to bolster the influence of his National Socialist Party by merging with Wu Xianzi's Democratic Constitutionalist Party, which traced its lineage back to Liang Qichao's mentor Kang Youwei and enjoyed a strong following among Chinese Americans.[28] Their new China Democratic Socialist Party, headquartered in Shanghai, led a southern faction of Third Force elements that joined the inaugural session of the National Assembly in September 1946. Zhang Dongsun, cofounder of the original NSP, led a northern faction of third parties that boycotted the assembly in solidarity with the CCP.[29] It was a bad omen.

Splendid Group of Men

As centrist intellectuals weighed their options between Mao and Chiang, an influential circle of American journalists, US government officials, and China Hands debated the viability of the Third Force and its implications for China policy. There were plenty of obvious drawbacks, starting with the incessant squabbling—Carsun Chang kept the US consul apprised of the crippling internal splits.[30] US ambassador John Leighton Stuart, who knew Carsun and others from Yenching University, offered a harsh assessment in his memoirs, *Fifty Years in China* (1954). "Not unlike our own discredited practice of spoils of office, these minor parties wanted jobs for their members, nor were the new ministers and their subordinates any improvement over the displaced Kuomintang officials," Stuart complained.[31] Calling them "pathetic," Stuart condemned third parties as "woefully impractical":

> Someone has answered the query why Chinese liberals cannot organize themselves by pointing out that it is precisely because they are Chinese liberals. In other words, there seems to be something about their social heritage and intellectual characteristics that makes them so individualistic, so suspicious or jealous of one another, so timid, that they lack the capacity for cohesion and action. Another deterrent was their lack of funds and a constituency from which these might be obtained without vitiating their objective.[32]

Unlike Ambassador Stuart, Professor Fairbank held the Third Force in higher regard, arguing that Nationalist repression, rather than the weakness or vanity of Chinese liberals, held them back. In the lead-up to the inauguration of the National Assembly in 1946, the streets of Kunming ran red with dissidents' blood: the China Democratic League leader Li Gongpu was shot and killed in July, and the famed poet Wen Yiduo (along with his son, who narrowly survived the attack) was shot at point-blank range by a team of assassins on the day of Li's funeral.[33] Fairbank pointed out that these assaults were "only the most prominent of many beatings, abductions, and assassinations aimed at the intimidation of Chinese liberals."[34]

The journalists Jacoby and White described the White Terror carried out by the Nationalists that year:

> The Kuomintang seemed determined that in their final choice the Chinese people should have no alternative to rule-by-terror except rule-by-Communism. All through the summer months, wherever the government's machinery of dictatorship could trap them, the liberals and democrats who offered the only non-totalitarian leadership in the land were either killed, imprisoned, or silenced by fear. Secret assassins singled out for cold-blooded murder not Communists but defenseless members of the Democratic League who had spoken their minds too freely.[35]

Jacoby and White's best-selling *Thunder Out of China* (1946) ended with a paean to the peace-loving men of the middle group, the "sincerest friends of America": "Between the extreme right of the Kuomintang and the disciplined Chinese Communists on the left stands a mass that seeks a middle way. It includes the Kuomintang moderates, the intellectuals, and nonpartisan liberals, the splinter groups of the Democratic League. A huge proportion of the Kuomintang rank and file belong to this group, as do most thinking people in China. This middle group, whose members are the sincerest friends of America, is surest of being wiped out in civil war."[36] Jacoby and White maintained that while Third Force liberals would over time naturally come to dominate a stable China, they lacked the political organization to bring about conditions of peace. "They lack an army, a political machine, roots in any social class. Only the spread of education and industry can create enough men of the modern world to give them a broad social base. Their entire future depends on the reconstruction of China."[37]

The American hero who was supposed to bring about those conditions of peace, George Marshall, ended his failed mediation mission in agreement with Jacoby and White. Marshall met multiple times with Carsun Chang and relied on Third Force actors to act as middlemen with Chiang and Mao—to no avail.[38] Marshall's dour final report in January 1947 left one sliver of hope for China's political future: the Third Force. Only this "splendid group of men," as he memorably called them, could redeem the nation: "The salvation of the situation would be the assumption of leadership by the liberals in the Government and in the minority parties, a splendid group of men, but who as yet lack the political power to exercise a controlling influence."[39] Behind closed doors, Marshall offered a variation on the Third Force idea, telling his counterparts in the War Department that "the only possible solution for China's troubles was to oust the reactionary clique within the Central Government and replace them by liberals from both the Kuomintang and Communist parties."[40]

In the summer of 1947, as George Kennan's *Foreign Affairs* article heralded the doctrine of containment, Minister-Counselor Walton Butterworth collected his things at the US consulate in Nanjing in preparation for the long voyage home. He was carrying home a memorandum calling for a fundamental reconsideration of China policy in light of realities he had witnessed on the ground—above all, the "current accelerated deterioration of the political, economic, and military position of the Central Government." The Nationalists were myopic in their political vision, inept at economic management, and bankrupt in terms of popular legitimacy. The US government was stuck holding a broken vessel—there was no point trying to fill it with water or putting the shattered pieces back together again. The bitter truth was that Free China was a liability, not an asset, and the realistic policy objective should be to ensure it was a "minor liability" rather than an exorbitantly costly one.

Like Marshall, Butterworth could see only one moderately hopeful course to pursue: encouraging the Third Force. This option, he acknowledged, did not really exist except in theory. A middle road would have to be blazed by proactive American support and might succeed only thanks to luck: "At best a middle group might be able to restore a modicum of stability in China. Even though the latter may appear to be a fairly remote possibility viewed in the light of recent events, it cannot be dismissed and offers for the United States a constructive middle course between the extremes of all-out aid to the present Government and cessation of all aid thereto." Although the Nationalist Party was "stagnant," it contained the seeds of a new leadership. Butterworth concluded that it was time to cut off Chiang Kai-shek and nurture an alternate leadership out of "key individuals"—generals such as Li Zongren and Zhang Fakui and intellectuals like Hu Shi. This future leadership needed to understand "that the United States is prepared to support extremism neither of the right nor the left, but believes that the best defense against either is broader participation in government by all classes and an energetic attack against social and economic evils."[41]

Soon after Butterworth left Nanjing, his boss, Secretary of State Marshall, dispatched a special emissary to Chongqing. General Albert Wedemeyer was sent as a signal of support for the alliance with Chiang, but he returned to Washington with a disturbing report indicating that the only hope was to find a substitute for the generalissimo. "I do not think it would be sound policy to suggest piecemeal assistance to China. It would be like plugging up holes in the rotten hull of a sinking ship. Our assistance should then be based upon a program that would make possible a new hull for the ship and would be predicated upon an able, honest captain and an efficient crew," Wedemeyer reported to Marshall.[42]

As the Civil War between the Nationalists and Communists intensified, Chiang's government continued to suppress Third Force elements, outlawing the China Democratic League in October 1947.[43] When Truman sent the China aid bill to Congress in early 1948, the middle parties came out in opposition to giving Chiang a blank check.[44] And as Mao marched toward victory, more and more Third Force figures gravitated toward the CCP. A prominent group of "democratic personages," as the CCP labeled them, including the philosopher Zhang Dongsun and the sociologist Fei Xiaotong, visited Mao's temporary headquarters in Xibaipo in January 1949, which symbolized a larger shift in liberal allegiance to the CCP.[45] Minor party leaders holding out in Hong Kong began trickling north in the following months.[46]

Professor Fairbank had been watching these developments from a safe distance in Cambridge since he left China halfway through the Marshall Mission. Stimulated by conversations with his brother-in-law Schlesinger (who was "deeply involved in the organizing of a 'non-Communist left'"), Fairbank agonized over the proper role that Third Force elements could realistically play in China policy.[47] He shared the anxieties of the realists about the damage that the wrong foreign policy could do to American politics and society. Writing for the Institute of Pacific Relations journal in 1947, Fairbank worried aloud about how "American efforts to save China from totalitarian communism" would not only "oblige the revolution to follow more ruthless, dictatorial, and totalitarian leadership than would otherwise be the case," but also risked reinforcing "a trend toward anti-communist authoritarianism"—even "an American style of fascism"—at home.[48] Fairbank's sympathies were with China's liberals, but he was realistic about their limited political power. Indeed, he became increasingly concerned that centrists would not be able to survive the Civil War.

Fairbank posed the question starkly in *The United States and China* (1948), picking up where Jacoby and White left off: "Observers have therefore questioned whether Chinese liberals as a 'non-Communist left' in or out of the government can really influence policy. They lack a tight party structure or mass following. They have no army nor secret police. Ground between two warring regimes, how can they play a decisive role?" As a historian of dynastic China and friend to Chinese academics, Fairbank feared he was bearing witness to the death of the Confucian scholar-official tradition in its twentieth-century reincarnation as liberal intellectual: "Have the liberal intellectuals a significant future in China? To any Chinese scholar who appreciates the tradition of scholar government, this question would be outrageous. Yet in these cataclysmic times it must be asked, for China is plainly undergoing a violent reshaping of her class structure, against which the liberal's future status must be gauged."[49]

Fairbank insisted that Third Force intellectuals and professionals were the best thing to come out of decades of American involvement in China, "our greatest stake there."[50] Even though their immediate political role was marginal, Americans should not lose sight of them. On the eve of the Korean War, Fairbank wrote:

> The chief fruit of the American investment in missionary education and humanitarian good works in China during the last century has been the modern-minded Western-trained academic and professional personnel who still form a major portion of the Chinese upper class. There is no prospect today that these individuals will be able to form a third force or a political alternative to the CCP as the holder of final power. But their present position and future prospects should be both instructive and of melancholy interest to us. The fate of these intellectuals, and of their formerly pro-Western or "liberal" political views, has an important bearing on the efficacy of the traditional Western ideology in its modern application to Asia.[51]

Fairbank reasoned that the large-scale defection of liberal intellectuals to Mao's side in the Civil War could not be attributed to fear of the CCP thought police alone. There had to be some element of genuine attraction to the Communist cause.[52]

Like Fairbank, Owen Lattimore was a firm believer in the Third Force in China. Indeed, he argued that Blum's *Troisième Force* was better suited to nationalist Asia than capitalist Europe. Unaware of the CIA's political warfare to check communist parties in Italy and France, Lattimore concluded that "eventually France and Italy might become third countries as part of a general trend, although they cannot be made into such countries by the third-force parties which they have at present."[53] It was not Western Europe but the Far East that was ripe for what Lattimore termed the "third quotient of power":

> This third quotient of power is something that has much more vigor than the vague and listless "third force" of Europe. The third force in Europe is led by a hesitant and dwindling fraction of the middle class and leads a harried life between the revival of big business interests which always put money above patriotism, and the growth of a tough, proletarian, class-conscious, and aggressive Communism and left-wing socialism that is not so much disloyal to old standards of patriotism as utterly contemptuous of them. The "third quotient" of power is an utterly different phenomenon. It is a heritage that has fallen to whole peoples, rather than to classes. These people are infused with a vigorous nationalist loyalty that the upper classes of Western Europe no longer have and the proletariat of Western Europe does not want; because throughout Western Europe international class loyalties have either superseded old national loyalties or are fast superseding them.[54]

Although a passionate defender of Third Force ideas, Lattimore was wary about the US role in promoting its spread. He cautioned policymakers against supporting moderates, openly at least. Doing so "would defeat the aims of American policy. . . . They would be tagged as agents of America. Everything they advocated would be suspiciously rejected as a disguised American move, detrimental to the interests of China. Any attempt to use individuals as the spokesmen of American policy would also contribute to the horrible process by which a political secret police is built up."[55]

Lattimore anticipated that Mao's Communists would eventually prove as brutal as the Nationalists in suppressing dissent once they gained sufficient power. US-backed moderates would be the first to suffer. "The danger of malignant secret police development begins when, after victory, a revolutionary government feels that it has to keep watch on all kinds of people who have foreign sympathies or may be receiving foreign support."[56] According to Allyn Rickett, the US government was doing exactly as Lattimore feared, launching a "big campaign" in the summer of 1949 "to separate these liberal intellectuals from the Communists and, by uniting them with so-called reform elements among the Nationalists on Formosa, to patch together a 'third force.'" Rickett claimed that "American intelligence personnel" sought his help in identifying "any possible dissident elements within the Communist Party itself who might fit in with this 'third force.'"[57]

As Lattimore predicted, the CCP began constricting the space for the middle parties as their power increased. Mao's "leaning to one side" speech in June 1949 contained an ominous message for Third Force elements. As Mao put it bluntly, "There is no third road." It was time to choose. In place of Blum's international Third Force and Schlesinger's vital center, Mao offered something different—an "international united front" under Communist leadership. Carsun Chang translated the relevant bits of Mao's speech in *The Third Force in China*:

> In the light of these experiences the Chinese people must fall in either on the side of Imperialism or of Socialism. There can be no other alternative. It is impossible to sit on the fence; there is no third road. We oppose Chiang Kai-shek's reactionary clique, which inclines on the side of Imperialism. We also oppose illusions about a third road. Not only in China but throughout the world without exception, one either inclines toward Imperialism or towards Socialism. Neutrality is a mere camouflage; a third road does not exist.[58]

Mao's rejection of a "third road" was a blow to the hopes of Third Force figures in Hong Kong as well as Titoist strategists in Washington. The Indian ambassador K. M. Panikkar described the reaction of the US ambassador John Leighton Stuart as they sat in the Canadian embassy in Beijing hearing Mao's speech: "That good man had hoped against hope that the communists, many of whom had been his students in Yen Ching university, would take a moderate line. But Mao Tse-tung's speech finally shattered that hope. Dr. Stuart was a broken man. He told me that he had made up his mind to leave early and had asked that his private aeroplane might be allowed to be repaired for this purpose."[59]

For Carsun Chang, Mao's Leaning to One Side speech "exploded any dreams of cooperation with the Western democracies on the part of the fellow-travelers."[60] Many Third Force moderates, however, felt they had little choice but to continue to hope for the best from the CCP. Eleven non-Communist parties were given representation in the inaugural session of the CCP-led multiparty governing institution, the Chinese People's Political Consultative Conference, when it opened in September 1949.[61] Mao and Zhou seemed to be honoring their commitment to "coalition government" in giving the Third Force a seat at the table.[62] Doak Barnett, who was born in Shanghai, studied at Yale, and returned to the Far East during the Chinese Civil War, assessed the situation in early 1950: "The Communists have shrewdly put them to work in all sorts of activities, and many politically conscious intellectuals feel for the first time that they are playing a real political role."[63]

A Third Force for China

Carsun Chang epitomized the kind of Third Force gentleman who George Marshall, John King Fairbank, and Owen Lattimore hoped might one day in the future be the salvation of China. But he would have to flee it again first.

Chang abandoned Shanghai on April 25, 1949, in advance of Communist liberation, and found a temporary haven in Macao.[64] He traveled onward to India in November at the invitation of the Nehru government to lecture at Indian universities on Asian philosophy and Chinese politics. Carsun resigned as head of the Democratic Socialist Party, which was transforming itself into a loyal minor party in Chiang's Nationalist-controlled regime in Taiwan. He was lying low in the Himalayan hill station of international intrigue, Kalimpong, when the Korean War erupted.[65]

In December 1951 Carsun Chang set off on a world tour, spending a few months in Southeast Asia and Australia before landing in Hong Kong, the unofficial headquarters of the embattled Third Force movement, in March 1952.[66] From there he stopped in Japan en route to his final destination of the United States, where he would serve as unofficial emissary of the Third Force. Having met George Marshall during the mediation mission, Chang, a bit naïvely perhaps, hoped he could count on the retired high official and war hero to be an ally.[67]

As Carsun lobbied for his cause and did research at the Library of Congress, he saw through the publication of an English-language book laying out the case for the Third Force in sweeping terms—explaining everything from its roots in Confucian philosophy to its relevance in contemporary Chinese politics. Published in New York in late 1952, Chang's *Third Force in China* replaced the murky question of who lost China with a clear strategy for how to win China back. As Chang put it, the question was "how to bring about and strengthen the internal forces for democracy in China . . . [and what] other countries can do to help in setting up this democratic government."[68] Drawing on a potpourri of Confucian political thought and Cold War geopolitical analysis, his answer boiled down to aiding the Third Force.

Writing for a Korean War–era American audience still in the throes of McCarthyism, Chang was careful to pre-empt criticism that he harbored sympathy for the Reds. "It is best for me to say at once that I am against Communism in China," he wrote, perhaps a bit too defensively. Throughout the book, his harshest judgment was reserved for Chiang Kai-shek. "I have never known a mind more unsuited to cope with the problems of the modern world," he writes of the generalissimo. "Personal power is all that Chiang understands. Under such a leadership, how can there be an efficient government in China—let alone a constitutional government?" Chiang perverted the original concept of tutelage, which was intended by the Nationalist Party founder Sun Yat-sen to be a temporary stage in the passage from imperial rule to constitutional democracy. Instead, the generalissimo turned tutelage into a permanent excuse for totalitarian rule.[69]

Chiang's megalomania retarded the development of civic life and self-government, and China's only hope lay in liberation from his dictatorship. Justifications for Chiang, like those offered by David Nelson Rowe, had it completely wrong:

> What is urgently needed to overcome the present crisis in China is not a "strong man" whose twenty-odd years of arbitrary rule has brought nothing but a deluge of corruption and a red inundation, but rather the cultivation of law-abiding habits, a willingness to submit the main issues of national life to open and intelligent discussion so as to reach a just and equitable solution, a consciousness at least among the leaders of the importance of constitutional and parliamentary processes, and a substitution of rational understanding for unstable, unreliable, and whimsical practices. This can come about only when the nation's intellectual resources are gathered together for maximum exploitation and unhampered expression and not smothered under the weight of an enlarged ego.[70]

Carsun Chang's contempt for Chiang Kai-shek did not blind him to the sins of the CCP. He rejected the idea that Mao enjoyed democratic legitimacy or a popular mandate. The Communists ruled "by means of bayonets" and were prone to paranoia. "The principal concerns of the Chinese Communists are party discipline, military power, spying, and infiltration," he wrote. Because it ruled by fear and repression, the CCP's grasp on power was tenuous. "Their hold on the country is effected through the secret police; it is not rooted in the hearts of the people. Their government is a house built of bamboo and mud, and can very easily be pulled down. . . . Can such a government last? No, it cannot last."[71]

Chang's conviction that Communist rule would falter grew out of his view of Chinese culture. He was convinced the Chinese masses were ripe for a counterrevolution against "Communist imperialism." He grounded this assertion in a reinterpretation of traditional Confucian culture, which, he argued, inoculated the people against the temptation of "Communist materialism" and prepared them for democratic self-government.[72] "I am firmly convinced that 90 per cent of the Chinese population will be glad to see China a democratic country and would much prefer to have nothing to do with revolution and conquest," he insisted.[73] Chinese people inherited a culture and history that was not authoritarian, as often claimed; rather, it had been "laissez-faire for thousands of years." Traditional China was an empire of negative liberty. "Knowing the long history of China and the characteristics of my own people, I think that they cannot be happy under the new dispensation, and sooner or later, in a manner which may not even be predictable, they will rise against the new oppression."[74]

The Third Force in China played on American fears of Soviet influence, invoking domino theory to warn that Mao's victory "opens the way for China's active cooperation with Soviet Russia in forming a base from which to threaten her neighbors—Korea, Indo-China, and all of Southeast Asia. Russian hegemony over the huge land mass of her own territory added to that of China also has important consequences for India, Pakistan, and the Near East." Chang presented Chinese communists as Stalin's willing pawns, unable to resist the Kremlin even if they wanted to. "Mao Tse-tung and Chou En-lai are insects in a spider's web; the more they struggle to free themselves, the more entangled they become. Anyone who proclaims the hypothesis that Mao Tse-tung can become a Tito has no true understanding of the situation and does immeasurable harm to the cause of democracy."[75]

If Chang was optimistic that the Chinese masses would inevitably rebel against CCP rule, he was apocalyptic in anticipating that World War III was similarly unavoidable. "It is quite certain that all the protagonists in the coming war will plunge in at the same time all over the world."[76] He proposed immediate measures to "restrict the scope of the coming disaster" and "perhaps stimulate the Chinese people to free themselves from their present slavery."[77] When the war came, America's duty would be to aid China's non-Communist liberals.

> We must always bear in mind that it was the denial of freedom and democracy, followed by all manner of corruption and incompetence, that precipitated the present crisis. This feudalism and absolutism can and must be uprooted by the liberal forces which are not under the immediate control of the Nationalist Government in Formosa. On the international side, the Soviet Union is backing up the present regime in Peking which it will not under any circumstances abandon. To combat this, the Western democracies should, in their own interest, give as much sympathy and assistance as possible to non-Communist China. The least the Western democracies can do is not to kill the seeds of anti-Communism, which are their greatest potential assets, and not to encourage Communism, which is their greatest enemy.[78]

As Chang explained at the outset of the book, he was writing for an audience of "forward-looking Americans" who could be persuaded to "join in the task of creating the proper atmosphere in which real democracy may flourish in China."[79] He offered up the Third Force as a "new movement" that could lead the 90 percent of Chinese people who rejected the totalitarianism of the right and the left and who craved liberal democracy with Confucian characteristics.

Published not long after Hannah Arendt's *Origins of Totalitarianism*, Chang's *Third Force in China* identified two strains of totalitarianism running rampant in China: the conservative totalitarianism of Chiang's Nationalist Party and the radical totalitarianism of Mao's Communists. The solution to the problem of two totalitarianisms was supporting the Third Force:

> I can assure him [the thinking American] that we in China are not only working wholeheartedly for the new political and social movement—the Third Force—but that we are fully confident of its ultimate success. This new force is more widely spread and has more support than is ordinarily realized. The sponsors are now scattered, and some are even within the sphere of Communist control. But the time has arrived when they will be glad to be brought into a new unity of purpose. Their experiences have taught them that neither the conservative type of totalitarianism, enforced by the Kuomintang rule for the last quarter-century, nor the radical type of totalitarianism of the last three years so ruthlessly imposed by the Communist regime, can ever solve the problem of China. Their aim is the creation of a new China, based upon the principles of democratic constitutionalism, which can be brought into consonance with the traditional spirit of Chinese culture.[80]

As *The Third Force in China* went to press in the fall of 1952, Carsun Chang's name also appeared as co-author of a twelve-point manifesto drafted on behalf of a political organization newly established in Hong Kong. The Manifesto of the Fight League for a Free and Democratic China resolved "to overthrow the totalitarian and party-dictatorship as practiced by the Chinese Communist regime" and replace it with a liberal democratic government and socialistic economic system.[81] The manifesto essentially ignored the existence of Chiang Kai-shek's regime on Taiwan and offered itself as the alternative to Communist rule.

The CIA, meanwhile, was knee-deep in an array of covert operations to make counterrevolution against Mao, looking for ways to support the Third Force in Hong Kong, the Nationalists in Taiwan, and resistance against the CCP wherever it could be found.

7

MAKING COUNTERREVOLUTION

As Carsun Chang was writing about the Third Force, the CIA was funding it. The ties linking US intelligence officers to Third Force elements dated back to WWII, and during the Chinese Civil War, General Claire Chennault lobbied Washington to back what he called a belt of resistance of those willing to fight the Communists. But it took the Korean War to make a policy of making counterrevolution, one that was kept secret from the American people. General MacArthur's top intelligence adviser Charles Willoughby was a key figure in urging the CIA to arm the Third Force. In the meantime, covert assistance was flowing to Taiwan to support Chiang Kai-shek's stratagems for destabilizing the mainland, from Operation Paper targeting Yunnan Province to Operation Octopus reaching its tentacles across the Taiwan Strait.

"Belt of Resistance"

The seeds of the idea to provide covert paramilitary assistance to a Chinese Third Force were planted in the final stages of WWII. Although US military intelligence and OSS operatives focused mostly on the Nationalists and Communists, Third Force possibilities did occasionally pop up on the radar. Oliver J. Caldwell, an OSS officer operating out of Chongqing, developed contacts with underground secret societies that opposed both Chiang and Mao and advised American support for a "moderate government" led by Nationalist General Li Zongren.[1] Caldwell wrote up the case for aiding a Third Force in a report that his superior,

Colonel John Coughlin, the head of OSS in the China Burma India Theater, forwarded to Washington.[2] In the spring of 1945, Caldwell assisted in Jedburgh-style infiltrations flown out of Xi'an, a hinterland city not far from the CCP base.

> It was a common evening ceremony for most of our Sian detachment to jeep over to the Fourteenth Air Force base and take pictures of a sheepish young American standing in the doorless opening to our old beat-up C-46, together with one or more Chinese. They would be flown under cover of night across the enemy lines only forty or fifty miles away until three bonfires were seen below. Our saboteurs would then be dropped in the triangle between the fires and would join guerillas, Communist or Nationalist. These groups carried radios, light weapons, and explosives. Some of them performed spectacular feats.[3]

Frank Lilley was posted to Yunnan Province for artillery training of Nationalist forces. In June 1945, on a visit to Kunming, Frank was invited by a friend working for the humanitarian group American Field Service to meet a group of Chinese "moderates" who opposed both Mao and Chiang. According to Frank's brother Jim (who would join the CIA after graduating from Yale in 1951), Frank was told, "It is very confidential, and people will get hurt if the nationalist leaders find out. The group is preparing to call for a coalition government to be controlled by moderates instead of the KMT [Kuomintang, or Nationalists], on the one hand, or communists, on the other. You are free to come if we can trust you not to talk about it.'" Lilley spent the day with the group of professors and businessmen—Marshall's "splendid group of men"—and was told there were more of them out there. "The Chinese cited a number of friends whom they considered good people who had gone over to the Communist side. They were hoping that these people, if convinced of the possibility of a workable coalition government, would come back."[4]

It was hard to keep track of the Third Force during the Chinese Civil War. There were precious few American intelligence officers left in China by the time the CIA opened its doors in September 1947, and the China stations had to close not long after the creation of Wisner's OPC in June 1948. John Singlaub, the CIA station chief in Shenyang, had to abandon his post in early September. Shortly after the fall of Shenyang to the CCP, the Nationalist commander Wei Lihuang secretly brought Singlaub to a country manor outside Beijing for a meeting with Fu Zuoyi, the commander for north China. Generals Fu and Wei begged for supplies from the US depot in Okinawa so that they could regroup and resist the PLA onslaught about to rain down on the Beiping Garrison. Fu and Wei knew Washington had lost faith in Generalissimo Chiang, telling Singlaub, "We understand your government's feelings about the Kuomintang." They offered themselves as the core of a new Third Force, as Singlaub explained in his memoir, *Hazardous Duty*: "Wei concisely outlined their plans. They hoped to create a 'Third Force,' a democratic, anti-Communist option to Chiang's Nationalists. This force, he said, would form an impenetrable buffer between the Communist armies in Manchuria and the KMT forces in the south. They would hold the old capital of Peking, the city of Tientsin, and the port of Taku. With their field armies supplied with modern American equipment, neither the Nationalists nor the Communists could dislodge them."[5]

Singlaub briefed Admiral Oscar Badger, the Naval Forces Far East commander, in Qingdao the following day, and Badger was "excited by the prospect of a viable third force in China." Far East Command in Tokyo gave approval for the transfer of supplies from Okinawa. Singlaub wired a top-secret cable back to CIA headquarters urging consideration of the Fu/Wei Third Force proposal as part of an admittedly "desperate" strategy to stop the Communist advance.

> From my discussions with Admiral Badger, I believed their offer represented the only viable option to preventing a complete Communist victory in China. Clearly, America's lack of confidence in Chiang after the Manchurian defeat augured poorly for our support of his government in the inevitable battles to be fought in the south. If General Fu's armies could physically separate the two forces, a partition of China between the three political elements might be possible. It was a desperate alternative. But no one could deny these were desperate times.[6]

Nothing came of the desperation plan. When Singlaub reported back to Washington early the following year, he was told that the generals' proposal had "sent the State Department into shock."[7] The National Security Council did consider a draft plan in November 1948 to back "regional anti-Communist regimes in Xinjiang and Manchuria, particularly Manchuria."[8] But facts on the ground were changing too fast for policy planning in Washington. Communist troops encircled Tianjin, forcing General Fu to make a last stand in Beiping. Facing certain defeat, and prodded by his daughter—an undercover agent for the CCP—General Fu surrendered over two hundred thousand troops under his command to the Communists, saving the city from destruction.[9]

While General Fu was rewarded by the Communists for making a separate peace, General Wei Lihuang was imprisoned by the Nationalists for the loss of the Manchurian cities Jinzhou and Shenyang.[10] General Wei may have also been guilty of war profiteering—according to Carsun Chang, at least, who claimed that Wei was taking "tons of banknotes" flown by Chiang Kai-shek's government to Manchuria for food purchases and flying the money to Shanghai "to be invested in commodities, which he hoarded."[11] Carsun further claimed that General

Wedemeyer "obtained evidence of utter corruption" on Wei's part—which might have been a factor in Singlaub's telegram getting no traction in Washington. General Wei was released from prison by Li Zongren and fled to Hong Kong in 1949.[12]

As the National Army imploded and Communists swept across the mainland, a man with a grand plan to arm the Chinese counterrevolution arrived in Washington. Major General Claire Chennault was a WWII hero famous for setting up the American Volunteer Group, better known as the Flying Tigers, a few hundred US airmen who flew for Chiang Kai-shek against the Japanese *before* Pearl Harbor. Chennault served as an adviser to Chiang before the war and returned to that capacity after VJ-Day, setting up a civilian airline, Civil Air Transport (CAT), that could serve Nationalist needs—starting with logistics transport in the Civil War. CAT planes were instrumental in the airlift operations to ferry troops and resupply Shenyang in the spring of 1948, and they did the same for the southeastern city of Suzhou later that year.[13] By the spring of 1949, when General Chennault went to Washington to present his plan for counterrevolution, Communist troops had conquered Chiang's erstwhile capital of Nanjing and were poised to take Shanghai. To Chennault and his backers, Mao's success only added urgency to the plea.

Chennault spoke before Senate committees on May 3, 1949, at the invitation of Bill Knowland, a California Republican known as "the senator from Formosa" for his close ties to Chiang Kai-shek, and Pat McCarran, a McCarthyite Democrat from Nevada nicknamed "the senator from Madrid" for his support for the fascist leader Francisco Franco. Chennault conjured up a harrowing vision of Asia falling to Communism. To prevent it, he pushed just the kind of expansive strategy that realists like Kennan and Morgenthau cautioned against. For a mere $700 million, the general told the senators, anti-Communist forces could hold the line against the Reds.[14]

Chennault lobbied the Truman administration directly in a meeting with Assistant Secretary of State Dean Rusk the following week, laying out his plan to fortify a "long belt of Chinese territory" in order to "contain communism in the remainder of China where it might fall eventually of its own weight." The alternative was the loss of not only China, but the whole of South Asia, Indochina, and the Pacific: "If the communists are able to occupy Yunnan Province, the most westerly province of China, it will then command the approaches to Indo-China, Siam and Burma. They will be able to extend communism through these areas into Malaya, possibly Indonesia, and the other islands of the Pacific and westward through Burma into India." Chennault guaranteed that the loss of China could be prevented if the United States would only help the 150 million restive people inside China's borders, from Muslims in the northwest to ex-Nationalist soldiers in the deep south ready to fight communism "to the death."

Chennault thought that without help, the Nationalists could hold Guangdong Province for another three months and the western regions for half a year. That was the window of opportunity open to the United States to make counterrevolution. Chennault excluded Tibet from his list of recipients of military assistance on the grounds that "they are not good soldiers; they want to be left alone."[15]

Having lobbied government officials directly, Chennault made his case to the public in a book published that same year, *Way of a Fighter* (1949). Offering an early version of the domino theory, Chennault classified China as the pivotal tile whose fall would trigger a chain reaction. "A complete Communist victory in China will channel the undercurrents of native unrest already swirling through Burma, India, Malaya, and Indonesia into another rising tide of Communist victories. The ring of Red bases can be stretched from Siberia to Saigon. Then the stage will be set for the unannounced explosion of World War III." Chennault insisted that Stalin's eyes were on Asia (in reality, the Soviet leader was focused on Europe, although Stalin did see the usefulness of Asia in diverting the energies of the West). "China is the key to the Pacific," Chennault wrote, playing the role of geostrategist. "There is growing accumulation of intelligence to indicate that Soviet leaders already consider their Asiatic victories of sufficient strategic importance to tip the world balance of power decisively in favor of Russia." To prepare the battlefield for World War III, the US would need China as a base for taking the war to Moscow's doorstep. A devotee of air power, Chennault argued that "from Okinawa, Japan and the Philippines, American airpower can only peck away at the perimeter of Russia's vitals. From North and central China the same force could strike deeply into Russia's industrial heart." It was not too late to save China: "The recent history of China is studded with examples of how small, technically well-equipped forces can exert decisive influence in China out of all proportion to their size."[16]

Secretary Dean Acheson dismissed Chennault's idea in public comments, and the Chennault plan found few takers in the Department of State.[17] Ambassador Stuart telegrammed from Nanjing dismissing the plan as unrealistic—Yunnan Province, for example, was almost certain to fall to the Reds. The US minister-counselor in Canton piped up cynically to add that the plan might be good business for the general's commercial airline, but it was bad policy for US interests. The Communist revolution would keep spreading, and the Chennault plan would only succeed in aligning the United States with detested overlords.[18] A CIA forecasting report was similarly sobering as it tallied the likely diplomatic cost to an "overt" subversive strategy: "Overt aid to anti-Communist forces in China would compromise the maintenance of normal diplomatic and commercial relations with the Communist-controlled regime, in the event that the US should choose to follow a policy of recognizing such a regime."[19] In June 1949, Mao

Zedong claimed that the PLA wiped out 5.5 million Nationalist troops, leaving some 1.5 million regulars, irregulars, and cadets. "It will still take some time to mop up these enemy remnants, but not long," Mao promised.[20]

Despite the frosty reception at the State Department and pessimistic intelligence estimates, the Chennault plan continued to circulate in government circles. Senator McCarran kept counterrevolution on the mind of Congress as the Senate debated NATO ratification in July, entering into the *Record* a long letter from Chennault that rehashed the case for aiding a "belt of resistance."[21] In August, Chiang Kai-shek's envoy to Washington, Ambassador Wellington Koo, made a formal request for $287 million in military assistance to maintain a firewall of anti-communist resistance from Xinjiang to Guangzhou.[22] But when the Defense Department submitted a feasibility study of the Chennault plan in October, it was dismissed as vague, while the CIA estimated that Mao's "enemy remnants" along the frontiers and on Taiwan would be completely eliminated by the end of the 1950.[23]

"To Activate a Third Force"

If the overt method of the Chennault plan was a nonstarter, that left covert options for making counterrevolution. Walton Butterworth, promoted to assistant secretary for the Far East since he returned from Nanjing, argued that the $75 million allotted by Congress for assistance to China would be wasted on Chiang, but some portion should be set aside "for possible use in supplying *covert* military assistance to promising resistance groups within China if and when an opportunity to do this arises."[24] Frank Wisner at the OPC was a step ahead of Butterworth, having met with Chennault and worked out a plan to save the general's airline from bankruptcy. Wisner's men needed a way to move around Asia hiding in plain sight, and CAT needed an angel investor. So the CIA bought itself a cut-out air transport system. On October 10, 1949, the same day Mao proclaimed the founding of the People's Republic of China, CAT flew its first secret mission for the CIA.[25]

Secretary Acheson remained adamantly opposed to a counterrevolution strategy for China, especially one that relied on Chiang Kai-shek. At a showdown with top brass on December 29 over Far East strategy and the fate of Taiwan, Acheson challenged General Omar Bradley and the Joint Chiefs to defend Taiwan's strategic value in terms of US national interest. He wanted more than a generic insistence that Taiwan was the last bulwark against all Asia falling to Communism. The service chiefs failed to provide compelling strategic reasons why the US had to hold onto Taiwan—or Korea for that matter. Acheson maintained that Mao's victory was a fait accompli and Chiang Kai-shek was a lost cause, and the wisest course was to buttress Southeast Asia against subversion by supporting nationalist movements. Echoing Professor Lattimore's *Situation in Asia* and contra General Chennault's *Way of the Fighter*, Secretary Acheson concluded:

> I pointed out that the Communists now in fact control China and that the conquest has not primarily been by force but due to the collapse of the Kuomintang and the existence of a long-smoldering agrarian revolution on which the Communists have capitalized. We must face the fact that there is no Chinese basis of resistance to Communism. We must also face the certainty that throughout Southeast Asia the Communists will seek to extend their domination, probably by subversive methods and not invasion. We must do our utmost to strengthen the neighbors of China. What we have to do is build up their internal stability, help them to produce more food and raise even moderately their standard of living. Above all we must get ourselves on the side of Nationalist movements, a task which is easier now that the dead hand of European colonialism has been removed.[26]

Acheson was not a fan of covert alternatives and was quick to shoot down the prospect of anti-Communist resistance on mainland when the Joint Chiefs mentioned Taiwan's utility as a springboard for covert operations. "The possible covert support of guerrilla activities on the Mainland came up and it was indicated to the Joint Chiefs that we did not feel there was present basis for such support."[27] Having given the Joint Chiefs a final chance to explain why Taiwan's defense was essential, President Truman decided to tell the public in plain language at the beginning of the new year that no military aid or advice was being provided to Taiwan. The following week, Secretary Acheson delivered his infamous speech at the National Press Club defining America's defense perimeter in Asia so as to exclude Korea and Taiwan, what would become known as the Acheson Line.

Belying the public signaling of the president and secretary of state, the CIA continued to develop options for covert activities supporting anti-Communists in China. Orders arrived on the desk of Alfred Cox, "a relaxed, unassuming American with a wrestler's physique . . . a hint of sadness in his eyes and sensitive mouth," who was serving as the OPC chief in Hong Kong while posing as a CAT executive for cover.[28] Cox later wrote an in-house CIA history of CAT, in which he recalled receiving instructions, dated March 10, 1950, to be on the lookout for clandestine opportunities. "Activity should be directed at the negation and eradication of Soviet influence in China, and the diffusion and diversion of Chinese Communism to the point where it would be replaced by Chinese

Nationalism and some form of indigenous democracy."[29] Some Truman administration officials, agonizing over whether Taiwan could be defended (short of military intervention), daydreamed in the spring of 1950 about the possibility that a coup against Chiang might put a fresh face on the Nationalist cause.[30]

The outbreak of the Korean War changed the equation, injecting the desultory debate over making counterrevolution in China with a military raison d'être. Even before Chinese forces crossed the Yalu River, the Joint Chiefs recommended to the Secretary of Defense that the CIA "be authorized to exploit guerilla potential on the Chinese Mainland to accomplish the objective of reducing the Chinese Communist capabilities to reinforce North Korean forces."[31] The CIA in Tokyo received authorization on July 10 for "initiation of operations" that might reduce Chinese capacity to help their Korean comrades.[32] Truman's approval of NSC 68 in September included orders for the "general intensification of intelligence and related activities to meet the requirements of a national emergency."[33]

After China's surprise intervention in the war forced a humiliating retreat by US forces in December 1950, the Truman administration's Asia policy came under harsh scrutiny. The leading Republican presidential contender Senator Robert Taft (R-Ohio) used a major foreign policy speech to re-up the Chennault plan. His remarks on the Senate floor calling for overt aid to Chinese counterrevolutionaries in January 1951 set off a "great debate" in foreign policy circles over the use of naval and air power against mainland China.[34] President Truman was careful to avoid publicly threatening to strike targets on PRC territory, just as China left alone Japan and Okinawa, the staging grounds for America's war effort. Truman was, however, open to covert options. In preparing "Courses of Action Relative to Communist China and Korea" (NSC 101), General Bradley and the Joint Chiefs recommended to "furnish now all practicable covert aid to effective Nationalist guerilla forces in China."[35]

But how much was "practicable"? And what defined "effective"? Sobering answers could be found in the National Intelligence Estimate (NIE-10) accompanying NSC 101, an early product of Sherman Kent's Office of National Estimates (ONE). The ONE classified Mao's regime as "stable." Anti-Communist resistance had still not been eliminated entirely, but it had been cut in half since Mao's estimate in June 1949 of 1.5 million. The ONE's analysts hedged on the question of whether these restive elements remained loyal to Chiang Kai-shek or were autonomous actors. Either way, they were not a major threat to regime stability or legitimacy.

> On the basis of the slight evidence available, it is estimated that about 700,000 men may be engaged in active resistance operations, ranging from local banditry to organized guerrilla warfare. There is insufficient

> evidence either to substantiate or deny Nationalist claims that a considerable number of these are associated with the Nationalist regime on Taiwan. These forces are creating widespread disorders and are handicapping the Chinese Communist program despite the fact that they are uncoordinated, lack effective top-level leadership, and so far have developed no constructive political program. By themselves and under present conditions these resistance forces do not constitute a major threat to the Chinese Communist regime.[36]

Applying Sherman Kent's formula from *Strategic Intelligence* that strategic posture minus specific vulnerabilities equals courses of action, the ONE assessed that given Communist China's vulnerabilities, assisting internal armed resistance might be sufficient to divert a bit of Beijing's strength from the fight in Korea. But without a viable organization and dynamic leadership, the counterrevolution would never be able to overthrow Mao and the CCP.

> By supplying the active anti-Communist forces already present in mainland China with effective communications, military equipment, and logistical support, Communist military strength could be sapped, and their capabilities for operations elsewhere could be reduced. Even under these circumstances, these opposition groups would be unlikely to overthrow the Chinese Communist regime in the absence of an effective counter-revolutionary movement, a political program, a clear-cut organization, competent leadership and a plan of action.[37]

In addition to aiding counterrevolutionaries on the mainland, the ONE identified three specific vulnerabilities in China that the US could exploit as a means of applying subversive pressure on Beijing. First, Washington could assist Chiang's five hundred thousand troops on Taiwan. Second, the US could wage seaborne "economic warfare" against the mainland in the form of a blockade, offshore bombardment, and/or sabotage operations. Third, the US could prolong the Korean War in order to drain PRC resources, damage its prestige, and generate tensions with Moscow. By pursuing all four actions, the US "would imperil the Chinese Communist regime"—but at a heavy cost and enormous risk. "These actions, however, create a grave danger of Soviet counteraction and would increase the danger of a global war."[38]

NIE-10 appended a giant question mark to NSC 101's call to arm the counterrevolution. But the US military was in warfighting mode, and conventional warfare was not yielding victory in Korea. So, despite the skepticism in the intelligence analysis, planning on covert options moved forward. The Pentagon's strategic planners recommended aid to anti-Communist guerillas to the Joint

Chiefs of Staff in February 1951. Military intelligence opined that "external logistic support would probably accelerate the tempo, increase the combat effectiveness, and widen the area of guerilla activity" of an estimated six hundred thousand anti-Communist forces, about half of whom were thought to bear no allegiance to Chiang Kai-shek.[39] The Joint Strategic Plans Committee proposed $300 million, less than half of the bill Chennault put before the Senate, to aid anti-Communists of all stripes. The Pentagon lifted language from NIE-10 by acknowledging that "covert activity within China would be unlikely to overthrow the Chinese communist regime in the absence of an effective counter-revolutionary movement, a political program, a clear-cut organization and competent leadership—none of which the Chinese Nationalists appears capable of providing at this time."[40]

But what if the counterrevolutionary movement to overthrow Mao were led not by Chiang Kai-shek, but rather by the Third Force? At the CIA director's meeting on March 23, 1951, Beetle Smith, Allen Dulles, and three senior Agency officials discussed a proposal by General Charles A. Willoughby, MacArthur's intelligence chief at Far East Command in Tokyo, the man who missed Chinese intervention in Korea until it was too late. The Willoughby proposal was "to activate a Third Force in China."[41] It came at a pivotal moment in the delicate relationship between Willoughby's and Beetle's bosses—the very next day, MacArthur would undercut and infuriate Truman by publicly calling on Beijing to admit defeat. Adding fuel to the fire, US eavesdropping picked up transcripts of MacArthur boasting to the Spanish and Portuguese embassies in Japan that he would expand the war to China.[42] When Truman fired MacArthur on April 11, the simmering Republican criticism of Asia policy boiled over into national outrage. The deposed general returned home the following week to a hero's welcome, declaring to a joint session of Congress that "old soldiers never die" and basking in the adulation of a million flag-waving admirers on hand to greet him in San Francisco. Arthur Schlesinger wrote at the time, in a book co-authored with journalist Richard Rovere, "It is doubtful if there has ever been in this country so violent and spontaneous a discharge of political passion as that provoked by the President's dismissal of the General and by the General's dramatic return from his voluntary, patriotic exile."[43]

As the drama of strained civilian-military relations and polarized party competition played out in public, the Joint Chiefs, the NSC, and the CIA quietly worked on covert counterrevolutionary planning along the lines of the Willoughby proposal.[44] Truman signed off on a new strategic plan, "United States Objectives, Policies and Courses of Action in Asia" (NSC 48-5), on May 17, 1951. The strategy called for aiding resistance and encouraging subversion inside the PRC—leaving open the question of whether to back the Nationalists or the Third Force:

> 1.b. Expand and intensify, by all available means, efforts to develop non-communist leadership and to influence the leaders and people in China to oppose the present Peiping regime and to seek its reorientation or replacement.
>
> c. Foster and support anti-communist Chinese elements both outside and within China with a view to developing and expanding resistance in China to the Peiping regime's control, particularly in South China.[45]

Wary of monkey business and keen to focus on the "primary mission" of strategic intelligence, Beetle Smith was not excited at the prospect of fomenting counterrevolution. Citing the example of guerrilla warfare in China, he complained on the one-year anniversary of the Korean War to senior NSC staff that the CIA was in danger of becoming a "covert War Department." Paul Nitze, Kennan's replacement as head of policy planning, was briefed on the CIA director's complaints:

> He [Smith] stated that it was possible that these operations might develop into a very large military effort involving perhaps two or three hundred thousand men who would have to be equipped and supplied. If this situation did in fact develop it would naturally involve a large production program for specialized light weapons and would mean in addition, a large-scale training, shipping and air-supply and re-supply program which would amount to a military operation. In other words an "operation of war" on a grand scale. General Smith doubted that the CIA was the proper agency to undertake such a program.[46]

Acutely aware of the danger that covert action could overwhelm strategic intelligence—of Dulles eclipsing Kent—Beetle worried that the "operations tail are now starting to wag the intelligence dog."[47]

Although the NSC policy encouraged covert action, the CIA continued to receive mixed signals over whether to back a Third Force over the summer of 1951. The OPC chief Frank Wisner reported in July that "the matter of assistance to the Third Force is all up in the air. State Department is of a divided mind. The DCI believes that the Third Force must be kept alive but that this is a political decision for State Department."[48] There were, after all, considerable diplomatic sensitivities involved if the United States government were to aid Third Force elements, even covertly. Such aid would represent a rebuke, if not an abandonment, of Chiang Kai-shek, who was competing for influence over Third Force holdouts in Hong Kong not only with Mao, but also against rivals within his own Nationalist Party.

The Nationalist Party's intelligence service—the Bureau of Investigation and Statistics (Pao Mi Chu) headed by Mao Renfeng—employed Hong Kong–based front organizations like the Anti-Communist and National Salvation Sub-League of Chinese Youth to ferret out Third Force figures.[49] The CIA station in Taiwan assessed that Chiang's "fear of defections to the Communists or 'Third Force' groups" was leading him to rely more heavily on the parallel intelligence service led by his son, Chiang Ching-kuo.[50] The rivalry between Chiang Ching-kuo's Political Department and Mao Renfeng's Bureau of Investigation and Statistics degenerated into a no-holds-barred "struggle for supremacy." The Chiang family network was strong in Taiwan, but "its intelligence service in Communist China is weak." As far as the CIA could tell, the Bureau of Investigation and Statistics might be trying to organize its own Third Force on the mainland in hopes of securing American support, in a complex power play against Chiang: "The Pao Mi Chu . . . is attempting to use its guerrilla force to build up a third force in order to break the CHIANG family control of the government. In an attempt to overthrow CHIANG Ching-kuo, again MAO Jen-feng and MAO Sen-FENG are working together secretly in an effort to secure U.S. backing for a third force. With such backing the Pao Mi Chu hopes to regain its prestige."[51]

As UN Command forces in Korea fought a war of attrition, the NSC recommended in October 1951 that the CIA oversee an intensification of covert operations and "develop underground resistance and facilitate covert and guerrilla operations in strategic areas to the maximum practicable extent."[52] James Lilley, a CIA recruit fresh out of Yale, arrived in Tokyo not long afterward to serve as "a foot soldier in America's covert efforts to keep Asia from being dominated by Communist China." He was part of the CIA's "three-pronged" approach: working with Nationalist intelligence out of Taiwan to assist stranded soldiers on the mainland; aiding ex-Nationalist Third Force elements; and conducting its own espionage. "There was precious little information coming out of China," Lilley recalled. "The CIA proposed to use communications intercepts, air reconnaissance, and human agents to redress the problem."[53]

Frontiers of Subversion

After a year of fighting the Chinese in Korea, Sherman Kent's analysts remained pessimistic about the prospects for counterrevolution in the PRC. "The Chinese Communists have succeeded in greatly reducing the strength of guerilla forces throughout China and these forces do not now have a significant operational capability," a special estimate read in December 1951. "Even if guerilla capabilities were developed, the guerillas could be employed effectively only in conjunction with other courses of action directed against Communist China."[54]

But the OPC had cash to spend—as much as $25 million was allocated for covert ops in China in 1951, with more in the pipeline.[55] Restive frontier areas looked ripe for resistance, especially Guangxi Province, on the border with Indochina, which was home to a large ethnic minority population and a clique of Nationalist leaders who resisted the dominance of Chiang Kai-shek. A CIA report enthused that "some have even shifted over to the Third Force and have engaged in guerrilla activities against the Communists. The United Front considers the situation serious because it appears that various political parties in Kwangsi can easily be won over by the Third Force."[56] Geography, unfortunately, made it difficult for the CIA to link up with the Guangxi resistance.

Another target was Muslim-majority Xinjiang Province in the far northwest, bordering the Soviet Union. In *Way of a Fighter*, Chennault pinned great hopes on Xinjiang counterrevolutionaries, predicting confidently in his 1949 book that "in the near future I am certain C.A.T. will bring the Moslems of Sinkiang what they need from the ports."[57] By the time Truman came around to the idea of sending covert aid to the Muslim resistance, it was too late—the regional strongman, Ma Bufang, had fled the provincial capital of Xining.[58] Chennault did eventually made good on his promise when a CAT plane flew Nationalist agents on a mission to the northwest in March 1952.[59] But the agents of subversion were never heard from again. By one tally, the CIA was involved in some two dozen infiltration flights over the northwest operating out of Taiwan during the second half of the Korean War.[60]

Along with Xinjiang and Guangxi Provinces, Tibet was a third obvious possibility for making counterrevolution along the Chinese frontier. During WWII, the US government was not supportive of Tibetan autonomy, which could undermine their ally Chiang's Republic of China, but the calculus changed as CCP victory in the Civil War appeared imminent.[61] The new problem was lack of channels of communication with the Tibetan leadership, which was a quilt of aristocratic and theocratic elements, at the center of which sat the fourteenth Dalai Lama. The British and Indians were logical intermediaries given their ties to Lhasa, but both Delhi and London were keen on working out an accommodation with Mao and wary of the Tibetan issue. The US ambassador to India Loy Henderson tried to contact the teenage Dalai Lama via his elder brother Gyalo Thondup, to no avail.[62]

People's Liberation Army soldiers marched into eastern Tibet in October 1950—simultaneous with the Korean intervention—and quickly "pacified" Tibetan troops in the Cham region. The Tibetan commander, Ngapoi Ngawang Jigme, headed a delegation to Beijing where he signed the Seventeen-Point Agreement acknowledging PRC sovereignty in May 1951. Tibetan leaders split over the accommodation and the Dalai Lama vacillated, holing up in a monastery near the India border. His eldest brother Thubten Norbu was whisked out of India to the United States in the summer of 1951 on a trip funded by the CIA-backed

Committee for a Free Asia (later known as the Asia Foundation). Secretary Acheson promised full-throated support for the Tibetan cause if the Dalai Lama would go into exile to be its standard-bearer.[63] But the Dalai Lama declined the invitation to become an agent of subversion. His message was relayed to Director Smith on October 1, 1951: "The Dalai Lama of Tibet has responded to the State Department message conveyed to him in July by his elder brother offering covert US assistance to maintain the autonomy of Tibet. The response expressed deep regret that the Dalai Lama was unable to take immediate advantage of the US offer. The Dalai Lama said that he was forced by circumstances and the needs of his people to return to Lhasa but hoped that the US would not lose confidence in him and would continue to be friendly."[64]

Tibet was a no-go for the time being. But Chennault was wrong about Tibet's lack of will to fight. There were in fact sporadic uprisings across northeastern Tibet, far from the Dalai Lama's reach, as the historian Benno Weiner shows. Armed insurrection in Tibetan areas of Qinghai Province would not be quelled until the spring of 1953.[65]

The fourth logical frontier of subversion for "practicable" delivery of "effective" covert aid, as required in NSC 101, was the southwestern province of Yunnan, which shared a border with the newly independent Union of Burma. As the vast majority of Nationalists—some two million people—fled to Taiwan in 1949, a ragtag force of a couple thousand National Army soldiers scrambled across the Yunnan border to reassemble in the remote northeast corner of Burma, a country grappling with ethnic division and armed rebellion. Yunnan-born Lieutenant General Li Mi won Chiang Kai-shek's blessing to use Burma as a base from which to plan a re-invasion of Yunnan—so long as he could raise the money for it.

Li Mi was in regular contact with CIA officials in Hong Kong and Bangkok in early 1950. In June, just ahead of North Korea's invasion of the South, the Burmese government sent troops to expel Nationalist soldiers from its borders. As rumors swirled of covert American assistance to General Li Mi, Burma's prime minister pressed the US ambassador, David Key, to intercede with Taipei to disband Li's army-in-exile. Li Mi met with US officials once again in Hong Kong and Bangkok in September. His fans at the CIA included the OPC Far East Division chief Colonel Richard Stilwell and deputy Desmond FitzGerald, who had fond memories of leading Chinese troops in Burma with the OSS. According to Evan Thomas, the intelligence gatherers in the OSO were not eager about another reckless OPC adventure. Tensions on the ground between the OSO and the OPC at Bangkok Station would erupt into an open fight the following year.[66]

The decision over whether to aid General Li Mi's Yunnan Anti-Communist National Salvation Army went all the way to the Oval Office. According to William Leary's research, President Truman gave the green light—over the objections of Beetle Smith—to Operation Paper late in the year.[67] Frank Wisner went to work with alacrity and the operation kicked off in February 1951, when CAT planes flown by civilian employees, men like Norman Schwartz and Robert C. Snoddy, transported munitions from Okinawa to Bangkok. The operation was coordinated by the CIA's shell organization the Overseas Southeast Asia Supply Company (run by the OSS Burma veteran Sherman B. Joost).[68] CAT C-46 planes made nearly a dozen weapons drops through the early summer of 1951.[69] The Thai police chief was only too happy to look the other way, as Operation Paper promised to deepen his network in northeast Burma with its profitable opium trade.[70]

After all the debate and planning, Li Mi's actual invasion in late spring and early summer 1951 didn't get far before being easily repelled by PLA troops in Yunnan.[71] The military defeat was compounded by diplomatic embarrassment for the United States. Secretary Acheson cabled Ambassador Key in Burma, denying allegations of US aid to General Li. Beetle Smith did the same to his British counterparts. The Burmese government was outraged that the United States was covertly supporting a renegade Chinese army inside its borders and took the matter up at the United Nations. While publicly denying any role, the State Department reauthorized the CIA to pass hard currency to Li Mi's army via his representatives in Thailand in September.[72] The CIA was also given the go-ahead for a Southeast Asia sabotage operation against merchant ships linked to the PRC. If a trial run at placing "facsimile packages" in the cargo during loading in Manila or Bangkok were to go smoothly, then State would consider "granting policy clearance for sabotage operations against Chinese Communist vessels outside of Chinese Communist waters generally."[73]

All the activity was getting hard to keep hidden. By early 1952, newsmen for the *New York Times* and the *Observer* began to peel back the veneer of official denials of US involvement with the tiny invasion force in Burma.[74]

Island of Subversion

As the CIA funneled arms and money to Chiang's satellite army in Burma, the Truman administration ramped up covert assistance to the bulk of his forces on the island fortress of Taiwan. Chiang had Kim Il Sung to thank for this reversal in fortune. As of early 1950, Truman and Acheson were prepared to write off Taiwan. But immediately after the North Korean invasion, Truman announced that the mighty US Seventh Fleet would be steaming into the Taiwan Strait to deter a Communist assault on the island. Chiang was kept on a leash—Truman pointedly refused Chiang's offer to send Nationalist troops to fight in Korea and publicly announced, "I am calling upon the Chinese Government on

Formosa to cease all air and sea operations against the mainland."[75] But under the exigencies of war in Korea, especially once it started going badly for the Americans, Taiwan proved irresistible as a covert base for making counterrevolution on the mainland.

The US embassy in Taipei got wind of Chiang Kai-shek's plans for raids on the China coast around the time Mao secretly sent troops to Korea. The top-ranking diplomat, Karl Rankin, saw potential benefits, including "relieving pressure on Indochina, interrupting enemy communications with that theater, and perhaps even bringing about the diversion of some Chinese communist units from Korea."[76] As the war in Korea stalemated in early 1951, covert assistance to Taiwan-based efforts to harass the mainland gained traction. The CIA established a front organization on the island, Western Enterprises Inc., that within a year would come to employ six hundred personnel "providing guerilla training, logistical support, overflight capabilities, facilities for propaganda coverage of the mainland by radio and leaflet balloon, and doing other tasks," according to Joseph Smith.[77] As James Lilley remembered it, "the CIA started to receive virtually unlimited funding for its collaborative efforts with Taiwan's intelligence and special operations units. As the war in Korea progressed, Taiwan became the principal base for launching clandestine military operations against mainland China."[78]

Code-named Operation Octopus, the CIA-backed operations out of Taiwan took three main forms: aerial surveillance, leaflet drops, and commando infiltrations. Immediately after the outbreak of war in Korea, US Navy surveillance planes made secret overflights along the Chinese coast to monitor for an imminent invasion of Taiwan. After Chinese intervention, the Far East Air Force (FEAF) asked permission to make overflights into Manchuria to identify possible targets for nuclear bombing, but it was not until May 1951 that RB-45s based out of Yokota, Japan, got permission for aerial surveillance over the Chinese mainland. A summertime mission flew south to spy down on the coastal cities Shanghai, Hangzhou, Ningbo, and Xiamen.[79] Soon the CIA was acting as intermediary, outsourcing FEAF aerial surveillance to Chiang Kai-shek: "Arrangements have been made with the Chinese Nationalist—Air Force for night and possibly day photographic missions over the Chinese mainland with [*sic*] the next two months. Western Enterprises Inc., the BGMARQUE cover organization, will furnish photographic equipment and technicians. The U.S. Military Attache at Taipei will furnish FEAF with copies of photographs taken. The Military Attache will also establish a symbol to be affixed to the photographs which will give Western Enterprises a credit line."[80]

Many of the CIA-directed Nationalist planes that took pictures over the mainland also left propaganda leaflets behind, dropping as many as seventy-five million pieces of paper in psychological warfare operations during the Korean War years.[81] This was the heyday of balloon launches in Eastern Europe—the CIA front organization Crusade for Freedom lofted millions of leaflets into Czechoslovakia and hundreds of thousands more into Poland.[82] Typical missions from Taiwan dropped ten thousand pounds of leaflets, papering southern Fujian Province with anti-Communist propaganda. In one busy month, 145,000 leaflets rained down from the skies.[83] The CIA was assured that locals were "very excited" by the drops and Communist authorities were "rushing collectors to gather the leaflets dropped and issuing orders to the people not to read them."[84] The leaflet drops, using CAT planes, were reported to Beetle Smith as a great psywar victory: "BGMARQUE is receiving excellent reports on news and leaflet drops on mainland. Since people are actually paying for the news bulletins, we are planning to have Civil Air Transport fly a full load over the coastal provinces of Chekiang and Fujian the week of 17 Dec. If successful, we will schedule one full load of approximately 10,000 lbs. thereafter. Up until this date, all leaflets have been dropped in the area surrounding Chin-Min Island for a radious [*sic*] of 60 miles."[85] The geographical reach of the leaflet missions was not limited to the coastal provinces directly opposite Taiwan. According to an internal CCP report, Nationalist planes dropped propaganda as far inland as western Hunan Province over two dozen times during a six-month period of 1951, "with a peak just before National Day when 11 counties were bombarded with propaganda against the Sino-Soviet dialogue and Peace Conference."[86]

The third prong of Operation Octopus consisted of paramilitary covert action. Raiding parties, trained on Taiwan and Jinmen Island (also known as Quemoy) with CIA assistance, parachuted out of planes or landed furtively by boat along the southern coast. According to internal CCP reports, one bizarre scheme called for lepers from Hong Kong, armed with US weapons, to be infiltrated by boat at night and wreak havoc on villages in Guangdong Province.[87] According to a comprehensive counterintelligence survey distributed among party members, the US set up a training program in Taiwan for Nationalist commandos in early 1951 led by three American instructors, covering guerrilla strategy and tactics, paramilitary warfare, weapons and parachuting, explosives and sabotage, emergency medical aid, and psychological warfare. A small team of American instructors opened a second training program in May 1951 on Jinmen in hopes of achieving better security than on Taiwan. In addition to training commandos, Western Enterprise agents carried out intelligence gathering with visits to offshore islands and debriefing of fishermen and businessmen.[88]

Internal CIA logs confirm that by the second half of 1951, CIA-trained commandos and operatives were landing on the mainland on a regular basis. A major coordinated assault under Operation Octopus, code-named Tentacle No. 2, was planned for September but had to be aborted because of a security breach ("the Communists possessed detailed information on TENTACLE No. 2 including landing point and size-of force. The Communists were reported rushing troops to the landing area").[89] Op-sec was a recurring problem: "Chinese Nationalist guerrillas returning from CIA-directed mainland operations report that the Communists are generally forewarned of guerrilla operations. The field reports its awareness of this situation and stresses the extreme difficulty of maintaining the security of landing operations."[90] Another challenge was getting reliable after-action reports—aerial reconnaissance or follow-on infiltration agents had to be sent to double-check reports of success.[91] Many infiltration parties simply disappeared without a trace, and the successful penetrations required contact teams in order to maintain communications.[92]

CIA-trained and -directed guerrilla warfare teams from Taiwan made night drops on the South China Sea island of Hainan, northward up the coast into Zhejiang Province, and as far inland as the Hubei-Henan-Anhui border, four hundred miles west of Shanghai.[93] The Jinmen base trained a one-thousand-man strong contingent known as the Fujian Anti-Communist National Salvation Army, the lost twin of General Li Mi's Yunnan National Salvation Army. The Fujian Anti-Communist Army staged a series of diversionary raids, including a major amphibious attack on Nanri Island in December 1951. According to the after-action report received at CIA headquarters, "the raiders withdrew after eight and a half hours of combat which resulted in Chinese Communist losses of 100 dead and wounded and the capture of fourteen regulars of the 249th Regiment, eighty-three civilians, one radio operator and a number of militia to Chinese Nationalist losses of eight dead and twenty-three wounded."[94] The historian Hsiao-ting Lin argues that the US military, frustrated over the stalemate in Korea, asked for more attacks on PRC territory than Chiang was willing to offer. Pushed to order a full-scale amphibious assault to regain Hainan Island in the spring of 1952, for example, Chiang resisted—while maintaining his public image as a revanchist who needed to be kept on a leash.[95]

Small-scale paramilitary operations continued, including a successful raid on the offshore island of Meizhou in July 1952.[96] A second, larger operation against Nanri Island on October 11, 1952, was a major success, with over seven hundred Communist prisoners taken in the fighting.[97] Meanwhile, CIA-trained agents were flying from Taiwan deep into the hinterland for penetration operations. One midnight in October 1952, an unmarked plane dropped a parachute team into a mountainous area of the Taoyuan district of Hunan Province. Villagers found their supplies in the morning and reported it to local officials. Within twenty-four hours, the Public Security Bureau team organized a manhunt with the assistance of locals, resulting in two infiltrators shot dead and one captured.

Two more paratroopers were captured carrying radios, pistols, carbine rifles, gold, cash, and rations. All five men were Hunanese, and three of them were Taoyuan natives. An agent already under detention in the provincial public security office confessed that the plan called for a seven-man team, so the search for the remaining two continued.[98]

With Operation Octopus spreading its tentacles out from Taiwan and Operation Paper threatening invasion from Burma, the CIA could claim to have opened two fronts in covert warfare against CCP control, as the overt war against Chinese People's Volunteers by United Nations Command forces bogged down in Korea. Optimistic assessments in Washington estimated that US-backed Nationalist paramilitary operations were "immobilizing" as many as two hundred thousand Communist troops that might otherwise be free to join the fight in Korea.[99]

There was a third front opening up, as well. Another border area to probe for counterrevolutionary potential was Manchuria, the staging ground and supply conduit for the Korean battlefield. The CIA effort to exploit its subversive potential would rely on the Third Force, and originate two thousand kilometers to the south in the British Crown Colony of Hong Kong.

8
HONG KONG FIGHT LEAGUE

To find Third Force agents of subversion willing to make counterrevolution on the mainland, the CIA encouraged a collection of anti-Communist, anti-Nationalist figures based in Hong Kong to come together in a unified organization. Monitored warily by the British authorities and Communist spies, members of the Fight League for a Free and Democratic China published journals to use in the propaganda war and recruited volunteers to train as Jedburghs willing to venture into Mao's China.

In the Crown Colony

According to the British double agent Kim Philby, Frank Wisner once told him, "Whenever we want to subvert any place we find that the British own an island within easy reach."[1] Wisner was alluding to Malta's utility in plotting to overthrow Hoxha's communist government in Albania, but he could just as well have been speaking of Hong Kong and the plot to overthrow Mao.

The British in Hong Kong were not exactly thrilled to offer this convenience to their American cousins (to use the le Carré-ism). British and American interests, after all, diverged sharply over China policy. China had been a mild irritant in the friendship between FDR and Churchill, who called Roosevelt's faith in Chiang Kai-shek "the great American illusion."[2] Trying to hang on to as much of its empire as possible—Hong Kong in particular—Great Britain offered recognition to the People's Republic of China on January 6, 1950 (although Beijing held out on reciprocating). Humphrey Trevelyan, the senior British diplomat in Beijing, watched coldly as the Americans struggled to accept their loss of China:

> It was like a love affair gone wrong. Generations of Americans had given their lives to China. American money had been poured out to improve Chinese health, education and agriculture. Generations of Chinese had looked to American-run schools and hospitals in China and to American universities in China and the United States for their higher education. American men, arms and supplies had supported the tottering Chinese effort to throw the Japanese out of their country and to relieve the distress caused by war. America had prided itself on being a non-colonialist, non-imperialist country which had not tried to dominate, but which had saved a moribund China from partition by the predatory European powers. Now the "open door" had been slammed in America's face.[3]

Mirroring the Anglo-American divergence in China policy, intelligence relations across Asia could be a bone of contention between the Americans and the British.[4] Americans might still feel like the junior partner coming out of WWII—Ray Cline, for example, considered the British intelligence system "more mature" when he was posted to London in 1951.[5] But as the Cold War heated up, it was the Americans who possessed greater wealth, power, and confidence. Beneath the veneer of a special relationship, spies found themselves jockeying for influence in numerous points on the globe where the sun of the British Empire was setting and the American Century was dawning. Third parties had to navigate with care. Take, for example, Sultan Hamengkubuwono IX, the Javanese monarch who shrewdly survived Dutch colonial rule, Japanese wartime occupation, and the birth of a secular Republic of Indonesia: "The British High Commissioner to Southeast Asia recently sought a meeting with the Sultan of Jogjakarta to offer British assistance in an intelligence training program. The Sultan, a key figure in OSO plans to gain eventual control of Indonesian security and intelligence forces, declined on the grounds that he could not, as a private citizen, reply to such an offer. OSO Djakarta believes he prefers to cooperate with the U.S."[6]

Anglo-American tensions played out on a regular basis in Hong Kong, the spy heaven of the East, as Allen Dulles recollected fondly in his memoir, *The Craft of Intelligence*.[7] Trevelyan observed, "If it was a Nationalist base for spying on the mainland, it was also a Communist base for spying on Taiwan," omitting that Hong Kong served the same purpose for the British and Americans.[8] The US covert effort was run out of its largest consulate in the world, a listening post and propaganda platform located on Red China's southern doorstep. The State

Department built up the Hong Kong consulate rapidly after expulsion from the mainland, giving their British hosts the jitters. The US consulate numbered close to one hundred staff by September 1951, who provided services to a mere thousand US citizen residents (as London noted in dismay).[9]

To be sure, there were important areas of intelligence cooperation—the Americans and the Aussies were free to use the product scooped up by the British signals intelligence center in Little Sai Wan, for example.[10] But Washington was not content to use Hong Kong as a listening post. The Americans saw the colony as a loudspeaker for anti-Communist propaganda and a launching pad for covert operations—both of which put British colonial authorities ill at ease.[11]

Having warned the "cousins" over the summer, British frustration seemed to be reaching a head in November 1951, as reported to CIA headquarters:

> British authorities in Hong Kong appear to be making a determined bid to reduce the scope of CIA activities there. Whether the instigation for these British activities stems solely from the policy of the local Hong Kong Government or has been directed from London cannot yet be determined. The OSO representative has reported the above situation to Washington in detail and has requested that Headquarters undertake a review of our Hong Kong liaison arrangements with the British in order to protect our intelligence assets. Such a review is in progress and recommendations will be made for the handling of this situation.[12]

As historian Chi-kwan Mark points out, colonial authorities complained to London a few months later, "We dislike its [US] under-cover activities—e.g., its habit of purchasing fictitious 'intelligence' from Third Force elements who make their living by concocting intelligence for United States benefit."[13]

British disapproval was not going to prevent the CIA station from carrying out its assignment to recruit a Third Force contingent that would be sent for training in Okinawa or Saipan, and then airborne infiltration into Manchuria to make counterrevolution. The proposal "to activate a Third Force" required a combination of liberal intellectuals, experienced generals, and willing foot soldiers: Hong Kong was home to all three.

Hong Kong had been a safe haven for intellectuals for decades, especially since the "great exodus" in 1941 when fighting resumed between the Nationalists and Communists. "From all over the country, progressive politicians, writers, artists and newspapermen made their way to the British Colony," newsman Israel Epstein wrote.[14] During the Chinese Civil War, Hong Kong could feel like a giant displaced persons camp, like the ones in Europe where the CIA did its best recruiting for infiltration agents to work behind the Iron Curtain.[15] Desperate soldiers and disillusioned generals fleeing the Chinese Communist army made their way south via Canton to Hong Kong rather than surrender to Mao or follow Chiang to Taiwan. The historian Frank Dikötter estimates that one million refugees flooded Hong Kong—including "several thousand soldiers, many crippled and disabled. The regime in Taiwan viewed them as a security risk and refused them entry."[16]

Hong Kong had a promising pool of recruits; the problem was, who would lead the Third Force? The most obvious candidate as the non-Communist alternative to Chiang Kai-shek was the Guangxi Province native Li Zongren, a respected National Army general who defied President Chiang's wishes by running for the post of vice president in April 1948. Chiang's resignation in January 1949 left Li holding the bag as acting president in the final stage of the Civil War. Li's options militarily and politically were grim, and illness forced him to evacuate via Hong Kong to New York to seek medical treatment. Before leaving, Li Zongren gave HKD 200,000 to the former economics professor and Nationalist Party apostate Gu Mengyu to set up a Third Force group in Hong Kong, to be called the Freedom and Democracy Grand Alliance.[17]

While recovering in New York, Li submitted a memo to President Truman requesting aid to Third Force elements in Hong Kong, outlining a four-point program to support guerrilla training, underground activities, overseas Chinese, and liberalization.[18] Truman and Acheson invited Li for a state dinner at the White House in March 1950; a few days prior, Chiang Kai-shek, who had ears and eyes all over Washington, had announced he would resume the office of presidency.[19]

Another promising option to lead the Third Force, one who was based in Hong Kong rather than New York, was General Zhang Fakui, with whom US consulate and CIA officials had been trying repeatedly to meet over the course of 1950.[20] A military commander in his native Guangdong Province since the 1920s, Zhang had never been happy with Chiang Kai-shek and over the years moved in and out of various anti-Chiang coalitions, sometimes aligned with Li Zongren's Guangxi clique.[21] During WWII, he led Nationalist troops in Guangdong and Guangxi against the Japanese, working with General Wedemeyer to strengthen the Fourth War Area. After Tokyo's surrender in August 1945, Zhang received Japanese surrender at Canton and would have been in charge of liberating Hong Kong if Chiang had not let the British race ahead and reclaim their colony.[22] By the final year of the Chinese Civil War, as Chiang plotted his flight across the Taiwan Strait, Zhang was left behind as commander of forces defending Guangdong Province against the final push by Communist forces. He appealed to Li Zongren to bring Chiang Kai-shek to Canton and arrest the generalissimo.[23] Not surprisingly, rather than follow Chiang to Taiwan, Zhang Fakui chose the Crown Colony of Hong Kong.

Zhang Fakui finally agreed to a meeting in December 1950 with James McClure Henry, a prominent American missionary educator acting on behalf of the CIA. For two decades, Henry helped run Lingnan University, founded in 1888 as the Christian College in China.[24] Henry would work for the Committee for a Free Asia, a CIA front organization. Fluent in Cantonese, Henry met Zhang at Hong Kong's Foreign Press Club, where he asked if the general would be willing to lead anti-Communist guerilla activities on the mainland. Zhang told Henry flatly that a counterrevolution was impossible—the population supported the CCP and guerilla war depended on local support. "Anyone who lands on the mainland will be captured," the general told the missionary. The real masters of guerilla warfare were the Communists, who could not be beaten at their own game. Henry probed for Zhang's view of whether Chiang Kai-shek had any chance of recapturing the mainland. Zhang opined it would be nearly impossible for Chiang to regain the mandate, having lost it once. Henry was in no mood to quarrel—he agreed that Chiang was too dictatorial.

So what was to be done?, Henry asked, invitingly. Zhang suggested forming a secret political organization and military force, focusing on cultivating future leadership and training an elite force. A half-dozen men could form the Third Force nucleus, Zhang told Henry, rattling off names like Gu Mengyu, Zhang Guotao, and Wu Xianzi. What about Carsun Chang? Henry asked. Zhang expected he would probably join as well. Henry was heading back soon to the United States and promised that he would report on their meeting in Washington and write later with good news. Zhang recalled that at the time he felt like the Chosen One in America's effort to create "what the outside world from this point on called 'the Third Force.'"[25]

During their meeting at the Foreign Press Club, Henry suggested that Zhang reach out to another Chiang Kai-shek rival, General Xu Chongzhi, who was lobbying the US consulate for assistance for his own Third Force group.[26] Having graduated from the Tokyo Military Academy, Xu was well connected in Japan and thought to have underworld connections in smuggling and narcotics from the days of occupied Hong Kong, although the CIA assessed that he had cleaned up since that "dissolute" phase of life. Unlike Zhang, Xu expressed boundless faith in the counterrevolution: 450,000 soldiers in north and central China would rise up against the Reds if only he were given resources to start a campaign in the south. Generals Fu Zuoyi and "numerous (unnamed) former Nationalists who defected to the Communists because of opposition to Chiang Kai-shek" would come over to the Third Force.[27] Xu Chongzhi agreed to join forces with Zhang Fakui, as did Carsun Chang.

A few months after the meeting with James McClure Henry, another quiet American—Scandinavian-looking, in his fifties, with passable Chinese—paid

Zhang Fakui a visit. Going by the name Hartmann, the mystery man claimed to represent the American people, not the US government, and wanted to introduce Zhang to two other men, who similarly represented the American people, not the government.[28] Zhang insisted that Xu Chongzhi be included in the follow-up meeting, held at a secluded Hong Kong villa. Zhang knew one of the Americans from the war—a colonel in Chennault's Flying Tigers serving at Nanning air base. The other man was barely thirty. They inquired about Hong Kong's leading "democratic personages" and how the American people could help. Zhang repeated the speech he had given Henry, talking about the need to take anti-Communist activities overseas. Can you get the leading men together, they asked? And what about intellectual types like Carsun Chang and Gu Mengyu? Zhang assured them Carsun Chang would come to Hong Kong, and that they could talk to Gu Mengyu themselves. Xu Chongzhi promised to draft a work plan.[29]

Zhang was never told what US entity he was dealing with. When Xu came back to the Americans with a plan, they demurred, saying they did not have the authority to approve it and needed to consult "the American people." By the time they made an offer for funding, Zhang refused it, infuriating Xu, who needed money to cover debts from his other group. Gu Mengyu, Zhang Guotao, and other core members wanted Xu out. When Zhang told the Americans about the expulsion, they said, "The Third Force is your baby. We won't interfere in how to raise him into a grown man." A group of two dozen leading figures in the dissident cliques of ex-Nationalists, ex-Communists, and various minor parties slowly coalesced, forming an unofficial Group of 25 in May 1951.[30]

But solidarity within the group was fragile. One core member got cold feet after feeling pressure from colonial police and dropped out, and Zhang had to assuage the others. If Hong Kong became unlivable, the fallback plan was to reorganize in the Philippines.[31] Meanwhile, from his residence in Riverdale, New York, Li Zongren wrote letters to Truman and Acheson alleging that Xu Chongzhi was secretly working for Chiang Kai-shek. Li claimed that Xu was manipulating Zhang Fakui to trick the group into setting up a base in Manila (with Hartmann's unwitting support) as means to destroy the Third Force in Hong Kong.[32]

Then there was the question of what the group should actually *do*. Since the days of Liang Qichao, liberal intellectuals and their centrist parties often got no further than founding a journal, which is what Third Force members did, with support from the Americans. Gu Mengyu launched *Independence Forum* in 1950 with a monthly stipend of HKD 8,000. Carsun Chang received HKD 6,000 a month for his journal *Renaissance*. CIA financing also helped set up the journals *Voice of China*, which put out its first issue on October 11, 1952, and *Overseas Chinese Bulletin*. The four publications together reached about 1,200 readers in Hong Kong and another 800 abroad, targeting young, educated arrivals from the mainland who found Third Force messaging appealing.[33]

The Americans conferred regularly with Zhang, doling out monthly salaries and sharing counterintelligence. Zhang was under constant surveillance but kept on good terms with police commissioner Duncan Macintosh.[34] When Commissioner Macintosh probed for basic information about the Third Force organization, Zhang was evasive, fibbing that the headquarters was Tokyo, acknowledging about three hundred members in Hong Kong, and exaggerating a bit to claim another one to two hundred more abroad. He showed Macintosh the political outline of the group and assured him it posed no threat to Hong Kong's security or British interests. Macintosh was no great fan of either Mao or Chiang and was willing to look the other away.[35]

In organizational terms, Carsun Chang's month-long visit to Hong Kong in the spring of 1952 on his journey from India to America marked a step forward, formalizing the association into a political entity. The scholar Chang met frequently with the general Zhang, and together they settled on an official name for the group: the Fight League for a Free and Democratic China. Carsun Chang drafted a twenty-five-page manifesto and then headed off for Tokyo and Washington in search of patrons—both financial and political.[36]

Recruiting Agents of the Counterrevolution

From his contacts in Hong Kong, Zhang knew the Americans were keen on doing more than subsidizing journals. They wanted intelligence.[37] Hong Kongers, after all, could visit the mainland with nothing more than a travel permit, which created opportunities for low-grade espionage. But the intelligence collection efforts left much to be desired. The Americans made a request for information on the PLA presence along the Guangdong–Kowloon railway, for example, and the Third Force "military affairs bureau" assigned the job to an agent who drafted his report . . . from the safety of Hong Kong. Americans caught onto him only because one of the special forces mentioned in the report was known to be stationed in Manchuria. In another case, the Americans outed a Third Force agent who had been assigned to set up a wireless transmission from Guangdong, after they traced his signal to a fishing boat in Hong Kong harbor.

By Zhang's estimate, 90 percent of the intelligence coming out of Hong Kong was unreliable, if not outright fake. Linkages between the espionage underworld and drug dealing muddied the waters even further.[38] The problem was hardly unique to Hong Kong. The OSO chief Richard Helms described how the demand for information on Soviet intentions and capabilities created "a legion of political exiles, former intelligence officers, ex-agents, and sundry entrepreneurs . . . turning themselves into intelligence moguls, brokering the sale of fabricated-to-order information to the various official intelligence services."[39]

In any case, Zhang Fakui's quiet American friends were not satisfied with information alone. They wanted agents of subversion willing to bring the fight to the mainland. Zhang received a request for twenty to thirty volunteers, preferably single, ideally with a background in wireless radio operation, willing to go to Okinawa for training to become Third Force Jedburghs making covert counterrevolution on the mainland. Zhang found the recruits, some married, most of whom went for the money.[40]

Zhang's American handlers urged him to join forces with Cai Wenzhi, a Nationalist officer who had fled Hong Kong for the safety of US-occupied Okinawa.[41] Zhang agreed begrudgingly to meet with Cai's representative in Hong Kong, a mutual acquaintance and former Nationalist Air Force officer named Huang Bingheng.[42] Huang explained that Cai's Okinawa-based organization, the Free China Movement, was ready to initiate guerilla warfare on the mainland and already had men on the payroll in Hong Kong. Zhang described himself and Cai as a "pair of nostrils"—that is, working in parallel—and the Americans clearly wanted the two groups to cooperate, so Zhang accepted Cai's invitation to send a representative to Okinawa.[43]

Zhang's doubts about Cai grew after the Free China Movement lost one of Zhang's recruits, who was sent on a covert mission to Zhang's hometown near Shaoxing, Zhejiang Province, in April 1952. The agents were quickly captured by unfriendly villagers and turned over to authorities. Put on trial, Zhang's recruit, a man named Hua, was summarily executed, and the radio operator was imprisoned in Guangzhou. In an even more spectacular failure, Cai dispatched thirty paratroopers, including some of Zhang's recruits, on a mission to Hainan Island, where they were promptly captured and executed.[44] Cai Wenzhi was getting money from Americans in return for sending young Chinese men to their graves, just as Mao Zedong said.

Despite his reservations about Cai, Zhang Fakui worked with his American contacts to develop a recruitment and training program for agents of subversion. He envisioned sending promising young mainland refugees in Hong Kong for advanced training to form an elite commando force that would be useful in a future invasion of mainland China or as US-allied Chinese diaspora units deployable across Southeast Asia. His American handlers offered USD 100 per month to trainees.[45] About eighty young men were sent off after passing counterespionage examinations. As the program continued, Zhang grew increasingly hostile to Cai, who seemed to be misleading the Americans into thinking that clandestine work was underway throughout Guangdong Province, on which basis the Americans naïvely planned to infiltrate agents, armed with wireless radio sets to gather intelligence.

One of the few covert operations Zhang directed was led by an eager group of young refugees willing to return to Guangdong Province to make counter-revolution in the name of the Third Force. The Americans gave funding at Zhang's request, and the team leader, Chen, trained his band of seventy men. The seas were stormy on the night of the first attempt at a landing and the American ship with weapons failed to show at the contact point in international waters, so Chen's men had to turn back. On the second attempt, the Hong Kong coast guard stopped the transport ship and detained the crew, once again foiling the operation before it could get off the ground. The Americans allowed Chen to sell the ship and use the proceeds.[46] While Cai's Free China Movement sent numerous teams into the mainland, Zhang Fakui and Carsun Chang's Fight League mounted only this one aborted paramilitary operation. Nothing was achieved. But at least no one died.

Tensions between Zhang Fakui and Cai Wenzhi eventually boiled over into a rupture. Zhang wanted Cai to dissolve the Free China Movement and place his men under the political leadership of the Fight League. Cai refused and tried to poach Fight League members like Zhang Guotao and Gu Mengyu. The Americans continued to fund both Cai's militia in Okinawa and Zhang's "cultural movement" in Hong Kong. When Cai detained a group of Zhang loyalists in Okinawa and put them under surveillance, the Americans interceded at Zhang's request and secured their safe passage back to Hong Kong. Gu Mengyu relocated to Japan in March 1952, around the time of Carsun Chang's visit to Hong Kong, and Zhang hoped he would found a Fight League branch there, but nothing came of it.[47] Carsun Chang hoped the League would establish a Third Force headquarters in the United States, where he officially registered the organization. But Zhang and the others rejected that idea.[48]

The Primary Mission

Monitoring all this activity, Sherman Kent's analysts at the ONE were not terribly impressed. Reporting Carsun Chang's arrival in the US on a quest for recognition, they commented, "There is no cohesive group of ex-Nationalist figures of sufficient stature to qualify as a 'third force.'"[49] The most prominent ex-CCP figure, Zhang Guotao, stopped participating in the Fight League. Third Force unity was unraveling. By one estimate, there were about five thousand core members and fifteen thousand more adherents of the Third Force in Hong Kong, but they remained dispersed across a cacophony of almost one hundred "small groups."[50] Neither the generals nor the philosophers nor the politicians could bring them together as one.

Beijing's analysts and spies were also paying close attention to Third Force activities in Hong Kong, along with American involvement and British ambivalence. A detailed report to Communist Party officials, "Developments of Bandit Chiang and Imperialist Special Agents in Hong Kong," appeared in the CCP's *Internal Reference* bulletin on March 27, 1951. The report mined open-source accounts of the "so-called Third Force" in Hong Kong's anti-Communist newspapers, separating them into two major groups—those with Anglo-American backing and those backed by Chiang Kai-shek.

In the CCP's eyes, the Americans were considered the most active, running three parallel intelligence operations. The State Department focused on collecting PRC materials for research and analysis via the consulate and the US Information Service, while disseminating propaganda through Voice of America broadcasting, newspapers, documentary film, and writers' groups. The Defense Department sought to organize the Third Force as a military organization, with help from the FBI so as to ensure no spies crept into the organization. Finally, Far East Command intelligence out of Tokyo collected military intelligence and carried out coastal military operations. As for the British networks, these focused on political and military intelligence and counterespionage. The Hong Kong colonial government also used undercover agents to suppress progressive figures with communist sympathies. The report claimed there was an intelligence-sharing group composed of British, American, Taiwanese, Philippine, Burmese, and Indonesian representatives.[51]

"Developments in Hong Kong" failed to appreciate the tension between Chiang Kai-shek and the Third Force or the awkwardness of the American role in supporting both. The report also mistook Zhang Fakui for an agent of the Nationalists, exaggerating the seamless organization of spying and subversion by Taipei and Washington: "The bandit Chiang's espionage units in Hong Kong include 'Third Force' like Zhang Fakui etc. directly under American imperialist control."[52] Party cadre readers were warned that Zhang Fakui was getting aid from the Americans to build up a guerrilla force along the Guangdong–Kowloon road called the Anti-Communist National Salvation Army—a counterpart to the NSAs targeting Yunnan and Fujian. Zhang's National Salvation Army was reported to have a dozen detachments and large monthly budget. Li Zongren was reported to have a smaller militia of two hundred men, bankrolled with USD 6,000 monthly. Many key figures in the Fight League were mentioned, as were ties to mobsters like Yuan Jiu, who was helping the British defend Lantau Island.[53]

Beijing monitored the Third Force in Hong Kong but largely left them alone. Owen Lattimore offered a cynical explanation of Mao's strategy: "The 'splinter groups' of liberal exiles in Hong Kong will have a limited and specialized importance. They took refuge in Hong Kong because they opposed Chiang Kai-shek but did not have the power to oppose him actively. They are therefore unable to make power bargains with the Communists. They will be primarily symbols of the fact that the Communists are not using their own power to exterminate political liberals and the educated middle classes."[54]

As Zhang Fakui tried to unify Third Force leadership in Hong Kong, Cai Wenzhi trained Third Force Jedburghs in Okinawa, and Carsun Chang promoted the Third Force cause internationally, Beetle Smith gathered his senior staff one Monday morning in late October 1952 for a stern lecture on mission drift at the CIA. The operations tail was wagging the intelligence dog. Covert ops—monkey business fueled by Lawrence of Arabia delusions—was getting out of hand. Mentioning "some difficulties in various parts of the world," Beetle warned against "the use of improperly trained or inferior personnel." He wanted fewer operations so that "it could do well rather than to attempt to cover a broad field with poor performance." Sounding like a schoolmarm, the irritable director "reminded the meeting that the Agency's primary mission was intelligence."[55]

Beetle had been waging bureaucratic warfare to protect the CIA's "primary mission" since the day he took over the Agency two years earlier, trying to prevent it from becoming a "covert War Department." In early 1951, he proposed a budgetary distinction between covert actions with or without intelligence value, with the latter to be paid for and justified by State and Defense. It got nowhere. In a progress report from April 1952, Beetle reminded the National Security Council that covert ops were not "essential" to the Agency's intelligence responsibilities and "will inevitably militate against the performance by Central Intelligence Agency of its primary intelligence functions."[56] In the fall of 1952, he suggested tasking a murder board with the job of slashing one-third of the OPC's projects. New OPC missions could move forward only after being scrutinized by an internal CIA committee, submitted to the OPC chief, approved by the director, and finally, reviewed and approved by the Psychological Strategy Board.[57] Extra layers of approval might translate into fewer adventures in cloak-and-dagger intrigue.

A few weeks after Director Smith chided his deputies about the need to focus on the "primary mission," President Harry Truman gave a valedictory speech to staff working at the Agency that had been created by the stroke of his pen. Held as a lunch event in the Department of Agriculture auditorium on November 21, 1952, Truman began his remarks to the men and women of the CIA in the audience on an expansive note, reflecting on the awesome power residing in the hands of the president of the United States of America—the kind of power that gave realist thinkers pause. As president of the world's most powerful nation, the plainspoken man from Missouri had ordered the incineration of two Japanese cities with atomic bombs, initiated political warfare in Europe and covert action around the world, and sent hundreds of thousands of young men to the battlefield in Korea, risking the start of World War III. Truman left office intensely aware of American imperial power. "Genghis Khan, Augustus Caesar, great Napoleon Bonaparte, or Louis Fourteenth—or any other of the great leaders and executives of the world—can't even compare with what the President of the United States himself is responsible for, when he makes a decision. It is an Office that is without parallel in the history of the world," he told the nation's top spies and analysts.

Truman was not intoxicated by the power of the office he was leaving. A Niebuhrian anxiety lurked beneath his sense of awe. Presidential decision making involved inordinate complexity. One wrong decision could usher in catastrophe, returning the world to war. Echoing Beetle Smith, Harry Truman reminded the CIA of their primary mission, their sacred duty to keep the president informed so that the nation could avoid catastrophe: "It is our duty, under Heaven, to continue that leadership in the manner that will prevent a third world war—which would mean the end of civilization. . . . You are the organization, you are the intelligence arm that keeps the Executive informed so he can make decisions that always will be in the public interest for his own country, hoping always that it will save the free world from involvement with the totalitarian countries in an all-out war—a terrible thing to contemplate."[58]

9

MANCHURIAN MANHUNT

Among the Third Force foot soldiers recruited from Hong Kong's refugee population were eight Nationalist Army veterans who originally hailed from Manchuria: Li Junying, Luan Hengshan, Man Zhihui, Wang Donghua, Wang Jinsheng, Xu Guangzhi, Yu Guanzhou, and Zhang Zaiwen. They were flown out of Hong Kong by CAT with the cover story of being construction workers employed by Far East Industries (a CIA front organization) for a job on the island of Guam. In reality, they were bound for a top-secret $28 million CIA facility with the nondescript name "Naval Technical Training Unit," located on the Pacific island of Saipan, one of a number of secret training sites where aspiring agents of subversion could master the arts of making counterrevolution in mainland China.[1]

Archipelago of Subversion

The remote island of Saipan was a vital piece in what the historian Daniel Immerwahr calls America's hidden empire across the Pacific Ocean.[2] In modern times, Saipan had passed from the imperial clutch of Hapsburg Spain to Wilhelmine Germany to Showa Japan, only to be seized by the US military after a gruesome battle against Japanese defenders in July 1944. Saipan took on strategic significance as the launchpad for US B-29 bombers to strike cities on the main islands of Japan. After WWII, the United States held on to its new Pacific acquisitions, and in April 1947—a month after the Truman Doctrine speech to Congress—the United Nations Security Council designated Saipan and other former Japanese possessions as a "strategic area" to be administered by the US government as the Trust Territory of the Pacific Islands. The trust was put to good use by the Pentagon and the Agency. In addition to the CIA training camp on Saipan, Guam hosted an airfield and submarine base, Kwajalein Atoll was used as target practice for missile tests, and the Pacific Proving Grounds were subjected to repeated atomic weapons testing. Elugelab Island was vaporized by Operation Ivy's Mike shot on November 1, 1952, in the first test of a hydrogen device, which was seven hundred times more destructive than the bomb dropped on Hiroshima.[3]

The CAT pilot Felix Smith flew Chinese recruits in and out of Saipan and left a vivid account of arriving for the first time at the redoubt via Andersen Air Base in Guam.

> We flew north, over a hundred miles of Micronesia's coral reefs and islands and ocean, and when we sighted Saipan, Gilbert said, "Ignore the main runway. I'll point out the strip." We reached their camp via a narrow road covered with migrating snails that popped when we ran over them. We crewmen were given separate rooms in a corrugated-metal Quonset hut on a beach. . . . The customers [CIA officers], some with their wives, lived in larger Quonset huts. A central building, decorated with shells, was a dining room and bar where we found casualness and camaraderie. . . . Guerrillas of a few other free nations in training had their own ethnic mess halls, which the customers enjoyed sampling.[4]

According to Zhang Fakui, the CIA camp on Saipan hosted two classes of Third Force trainees—127 in the first group and 182 in the second—guided by twenty instructors with the help of eight interpreters.[5] The historian Roger Jeans determined that most of the trainees in Saipan were bound for missions in Manchuria, while others went through a facility on the Japanese island of Okinawa (then under US military administration).[6] The Saipan training program was modeled loosely on what CIA trainees went through back at The Farm in Virginia. In addition to ideological instruction on the falsehoods of Marxism, recruits focused on paramilitary skills: parachuting, communications, explosives, firearms, and guerrilla tactics. The pilot Felix Smith recalled, "They taught techniques of blowing up all kinds of structures, escape and evasion, the Morse code, the vagaries of small radio transmitters. Gold bars to be used for bartering or bribes were inscribed with the logo of whatever mint existed in the area."[7] A high-ranking Nationalist propaganda official arrived in Saipan from Hong Kong in 1951 to run the political education program.[8]

Naturally, the CIA endeavored to keep its facilities shrouded in mystery, which in the case of Saipan involved elaborate schemes to prevent trust territory administrative officials from seeing anything during their occasional inspection visits to the island.[9] The Agency had a close call in the late summer of 1951 when an Associated Press reporter and photographer, working on a story about Interior Department work on the island, began snooping around. "They are known to have inquired from natives about the Interior Department camp," Beetle Smith was informed. But the cover held. "However, they have neither visited nor requested permission to visit CIA's Saipan paramilitary training camp."[10] A couple of months later, a percipient attorney at the Interior Department began an inquiry into Far East Industries, which he alleged, quite accurately, was "training Chinese guerrilla warfare personnel for future use against the Communist regime in China."[11] The Interior's local administrator on Saipan, who knew the true nature of company, was put in the awkward position of being interrogated by a government lawyer who was not in the know. The Agency had to make a call to the top of the Interior Department.

If exposure was a public relations liability, infiltration was a mortal danger, and the CIA struggled to maintain operational security at the Saipan camp. One American staff member in charge of communications had to be brought back to Washington "for breaches of security and publicized marital difficulties."[12] Zhang Fakui was convinced there was a Communist plant in the second cohort of recruits, and his warnings reached CIA headquarters in early September 1951. General Zhang took his own counterespionage measures, keeping the CIA apprised: "Chang [Zhang Fakui] does not know the suspect's name but knows him to have been recruited by Wu Shao Ming who saw him depart from Tokyo Airport. Chang believes the suspect was sent from the Ta Hwa Watch Company 794 Nathan Road, Kowloon. Chang has requested his deputy at Saipan to investigate, and his deputy in Hong Kong to arrange for an investigation of Wu Shao Ming."[13] Felix Smith recalled on one flight a Chinese agent was pushed out of the plane (in a real-life version of the scene in the OSS-inspired 1947 film *13 Rue Madeleine*). "I supposed our customers had discovered a double agent," he concluded.[14]

CAT security protocols mandated blindfolds on passengers and forbade inflight conversation. It was feared that both Communist double agents and Nationalist moles were trying to infiltrate the Saipan operation. Adding a final layer of intrigue, CAT's CIA liaison had to ensure that the airline's boss, Claire Chennault, was kept in the dark about any operation involving the Third Force, lest he pass information on to his friend Chiang Kai-shek. According to Felix Smith, "Worrying over Chennault's loyalty to the CHINATS, customer headquarters invented reasons for him to be in Washington during a Third Force operation."[15] The dual risks of infiltration and exposure converged in November 1951, when the family of a suspected Nationalist agent working at the camp barbershop caused a ruckus. "His family in Hong Kong is concerned about his whereabouts and has demanded a letter from him. If this is not forthcoming, the family threatens legal action through the Hong Kong police to ascertain his whereabouts or otherwise investigate with a resultant threat to the security of the Saipan base."[16]

Jack Downey visited the Saipan camp in the spring of 1952 and selected eight men from Manchuria to head back with him to CIA regional headquarters in Atsugi, Japan, where three more members joined the team—Niu Songlin, Wang Weifan, and Zhong Dianxin.[17] Atsugi naval airfield was one of the busiest in the world, which provided useful cover for the activities of the Joint Technical Advisory Group (JTAG), as the CIA base set up by Hans Tofte was formally known. JTAG-Atsugi was the hub for North Asia operations, the center of a web connecting frontline stations in Seoul and Pusan, supply depots and training facilities on Okinawa, refugee recruitment operations in Hong Kong, myriad endeavors of Western Enterprises on Taiwan, and the training camp on Saipan.[18] A small facility at Chigasaki—part of the Atsugi complex—assisted in training hundreds of Third Force agents in guerrilla tactics and communications.[19] Jack Downey, who had arrived in Japan in 1951 after summer training, was a member of the cadre of American officers who oversaw their training and deployment.[20]

The program of recruiting Third Force agents in Hong Kong for training in Saipan and infiltration into Manchuria was code-named Operation Merlin. It was funded out of a $10 million advance on $50 million apportioned for an array of covert operations in the China theater, including Operation Octopus in Taiwan.[21] In addition, the Hong Kong station hoped to raise a huge fund thanks to the defection of a former Chiang loyalist, General Mao Bangchu, who had been in charge of Nationalist air force procurement in Washington. As reported to Beetle Smith, "OPC Hong Kong suggests that if HTMERLIN has reached the overt stage at this time, it appears probable that General Mow would rally to the flag, bringing the 19,000,000 bucks with him."[22] General Mao (known in the American press known as P. T. Mow) had recently been accused by a Nationalist government spokesman of embezzling $19 million, triggering a diplomatic incident and feeding the partisan fight over who was to blame for the loss of China. Liberal China Hands defended General Mao as a victim of Chiang's corruption, while conservative China lobby voices defended Chiang. Mao's executive assistant, Colonel Hsiang Wei-hsian, had been working with a congressional investigation since late 1950 to expose the corrupt practices of Nationalist military contracting, and he fed information to *Washington Post* reporter Alfred Friendly, whose four-part series on the case was entered into the *Congressional Record* in September 1951.[23] Fearing extradition to Taiwan, Mao fled across the border in January 1952 to Mexico, where he would fight legal battles from a luxury prison cell. Rumors circulated for years that Mao ran off with Third Force funding; despite the hopes of the OPC Hong Kong, there is no evidence that General Mao ever shared his $19 million with the CIA.[24]

Into Manchuria

Approval to violate PRC airspace for covert paramilitary operations came in early September 1951, when Agency leadership was informed that "State Dept. has authorized flights over the Chinese mainland by CAT aircraft when they are supplying guerrilla units."[25] Isolated airborne operations ensued: a lone OSO agent was dropped into Henan Province; an agent was flown over Shenyang but refused to jump.[26] In October 1951, agent teams were dropped in the far northeast corner of North Korea with a mission to hike into China for espionage and conduct search and rescue of downed pilots.[27]

Logistical planning moved ahead on aerial infiltration of counterrevolutionary teams into Manchuria. CAT would be doing the flying under the code name Operation Tropic. In March 1952, the CAT director of operations Joe Rosbert flew to Tokyo to finalize plans. He confessed to his diary, in a passage found by the historian William Leary, that he shared his boss Chennault's objections to supporting the Third Force: "We'll never learn that you can't win the faith of a people by stupidly dividing the house. Why not get the third force elements into the 1st force? Because we were divided before, the 2nd force (communism) has all the Mainland. I'm really burned on this type of thinking. . . . I'm disgusted with the so-called thinkers in Wash. who work out these utterly stupid plans."[28]

A Third Force Jedburgh team landed somewhere in south China in April 1952 in what was perhaps the earliest parachute drop, but no contact was ever established with the four-man unit.[29] A retired CAT pilot, E. C. Kirkpatrick, interviewed by Leary in 1980, recalled making four or five drops, "mainly in eastern Manchuria," starting that spring.[30]

Manchurian skies were familiar territory for CAT, which had supplied isolated Nationalist forces in Shenyang during the Chinese Civil War. Now with the Korean War at its height, PRC security in the northeast was on the lookout for American planes. According to Jilin Province records, a US military aircraft that crossed into Tonghua County on June 26, 1952, was shot down by air defense; the crew bailed and was captured alive by local people's militia.[31] Three weeks later, an unmarked plane was reported crossing the border and then heading south. Spotters had presumably seen the CAT C-47 that flew into Manchuria on the night of July 14, 1952, dropping a five-man group known as Team Wen, consisting of Man Zhihui, Niu Songlin, Xu Guangzhi, and Yu Guanzhou, and led by Wen Shijie (alias for Zhang Zaiwen). Recruited in Hong Kong, trained on Saipan, and deployed out of Atsugi, they leapt from the cargo hold over the wilds of Laoling Mountain on the Jilin Province side of the border with North Korea. As the CIA's in-house study *Missing in Action* (1974) explained, their mission, code-named ST/AROMA, combined intelligence and subversion: "collect operational intelligence and, also, determine the extent of, and organize, resistance activity."[32]

Team Wen relied on survival skills and supplies from their initial drop to endure the first few weeks of midsummer on Laoling Mountain. By early August, they were sending urgent radio messages to Japan requesting resupply. "Desperate/men sick/hungry. Please coordinate supply drop in next 2 days. Advise airplane type, number of drops, and drop time." Hearing no reply, Team Wen sent a shopping list of needed supplies: corn, noodles, dried fish, egg power, sugar, salt, sugar, oil, wine, raingear, gloves, cigarettes, aspirin, lighters, maps, military caps, emergency kits, a transistor and handheld radio, ink, RMB 50 million, a calendar, soy sauce, vinegar, milk powder, coffee.[33] Their fate depended on the fickle gods of long-distance wireless radio transmission, in a purgatory of waiting for the generator, tapping out a message (at about a dozen words per minute), and switching over to listen in intervals for acknowledgement.[34] Time spent listening for the faint, high-pitched reply was limited by the power of one's battery and the risk of enemy direction-finding devices. This "thin vulnerable link," as one Korean War operative put it, was all Team Wen had as a lifeline.[35]

Team Wen eventually received a response from headquarters. "Rations and medicine requested will arrive between 2400 and 0100 hours on August 14, 15 or 16; request you signal safety for landing with triangle fire signal." Two days later, the team picked up a follow-on message: "Using same plane. 'Bu' is package number one. Two packages of supplies. 'Bu' will carry a letter from me and from 'X.' Stay strong, endure the hardship to enjoy the sweetness." Bu was the code name for a sixth agent, Li Junying. But two days later, Team Wen was informed by their control at HQ, named Chen Wen, that liaison Li—referred to by his numerical code name 5774—would not be coming after all—not yet, anyway.

On August 14, a month after their original landing, Team Wen's resupply drop arrived.[36] Jack Downey was on board the flight, based on what he called "a certain unofficial authorization." According to the CIA study: "His immediate superior in the field, [redacted] had complained that he had only one jumpmaster for the mission. Downey's offer to fly the mission was accepted with the admonition, 'If you are caught by our bosses, you have got to say that it was unauthorized. You just wanted to go along for the ride for fun and games.'"[37] The CAT plane with Downey on board swooped overhead as planned at half-past midnight, disgorging two crates stuffed with essentials: a transmitter-receiver, weapons, rations, medicine, gold bars. Team Wen also found a crudely written note of encouragement from Chen Wen and a more poetic one from Cai Wenzhi.[38]

The resupply afforded Team Wen a new lease on life, but within a couple of weeks they had eaten through their supplies once again. Gold and cash would be of little use once the harsh Manchurian winter hit. Making contact with locals risked exposure to the PRC's public security apparatus, designed to mobilize the masses for surveillance. And what about the mission? If the team remained hidden away in the wilds of Laoling Mountain, how could they incite counterrevolution?

Hunger encouraged risk taking. One day, an elderly Korean-Chinese man out foraging for mushrooms encountered a member of Team Wen, who asked to buy food from him. The forager refused, so later the team member took rice from the man's storage place and left money as payment. The elderly man promptly filed a report with the local Public Security Office in Helong County.[39]

As Team Wen coped with surviving in the Laoling wilderness, a second band of Third Force Jedburghs landed in Jilin Province sometime in September 1952. Known as Team Shen, after its leader Shen Hengnian (alias for Luan Hengshan), Wang Donghua, Wang Jinsheng, Wang Weifan, and Zhong Dianxin jumped from a B-17 transport in the Longwan area of Jingyu County.[40] Meanwhile, an unmarked C-47 returned to Laoling Mountain to resupply Team Wen on the night of September 20, dropping rations, winter clothing, and renminbi cash. This time, the CAT plane also dropped Bu, the liaison agent Li Junying.

Li Junying was originally from the city of Liaoyang, south of Shenyang. He was older than many of the other agents, at forty-four years of age, and had served as battalion and deputy regimental commander in the National Army before fleeing to Hong Kong during the Civil War. Li's assignment was to check in with Team Wen, reconnoiter with Team Shen, coordinate efforts between the two groups, and report back to headquarters as soon as possible. After landing safely and inspecting Team Wen's progress, Li headed off to find Team Shen's base camp.[41]

Seeing like a Party-State

Covert operations require the kind of mastery of detail in which even death must be disguised to perfection. The classic example was a WWII caper known as Operation Mincemeat and described by Ewen Montagu in the book *The Man Who Never Was* (1953). British intelligence placed a uniformed corpse floating off the Spanish coast, gambling that his briefcase of (fake) secret plans for an Allied invasion of Greece would be turned over to German intelligence and distract Nazi High Command from the actual Allied plan to land in Sicily.[42] Everything about the man who never was had to be convincing, down to the degree of decomposition of his skin, and the ruse succeeded. But the deceased British agent was luckier than many living ones, like the operative captured behind enemy lines because the arch supports in his shoes were too new. The OSS agent Donald Downes explained: "Our British allies had warned us early in the game of the great danger which lay in overlooking details in preparing a mission to enter enemy territory. Among the most serious and dangerous of these details were the equipment, clothes, baggage, tobacco, everything carried along by a mission."[43]

The fateful detail in the unfortunate case of Li Junying had to do with paperwork. Even though he was traveling in a frontier wilderness, Li was surprised at the number of checkpoints as he made his way toward Team Shen. Chairman Mao's minister of public security, Luo Ruiqing, had been working hard to create a nationwide surveillance infrastructure. The northwest region, in fact, was singled out for praise at the 1952 security conference as a model for the rest of the country. Liaison Li was putting it to the test.

Li carried a Shanghai municipal government ID and a Shenyang city government passport, but two female officers checking his papers at a wildfire control point in Erdaobaihe, Antu County, asked for his mountain travel permit. According to regulations, anyone traveling in wilderness areas had to carry a Public Security Bureau–issued mountain passage permit. Li was told to register at the forestry office, where the manager, finding Li suspicious, offered to introduce him to the Public Security Bureau officers for the Sixth Ward, which had jurisdiction over the area. The PSB office head Jin Zhongzhe discovered another missing detail in the paperwork: Li had no letter of introduction explaining that he was traveling on official business, which should have accompanied his work identification papers. Li's behavior was raising red flags as well. Jin Zhongzhe feigned wanting to help Li by offering him a ride the following morning to the county-level PSB office, where he could apply for a mountain travel permit.[44]

Li Junying's difficulties dissembling his way through bureaucratic surveillance in the remote parts of Jilin Province testified to the success of the PRC in terms of what political scientist James Scott calls "seeing like a state"—the attempt to register, monitor, and organize a population by the state apparatus in its quest to increase the "legibility" of society.[45] Ironically, Communist Party propaganda had once criticized the Nationalist government's system of identity cards as fascist. But now that Chairman Mao was in command, he wanted as much information as possible about the masses. The PRC government introduced a residency card system and the police ran an all-purpose household registration system.[46] But legibility was painstaking work. Mao's surveillance and security apparatus remained a work-in-progress in 1952—the household registration system had spread through cities only a year prior and would not be extended into rural areas until 1955.[47]

As bureaucratic systems of registration and surveillance gradually came into place, the party supplemented formal administrative legibility with guerrilla methods of mutual surveillance and self-criticism. As the historian Frederic

Wakeman pointed out, the key feature of the CCP public security regime was its success in mobilizing citizens to monitor one another.[48] The China Hand Doak Barnett watched the formation of the culture and structures of mutual surveillance from his observation post in Hong Kong, where he conducted exit interviews with refugees from the mainland. Barnett was trying to work out how public order was maintained at the village level. He identified multiple layers of surveillance and, as necessary, repression. His report "Social Controls" (April 1953) identified peasant associations, village militia units, public security bureaus, village public security committees, and Committees on People's Supervision, all working to keep an eye on the masses. "They have constructed an organizational apparatus that reaches deep into the grass-roots levels of the country and into the privacy of people's lives," Barnett concluded.[49] As an added layer of surveillance, there was the Maoist practice of self-criticism. Written self-criticisms submitted to party officials in effect mobilized individuals to create their own dossiers, while group criticism sessions could function like organized neighborhood snooping.

Operation Merlin was stress testing the culture of mutual surveillance and organizational apparatus of public security in Manchuria. The system may have failed the first test by allowing unmarked enemy planes to fly across the border and drop agents of subversion within PRC territory, but once Li Junying tried to move from one isolated hideout to another, he was caught like a fly on a spiderweb.

It did not take long for the fly to give in. Waking up at the Sixth Ward on September 27, Li Junying asked to meet the head of public security. Jin took him to the office of his supervisor, Lian Chenglian. Standing at attention, Li blurted out: "I am a special agent sent by the American CIA; I want to surrender to the people's government and ask the nation to handle me mercifully."[50] The game was up.

Sixth Ward officials transported Li to the public security office in the county seat, where the county party secretary Han Jincai and PSB deputy head Qian Longjiu spent the night interrogating the detainee. Li revealed what he knew about the July, August, and September drops, including Team Wen's mission, agent names, duties, and current location. Yanbian Prefecture public security head Yao Ting hurried to Antu County to interrogate Li in person. Yao sent a report to his superiors at provincial headquarters and had Li transferred to the provincial capital. The Jilin Province public security chief sent his deputy to Shenyang to make a report to the Northeast Region head of the Political Protection Bureau (also known as the First Bureau), responsible for counterintelligence and anti-subversion. Northeast public security bureau chief Wang Jinxiang called an emergency meeting and organized a team to sweep the Laoling mountains for special agents. Jilin Province deputies for public security (Wang

Jieren) and political protection (Lu Tian) were put in charge of the dragnet, and Li Junying was transferred to custody at regional headquarters in Shenyang.[51]

Within a week of Li's confession, Team Shen seems to have been rolled up, although details are sparse. Chinese accounts are silent about their capture, and the CIA histories have nothing to add. There is a fragmentary record in the *Jilin Province Annals*: "October 4: A joint search operation by the Public Security Bureau and People's Militia in Jingyu, Huinan, Linjiang, Liuhe, Tonghua, Changbai for agents dropped by a US-Chiang Kai-shek plane over Jingyu County, Longquan Township led to the capture of five agents led by Shen Hengnian, along with their firearms, radios and supplies."[52]

Team Wen proved to be a harder target than Team Shen for the public security dragnet, and extant sources provide more—if slightly divergent—details. According to a local history, Antu County mobilized five hundred soldiers and forty public security officers and police beginning on October 1 for a manhunt organized out of Sandao Gully Village and led by the prefectural public security head, Yao Ting. The Jilin Province public security deputy chief Wang Jieren took over after five days of fruitless searching and mobilized three thousand local soldiers and militia for a thorough sweep of Laoling. The search party found traces of campsites and then (on October 10) discovered a hidden supply depot. Spotted as they headed toward their hideout five days later, the agents of subversion fled after being fired on, but the pursuit was delayed by rain and snow until October 18.[53]

According to the oral history version made available by the Jilin Public Security Bureau, the underground cache—complete with carpentry and fishing tools, food canisters, year-round clothing in farmer, worker, student, and PLA styles, small arms, fake residence papers, and cash—was discovered on October 13, and villagers in the search party had to redirect their energies toward a major tree-cutting operation, which may have tipped off the agents to the location of the manhunt.[54] Both accounts, the local history and the public security history, agree that for the next ten days, the dragnet made no progress.

The public security search party had one very useful bit of information: Li Junying told his interrogators where he was supposed to rejoin Team Wen on October 30. The search party staked out the meeting point a couple of days in advance. Hunger flushed out one of the agents, who was apprehended as he approached a fisherman begging for food. It turned out to be Zhang Zaiwen, aka Wen Shijie—head of Team Wen, a twenty-eight-year-old native of Jiutai County, Jilin Province. Zhang was a former company and deputy battalion commander in the National Army who ended up in Hong Kong at the end of the Civil War.[55]

A second team member was shot dead as he ran away after spotting a soldier in the search party. On his corpse was found a revolver, a knife, a compass, a wad of cash, and two bars of gold. Zhang Zaiwen confirmed that the body was that of Man Zhihui, aka Ke Jing, a twenty-six-year-old former Nationalist officer from Andong on the China–North Korea border who had signed up for Third Force covert action in Hong Kong.[56]

The interrogation of Zhang Zaiwen yielded more clues to help in locating the three remaining special agents. On November 4, a sixty-man squad came upon three unidentified men in the wilderness—one was captured alive in his shelter and the other two, who had been tending a fire, escaped after a firefight. The captive was Niu Songlin, alias Chen Chongpei. Originally from Zhuanghe County in neighboring Liaoning Province, Niu was the old man in the unit at forty-seven. He served as the radio operator, using his training as a communications officer in the National Army. Niu confessed that the team had been preparing for a supply drop due to arrive at 1:30 a.m. His captors quickly performed so-called political work on the captive, explaining that the party and government would be lenient if—for the sake of the nation and the people—Niu maintained normal radio contact with headquarters in Japan.

Niu agreed, becoming a double agent on the spot as he radioed confirmation of plans for the resupply drop after midnight. The signal fire was prepared as instructed and the unmarked CAT plane dropped eight large packages of supplies. As far as HQ knew, Team Wen was successfully resupplied.[57] (According to CIA records, Team Wen received a resupply drop sometime in October.)[58] In reality, the radio operator had been turned, the team leader captured, one member was dead, and the last two agents in the unit were on the run.

Public Security put villages and towns west of Laoling on alert to look out for two fugitives. Within twenty-four hours, the village militia sentry Jin Shoulie stopped a suspicious young man who put up a fight. Sentry Jin overpowered the stranger, who turned out to be Zhang Zaiwen's second-in-command and fellow Jiutai County native Xu Guangzhi (alias Si Xueshen), a former company commander in the National Army.[59] Later that day, the farmer Liu Haiting was riding his oxcart home from the fields when, about two kilometers out from his village in the Third District, a stranger called to him asking for food and promising to pay in cash or gold. The stranger introduced himself as a soldier returning from Korea and trying to get to Fusong County. Farmer Liu was wary, having heard the warning of bandits in the area, and he stalled for time, telling the stranger he could stay the night and head out in morning. Just then, Liu's little brother Haichun came down the road wearing a people's militia uniform, making the stranger anxious. A scuffle broke out and the stranger pulled a gun on the Liu brothers, but was unable to get off a shot before they subdued him. The final member of Team Wen—Yu Guanzhou (aka Jiang Dazhi), from Kuandian County, Liaoning Province—was now captured.[60]

The Public Security Bureau's countersubversion operation had lasted over a month, mobilized thousands of locals, and absorbed the attention of provincial and regional public security authorities.[61] The efforts ended in success: all five agents of subversion in Team Wen had been captured or killed, and their guns, gold, and counterrevolutionary paraphernalia seized. Best of all, thanks to the cooperation of Niu Songlin the radio operator, the CIA had no idea anything was awry with their covert mission in the Manchurian wilderness.

CIA operations continued, targeting an "ocean of forest" along the Laoling, Jingyu, and Tianchi sectors of the Changbai mountain range—impenetrable mountains, sparsely populated, snow-covered much of the year, difficult even to hike through.[62] According to Chinese sources, there were other agents of subversion apart from the Third Force teams trying to infiltrate into Manchuria in late 1952, including Korean groups. Twenty commandos in a South Korean partisan unit, suspected of having CIA backing, entered the Baituoshan Tianchi area in October on a mission to set up an observation post, but were quickly discovered. In mid-November, signal fires and an unidentified aircraft were spotted west of Tianchi. A security dragnet caught an agent team two days later, capturing three men and killing a fourth. The captives, surnamed Kim and Li, confessed to being part of a grand plan to link up a resistance movement loyal to South Korean president Syngman Rhee. Eventually, fifteen men were caught, and one managed to escape across the border into North Korea.[63]

Another plot foiled earlier that autumn in Manchuria may have been a Nationalist operation based out of Taiwan. PRC sources record agents being captured after parachuting in much further west in Jilin Province, in Jiaohe County, in the first week of October.[64] According to the *Jilin Province Annals*, "Under the supervision of the provincial public security office, US-Chiang special agents Colonel Wen Jiachuan and Lieutenant Wang Tianxi were captured in Jiaohe County, along with a wireless radio, five rifles and revolvers, 476 explosives, 127 pieces of gold, and a large amount of dollars, yen and renminbi."[65] This may have been the same infiltration operation mentioned by James Lilley, who had been based on Taiwan since May. After an earlier aborted drop, Lilley's agents jumped on target in October. "They came up once on the radio, and then we never heard from them again. We guessed they assimilated into Chinese society or had been caught."[66] Lilley was careful to avoid leaving American fingerprints on the operations he directed, recruiting foreign pilots to fly into Manchuria.

The threat posed by subversive operations helped the CCP make the case in relentless propaganda railing against special agents sent by the American imperialists and the bandit Chiang. The covert missions also seemed to bear out Mao's quip that "the United States of America supplies the money and guns and

Chiang Kai-shek the men to fight for the United States and slaughter the Chinese people." According to CIA records viewed by Evan Thomas, of 212 Third Force agents of subversion air-dropped into China during the Korean War years, 111 were captured and 101 killed.[67] The PRC Ministry of Public Security offered a slightly different tally of the fate of CIA-backed paratrooper operations, including Third Force as well as Nationalist commandos, claiming that 124 special agents had been captured and 106 killed from 1951 to 1954.[68]

There is no evidence that the "martyrs," as Allen Dulles called them, who were sent into Red China actually succeeded in fomenting counterrevolution. Their presence was, however, a powerful argument in favor of enhanced surveillance and repression, which were eagerly organized by the CCP through the Campaign to Suppress Counterrevolutionaries. According to Jilin Province statistics, by the time the campaign concluded in December 1952, authorities had caught 7,751 counterrevolutionaries, of whom 1,678 were killed.[69]

"Anxious Autumn for America"

As unmarked CAT planes made monthly runs on behalf of the CIA into Chinese airspace, tossing Third Force Jedburghs into the Manchurian wilderness during the summer and fall of 1952, the war next door in Korea ground to a bloody stasis. Armistice talks between the US, China, and North Korea had been meandering along without much progress for a year when, on October 8, 1952, the Americans declared the negotiations indefinitely suspended. The sticking point was what to do about POWs. American negotiators insisted on voluntary repatriation, allowing each prisoner to decide which side he wanted to be released to. Beijing insisted that repatriation should be obligatory and automatic—in line with the recently signed Geneva Convention. When Beijing was tipped off by a mole that the United Nations Command was recruiting POWs to serve as agents after repatriation, it had the additional fear that spies were coming home along with soldiers.[70] Frustrated over the stalemate, the US suspended the talks amid a flurry of hopes that battlefield successes might generate leverage in resumed negotiations. In that spirit, General Mark Clark signed off on a plan for a "small victory" in taking a location along the DMZ called Triangle Hill, known to the Chinese as Shanggan Ridge.

The Battle of Triangle Hill became a defining moment of the Korean War for the Chinese People's Volunteers, who held out against punishing assaults by American and South Korean forces for over a month—at the same time when, across the border in Manchuria, the manhunt for Team Wen went into full gear.[71] The UN Command's Operation Showdown employed artillery barrages and infantry attacks designed to enable Clark's battalions to take two positions—Hill 598 and Sniper Ridge. Though tactically advantageous, the promontories had no strategic significance to the wider war effort for either side.

The Chinese dug in, turning the defense effort into a morale booster. US troops were dismayed at the enemy's capacity to absorb pain and death—some Americans thought they must be on drugs.[72] A month of offensives yielded nothing but casualties. Finally on November 18, South Korean units seized bits and pieces of Sniper Ridge, although the Chinese clung to Triangle Hill. A week later, the UNC called off the ill-fated offensive after suffering nine thousand casualties and inflicting an estimated nineteen thousand on the enemy. Even the official US Army history recognized Shangganling (immortalized in a 1956 PRC film by that name) as a morale victory for the Chinese. "At Triangle Hill they gained face as their tenacious defense reversed the offensive defeat at White Horse and forced the U.N. Command to break off the attack."[73]

While Chinese morale got a lift from Triangle Hill, public opinion in the US was further deflated, even by small victories like the American defense of White Horse Mountain. White Horse, too, was a strategically insignificant promontory that required significant casualties to hold on to. By the fall of 1952, the war was deeply unpopular, just as the Republican presidential candidate Dwight Eisenhower's campaign was hitting its stride. Stalled talks, battlefield stalemate, and public despondency reinforced Eisenhower's sense that what the US needed was an exit strategy.[74]

With election day barely a week away, Ike opened his campaign speech in Detroit, Michigan, with an appeal to the public's negative feelings about the war: "In this anxious autumn for America, one fact looms above all others in our people's mind. One tragedy challenges all men dedicated to the work of peace. One word shouts denial to those who foolishly pretend that ours is not a nation at war. This fact, this tragedy, this word is: Korea."[75] Eisenhower made it clear that his goal as president would be "an early and honorable end" to the war. As to *how* exactly that would be accomplished, he didn't say, except to promise, in MacArthur-esque fashion, "I shall go to Korea."

Another thing Ike promised on the campaign trail was to do more psywar. In Detroit he talked about the need to "shape our psychological warfare program into a weapon capable of cracking the Communist front."[76] At a campaign stop in San Francisco earlier that month, Eisenhower offered a sweeping vision of psychological warfare. "We wage a 'cold war' in order to escape the horror of its opposite—war itself," he explained. Eisenhower defined the essential nature of cold war as a "struggle for the minds and wills of humanity"—in a phrase, psychological warfare.[77] Having orchestrated total war as supreme commander of allied forces in Europe, having witnessed the wreckage of firebombed cities and the horror of concentration camps as military governor of occupied Germany, Eisenhower had acquired an ironic appreciation of the *limits* of power. In his own way, trained in the discipline of military affairs, Ike shared the sense of restraint advocated by the realists. He was determined to avoid atomic war, world war, or large-scale conventional war in Korea or anywhere else. But as commander-in-chief, as leader of the Free World, Eisenhower would need tools, weapons, to use in the fight against communism. Psywar was a way to fight the enemy without risking WWIII.

On his way out of the White House, Truman added a weapon in the future president's arsenal for covert foreign policy. With the blessing of Beetle Smith and his senior cabinet members, Truman secretly signed off on the creation a new instrument for surveillance, the National Security Agency (NSA), housed in the Defense Department, designed to do for communications intercepts and signals intelligence what the CIA did for all-around intelligence.[78]

Ike's "go to Korea" speech garnered national praise, giving him a boost heading into the final campaign stretch. It was the icing on the cake as he cruised to a landslide victory on November 4, 1952. Liberals like Arthur Schlesinger were crestfallen at the defeat of Adlai Stevenson, a "vital center" Democrat. But at CIA headquarters, the boys at the OPC were thrilled, having heard Eisenhower's message in San Francisco loud and clear. Joseph Smith was in the Far East Division and described the elation after Ike's victory: "On the morning of the election of Eisenhower one of the senior paramilitary officers home from the SEA Supply Company in Thailand ran through the offices shouting, 'Now we'll finish off the goddamned Commie bastards. We'll get rid of the fucking pinkos in the State Department and around this place too. They'll all be as dead as that little bald-headed son-of-a-bitch who said he thought he was going to cry last night when he had to concede to Ike.'"[79]

Part III

ROAD OF TRIALS

10

EXFILTRATION

President-elect Eisenhower wanted to get his campaign promise to go to Korea over with as soon as possible—before inauguration, in fact. It would be the first presidential trip to Asia since the final leg of Ulysses Grant's postpresidency world tour in 1879. But unlike former president Grant's port calls in China and Japan, which were accompanied by much pomp and circumstance, future president Eisenhower's voyage to Korea would be carried out in strict secrecy—a prelude to the countless covert operations of the Eisenhower era. In a curious case of synchronicity, as the presidential plane left in stealth for Korea, another airplane of Americans left Korea bound for Communist China.

Two Flights in November

Eisenhower's preparatory meetings ahead of the long trip to Korea included sessions with Truman's director of central intelligence, Beetle Smith. It was a reunion of brothers-in-arms: Smith had served as Ike's chief of staff in Europe during WWII. For their first meeting, Beetle and his assistant furtively boarded Ike's train from Washington to New York. Beetle later secretly visited Eisenhower for a second session on November 28 at the Commodore Hotel in Manhattan, spending an hour updating him on the situation in Korea.[1] Ike tasked Beetle with carrying out a comprehensive "reappraisal of 'cold war activities.'"[2] Meanwhile, the transition team put out a story that the president-elect needed a few quiet days working at his residence in New York City to decide his cabinet appointments.

Staff came and went from the building according to carefully coordinated schedules, with nothing to do once inside. The trip would not be announced to the public until Ike was safely on his way home.

A day after his session with Beetle—on Saturday, November 29, 1952—Eisenhower slipped out of the city, headed for Mitchell Field on Long Island, where he boarded a Constellation plane that would lumber halfway across the world, making stops in San Francisco, Honolulu, Midway, and Iwo Jima.[3] Improvements in long-distance air travel had dramatically shortened the time it took to reach the Far East, making Eisenhower's visit to Korea feasible in the first place. The great air-power afficionado Claire Chennault bragged that it took a mere fifty-one hours to fly the Great Circle course from Shanghai to Washington, as compared with the fourteen-day steamship passage across the Pacific he had made a decade earlier.[4] Still, Ike's flight was measured in days, not hours.

Eisenhower finally touched down at the airfield in Seoul on the evening of December 2 local time.[5] He met of course with the embattled South Korean leader Syngman Rhee, who was desperate to show off his ties to the US.[6] Like Chiang Kai-shek, Rhee cultivated the image of a revanchist, anti-Communist firebrand. Ike recalled dismissively that Rhee "of course, was for all-out, full-scale attack." Eisenhower had a very different theory of victory. As he explained in retrospect, "At this time—December 1952—it had been tacitly accepted by both sides, including all of the Allied governments providing troops for the war, that we were fighting defensively and would take no risks of turning the conflict into a global war, which many feared would occur should we undertake offensive operations on a scale sufficient to win a decisive victory."[7] After all, as he had put it in San Francisco, the point of cold war was to avoid its evil twin—world war.

Eisenhower spent more time with his former subordinate from WWII days, General Mark Clark, now commander-in-chief, Far East, who lobbied for an aggressive campaign, including attacks on Manchuria and bringing Nationalist troops from Taiwan to Korea.[8] Ike went up by light airplane for an aerial survey of the front and reviewed troops as a morale boost—and to improve public opinion back home.[9] He ate chow with the Fifteenth Infantry, whose First Battalion Ike once commanded as a lieutenant colonel. Eisenhower's son John was a major in the Fifteenth (he was luckier than Mao Anying, the son of Chairman Mao, who was killed serving in Korea in November 1950). The First Son's mates did not try to put a pretty face on things, Eisenhower recalled: "The men freely told me about their daily lives in that mountainous and exposed terrain and described the discomfort they suffered because of the cold and the difficulty of maintaining underground shelters in decent condition."[10] Eisenhower witnessed the value of a new weapon of war, the helicopter, which was used extensively in Korea's mountainous terrain to ferry reinforcements in and casualties out. Just prior to Ike's visit, evacuation choppers had saved the life of another unfortunate son—Second Lieutenant Allen Macy Dulles, the twenty-two-year-old son of CIA deputy director Allen Dulles, who was severely injured by mortar fire in Korea and rushed to Japan for treatment.[11]

At a predeparture press conference in Korea, Eisenhower used a careful formulation to define his objective as achieving "a positive and definite victory without possibly running the grave risk of enlarging the war."[12] There were no "tricks" or "panaceas"—no easy answers. He departed on the evening of December 5, flying for Guam to board the cruiser USS *Helena*. The first stop was Wake Island, where, on the eleventh anniversary of Pearl Harbor, Eisenhower was joined by his nominee for secretary of state, John Foster Dulles, and other close advisers. Steaming across the Pacific, the men worked out their plans for the new administration, starting with the question of how to bring an honorable end to the unpopular and unwinnable war in Korea. Their Korea strategy would be to increase military, political, and psychological pressure on the Communist bloc—the Soviets, Chinese, and North Koreans—in order to soften their negotiating positions on an agreement to end the fighting.

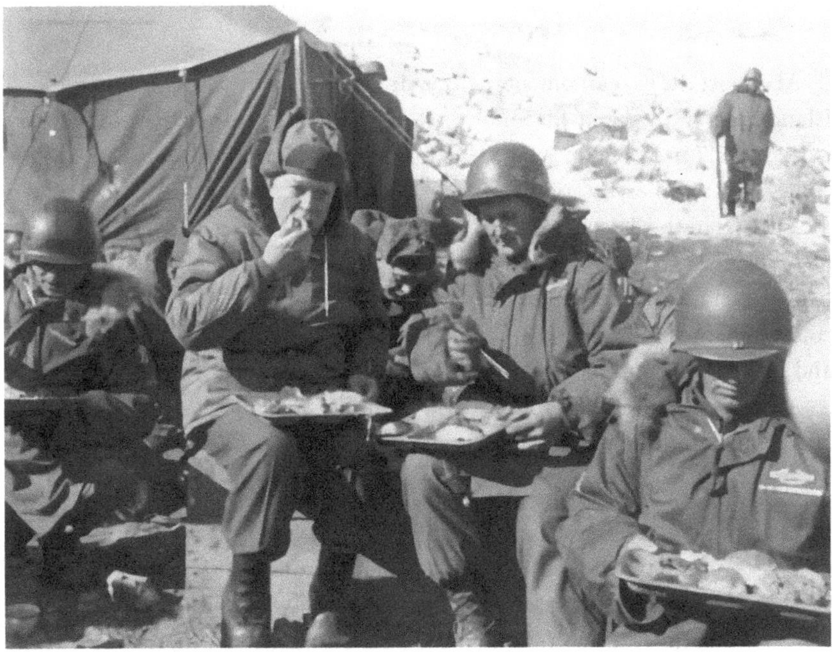

FIGURE 6. President-elect on the front line (1952). Photo by US Army Pictorial Agency.

FIGURE 7. The moment of capture: Downey and Fecteau (1952). People's Daily.

At almost the exact moment the US Air Force's Columbine II departed Long Island carrying Dwight Eisenhower to Korea, Jack Downey boarded an unmarked C-47 in Korea for what was supposed to be a round-trip flight to Manchuria. It was an exfiltration mission, planned in response to a wireless radio message from the liaison Li Junying requesting pickup. Downey was accompanied by another CIA officer, Richard George Fecteau, of Lynn, Massachusetts, two years his senior. Dick Fecteau had transferred from the US Merchant Marine Academy to Boston University, where he played guard on the football team and graduated in the class of 1951.

American and Chinese sources give slightly divergent details on the timing and content of the request. According to the CIA in-house study:

> On 11 November 1952, a radio message from the team leader, STAROMA/6, stated that he had returned safely from a trip to Linchiang and that he had been successful in obtaining official credentials and other needed operational documents. However he also reported that exfiltration routes through Korea were blocked and it would be impossible to carry the documents out through Hong Kong. The agent requested that he be exfiltrated by air, and that supplies be dropped to the rest of the team to carry them through the winter.[13]

The CIA staff historian Nicholas Dujmovic added the detail that the exfiltration request also mentioned having made positive contact with a "local dissident leader."[14] Don Gregg had dinner with Downey the night before the exfiltration and remembered it differently. Jack's mission was to "drop supplies to an agent team, recently parachuted into Manchuria, that had sent an SOS message that its supplies had been lost in the snow."[15]

According to the Jilin Province public security account, Team Wen's radio operator, Niu Songlin, posing as Li Junying, sent a message on November 20 requesting pickup by air on November 29 at Sandao Gully in order to report in person on developments, and he received confirmation from headquarters on November 26.[16] CIA records indicate that Atsugi station radioed on November 20 to confirm the pickup date nine days later.[17]

The decision to send an exfiltration mission was made at a moment of distraction for the CIA's senior leadership back in Washington, complicating the question of just how far up the chain of command knowledge of the impending operation might have gone. Director Beetle Smith was busy with the delicate dynamics of the Truman-Eisenhower transition; it was the first time the White House was passing from Democrats to Republicans in two decades. Smith submitted his letter of resignation as director of central intelligence on November 1, but was keeping Eisenhower up to speed on intelligence matters in the months leading up to the inauguration. Beetle was also preparing for his own transition to the State Department, where he would serve as number two under John Foster Dulles.[18] Even if Beetle had been aware of the exfiltration mission, and that it would be taking place as Eisenhower was en route to Korea, would he have deemed it significant enough to be included in their one-hour discussion at the Commodore Hotel? The answer remains locked in a vault of silence. When John Foster Dulles asked Smith how his session with the president-elect went, Smith curtly replied, "That's between him and me."[19]

Under normal circumstances, Beetle's deputy Allen Dulles would have been keen to involve himself in the details of an exciting field mission like the experimental exfiltration of Operation Aroma. But adding to the stress of preparing to assume Beetle's place as director, Allen learned in the second week of November about his son's life-threatening injury in Korea. He would be heading to Japan in December to be by his son's bedside. Next in line was Frank Wisner, deputy director of plans, who may have known of the operation, but his hands were full with the administrative nightmare of trying to fuse the OPC and the OSO into what was now called Clandestine Services.

As if all these distractions weren't enough, the Far East Division was in a period of turnover. Colonel Richard G. Stilwell had been replaced as division chief by Lloyd George, who was subsequently transferred to Japan to serve as deputy head of what, since the summer of 1952, was being called North Asia Command, in charge of coordinating intelligence and covert operations across a vast region.[20] George Aurell rotated from Tokyo back to Washington to take over as Far East Division head, assisted by his adventurous deputy, Desmond FitzGerald.[21]

The exfiltration of liaison Li Junying would not necessarily require specific approval from Washington, considering that it was part of an ongoing, approved operation. The OPC recognized the need for field flexibility—as Allen Dulles later wrote, "An intelligence officer in the field is supposed to keep his home office informed of what he is doing. That is quite true, but with some reservations, as he may overdo it. . . . Only a man on the spot can really pass judgment on the details as contrasted with the policy decisions, which, of course, belong to the boss at headquarters."[22]

Ultimate field responsibility for the mission lay with the North Asia Command senior representative in Japan, Vice Admiral Harvey E. Overesch.[23] Wisner would later insist that the CIA's North Asia Command informed their military counterparts at Far East Command of the exfiltration: "This operational flight was approved in writing by General MacArthur's Chief of Staff, Lt. General Doyle O. Hickey, on November 28, 1952. . . . This flight was one of a number of similar flights contemplated under an operation program which had likewise been accepted and approved by the Command at a somewhat earlier date, with full knowledge of its purpose and significance."[24] The CIA's in-house history confirmed that the North Asia Command senior representative "properly notified" and received clearance from FEC, citing approval from a different officer (General Jacob E. Smart of the US Far East Air Force).[25] Indeed, the project concept itself originated with Far East Command, going back to March 1951 when MacArthur's G-2, Charles Willoughby, proposed to "activate a Third Force in China."

In addition to the intelligence officials with North Asia Command and military officers at Far East Command, a certain number of CAT employees had to know about what they called Operation Tropic—after all, they would be flying the plane. The CAT office in Hong Kong was also in charge of ensuring that Chennault did not know about the Third Force activities. CAT employees would sometimes receive CIA mission briefings in a secure room in the Miramar Hotel—the OPC chief and CAT executive Al Cox would sit on the toilet and brief crew members perched along the rim of the tub.[26]

Although CAT had flown into the PRC on covert missions before, the November 29 mission would be the first pickup, and a technically daunting one at that. Two pilots assisted by a two-man crew would attempt an experimental on-the-fly method of picking up the passenger *without landing*. According to the aviation historian William Leary, the idea originated with a system of picking up mailbags in the open fields of Pennsylvania without landing. The plane would come in slow and low, dragging a hook that would catch a horizontal nylon wire mounted to a pair of thirty-foot-tall poles spaced sixty feet apart, to which the mailbag was attached. During WWII, the US Air Force began tweaking the system to see if they could replace the mailbag with a man wearing a harness wired for pickup, and the British tried picking up spies with it.[27] The USAF and the CIA continued adjusting the method, making some practice attempts in Japan.

If the idea sounds like something out of a Bond film, that's because it later became one. In the final scene of *Thunderball* (1965), Sean Connery's 007 delays an embrace with Domino in order to attach her to a harness as she looks on, quizzically. The next moment, they are whisked into the air using a modified version of the no-landing pickup known as the "skyhook system." Bond made it look easy, but there would be no brunette in a bikini involved in the mission to extract Li Junying, who was meant to be waiting for pickup in the bitter cold of a narrow valley on the China side of the North Korea border.

How Downey and Fecteau ended up on the plane remains something of a puzzle. Originally, four CAT personnel were slated to carry out the exfiltration: the pilots Norman Schwartz and Robert C. Snoddy, along with crew members Doc Lewis and James Stewart, who were based out of CAT's Tachikawa Airfield, near Atsugi. According to Al Cox, "At a very late stage in the planning, [redacted] notified CAT that it had been decided to withdraw Lewis and Stewart from the operation and replace them with two US Army (CIA) civilian employees, John T. Downey and Richard Fecteau; both were hurriedly trained in carrying out the duties involved in the rear of the aircraft for such an operation."[28] The CIA in-house account similarly redacts the name of the individual responsible for assigning Downey and Fecteau, explaining that he was "wary of the two CAT men not having the proper clearances."[29]

Published memoirs offer alternative explanations. The Atsugi-based CIA officer Joe Kiyonaga was the one who suggested sending Downey and Fecteau after the two CAT men called in sick, according to his widow.[30] The CAT pilot Felix Smith, who was with Snoddy and Schwartz in Tachikawa as they trained for the mission, claims that Al Cox made the decision to drop Doc Lewis. "That's the customer's job, not yours,' Cox said, and grumbled, 'that damn Third Force operation.'"[31] Cox himself later wrote that the two CAT employees Lewis and Stewart were "very good personal friends . . . but from a purely realistic Agency point of view, they offered much less of a security risk for the Agency than did Downey and Fecteau."[32]

Whoever was responsible for the substitution, it came late in the game, and Downey and Fecteau had to do a crash course in the logistics of the pickup. It was just the kind of rushed operation that Beetle warned his senior staff against a month earlier, when he complained about "the use of improperly trained or inferior personnel."[33] The substitution was also a dangerous violation of the security-efficiency equation that governed communication in intelligence work. The most efficient form of communication, a face-to-face meeting, was the least secure, and had to be planned and executed with extreme precaution.[34]

Ambush

On November 29, two CIA officers would be flying into enemy territory, in gross contradiction of presidential promises to leave China alone, for an experimental exfiltration of a foreign agent. Downey and Fecteau would have no cover, no cutouts, and no exit strategy. As white Americans with minimal Chinese language skills, the two CAT pilots and two CIA officers would have nowhere to hide if anything went wrong and they ended up on the ground. Allen Dulles, reflecting his racist notion of what it meant to be American, observed in his memoir, "The Chinese are, of course, at the same disadvantage in operating against us as we are in attempting to operate against them. Physical and cultural differences make it quite difficult to camouflage the true ethnic status and national origin of intelligence officers or agents on either side."[35]

In addition to the previous CAT missions into Manchuria (one of which included Downey), there had been a smattering of cases of white Americans entering PRC territory on covert missions as early as October 1951, when Americans—presumably not of Chinese ethnicity—served as pilots and jumpmasters on infiltration flights out of Taiwan into Zhejiang Province.[36] In April 1952, the US Fifth Air Force set up a special psychological warfare unit (the 6167th Operations Squadron) to fly covert missions out of Seoul City Airfield. One veteran, navigator Major P. G. Moore, told the historian Michael Haas that he flew missions over Manchuria to infiltrate a blonde-haired, Chinese-speaking American: "There was a mountain range north of the North Korean–Chinese border that featured a saddle between two extinct volcanoes. There was a drop zone in the saddle and we went up there with parachutists more than once. Twice I took a blonde-haired American there. He wore an Army uniform without rank, and spoke fluent Chinese. I don't know who he worked for or how he got back."[37] Haas also interviewed a US Air Force rescue boat captain who inserted a Princeton graduate in his mid-twenties in waters off the China coast for a three-day covert mission. Like the Manchurian paratrooper, he was blonde-haired and fluent in Chinese. Dressed in peasant garb, the commando claimed—with Lawrence of Arabia swagger—that if spotted, he would be mistaken for a Manchu.[38]

The obvious danger of such missions may have appealed to the Agency's more romantic recruits. Don Gregg recalled his "muted sense of envy" at dinner in

Japan with an enthused Downey the night before the mission. "Jack was in high spirits, as he was at last 'going to see some action.'"[39]

As the Americans got ready for their flight into Manchuria, the Chinese public security team was completing preparations to welcome them at the pickup site. It was a moment of truth at least two years in the making, since the Ministry of Public Security's inaugural National Conference on Operational Work in 1950 stressed the need for patience and thoroughness in defending the country against special agents.[40] At the second national conference in July 1952, Minister of Public Security Luo Ruiqing, addressing Chairman Mao and the Central Committee, warned of "enemy agent activities in border areas, especially enemy agents using ethnic minorities as covert assets" and recommended to "specifically enhance reconnaissance work along national border areas and with ethnic minorities."[41]

Public security units from the county level up had been ordered to create a counterespionage investigative office responsible for case management. Security for Jilin Province fell under the Northeast Military Regional Command, headed by Gao Gang, with Wang Jinxiang serving as regional public security minister. The Northeast Command functioned as a laboratory for a range of policy experiments in the first years of the PRC, which included public security, with Chairman Mao singling out the Northeast Model for nationwide praise and replication.[42] Gao Gang used a vivid metaphor to describe his counterespionage method: "One should proceed as if pulling out a nail, which means pulling the whole thing out. One should not proceed as if picking apples, picking them off one by one."[43] Mao brought Gao Gang to Beijing at the peak of countersubversion operations, in October 1952, to run the State Planning Commission, part of the transition to a permanent structure of civilian provincial governments in place of the temporary system of six regional military-administrative commanderies.[44] The Northeast Regional Command, headquartered in Shenyang, remained in overall charge of the anti–special agent operation to lure the CIA into its Manchurian trap.

Northeast Command dispatched regional deputy commander Tan Youlin to run the operation, assisted by the Jilin Province deputy Wang Jieren, with an anti-aircraft artillery unit at their disposal. Units began positioning around the drop zone on November 6, and Anshan Barracks was ordered to bring eleven anti-aircraft guns. Wang Jieren selected a dozen men with combat experience and emplaced six heavy machine guns in Sandao Gully Village at the foot of Laoling Mountain. The pickup location, Nanda Ravine, provided ample forest and mountain cover to camouflage an ambush. On November 26, Antu County public security deputy Qian Longjiu led thirty police and militia up Laoling's Pillow Peak. Three lines of air defense were set up, with six heavy machine guns and seven submachine guns in the primary line, backed by eighteen anti-aircraft guns and six submachine guns in second and third lines.[45]

Everything was in place on the night of November 29. Signal fires were lit a little over twenty meters away from the pickup spot.[46] The on-site commander Tan Youlin, reporting to border defense command, oversaw four hundred men covering a three-and-a-half-kilometer perimeter.[47]

Downey and Fecteau's C-47 lifted off from Seoul at 9:40 p.m. and arrived at the pickup spot just after midnight, flying under a full moon ideal for navigating by rivers and lakes.[48] The two young intelligence officers would have been taught to look for signals. Joseph Smith explained, "At every step of the operational meeting procedure—approaching the meeting place, checking surveillance, checking the meeting place before the meeting takes place, countersurveillance of the meeting, during the course of the meeting itself, and following the meeting—signals need to be employed to indicate any signs of trouble or need to change plans or cancel the meeting."[49] There were no signs of trouble, and when they came within radio contact, Niu Songlin assured them, "Situation normal, everything ready, proceed according to plan."

Swooping back from the southwest for a pass over the pickup site, the signal fires could be spotted. Pilots Schwartz and Snoddy slowed the C-47 and dropped a large package with guns, rations, and the air-hook apparatus—two poles, nylon wire, backpack, illustrated instruction manual. There were notes for Team Wen, too. "Tonight's pick up of Li Junying will proceed in 3 tries; 1st is practice, 2nd is real. 3rd is contingency. Entire process will take less than half-hour."[50] A twenty-seven-year-old junior officer in the Public Security Bureau, Zhang Zhenbang—pretending to be Li Junying—set up the ground station, put on the harness, and lay down on the snow.[51]

As the plane came back for another approach, flying to within 150 meters elevation, the valley lit up with gunfire. The C-47 went down in flames, colliding into a bank of trees five hundred meters beyond the clearing where Zhang lay. The pilots Schwartz and Snoddy were dead. Downey and Fecteau walked out of the debris virtually unscathed and were quickly surrounded by a couple of dozen men. Fecteau remembered Chinese soldiers coming from all directions, screaming and shouting, and that a couple of shots were fired.

An officer struck Fecteau and drew a pistol on him when he cursed, saying, "You know your future is very dark." Someone snapped a photograph of the two secret agents, dazed looks on their faces, their hands behind their backs. The soldiers asked for Jack Downey by name.[52]

Downey and Fecteau were transferred to the prefectural office and then onward to regional headquarters in Shenyang. A truck drove out to the crash site to collect the plane parts. The ambush party celebrated with a round of *baijiu* rice liquor.[53]

On Mao's Orders

Mao Zedong received a briefing almost immediately on the results of the counterespionage operation. But the chairman was in no mood to celebrate. He sent a long memo to Public Security Minister Luo Ruiqing dated December 2 on the problem of US-backed subversive efforts and what needed to be done in response. Even Mao may have been taken aback by the gall the American imperialists showed in flying their secret agents well into Chinese territory on an exfiltration mission. He appended a half-dozen files of documents and maps, instructing Minister Luo to investigate further and report back to his secretary.

Mao's memo provides a sketch of known and suspected paratrooper infiltration operations, starting with a list of agents captured and killed in the five counties of Changbai Mountain as reported in what he refers to as "the Northeast documents." Mao warned that the enemy planned to drop agents in the Lesser Khingan Mountains of Heilongjiang Province (near the Russian border) and Lü Mountain in Liaoning Province to set up bases for sabotage and killings in urban areas. He mentioned reports of an airstrip in the grasslands of the far west being built to accommodate American planes by General Ma Liang, the leader of a Muslim insurgency (who in fact was in communication with Nationalist secret agents about forming a Southwestern Anti-Communist National Salvation Army).[54] A spy captured in Korea confessed that enemy planes had landed and picked up agents in western Xinjiang, along the border with Mongolia, in the Kham region of Garzê, and as far away as southwestern Tibet.

Mao warned his security chief Luo Ruiqing that the threat of covert subversion was approaching crisis proportions.

> These incidents have been happening across the new Soviet states, which had sounded the alarm to catch infiltrators. Judging from all this, it appears the enemy could use helicopters or large transport aircraft to make nighttime paradrops or landings in forests, deserts, grasslands, and uninhabited areas all across the country [lists 16 locations, spanning Gansu, Guizhou, Yunnan, Qinghai provinces and Tibet]. Even in non-mountainous areas there could be parachute agents. Reportedly drops have occurred even in the vicinity of Beijing and Tianjin.

Mao expressed little confidence that his young republic's borders were secure: "Apart from those we know about, it's hard to say how many more that we don't know about." The United States was subsidizing airborne espionage and subversion operations with USD 100 million earmarked for such purposes, he wrote.[55]

Chairman Mao instructed Minister Luo to come up with concrete methods to defend against incursions from the skies by US-backed operatives. He suggested one idea for starters: What about establishing surveillance positions staffed by armed, plainclothes units in vulnerable locations? Mao listed possible sites for outposts: the mountains of the northeast (Changbai, Khingan, Lü), the Inner Mongolian grasslands, and the Daba mountain range running through Central China between the Yellow and Yangtze Rivers. Every military region and province could be instructed to set up these kinds of strongholds to defend against enemy paratroopers. When things were calm, they could work and study in the mountain area. When an incident arose, they would be on hand to report and capture any infiltrators. Mao encouraged Luo to organize a conference in Beijing for personnel from relevant areas.[56]

A month later, in his New Year's speech to colleagues in public security, Minister Luo Ruiqing emphasized the need for vigilance in fighting the counterrevolutionary forces of infiltration and subversion: "Whether these special agents and bandits are dispatched from abroad, drop down from the skies, climb up from the seas, or are already hiding in our hinterland or hiding in the corners of our society, regardless of where they come from or where they are now, all of them must be attacked and eliminated in short order."[57] Catching spies and exposing counterrevolutionary plots would be the primary mission of the Public Security Ministry for 1953, Luo declared.[58] He sent a status report on antiparatrooper efforts to General Peng Dehuai in late February, and Mao added his own comment in early March, advising that a system of mountain watchposts with armed sentries be discussed by the CPV-KPA joint command for implementation in North Korea as well. "They should be specifically in charge of the struggle against paratrooper agents, and by periodically reviewing their experience and strengthening technology and tactics, completely eliminate airborne espionage," Mao instructed.[59]

As Mao suggested, the Ministry of Public Security convened the gathering, called the Conference on Countering Airborne Agents, where the central agenda item was the chairman's proposal of militia observation posts. Antiparatrooper work would include setting up posts, establishing command structures, mobilizing the masses, organizing local militias, and assigning aerial surveillance. While making allowance for local variation, every region was ordered to set up the posts on short order and to develop the mass characteristics of antiparatrooper struggle in order to thoroughly eliminate the threat posed by agents of subversion.[60]

As Chairman Mao and Minister Luo grappled with the question of how to defend against airborne infiltration, Jack Downey and Dick Fecteau were in shackles in Shenyang, where they would be held incognito, undergoing interrogation for five months.[61] Raja Hutheesing visited around the time of their incarceration, describing Shenyang as "a Japanese city with tall buildings and wide streets. On its cobbled road there was the constant rumble of mule carts bringing essential supplies. Occasionally a truck would tear down the street loaded with workers going to the factory. For the guests there were the latest models of American cars smuggled from across the sea."[62] Downey and Fecteau were held in ankle chains in the basement of a "tall ornate building with a big courtyard," of the kind Hutheesing admired from the outside.[63]

Underground, incommunicado, isolated from one another and the wider world, the grilling commenced. Interrogators reminded Downey and Fecteau that no one knew they were alive and they could do anything they wanted with them.[64] They sought the obvious information: names, locations, organizational structure, operational plans. These were details that only these two Americans could know.

Fecteau was quick on his feet and cool under the pressure of interrogation, concocting a fake story that shortened the amount of time he had been with the Agency, thereby limiting the scope of what he should be expected to know. He also, ingeniously, mentally renamed his CIA colleagues based on the roster of his Boston University football team—a mnemonic device that allowed him to be consistent in his deceit.

In their training, the men had been taught never to admit being CIA. But they were under intense psychological pressure, which was vividly described by the graduate student Allyn Rickett, who endured interrogation for espionage around the same time:

> Whenever my interrogator thought I was about to balk he quickly changed the subject to something I was willing to talk about, thus always keeping me off balance and never allowing me to come to a crisis, yet not relaxing his pressure. I found myself being led into a maze of truths, half-truths, and outright lies. Often I was unable to remember what I had said before and kept tripping myself up on details. Several times I tried flatly denying any knowledge of a person, only to give in later when I realized my relations with him must have been known. Sometimes, too, I really could not remember details which might have occurred three years before. Then, under the cynical, accusing stare of my interrogator I often felt even more uncomfortable than if I had been telling a lie. All the while, the haunting realization that a large part of what I said could be checked against the facts already in the judge's hands made me feel even more insecure.[65]

While Fecteau's football team trick helped him hold out, Downey quickly became confused. "I found it very difficult to keep track of my false stories. I was giving all kinds of false stories and using false names and I'd forget which name

I was giving to which guy," he recalled.[66] Questioning lasted up to twenty hours a day, and sleep deprivation was taking its toll. "I was extremely scared. . . . We were isolated and had no idea of what was going to happen to us and had no idea of what was going on in the world."[67]

Loneliness and uncertainty tightened their grip on Downey's mind. "I tried to hold back at first. I pretended that I thought I was in Korea. All the time I was trying to save what I could. I tried to delay. But they managed to scare the living Jesus out of me, and I could see no end to the interrogation." The interrogators were lucky to have *two* captives, allowing them to use prisoner's dilemma techniques. "From the interrogation I got feedback which I thought meant that Fecteau was talking a lot. . . . I sometimes had trouble remembering the stories I had made up to divert the interrogators."[68]

Downey and Fecteau had added reason to fear their interrogators given the American paranoia that Asian communists had mastered paranormal mind-control techniques referred to as "brainwashing," a literal rendering of the Chinese term *xinao*. Edward Hunter, a journalist with a WWII intelligence background and ties to the CIA, popularized the term in articles in 1950 and in his book *Brain-Washing in Red China*, published in 1951. "What actually is meant by cold war is warfare with unorthodox weapons, with silent weapons such as a leaflet, a hypnotist's lulling instructions, or a self-criticism meeting in Red China," Hunter explained in his best-selling book (an enlarged edition came out in 1953).[69] Brainwashing was a useful idea, as it could be used to engender sympathy for Korean War POWs by casting them as helpless victims of psychiatric manipulation. But it would also contribute to vilifying repatriated POWs as weak-willed traitors, even Red agents—an ambiguity dramatized on screen in films like *Prisoner of War* (1954) starring Ronald Reagan, and later exploited by the writer Richard Condon in his noir novel *The Manchurian Candidate* (1959).[70]

The CIA took brainwashing seriously—in the spring of 1953, Allen Dulles approved a mind-control research program called MK/ULTRA that would lead to at least one death from experimentation with psychedelics.[71] But the actual Maoist practice of brainwashing, also known as "thought reform," had nothing to do with serums, hypnotism, or sleeper agents. Downey and Fecteau would get a taste of such techniques later in Beijing, but not during their initial incarceration in Shenyang. There, they were subjected to textbook intelligence extraction using aggressive, but not abusive, interrogation techniques.[72] There was nothing mysterious about the questioning at all.

The weight of time, loss of hope, and welter of lies was enough to break Downey. "There was no end to what I was facing. There was no 'if I can hang on for a week it'll be ok' or 'the war is going to be over.' I was facing an indefinite period of incarceration. There was no way I could get out of it." Downey made no pretense to heroism. "I think it was the sixteenth day by my count I admitted I was in the CIA. I burst out crying at the time."[73] The details poured out, including names. Among them was Don Gregg, just starting his career in intelligence. As Gregg explained in his memoir, "In 1958, I was named as a CIA agent in a broadcast out of East Germany. I was part of a large group, all accused of doing Agency work, some of whom had nothing to do with CIA. I suspected that this information resulted from Chinese interrogation of survivors of the Downey-Fecteau crash. I later learned that this was exactly what had happened."[74] Gregg held no grudge. Quite the opposite: his envy of Downey at dinner in Japan the night before the doomed exfiltration mission turned into lifelong admiration, even years later when one man's confession blew the other man's cover.

As the winter of 1952 turned into the spring of 1953, Downey and Fecteau remained in a subterranean prison, suspended in a void of information and vacuum of time. There were few markers of the passage of events. Their guards may have donned black armbands on March 6.[75] But how would the CIA men have guessed it was in mourning for the death of Joseph Stalin? And how would they have known that the Soviet leader's passing would help clear the way to an armistice in Korea, signed at the end of July? The undeclared war between China and the United States came to an inconclusive end, with neither side able to claim victory or forced to admit defeat. It was a tragic example of war's senseless destruction, with the Korean Peninsula ending up divided along the same line as when it all began, after millions had lost their lives, homes, and loved ones.

Enmity between the United States and People's Republic would not abate once the artillery shells stopped falling along the thirty-eighth parallel. And the war's end was only the beginning of the trials facing the pair of quiet Americans in Communist China.

11

QUIET AMERICANS

What to do when a secret mission simply disappears without a trace—that was the conundrum facing the CIA's North Asia Command when the exfiltration flight failed to return from Manchuria. The Agency cobbled together a cover story about two civilian employees of the Far East Command having disappeared on a commercial flight between Japan and Korea. The Far East Air Force sent out a C-47 to simulate a nosedive into the sea, followed by search and rescue sorties over the fake crash zone.[1] At CIA headquarters, the Far East Division, certain that Beijing would make propaganda hay of captured American spies, assumed that the plane must have crashed without survivors.[2] Downey and Fecteau's next of kin were notified of their disappearance in letters of condolence on CIA stationery signed by Beetle Smith, dated December 4, 1952. The personnel department classified Downey and Fecteau as missing in action and maintained their pay and allowance.[3]

The timing of four Americans disappearing somewhere over Chinese territory could not have been worse for senior US officials. The Agency leadership was consumed by the presidential transition, with Beetle moving to number two at State (to help Ike keep an eye on John Foster Dulles) and Allen Dulles becoming acting director of central intelligence on Inauguration Day.[4] Allen's dream of a lifetime was made official in February when he was confirmed as the first civilian to serve as the nation's top intelligence official, realizing Sherman Kent's plan for "civilianizing" the CIA, as written in *Strategic Intelligence for American World Policy*.[5] The loss of Jack Downey, Dick Fecteau, Norman Schwartz, and Robert Snoddy, at least, was easy to keep quiet. They simply vanished.

The Arnold Eleven

Such was not the case with another crew of American captives, who from day one of the Eisenhower era could not be so easily imagined away. In his inaugural address on January 20, 1953, President Eisenhower called on his countrymen to steel themselves for a long fight against communism: "We shall never try to placate an aggressor by the false and wicked bargain of trading honor for security. Americans, indeed all free men, remember that in the final choice a soldier's pack is not so heavy a burden as a prisoner's chains."[6] The next day, his first morning in the Oval Office, the PRC media welcomed the new POTUS by announcing the capture of eleven Americans from a recently downed USAF B-29 Superfortress. "We knew it had been missing," Eisenhower recalled in his memoirs. "Now we knew that fourteen crew had parachuted out: three had been killed and eleven taken prisoner."[7]

Commanded by Colonel John Arnold of the 581st Air Resupply and Communications Wing, the B-29 had been flying near the China border dropping propaganda leaflets. Near the target of Cholson, North Korea, searchlights bathed the blackened plane in blinding light and a swarm of MiG jets shot it from the skies. Crew members would later question whether they might have intruded into PRC airspace. Navigator Steve Kiba insisted they were forty miles south of the Yalu River.[8] Sergeant Wallace Brown conceded that "perhaps while trying to evade the Communists' fighters, we had accidentally crossed the border into Red China."[9] Major William Baumer, Arnold's second-in-command, agreed they might have crash-landed on the China side of the border, but when his captors demanded a statement, he would only write: "I've been told we violated Chinese territorial air. If we did, it was accidental and due to a radar navigational error." Baumer heard the same line used on Downey and Fecteau—his interrogator screamed in his face, "You are a criminal! . . . Your future is very dark!"[10]

The questioning of the Arnold crew had a similar pattern to the grillings endured by Downey, Fecteau, and Rickett. Interrogators confronted Sergeant Brown with his moral culpability, demanding that he atone. "You and your crew have flown your damn B-29 over Chinese territorial air. You have invaded the Chinese People's Republic. You have committed a most serious act of aggression against the peace-loving Chinese people. You must pay for this!" After he had spent a month convalescing in a hospital bed, Brown's questioning intensified as he became more compliant. His interrogators dug for military information, alternating endless hours of little food and no sleep with "enlightening lectures." "Your damned airplanes have constantly provoked the peace-loving Chinese people by intruding across our borders, dropping germ bombs and attacking hospitals and schools. . . . How many men in your goddamn spy wing?"[11]

Brown's interrogators were not buying the story that the mission objective was limited to leaflets. "What is the mission of your wing? Why did your B-29 fly over the Chinese People's Republic? Can you deny that you were trained to drop spies? God damn your leaflets! You don't need training to drop leaflets! What have spies to do with leaflets?" On the ninth consecutive day of interrogation, Brown was forced to stand for fourteen hours. Then the topic turned to activities in Taiwan, and Brown was made to stand for six and a half days straight. "I had been under interrogation over sixty hours. I had slept less than an hour in almost a week. My body was so swollen that it looked more like a dead stump than a human being. The pain I had endured was much greater than I ever dreamed the human body could bear."[12]

Crew member Steve Kiba endured similar interrogation techniques designed to elicit a confession about the true nature of their unit. "The Red Chinese tried to force me to admit that 581st ARC Wing was involved in training, dropping, and supplying espionage agents. They kept insinuating that we were directly associated with a highly secretive non-military agency."[13] The case that the interrogators were trying to build linked the Arnold crew to the CIA, and they wanted to prove that Arnold's mission, code-named Stardust Four Zero, was related to Downey's Operation Aroma. Colonel Arnold would tell Kiba that his interrogators, too, tried to link their unit to the CIA, and "both Fecteau and Downey said that in many of their interrogations the Red Chinese tried to link them with us."[14]

The truth was more complicated than the crew members themselves may have known at the time. Based out of Clark Air Force Base in the Philippines, the 581st ARC Wing was activated by the US Air Force in the summer of 1951 as an experimental unit to assist with airborne psychological warfare, including intelligence gathering and covert operations support. The intelligence historian John Prados unearthed evidence that the USAF's first special warfare units, like the 581st ARC Wing, functioned as the military's equivalent to the CIA's relationship with CAT—using overt missions to camouflage covert infiltrations. Decades later, the reporter Robert Burns tracked down veterans of Stardust Four Zero in looking for links to the CIA. Even Colonel Arnold did not know that one of his gunners was a CIA contact. "I had known that some had associations with the CIA, but I didn't know which ones they were—and I didn't want to know," Arnold told Burns.[15]

The capture of Colonel Arnold and his crew triggered a security review at the CIA over who should be allowed in or near enemy territory. "The colonel possessed a number of high-level and sensitive clearances which gave him access to special information the Chinese would have been delighted to obtain," recalled Howard Hunt, who served in China with the OSS during WWII, supervised William F. Buckley Jr. during his postgraduate stint with the CIA in Mexico, and was assigned to OPC duty in Japan in 1954. "In such a case the operational assumption is that the captive has talked, told everything. . . . Following a final damage assessment, orders were established throughout the Far East Command curtailing travel into potentially hazardous areas by anyone possessing sensitive clearances."[16] In November 1954, Allen Dulles would claim that "the practice of using American personnel on overflights of hostile territory was discontinued by CIA about two years ago"—in other words, around the time of the Downey and Arnold incidents.[17]

Rectification

After a period of detention in the northeast, the Arnold Eleven were transferred to a facility in Beijing in early 1953, ending up in Caolanzi Hutong Prison.[18] Caolanzi was located in the heart of the city that could itself feel as orderly and soulless as a prison, at least in the eyes of visiting foreigners like Raja Hutheesing:

> The dust had been swept clean and though the haunting beauty of the temples and the gleam of the palace roofs remained, there was no easy laughter. Art and gentle living had disappeared and their place was taken by grim humorless men and women in blue cotton uniforms to be molded to one pattern of life. The scholar too had left and the slogan-shouting peasant had replaced him. New Forbidden Cities had been built within the ancient walls. Only the rickshaw coolies remained, sitting and smoking as they waited for customers.[19]

At the time the Arnold Eleven were transferred in, Jack Downey, Dick Fecteau, and Allyn Rickett were also being held in Caolanzi's five-by-eight-foot cement cells, each with an eyehole slit in the thick wooden door and a covered window. A single lightbulb was mounted above a straw mattress placed for sleeping on the floor. The compound was built on the site of a Buddhist monastery and had been used to imprison CCP revolutionaries before 1949. A tall wall separated it from the neighborhood.[20]

Downey was bound in iron chains for almost a year, his varsity football figure withering away under the physical and psychological strain. "The first three years were miserable," Downey recalled. He had "no knowledge of what was going on in the world, no contact with anybody else."[21] Speakers blared news and propaganda, but Downey could not glean much with his limited Mandarin—as an English major at Yale, he had not benefited from Professor George Kennedy's pedagogical innovations in teaching Chinese.[22]

Downey and Fecteau's incarceration regime bore little resemblance to the wartime POW camps in Korea, where physical violence had been widely used

FIGURE 8. Peking prison: Caolanzi Hutong. Photo by Edward Wong.

to induce powerlessness and degrade the captives. The brutality of the Korean camps may have reflected the influence of the Japanese imperial method, which was experienced across Asia and depicted vividly in the French novel *Le pont de la rivière Kwaï* by Pierre Boulle, published in 1952 (and later turned into the Oscar-winning film *The Bridge on the River Kwai*). But what the Chinese Communist prison experience lacked in terms of physical pain, it made up through an insidious and coercive regime of psychological pressure. As the historian Jan Kiely explains, Communist penal theory fused traditional Confucian and Buddhist notions of transformation with Soviet techniques of "dehumanizing bullying tactics mixing threats (with or without physical torture), lies and innuendo, making much of minor contradictions in different accounts, unrelenting continuous interrogation by multiple rotating interrogators—the 'wheel battle' (*chelunzhan*) tactic—pressuring and ganging up by groups surrounding a target, demanding a confession, spitting and shouting abuse in their faces."[23]

The penal method of transformation used on prisoners was analogous to thought reform and "rectification," terms used for the transformation of society as a whole. Mao Zedong launched the original rectification campaign in 1942 on the tight-knit CCP base camp at Yan'an, with assistance from his counterintelligence expert Kang Sheng, who had studied Soviet techniques in Moscow. Rectification was designed to induce "excruciating physical and psychological distress," leaving no exit except suicide or confession.[24] After the subject was guided toward self-annihilation, rectification then sought to insert a new self, predicated on total loyalty to Communist tenets and party discipline.[25] This method of political indoctrination based on intensive psychological pressure, described by the Yale professor of psychiatry Robert Jay Lifton as "ideological totalism," was the reality behind Orientalist myths of brainwashing. Professor Lifton based his analysis of thought reform on interviews in Hong Kong with Chinese refugees as well as with Westerners subjected to the method during prison terms on the mainland.[26]

Rectification was a tool of socialist transformation to be woven into all aspects of quotidian existence. Prisons offered the ideal laboratory for subjecting a captive population to thought reform techniques. Hannah Arendt observed in *The Origins of Totalitarianism* that concentration camps were "the true central institution of totalitarian organizational power," but Maoist penal institutions operated on a different principle from Hitler's concentration camps and Stalin's gulags.[27] Where Nazis used extermination (mass slaughter of Jews and others) and the Soviets used isolation (shipping troublemakers off to Siberia), Maoist camps demanded that wardens and inmates participate actively and energetically in the project of rectification.

As a practical matter, rectifying the huge number of counterrevolutionaries rounded up during the mass campaigns of the Korean War years created an administrative nightmare. The historian Frank Dikötter estimates that China's incarcerated population soared to two million by 1952—including 670,000 in so-called re-education through labor camps.[28] Prisons themselves became objects of rectification: the Three-Antis Campaign in 1951 included a crackdown on corrupt practices in prison management, and the public health campaign in the spring of 1952 addressed the need to improve prison hygiene.[29]

As the net of thought reform widened, a handful of Westerners submitted to the rectification, including the British citizen Robert Ford. Ford lived for years in Tibet before his arrest in December 1950 on espionage charges in Chongqing. Subjected to thought reform in prison, Ford came to believe more and more of his political instruction. "It is impossible to explain in so many words how anyone, already opposed to Communism, can become less so instead of more so when he is suffering agonies in a Communist gaol. Of course I hated them; but one gets used to everything, including hate," he explained in a memoir of the experience.[30]

Ford gave a succinct description of the theory behind thought reform in a letter from prison to his parents (dated May 14, 1954): "This policy is one of patiently re-educating the criminal—one of remoulding a criminal, a man shunned by society, into a new man—a new man who, when he returns to society, will not commit further crimes, but will be of use, and who, to atone for his previous misdeeds, will give of his whole strength for the betterment of society."[31] Ford noted the similarities between interrogation and rectification. "The method of extracting confessions and the technique of criticism and self-criticism sessions were completely analogous. . . . The victim was given guidance, but everything had to come from him. And everything he said had to pass the exacting tests of apparent truthfulness, dogmatic conformity, and, above all, sincerity."[32]

The American graduate student Allyn Rickett left an even more detailed account of what it was like to undergo thought reform in a Chinese prison, emphasizing the role played by his cellmates. Likening the process to group therapy, Rickett perceived a core element of traditional Chinese psychology sharpened by Marxist methods: "The entire process seems to have developed in a rule-of-thumb manner based on a common-sense insight into human character, something for which the Chinese have always been noted, a concept of self-criticism borrowed from the general Marxian principle and techniques which grew out of the need to reform the troops and intellectuals in the early days of the revolution."[33] Allyn and his wife Adele described a steady weakening of their psychological resistance until a point of moral and spiritual breakdown.

The researcher Doak Barnett debriefed the Ricketts on their release in Hong Kong and offered a clinical assessment that attempted to demystify their apparent brainwashing: "The Chinese Communists' methods of indoctrination are not basically esoteric or mysterious. Essentially, the technique is to control all that a person sees and hears, as well as to focus on any individual the full force of authority and social pressure, and to use both persuasion and threat to make a person confess past guilt, renounce previous attitudes, and wholly accept a new faith."[34] If the imperial secret agent analyzed by Arendt, the Lawrence of Arabia archetype, represented an escape from the agonies of selfhood, Maoist rectification similarly promised the security of a new self, whose actions would be guided by an omniscient party. The perfect spy and the good Communist had more in common than either might have liked to admit.

The Ricketts' postrelease interviews in Hong Kong would spark minor outrage in early 1955 due to the sympathetic description they gave of their prison experience and their insistence on their own guilt. Even more controversially, twenty-one American POWs and two Brits, free to go home after the signing of the Korean War Armistice Agreement, chose to defect to the People's Republic of China rather than be repatriated to the United States in January 1954. Just as the inability to free US prisoners held in Red China was a frustrating reminder of the limits of America's superpower status, the idea of the twenty-one "turncoats" freely choosing to live in a communist country threatened the sacred superiority of the American way.

Golden Age of Psywar

As Ford and Ricketts submitted to rectification, and Downey, Fecteau, and the Arnold Eleven endured incarceration, President Eisenhower and his secretary of state took a hard look at Far Eastern policy. John Foster Dulles shared none of his predecessor Dean Acheson's hopes that the communist atom could be split between Moscow and Beijing. In place of Titoism for China, Dulles advocated a hawkish strategy of strengthening the US alliance system in order to prevent the further spread of Communist influence, and with some luck, to roll it back—perhaps even in China. Eisenhower's worldview was perhaps less Manichean than Dulles's. As an elected politician rather than an appointed official, the president was also more attentive to the preferences of the public. Given the unpopularity of the Korean War and fears of WWIII, Eisenhower's top priority was bringing the war to an end and creating the "chance for peace" with the Soviets—America's real adversary.

To get a peace in Korea, however, Ike felt he needed to build up leverage. The Joint Chiefs offered him aggressive options including military strikes on PRC territory. But instead of conventional warfare, Eisenhower hoped to use psychological means to put pressure on Beijing to compromise in the deadlocked negotiations over a cease-fire in Korea. So Ike hinted he was ready to bring the war to China, and Secretary Dulles told Prime Minister Nehru to pass the message to Premier Zhou Enlai that atomic war was under serious consideration.[35] Eisenhower also offered a massive increase in funding for the South Korean military to bring their troop level up to 655,000 men, as a way to intimidate Beijing and Pyongyang while reducing the burden on the American military.

Covert support to counterrevolution in China was a natural weapon in the psywar arsenal for Eisenhower to draw on in trying to end the war in Korea. Clandestine activity initiated under Truman was continued by Eisenhower under the screen of plausible deniability. On the day of Eisenhower's inaugural address, PRC Public Security conducted a raid in Guangdong Province and captured seventeen Third Force operatives. Those taken alive confessed to being members of Cai Wenzhi's Free China Movement; two reported being recruited in Hong Kong and flown in February 1952 to Saipan and Chigasaki for training, then brought back to Hong Kong by submarine.[36] Chinese military histories record intensified parachute infiltrations on the North Korea and China coasts in early 1953, causing the

Sino-Korean joint command to promulgate an order in mid-February to enhance defense against subversive operations. A counterinfiltration campaign began in March, with the PRC Central Military Commission's "counterparatrooper program" teaching protocols based on "experiences with countering US and Chiang parachuters in China." The sweep yielded 66 commandos, 653 suspects, and a large haul of guns and radios.[37]

Finally, after three years of fighting, including two years of on-again off-again negotiations, the Korean War Armistice Agreement was signed on July 27, 1953, by General Mark Clark as UN commander, General Peng Dehuai as head of the Chinese People's Volunteers, and the North Korean leader Kim Il Sung. Eisenhower would claim in his memoirs that his atomic bluff made the difference in creating leverage to bring the armistice talks to a conclusion.[38] According to his biographer William Hitchcock, it was not entirely a "bluff" by mid-March, when Eisenhower was seriously contemplating tactical atomic strikes, but was spared a final decision by a shift in Communist strategy that led to progress in the Panmunjom negotiations.[39] The trigger for that shift, in turn, is probably best explained by one simple factor: the death of Stalin.

Ending the war in Korea freed Eisenhower and the Dulles brothers to devote greater attention and resources to psywar offensives elsewhere. Of the major foreign policy challenges that Ike recalled faced him on taking office—Korea, Indochina, Malay, Iran, Guatemala, Yugoslavia, and Italy—he would authorize major covert operations in virtually all of them.[40] The CIA official Richard Helms described the Eisenhower years as the "high tide of covert action," as the Agency racked up what seemed to be a string of stunning subversive victories.[41] These successes were achieved not by dropping Jedburgh commandos in the wilderness to foment counterrevolutionary movements, but rather by employing various forms of political warfare and psywar to dislodge leaders—including democratically elected ones—deemed unfriendly to the United States and vulnerable to subversive Communist influence.

The three best-known covert triumphs of the post–Korean Armistice years took place in Iran, the Philippines, and Guatemala. In August 1953, the CIA operative Kermit Roosevelt helped manufacture street protests in Tehran that contributed to the overthrow of Iran's democratically elected prime minister Mohammad Mossadegh.[42] In November, Defense Minister Ramon Magsaysay won the presidency of the Philippines with considerable assistance from his close adviser, the CIA officer Edward Lansdale.[43] In June 1954, the Agency helped Guatemala's defense minister stage a military coup against the democratically elected president Jacobo Arbenz.[44]

In his service under Truman, Beetle Smith had tried to prevent the CIA from turning into a mere "covert War Department." But under Ike, the new director,

Allen Dulles, was left free to play his favorite game—clandestine subversion. Dulles boasted about the regime change record of "America's Secret Agents" in a 1954 publicity blitz (arranged in part to defend the Agency's public reputation against Joe McCarthy's insinuations of communist infiltration of the CIA). Curiously, Dulles invoked the term "third force," but used it as a generic reference to anti-communist resistance anywhere in the world. He crowed about how the CIA "operates a superclandestine third force—the top-secret activity of aiding and abetting freedom forces where the patriotism of captive peoples may be fanned from a spark into action."[45] Dulles insisted that "the CIA's third force" was rooted in "indigenous freedom legions"—never imposed from outside—and cited "the visible communist setbacks in Iran, Egypt and Guatemala" as proof of concept.[46] The emphasis on humility and self-restraint found in the writings of Morgenthau and Niebuhr had little place in the brazenly secretive and ambitious world of Allen Dulles, for whom the possibilities of psywar were endless.

But if Dulles's CIA was making regime change look easy in some parts of the world, the East Asian continent seemed to tell a very different story. For one thing, the empirical basis for strategic intelligence about Asia was thin. As one CIA report summed it up in February 1954, "The picture for the major target area in Asia, i.e. Communist China, is very dark."[47]

Unfortunately, what was pretty clear was that well-armed, Soviet-aligned communist parties were firmly in control of mainland China, North Korea, and North Vietnam. Led by charismatic nationalists in the figures of Mao Zedong, Kim Il Sung, and Ho Chi Minh, Asian communism seemed impervious to Dulles's coup making and invulnerable to Eisenhower's psywar. Washington, in fact, had to worry about propping up pro-American governments in its own embattled protectorate states—Chiang Kai-shek's Republic of China, Syngman Rhee's Republic of Korea, and Ngo Dinh Diem's Republic of Vietnam. Chiang, Rhee, and Diem ran highly repressive regimes, and Washington had to excuse their authoritarianism as the price to pay for fighting communism.

The deep tensions in East Asia came to a diplomatic head in the spring and summer of 1954, when a recalcitrant Secretary Dulles, egged on by his British and French counterparts, accepted a Soviet proposal to include the PRC in a five-power conference that was to address the conflicts in Korea and Indochina. The Geneva Conference, hosted by neutralist Switzerland from April 26 to July 20, 1954, would afford Premier Zhou Enlai his first opportunity to represent the New China on the world stage—much to John Foster's chagrin.

Sherman Kent was a member of the US delegation to the conference and could not help but be impressed by the Chinese premier. Kent's stay in Geneva was part of a world tour that spoke to the Agency's global reach: in Guatemala, he met President Carlos Castillo Armas, who came to power in a CIA-backed coup in

June; in Cairo, he sat with Colonel Gamal Abdel Nasser, who seized power from King Farouk in a 1952 coup and was getting CIA advice on how to build up his regime's intelligence service; and in Tehran, he was briefed on the prospects for America's preferred leader, the shah, Mohammad Reza Pahlavi.[48] As an observer in Geneva, Kent found the North Korean delegate repulsive, comparing him to "a great big Chicago thug," but he was wowed by Zhou Enlai. "Boy, I often wish he was on our side and not with some of those types in charge of mainland China!" Kent later recalled.[49]

Like Dulles, Zhou Enlai brought along his intelligence chief. Li Kenong was in Geneva wearing his official hat as deputy foreign minister. Li was a hero of the CCP underground in the 1920s and the top intelligence official since the Civil War.[50] Unfortunately, Kent left no record in his memoirs of any impression Li made.

The first half of the conference, focused on the Korean question, ended in early May without any progress. The day before the Indochina phase of talks was set to commence, North Vietnamese troops dealt a crushing blow to French colonial forces by capturing the fortress at Dien Bien Phu. Desperate for an exit from its imperial nightmare, Paris conceded to a division of Vietnam at the seventeenth parallel. The Americans slipped effortlessly into France's shoes, becoming the new patrons of the South Vietnam government and military.

John Foster Dulles did his utmost to prevent Zhou Enlai from gaining prestige in Geneva, refusing to shake hands with the Chinese premier and leaving the conference early. But there was one issue that neither side could afford to ignore entirely: getting detained citizens back. Zhou managed to resolve most detainee cases with the British (Robert Ford being a notable exception), which put indirect pressure on the Americans to do the same.[51] Dulles left the talks in the hands of his undersecretary, Beetle Smith, who subsequently turned things over to Ambassador U. Alexis Johnson with instructions to maintain a hard line. But Johnson admitted that Zhou "had a bargaining chip he knew we wanted badly enough that we would relent on our social quarantine tactics to get it." More precisely, Zhou had seventy-six chips, one for each American thought to be held against their will in the PRC.[52]

Thanks to the intercession of the British diplomat Humphrey Trevelyan, Ambassador Johnson and his Chinese counterpart, Wang Bingnan, held five sessions on the sidelines of the conference in June, which constituted the first bilateral talks between the PRC and the United States.[53] Of the seventy-six Americans held in China, thirty-five detainees were military, and US diplomats worried that there could be scores, even hundreds more—POWs transferred from capture in Korea to camps in Chinese cities from Harbin to Canton. There were also a handful of mystery cases related to military incidents outside the Korean theater, such as US Navy Patrol Squadron 22, shot down off the China coast in

January 1953, and a Coast Guard rescue plane that crashed at sea on takeoff.[54] When reports filtered in of two American captives being displayed in bamboo cages during an anti-imperialism rally in Shantou, Guangdong Province, they were thought to be survivors of the crash.[55]

Adding up all the missing persons cases, State Department officials in Geneva handed a list of 944 lost Americans to Wang Bingnan, who responded with a list of his own of Chinese nationals held against their will in the United States.[56] The US missing list did not include the names Downey and Fecteau, maintaining the fiction that they had been on a flight from Korea to Japan. Anyway, the CIA was sure the men were dead, having reviewed their case and officially declared them deceased as of December 4, 1953.[57]

Chiang Kai-shek watched the incipient US-PRC contacts in Geneva with alarm. His allies in the China lobby stepped up pressure on the China bloc in Congress and Republicans close to the White House to offer the Republic of China a defense treaty, as Australia, New Zealand, South Korea, and the Philippines enjoyed, and as the generalissimo had formally requested back in March 1953.[58] But Ike worried that signing a treaty could trigger a hot war in the Taiwan Strait. Stoking his fears, the PLA staged an amphibious assault on a few islets in the Nationalist-held Dachen chain off the coast of Zhejiang Province on May 15, just a week after the Vietnamese Communist triumph at Dien Bien Phu.[59]

Mao escalated the confrontation a few months later with a bombardment of Kinmen Island, almost two hundred kilometers from Taiwan but only ten kilometers from the mainland coastal city of Xiamen. The artillery barrage on September 3 killed two US soldiers and made front-page news in the United States.[60] Sporadic artillery, air, and sea fighting continued throughout the fall. If Mao intended these aggressive moves to scare Eisenhower away from a stronger commitment to Chiang, he miscalculated badly. The Taiwan Strait crisis only pushed Washington closer to Taipei, convincing Eisenhower and Dulles to give Chiang the defense treaty he wanted dearly.[61]

If there was one clear loser from these developments—the Republican victory, the Korean War Armistice, the Geneva talks, and the Taiwan Strait Crisis—it was the Third Force.

Doubts about the efficacy of Third Force psywar could be heard at high levels of the US government at least as early as November 1952. Just weeks ahead of the ill-fated exfiltration mission into Manchuria, the National Security Council was informed that the Third Force "counterattraction" had failed as a weapon in political warfare against CCP rule:

> The sweeping actions of the Peiping regime against "counterrevolutionary" elements have been effective in eliminating sources of opposition.

> The United States has, so far as possible, sought to counter Chinese Communist propaganda and keep alive in the Chinese people an appreciation of their true interest through its media of information, notably through the Voice of America. However, it has not proved possible to develop any very promising counterattraction to Communism among the anti-Communist and anti-Nationalist Chinese in the so-called "Third Force" category.[62]

Although the CIA would continue subsidizing Third Force journals in Hong Kong and training recruits in Saipan, a shift was underway toward supporting the Formosa (Taiwan) option. As the National Security Council put it, "The efforts of the United States to help develop a counterforce to the Peiping regime have been increasingly directed to assisting the Chinese National Government in Formosa through military and economic assistance, advice, and the application of pressures to improve its effectiveness and its appeal."

Eisenhower's victory in November and the triumph of the Republican Party, whose members had for years attacked Democrats for failing to support Chiang Kai-shek, was another major blow to Third Force standing. Zhang Fakui's American contacts warned him after Ike's election that the new administration would be "supporting those who oppose the Communists but do not oppose Chiang."[63]

The armistice in Korea compounded Third Force woes by eliminating the military rationale for the US to consider anything and anyone so long that it might deplete Beijing's strength. The futility of fomenting a Third Force counterrevolution became harder to justify in peacetime, especially as the CCP seemed to have survived the initial transition from a guerrilla movement to a one-party state. Last but not least, there were the inherent weaknesses in the Third Force movement. Internal squabbling among Third Force generals, politicians, and intellectuals made a depressing contrast to the unity enjoyed by the Chinese Communists behind their leader, Chairman Mao, as well as the reconsolidation of power in Taiwan achieved by Chiang.

With all these factors working against the Third Force, the CIA slowly closed the spigot of support over the course of Eisenhower's first year in office. The CIA historian Nicholas Dujmovic refers to orders to end the Third Force program being relayed to Frank Wisner in 1953.[64] Cai Wenzhi's Free China Movement training program was decommissioned: according to Cai's private papers, reviewed by the historian Roger Jeans, his funding was sharply reduced from April 1954. Most of his men were resettled in Taiwan and Cai relocated to Washington, D.C., where he became a consultant to the Pentagon.[65] Zhang Fakui's Fight League objected to the CIA plan to "repatriate" Third Force recruits to Taiwan and helped some to be re-routed back to Hong Kong instead.[66]

Sporadic reports indicate continuing Third Force guerrilla activities even as the CIA was cutting off support, like a series of infiltration attempts in Guangdong Province from May to November 1953 that finally met with success in January 1954—only to be betrayed by a member of the group who was given seven million yuan and allowed to go home to his native village.[67] Eventually, General Zhang Fakui's American contacts stopped asking for meetings, and the Hong Kong channel closed.

Agency support for Third Force gray propaganda—the journals and cultural activities—ebbed along with the withdrawal of support for paramilitary training. Zhang Fakui stopped dispersing funds for his journal *Renaissance*, and the final issues of *Overseas Chinese Bulletin* and *Voice of China* came out in late 1953. As the pie shrank, Fight League members quarreled over the crumbs, while Carsun Chang and Gu Mengyu suspected the league had been penetrated by Nationalist moles. Zhang Fakui agreed to convert the league from an independent organization into an umbrella group in August 1954, and then dissolved it entirely. In the end, Zhang Fakui admired Carsun Chang's personal virtue but was "extremely disappointed" by his lack of organizing ability. "Other than Carsun Chang's book, where can people go now to find the Third Force?" the general asked plaintively in his memoirs.[68] But General Zhang was just as much to blame. The "splendid group of men" simply could not organize themselves into a serious political force, let alone a militarily viable one.

Unleashing Chiang

Decommissioning the Third Force did not mean terminating all covert activities directed against the People's Republic of China. Rather, the Eisenhower administration shifted to unequivocal support for Chiang Kai-shek's forces on Taiwan, exploiting the island's potential for infiltration, surveillance, and espionage on the mainland.

Eisenhower laid the groundwork for a policy shift toward Taiwan in his February 1953 speech to Congress, where he stated that he was "issuing instructions that the Seventh Fleet no longer be employed to shield Communist China. This order implies no aggressive intent on our part. But we certainly have no obligation to protect a nation fighting us in Korea." The *New York Times* front-page headline blared "Eisenhower Frees Chiang to Raid Mainland," and the press labeled Ike's new posture "unleashing Chiang."[69] During the last six months of the Korean War, Nationalist commandos staged frequent raids from offshore islands like Jinmen and Matsu, where they received training and assistance from the CIA and the US Military Assistance Advisory Group.[70] The CIA also helped set up the Special Mission Group under the Nationalist Air Force in June 1953, just prior to the Korean Armistice, tasked with leaflet drops, aerial reconnaissance, and infiltrations. The Special Mission Group in Taiwan would fly over 50 missions in 1953 and 126 in 1954, according to researchers Chris Pocock and Clarence Fu.[71]

A CCP counterintelligence report circulated internally in January 1954 conveys a sense of the magnitude of subversive threat that mainland authorities thought themselves to be facing. Like the earlier report "Developments in Hong Kong" (1951), the analysis divided sabotage efforts into those run by the Departments of Defense and State. The military program was thought to be run by the Far East Intelligence Bureau headquartered in Tokyo, with its branches in Hong Kong and Taiwan supporting Nationalist sabotage efforts and intelligence collection. The State Department's covert effort relied on embassies, consulates, and US Information Service offices across Southeast Asia and Hong Kong, with assistance from missionaries doing sub rosa intelligence work. The USIS in Hong Kong was reported as initiating a program in late 1953 of recruiting students and businessmen to return to the mainland for hometown visits, business deals, or study opportunities, using the trips as cover for low-grade intelligence collection. The CIA cover organization in Taiwan, Western Enterprises, was also reported to be actively recruiting, training, and deploying agents.[72] The CCP report detected internal conflict among the various Nationalist intelligence services in Taiwan, which benefited from CIA training, competed for US funding, and desired autonomy in determining intelligence targets. The report noted Nationalist fears of being co-opted by Washington. Chiang Kai-shek's son, Chiang Ching-kuo set up an advanced instruction program for CIA-trained agents in order to continue their "political indoctrination" and ensure they were not "Americanized."[73]

A supplementary report from the same internal bulletin tallied up covert penetrations of Fujian Province over the course of 1953, noting the Nationalist attack at Meizhou Island in February and the division-sized assault on Dongshan on July 16, when the assault unit from Taiwan took very heavy casualties.[74] According to the historian Hsiao-ting Lin, the Nationalists' "catastrophe" at Dongshan marked the last major assault of its kind; henceforth, the CIA and Nationalists stuck to small-scale raids.[75] PRC counterintelligence claimed that CIA operatives cooked up a plot to sabotage an electricity company in Xiamen in early October 1953, but the mission had to be canceled due to difficulties landing the infiltration teams.[76] Zhejiang and Jiangsu Provinces were reportedly infiltrated by offshore spies—a counterintelligence summary claimed that special agent insertions into Jiangsu increased by 50 percent in early 1954, and the coastal Zhejiang city of Wenzhou harbored three- to five-man espionage teams created by operatives who had entered legally via Hong Kong.[77]

Fujian Province remained the biggest target. Over two dozen agents were captured along the Fujian coast and tried in November 1954 for espionage and sabotage.[78] Fujian reported twice as many operatives making unwelcome arrivals in 1953 as compared with 1952, and double that rate again in 1954. According to CCP counterintelligence analysis of the operations against Fujian in 1954, the primary objective was military intelligence, targeting coastal military installations and critical infrastructure such as airfields, railways, ports, and roads. One secret agent in Xiamen, for instance, provided detailed information on military units, naval capabilities, and artillery positions. Subversive activities ("inciting rebellion") were deemed to be the number two priority, and of a dozen attempts in Fujian, five were classified as "successful." A third category of operations was described as trying to "establish a party behind enemy lines"—in other words, creating underground networks to link up counterrevolutionary elements like ex-Nationalist soldiers and dispossessed landlords. The fourth type of operation was "psychological warfare," with teams based out of Matsu Island who specialized in dropping leaflets and handbills as well as carrying out "terrorist activities" to undermine CCP rule. Cadre readers were pointedly warned that special agents would go to extreme lengths to insinuate themselves, including employing honeypot methods of seducing or even marrying senior cadres, as instructed by spymistress Ci Shuzhen.[79]

While keeping CCP counterintelligence focused on the provinces across the Taiwan Strait, Chiang Kai-shek did have one other front available for pricking away at the mainland. In the far southwest, General Li Mi's Yunnan Anti-Communist National Salvation Army staged intermittent incursions across the border and caused ongoing diplomatic embarrassment.[80] The government of Burma complained loudly to the United States as well as at the United Nations about the violation of its sovereignty. Secretary Dulles agreed to a four-power conference with the Kingdom of Thailand, the Union of Burma, and the Republic of China in May 1953, and sent Wild Bill Donovan to Thailand as ambassador in September to make arrangements for repatriating the Nationalist troops.[81]

Although General Li Mi officially dissolved the National Salvation Army and thousands of soldiers headed to Taiwan, a rump force remained behind.[82] In a classified CCP report from November 1954, the Yunnan Province information service complained that Li Mi's "bandits" continued to conduct "fairly serious" intelligence gathering and disruptive operations on PRC soil, with armed bands ranging in size from 250 to 800 men in pockets along the border area.[83]

In the background of covert paramilitary operations and agent infiltrations, the US and Nationalist militaries continued to carry out relentless offshore and overhead surveillance of the mainland, as well as blockades and harassment of PRC ships at sea. The tally on water for 1953 was 2,436 "incidents" staged by 3,605

US and Taiwanese vessels—a monthly average of 200 incidents involving 300 ships. In addition, there were 1,815 air incidents involving 2,109 US and Nationalist planes along the coasts and over the interior.[84] Mao Zedong complained about the covert air war in his private meeting with Indian prime minister Nehru, who was making his first visit to the PRC in October 1954:

> American airplanes fly to the air space over our interior and air-drop special agents. These special agents form groups of seven to ten persons and are equipped with radio sets. Recently, scores of such groups of special agents have been air-dropped in our interior provinces. In Sichuan Province and parts of Qinghai adjacent to Tibet, American airplanes have air-dropped not only special agents, but also weapons to aid the bandits there. All this shows that a small number of people in the US authorities are bent on harming us whenever they have the opportunity to do so.[85]

Nehru was keen to know more about the special agent infiltrations, and he asked Zhou Enlai later that day to share details. Premier Zhou acknowledged that the number of "intrusions" had decreased since the Korean War Armistice. But the problem was not gone. Zhou gave Nehru a heads-up that "thirteen" American captive spies would be exposed soon: "Special agents were air-dropped as well. America did not stop air-dropping until they had wiped out these bandits. America has also air-dropped special agents into the forests in our country. We have captured some of them. Among these special agents, thirteen are American. We are going to make an announcement soon."

The US military continued aerial surveillance and naval interdictions. But, contrary to what Mao and Zhou told Nehru, CIA enthusiasm for helping Nationalist Jedburghs infiltrate the mainland was waning by the end of 1954.[86] The Far East Division deputy chief Des FitzGerald found the CIA China Mission in Yokosuka listless when he arrived in the fall. His superior, Al Ulmer, recalled that FitzGerald's visit to Taiwan left him unimpressed: "We were dropping agents into China—two a month—but we weren't getting much. . . . Des wanted out. He had no use for the Chinese Nationalists."[87] The massive CIA front in Taiwan, Western Enterprises, Inc., was dissolved by early 1955, with the Pentagon's Military Advisory Group taking over all responsibility for training Nationalist commandos.[88]

The disinclination to continue dropping agents behind the Bamboo Curtain paralleled a similar shift in tactics for operating behind the Iron Curtain. Jedburghs were going out of style at both ends of Eurasia. Harry Rositzke, who headed airborne infiltrations out of Europe, recalled that "air dispatch of radio-equipped agents virtually ceased in 1954."[89] The Jed mode of penetrating small-unit agents of subversion had a high failure rate, low intelligence yield, and negligible counterrevolutionary impact.

Diplomatic calculus also factored in the shift. Eisenhower wanted to avoid provoking the post-Stalin leadership in Moscow, which showed signs of softening its foreign policy line under First Secretary Nikita Khrushchev. But Beijing had a surprise for Washington, one that would make it difficult to act as if the era of infiltrating agents of subversion was well and truly ended.

12

SUBVERSION ON TRIAL

As the CIA poked, prodded, and probed for vulnerabilities in Communist China, the American fliers, as the Arnold Eleven were known in the press, had little idea what was happening in the outside world. "We thought the only way we would be released was if the American army invaded China and captured Peking," Wallace Brown recalled. "As far as we knew, the Third World War might already be under way." The crew began receiving letters from family in early September 1954, a sign of progress toward release, perhaps, and proof that the world knew of their plight. Brown was made to sign his indictment the following month, confessing to "dropping supplies to spies and saboteurs."[1] The trial and sentencing of the eleven airmen along with the two spies would thrust the American prisoners into the center of the maelstrom of US-China relations.

Crime and Punishment

After nearly two years in limbo, the Arnold crew finally had their day in court in November 1954, appearing before the Chinese People's Military Tribunal to face charges. Colonel Arnold, playing the part of stoic captain, smiled at his second-in-command and said, "Good luck, buddy. Pass it on." The eleven airmen filed in front of a panel of military judges seated on an elevated bench; behind them was an audience, mostly in uniform. "Glancing to the right," Major Baumer recalled, "I could see parachutes hanging from the walls, along with various articles commonly worn by combat crews in Korea. Other items were displayed on tables. I suppose this equipment was ours."[2]

Standing alongside the Arnold Eleven were two strangers, fellow Americans: Jack Downey and Dick Fecteau, whose two years hidden from the world were about to end. On seeing Downey for the first time since their capture, Fecteau was ready with a quip. "Hey Jack, who's your tailor?" he asked.[3]

The case against Downey and Fecteau was clear-cut. A law on the Articles for the Suppression of Counterrevolutionaries, passed in February 1951, established unambiguous legal grounds for conviction.[4] The presiding judge questioned Downey directly:

> JUDGE: What was your profession before you were arrested?
> DOWNEY: I was in the Central Intelligence Agency of the United States.
> JUDGE: What training did you undergo?
> DOWNEY: I received espionage training, consisting of guerilla warfare, weapons, small unit tactics, sabotage, the use of explosives, intelligence surveying, radio operating, parachute jumping, unarmed combat, map reading, etc.
> JUDGE: Did you come in person to Northeast China in August 1952?
> DOWNEY: Yes, I did.
> JUDGE: Why did you come?
> DOWNEY: To drop supplies for the "Wen Team."
> JUDGE: Did you come once again in November 1952?
> DOWNEY: Yes.
> JUDGE: Why did you come to Northeast China?
> DOWNEY: We came to pick up the agent "Bu Jingwu" [alias for Li Junying] and bring him back to Japan.[5]

Li Junying and his fellow Chinese agents were given court-appointed lawyers, including law faculty from the recently established People's University in Beijing. Defending counsel for Downey and Fecteau was Zhao Xilun, whose legal strategy was for the two Americans to acknowledge guilt, demonstrate repentance, and plead for leniency. Downey commented caustically, "It was a show trial. . . . On the other hand I was not an innocent lad who fell into the hands of robbers. I'd been trying to overthrow their government."[6] The trial was brief and the accused returned to prison.

The men were bused back to the court in handcuffs for sentencing on November 23. The main party newspaper, *People's Daily*, broadcast the result to the nation and the world the following day, reporting that eleven US military officers, two CIA officials, and nine Chinese agents had been found guilty by the Military Tribunal of the Supreme People's Court for acts of espionage and endangering national security. The news report detailed how the nine former followers of the bandit Chiang Kai-shek in 1951 joined the Free China Movement, a US-backed spy organization in Hong Kong, from whence they were sent to Saipan and Chigasaki to receive special training. They were given weapons and radios and parachuted into China's northeast. Their assignments were to commit terrorist acts of sabotage, gather military and economic intelligence, and organize guerrilla unrest. According to the Xinhua (New China) News Agency report, the mission's ultimate objective was to "pave the way for the Great War" in which the US would expand its military activities onto Chinese soil. The CIA chief in Chigasaki reportedly said that he looked forward to entering the PRC accompanied by the US military.[7]

The radio operator and double agent Niu Songlin received a comparatively light sentence of fifteen years. Li Junying, Team Wen leader Zhang Zaiwen, and two members of Team Shen (Luan Hengshan and Zhong Dianxin) were sentenced to life imprisonment. Two members of Team Shen (Wang Jinsheng and Wang Weifan) and two members of Team Wen (Xu Guangzhi and Yu Guanzhou) were sentenced to death.

The Arnold Eleven were sentenced according to rank, with the longest sentence going to Colonel Arnold, who got a ten-year prison term.[8] An accompanying article in the *People's Daily* explained that the 581st ARC was responsible for airdrop, resupply, and communications with agents in the USSR and PRC.

The two CIA spies came in for considerably harsher sentences than the uniformed airmen. Jack Downey was described as "chief culprit" and given a life sentence. Dick Fecteau, "assistant culprit," got twenty years. Fecteau joked to an ashen Downey, "My wife is going to die childless"—blithely unaware that she had died in a house fire the previous year. Downey took the sentence hard. "When I was sentenced to life, it was a complete revolution in my expectations. I was really depressed when I went back to my cell that night. And I said to myself, 'Do you realize, old buddy, you've just been sentenced to life imprisonment?' I had this vision of myself as an old gray-haired man, speaking broken Chinese, shuffling about the prison, sweeping up."[9]

The sentences handed down to Downey and Fecteau could have been worse, based on precedents in PRC spy trials involving foreigners. The first major foreign espionage trial, in the summer of 1951, ended in executions. Coming at the high point of the Campaign to Suppress Counterrevolutionaries, the case involved a former Italian air force pilot named Antonio Riva and the Japanese bookseller Ruichi Yamaguchi, who were given the death penalty for conspiring to assassinate Chairman Mao Zedong. Their plot allegedly called for Riva to kill Mao at the October 1950 parade in Tiananmen Square using an old trench mortar that he kept in his Beijing residence. It was further alleged that behind the scenes, the real mastermind was US Army Colonel David Barrett, who had met Mao in Yan'an as a member of the friendly American outreach back in 1944. Ironically, at the moment of the trial in Beijing, Barrett's career in the US government was being destroyed due to the pervasive suspicion of China Hands inspired by Senator McCarthy.[10]

While the plot to kill Mao may sound outlandish, the Barrett network was not a mere phantom of Communist paranoia. The CIA closely monitored fallout from the Riva/Yamaguchi case, fretting when Riva's wife Catherine, a US citizen, went public to defend her executed husband's innocence, while at the same time indicating that Yamaguchi was guilty. Yamaguchi had, in fact, been an agent of External Survey Detachment #44, the OSS unit based out of Shanghai and maintained by the OSO until the end of the Chinese Civil War. Yamaguchi, however, was reported as having "had no contact with CIA since the Communist occupation of Peiping."[11] The OSO acknowledged that it was "probable that Colonel Barrett recruited Yamaguchi, together with Riva and others, in Peiping and will attempt to quash further publicity about the net."[12]

The party's decision to execute the Italian and Japanese assassins came at a time when the Hate America movement was at fever pitch, which probably contributed to the severity of their sentencing given the link to Barrett. As it turned out, Riva's widow's sister, Peter Lum, was also living in Beijing at the time, accompanying her husband who worked in the British diplomatic mission. She vividly described the atmosphere of rising anti-American sentiment in late 1950:

> "Spontaneous" anti-American rallies are also common, usually centering around a dejected character with a large false nose (all foreigners are believed by the Chinese to have enormous noses), wearing a red-and-white-striped top-hat, who is led through the streets to be laughed and jeered at by his companions. The anti-American theme runs through everything. Even some of the pedlars who roast chestnuts in the streets have fitted up their stoves with an ingenious paper lantern which is turned by the heat rising from the fire and which shows three American tanks retreating before a Chinese soldier with fixed bayonet. . . . One of the things that strikes you most strongly is that this Chinese fear of America seems in large measure genuine. They have convinced themselves that America is about to invade China through Korea, Formosa, and Indo-China. . . . Shop windows are filled with pictures of Korean infants reputedly machine-gunned by American troops, of American planes apparently dive-bombing hospitals clearly marked with red crosses, of Dulles talking to a soldier during his recent visit to Korea and "pointing towards the north," thereby clearly proving that he is planning an invasion of China.[13]

But even in this overheated atmosphere of anti-Americanism, the expat community was stunned by the executions of Riva and Yamaguchi, according to Lum. She could only guess at how locals saw it.

> The effect on Peking's small foreign community may be imagined. I feel that the effect on the ordinary Chinese has also been considerable, and perhaps not quite what was intended, but that we cannot know. Until now probably no one quite believed that the Government would go so far as to execute a foreigner, especially under such circumstances; that is, with no open trial, no one allowed access to him, no evidence on his behalf, and no mention even to his own family of what the charges against him might be until he was already dead. One cannot but wonder, what next?[14]

It was impossible for Peter Lum to divine how ordinary Chinese thought of the spy trials, but the party had methods of monitoring public opinion on sensitive matters through its domestic surveillance organs. According to internal reports, the executions of the foreign "conspirators" Riva and Yamaguchi were popular with the masses. Most people liked the show of strength and cheered Chairman Mao's boldness, although some voiced fears that the US might retaliate against overseas Chinese.[15]

There had been a few more foreign spy trials outside Beijing between the Riva/Yamaguchi executions and the sentencing of Downey, Fecteau, and the Arnold Eleven. Cases were heard in Tianjin in November 1953 and in Guangdong Province in January and April 1954. And then, an espionage case in Shanghai put an American in prison for life.

Hugh Francis Redmond was an international businessman arrested on espionage charges three years prior, around the time of the Riva/Yamaguchi executions. He was accused of running a spy ring on behalf of External Survey Detachment #44, involving seven local agents.[16] The material evidence presented before the Shanghai court read like something out of an Ian Fleming novel: "Five radio receiving and transmitting sets, spare parts for radio sets, 16 secret code books, six bottles of chemical developer for invisible messages, two copies of radio calling and wave-length tables, a case of machine gun bullets, a specially constructed suitcase, and 406 copies of information reports, instructions, credentials and certificates."[17]

Redmond had in fact been with the OSS during the war, and was remembered as a "likeable guy, but not terribly effective" by fellow agent Jack Singlaub, who overlapped with him in Shenyang. Redmond ended up in Shanghai by the end of the Civil War and volunteered to be a stay-behind agent, posing as an international businessman and enjoying newlywed life with his Russian wife.[18] After

Redmond's arrest in April 1951, the CIA received intelligence that he may have been executed: "A Portuguese DP who left Shanghai in mid-August has reported that a former U.S. paratrooper in Chinese military uniform is believed to be collaborating with the Chinese Communists in Shanghai. The man lives at the former Shanghai address of Hugh Redmond, a stay-behind staff employee previously reported arrested and possibly executed, who was also a former paratrooper. OSO is attempting to check the report."[19] It was bad intel—Redmond was being held in Shanghai's Ward Prison for over three years with no public statement from Chinese authorities until his sentencing. On September 12, 1954, he was given life. Two of his alleged local agents were sentenced to death.[20]

"Why Not Kill the Americans?"

With these precedents in mind, the Communist Party carefully observed the public's response to the trial and punishment in the capital of such a large batch of agents of subversion—thirteen American and nine Chinese. Special attention was paid, naturally, to the reaction in the northeast.

The Liaoning Province branch of Xinhua News Agency reported on the mood in Shenyang, where locals were consumed by news of events that had taken place around them. Most of those monitored found the sentence to be just, in the national interest, and proof of the country's independence. It struck a "heavy blow" against American imperialist aggression. Some residents, however, thought the sentence was too lenient. Zhang Huidong, the owner of True Likeness photography, called for no mercy. "This government captured them and should execute them all," Zhang said. Another resident, He Fucheng, grilled a police officer about why some of the Chinese agents were given death sentences, while the American spies were not. An assistant manager at a factory admitted to being impressed by the imperialists' ability to link up paratroopers from the air with agents working on the ground. "There's really nothing these guys cannot do," he commented. A gabble of locals was overheard saying, "The Americans are something else, it's really amazing how they can fly in and pick their agents right up from the ground." A factory manager, Song Junsheng, saw a longer play at work in sparing the spies capital punishment: "Why not kill the Americans? Maybe it's for a POW exchange between the two countries. Maybe China has sent spies to America, and in the future hopes for an exchange of personnel."[21]

It was a fair question—Why *not* kill the Americans? "Espionage is not tainted with any 'legality,'" Allen Dulles mused. "If a spy intrudes on your territory, you catch him if you can and punish him according to your laws. That applies without regard to the means of conveyance he has taken to reach his destination—railroad, automobile, balloon or aircraft, or, as my forebears used to say, by shanks' mare."[22] The US government, moreover, had proved itself willing to kill even its own citizens for spying, as President Eisenhower demonstrated in the summer of 1953 when he allowed the executions of Julius and Ethel Rosenberg. Arrested just after the outbreak of the Korean War and convicted in the spring of 1951, the Rosenbergs were sentenced to death on the basis of the Espionage Act of 1917. Decryptions of Soviet communications by government cryptanalysts in the top-secret Venona Project provided hard evidence of espionage activities by numerous agents in the US, UK, Canada, and Australia, including the Rosenbergs.[23] But while the Rosenbergs were convicted, the public and the courts were kept in the dark about the Venona evidence in order to protect the decryption program. There was considerable skepticism toward the government's prosecution, and sympathy for the Rosenbergs. Facing national controversy—Eisenhower remembered "Communist and anti-Communist demonstrations up and down Pennsylvania Avenue"—the president wanted to show the Russians that Americans were not weak-willed or vulnerable to subversion.[24] The United States of America would execute its own—women and men alike—if that was what it would take to win the Cold War.

While President Eisenhower used the Rosenberg executions to signal merciless resolve in the face of Communist subversion, Chairman Mao and Premier Zhou used the spy trials to assert the legitimacy of their legal system. Legality was a long-standing bone of contention in Sino-Western diplomacy, with the United States and European powers traditionally refusing to allow their nationals to be tried by Chinese courts on a principle called extraterritoriality. The "unequal treaties" signed by the Qing dynasty with the British, Americans, and other imperial powers were predicated on a Western prejudice against the Chinese justice system as fundamentally illegitimate. This imperialistic view was not far in the past at the time of Mao's spy trials. The US had renounced its treaty privileges only in 1942.

With questions of legality in the background, the party went to great lengths to convince the court of public opinion that Downey and Fecteau were treated in a way consistent with international laws and norms. Top legal scholars published articles laying out the case against the spies and delineating why the men did not qualify as POWs. Oxford-trained international law expert Chen Tiqiang explained: "Any one with the slightest familiarity with international law knows that only captured members of the armed forces of a belligerent can be considered prisoners of war by the captor side. No state of war exists between China and the United States. US spies who have intruded into China for espionage are not prisoners of war.'"[25] Wang Tieya, a professor of international law at Peking University, refuted the objection to treating the Arnold crew as spies since they were wearing military uniforms, citing a leading authority on international law, L. F. L.

Oppenheim of Cambridge University. "Even this bourgeois scholar admitted that it is chiefly the espionage activities and not the clothes that determine whether a person is a spy," Professor Wang wrote. "In international law, he [Oppenheim] asserts, every state has the right to punish spies. All international law experts, including bourgeois international law experts, acknowledge this."[26]

Bombshell

Why did Mao and Zhou wait two years and then decide to play their pair of aces alongside the Arnold flush at the particular moment of Thanksgiving 1954? One counterintuitive hypothesis at the time was to read the trial as a pretext for re-initiating dialogue with the United States. Fledgling contacts established with Washington on the sidelines of the Geneva Conference had petered out. The American negotiator in Geneva, Ambassador Johnson, thought the sentencing was timed "to test our depth of commitment to getting the prisoners back and to prod Washington into more aggressive courtship."[27] At the other end of the spectrum of interpretation, the revelation of captured spies could be seen as designed to humiliate Washington, damaging US standing with its European allies and at the United Nations. Perhaps the public relations damage—at a time of ongoing crisis in the Taiwan Strait—could even prevent Eisenhower and Dulles from offering a treaty alliance to Chiang Kai-shek.

Whatever the intent, Beijing's announcement of the sentencing of the American prisoners arrived at CIA headquarters late in the afternoon on Tuesday, November 23 like a bombshell. It would be a long Thanksgiving week. Shockingly, incomprehensibly, Jack Downey and Dick Fecteau were not dead. The confidence of Sherman Kent's analysts that the ChiComs would not be able to resist making propaganda hay out of a pair of captured American spies turned out to have been very wrong indeed. Worse, Chinese press reports indicated that the operation had been blown well in advance of the flight on November 29, 1952. The in-house history noted, "Chief/FE concluded that it was probable that the ST/AROMA team had been doubled immediately after their launching or that the Chinese Communists had obtained text of messages from the team operator or other team members by interrogation after capture." Rumors would bubble up in the Agency that Fecteau had gotten a lighter sentence because he talked. There was also watercooler chatter that neither man should have been on the plane, that they were on a "joyride."[28] The painful truth was that the Agency faced a counterintelligence disaster and public relations nightmare of global proportions.

For the Eisenhower administration, the sudden attention to the issue of lost captives was like rubbing salt in a wound. Eisenhower had been under pressure from Republicans in Congress all year over the issue of American soldiers still unaccounted for after the Korea Armistice POW exchanges were completed. The Massachusetts Republican Thomas Lane introduced a resolution in the House of Representatives in January blasting the White House for abandoning 944 "forgotten Americans." Lane put out a blistering press release: "American foreign policy is becoming so confused and so cowardly that we can't trust the government to protect our own citizens from the Reds. . . . It is nothing short of treason by our government toward the men it drafted for military services . . . and then abandoned to the enemy."[29] After Ambassador Johnson gave his list of 944 lost Americans to the PRC delegation at the Geneva Conference in June, the United Nations Command in Korea used the Military Armistice Commission to demand accounting for an even longer list of 3,400 UNC personnel, of mixed nationalities. The Communist side countered with their own list of 98,000 missing Chinese and Korean citizens.[30]

The sentencing of the Arnold Eleven and the bombshell announcement that Downey and Fecteau were alive poured fresh fuel on these flames. Fecteau was from Thomas Lane's congressional district, and the congressman wasted no time in firing off a letter to John Foster Dulles demanding that the State Department give the Chinese Reds an ultimatum: release the prisoners or face a blockade.

> Force is the only argument that will induce them to release our fellow citizens. I, therefore, ask that our State Department serve notice on the Chinese Reds that they will be given one week to fly these men out to freedom. If this demand is not complied with, we shall inform the Chinese Reds that we shall step [up] our aid to Chaing Kai Shek [*sic*], and permit him to engage in counter-offensive actions against the Chinese mainland, effectively sealing off all Red commerce. I am sure that such a realistic policy will convince the Communists that they must respect the legitimate rights of the United States and its citizens.[31]

Bill Knowland, the senator from Formosa, was now Senate majority leader. The *New York Times* ran his attack on Eisenhower for being soft on Communism on the front page on Thanksgiving Day, next to a report on Beijing's claims of subversive activities directed against them in recent years. Knowland had emerged as a key figure in the Asia-First Republican movement, which hammered away at Democrats, and sometimes fellow Republicans, for the loss of China and the failure in Korea. As the historian Joyce Mao explains, Asia-First Republicans sought to "internationalize" conservatism by linking their anti-communist, pro–Chiang Kai-shek agenda to a domestic platform of dismantling the New Deal welfare state, with its "socialist" underpinnings.[32] It was the antithesis of Schlesinger's vital center.

Under massive pressure from Congress and the press, the interagency Operations Coordinating Board (set up by Eisenhower in place of Truman's Psychological Strategy Board to oversee covert activities) convened an emergency session to craft a response to the "illegal and amoral action of the Chinese Communist Government."[33] The Defense Department offered three options to get the men home and reassert the US's "international position." The first was a set of military actions that could be undertaken unilaterally, such as a sea blockade, the seizure of ships and crews (to be held as bargaining chips), or an ultimatum threatening air strikes on ports or industrial facilities ("not as an act of war but as an act of retaliation"). The second option was to work through the United Nations, drafting a resolution to create a commission of investigation with a mandate to enter PRC territory. Option three was to support Nationalist-led retaliation, both overt (such as interdiction of the main southern rail line) and covert. "Covert U.S. support for Chinese Nationalist seizure of additional off-shore islands now held by the Chinese Communists as retaliation for the illegal imprisonment of Chinese and American individuals, to be followed by overt U.S. association with the action; Provision of support for a medium-scale raid on the China mainland by the Nationalists for purposes of seizing hostages followed by open U.S. support of such action."[34]

As the Operations Coordinating Board deliberated, John Foster Dulles sent his diplomats on the offensive. He tried the two readily available channels to get a message into the hands of Mao and Zhou: PRC representatives in Geneva and the British legation in Beijing. Hours after receiving the news about Downey and Fecteau via Radio Peking, Dulles sent a telegram to diplomats in Geneva with instructions to meet the ChiCom representative as soon as possible in order "to protest their action as groundless." "You should also point out Chinese Communists have never before mentioned Fecteau and Downey despite repeated requests they account for all Americans, and that this is an especially flagrant example of deplorable Chinese Communist practice of holding prisoners incommunicado."[35] The consul in Geneva was told to read the Chinese the riot act using the official press release. The statement offered a version of the story—that is to say, the lie—that the US government would tell about the Downey and Fecteau operation:

> American Consul General instructed to protest the sentencing of two civilians to life and 20 years respectively, on similar trumped up charges [of being espionage agents] as a most flagrant violation of justice. These men, John Thomas Downey and Richard George Fecteau were civilian personnel employed by the Department of the Army in Japan. They were believed to have been lost on a flight from Korea to Japan in November 1952. How they came into the hands of the Chinese Communists is

> unknown to the US but the fact of their detention was obviously known by the Chinese Communists and was deliberately concealed by them when the possible repatriation of Americans was discussed at Geneva in June of this year. . . . The continued wrongful detention of these American citizens furnishes further proof of the Chinese Communist regime's disregard of accepted practices of international conduct.[36]

What Downey and Fecteau were doing was to be left unspecified, except to establish a connection to the Korean War that would help to qualify them as POWs who should have been released in accordance with the Armistice Agreement in 1953. As the State Department put it to the British, "They were on a confidential mission in support of the United Nations Command. The mission was directly related to the United Nations defense against the Chinese Communist aggression in Korea."[37]

Consul General Franklin C. Gowan met with his Chinese counterparts at Geneva's elegant Hotel Beau Rivage five days after the news landed. When the PRC diplomat tried to interrupt, Gowan proudly cabled to Washington that "I drowned him out by continuing my protest in the loudest possible tone." Gowan's patronizing account leaves no hint of awareness that the Chinese had truth on their side. "After consulting among themselves Chinese said they could not receive protest. I said they had noted it and written it down. . . . Meeting thus ended at 5:45 with the Chinese mumbling among themselves and apparently at loss to decide if they had anything else to say."[38]

Meanwhile, in London, the US embassy asked the British Foreign Office to pass on a letter of protest, couched in the language of self-righteous indignation, demanding redress and claiming damages. It asserted that the US government

> vigorously protests the wrongful action . . . grossly contrary to the substance and spirit of all recognized international standards as to the protection of prisoners of war. The maltreatment of two civilian American citizens whose names were willfully and deceitfully withheld by the Chinese Communist representatives at Geneva last June from the list of American civilians held in Chinese Communist jails, is equally reprehensible. . . . The Chinese Communist authorities are under an obligation to redress in so far as possible the wrong they have inflicted on these American nationals and their families. The United States Government reserves the right to claim compensation as may be determined appropriate, and to demand the punishment of the Chinese Communist officials responsible for the denial of the rights of these persons.[39]

Chinese diplomats in London and the Foreign Ministry in Beijing refused to receive the American letter of innocence via the British.[40] "It is no secret that the United States is engaging in espionage in China," the British were told curtly in Beijing. "'Western [grp. undec.] [*Enterprises*, handwritten notation]' in Formosa and Nationalist-occupied islands, the enormous United States Consulate-General in Hong Kong, and Central Intelligence Agency's ATSUK Organization in Japan, are all well known centres of United States espionage activity against China."[41]

Even as Dulles asked the Brits for help, the State Department refused to designate the United Kingdom as its representative in dealing with Beijing, fearing an implicit recognition of PRC sovereignty. The American inflexibility stymied mediation efforts by the British chargé d'affaires, Humphrey Trevelyan.[42] Trevelyan later wrote, "We felt that the interests of Americans kept in China were more important than the American theoretical position, and said so. As usual, Mr Dulles was on Duck Island."[43] Internally, the British Foreign Office was not quite sure what to make of the case. Surely the Americans could not have been so reckless? "Little is known of them [Downey and Fecteau] either to us or to the U.S. Embassy here, but the Chinese claim them to be agents of the U.S. Central Intelligence Agency. We cannot at present say definitely that this is not so, but it is difficult to believe that the Americans would ever have attempted to land non-Chinese agents in China."[44]

Back in Washington, among the three options presented to the Operations Coordinating Board, the initial choice was to impose an offshore naval blockade, pending congressional approval, that would specifically exempt the port at Hong Kong and Soviet flag vessels destined for Port Arthur and Dairen.[45] But the blockade idea soon faced headwinds. The State Department's legal adviser, Herman Phleger, "found that certain of the individuals were connected with CIA and were not in uniform." So, while holding the Arnold Eleven might be legitimately construed as a violation of the Korean Armistice Agreement, such was not the case with Downey and Fecteau. Moreover, a blockade would constitute an act of war and a violation of the United Nations Charter. "Mr. Phleger concluded that we should not undertake a blockade, but should attack the action as a violation of the Armistice and the assurance given to us and the British, and should seek to line up the sixteen nations and demand adherence to the Armistice terms."[46] The international lawyer's advice was to focus on the Arnold crew and punt to the UN.

The CIA's estimate as to the likely impact of a blockade was no more encouraging. Analysts warned that Beijing would likely interpret a blockade as a prelude to attack, and that the US would be isolated internationally, given that China had the facts on its side.

> Peiping probably feels that it has a convincing case against the US prisoners, or at least against certain of them. More importantly, it would feel that its prestige as a leading Asian power had been directly challenged by the US blockade. Peiping would probably estimate that the blockade would offer possibilities for the Communists to isolate the US on this issue. Peiping would probably be surprised at the vigor of the US reaction and would be concerned lest it signified a US intention to take still more aggressive action against Communist China. In any case, Peiping would probably believe that the US was willing to proceed without its allies and that the US was psychologically prepared at the moment to attack the mainland in reaction to any attack against the blockading forces.[47]

Analysts anticipated that neutralist countries like India would harshly criticize a blockade, revanchists like Taiwan and South Korea might feel emboldened, and support from Great Britain and Japan could not be taken for granted.[48] Pacific Command, which would enforce a blockade, was similarly disinclined. The commander opposed retaliation for the sentencing, given that the "ChiComs may have good case in international court against some of these people."[49]

As State, Defense, and the CIA backed away from punitive measures, Congress continued to demand retaliation. Senator Leverett Saltonstall (R-Massachusetts) forwarded to Secretary Dulles a telegram from two Boston men ready to enlist for a war against Red China if the prisoners were not released in the next forty-eight hours.[50] Representative Thomas J. Dodd (D-Connecticut), who represented Jack's mother Mary Downey, called for an embargo. The day after getting a briefing from Allen Dulles, Dodd wrote to the president. His tone was respectful, but he demanded "strong and positive action." If a trade embargo failed, then next would have to be a naval blockade of the China coast. "The Chinese Communists will only respect strength."[51] The loudest voice in the outcry was Senator Knowland, who infuriated the president with his grandstanding. Years later, Ike wrote contemptuously of Knowland, "The hard way is to have the courage to be patient."[52]

Cloudy

After Congress, the next-biggest problem complicating the administration's efforts to clean up the mess of a botched covert operation was the press. A wire story out of Tokyo quickly poked holes in the paper-thin cover story put out at the time to explain Downey and Fecteau's disappearance. The Far East Air Force spokesman said on record that Downey and Fecteau were "hitchhikers" on a CAT plane flown by Captain Snoddy, whose family now wondered if Robert might be alive as well. The Air Force claimed ignorance about what had happened to the plane "after it vanished from the radar screens over the Eastern Korean coast." The United Press report repeated the cover story that search and rescue teams "scoured the Sea of Japan for two days after the plane disappeared," but drew attention to another inconsistency: Far East Command headquarters could not find a record for either Downey or Fecteau in the files of civilian employees.[53] What to do about these pesky reporters?

Two years earlier, at the staff meeting at CIA headquarters on the eve of the exfiltration disaster, Beetle Smith gave Allen Dulles and other senior deputies tips on how to handle the media. Beetle instructed them that when asked by the press about CIA-related activities, simply to say nothing. "In rare cases, however," the director added, "it might be necessary to go to the top man of a news organization in order to kill a story."[54] Now, as Director Dulles conferred with his brother Secretary Dulles in preparation for reporters' questions on the Downey/Fecteau case, it seemed like one of those rare cases. The transcript of conversation between John Foster ("Sec.") and Allen ("AWD") reads:

> The Sec. said he will be asked at his press conference about the 2 civilians. Do we say they were part of the UN operation? AWD said the story is they were civilian members of the Dept. of Defense. We generally refer them to Defense as one way of handling it. The Sec. said the Pres. sent word yesterday to [Secretary of Defense] Wilson he should refer people to the Sec. AWD said that the above was the story given out at the time of their supposed death and we have stuck to it. It was done, said the Sec, before this Adm. came in in 1952. . . . AWD said it would be best to find a way to avoid going into details—although it would be hard. It is difficult to change stories now.[55]

The State Department prepared a confidential fact sheet on Downey and Fecteau that obfuscated their employment at the time of the disappearance in language worthy of Kafka. Their status was "contract employee assigned as administrative assistant on classified technical research project." "Name of Contracting Agency: Project continues operative and classified—not releasable." Employed since June 1951, departed for Japan in December 1951. "Circumstances of Disappearance: Temporarily in Korea in connection with duties. Departed Seoul for return Japan at 1:00 a.m. about the first of Dec. 1952. Aircraft reported overdue off the coast of Honshu, Japan, three hours later. Search instituted on the same day revealed nothing." Schwartz and Snoddy were listed as pilot and co-pilot. "DC-3 belonging to Civil Air Transport, Inc., under military contract with the Far Eastern Air Force."[56]

Armed with these facts, Secretary Dulles escaped the press conference on December 1 relatively unscathed. He spoke by phone with the president shortly thereafter about the "terrible situation." Both men sounded confused about the Arnold mission, referring to it as "funny business." Dulles advised Eisenhower to keep blaming the Chinese for deceit and to cast aspersions on their motives for bringing the issue to the fore now.

> The Pres. asked what if they press as to the exact status of the prisoners. Both are worried about this. The Pres. suggested he say it seems probable the plane landed in such circumstances they can say they are not prisoners of war. The Sec. said that will put some people in the position of not telling the truth. Some were not in uniform nor in Korea. They agreed it was a funny business about the other plane as it evidently shouldn't have been so used. 13 were aboard to drop leaflets. Arnold had no business to be there. He was back here before doing that and told everything. They agreed it is a terrible situation. The Sec. said he thinks the Pres. is high enough up to shove some of it back to the Sec. Some is actually a matter of the War Dept. records. The essential thing said the Sec. is they agreed by the Armistice to return all prisoners of war. They have acted in a deceitful way. They supposedly gave all names at Geneva but didn't give the names of civilians. The Pres. can say it was brought out now to make it more difficult with our allies.[57]

Differences between the president and the Dulles brothers were on display at a freewheeling National Security Council session on Far East policy held that same day. Ike and Allen Dulles clashed over the big strategic debate at the heart of China policy: whether the Maoist regime could really survive, and if so, whether it might make a Titoist turn away from Moscow. Eisenhower was convinced that the PRC was weaker than it looked and "these totalitarian regimes were excessively rigid and have inherent weaknesses on which we should attempt to capitalize." Allen disagreed that sudden collapse was in the cards, but he did foresee "a chance of disassociating Communist China from the Soviet Union."

John Foster then debated the president over the value of promoting counterrevolutionary forces—not with commando paratroopers, but through psychological warfare. They argued over a line in the draft that read, "Creation in non-Communist Asia, and ultimately within Communist China, of political and social forces which will zealously spread the greater values of the free world and simultaneously expose the falsity of the Communist ideological offensive." How could anyone object, Eisenhower asked, when this is precisely what the US Information Agency was set up to do? Dulles thought it was unrealistic.

> The President replied that he was obliged to disagree with Secretary Dulles. Zealots, in this paragraph, did not necessarily mean evangelists of the Billy Sunday type, who would be running up and down the countryside in Communist China publicly proclaiming democratic ideals. The actual task could be done quite differently and perhaps with some effect.
>
> Secretary Dulles countered that he remained unconvinced, and the President said in that case why do we spend so much money to enable the Voice of America to beam messages to the captive Communist states?[58]

Next it was Eisenhower's turn to face the press (the president held weekly press conferences throughout much of his eight years in office). He began with a sweeping statement that framed the crisis over the American captives in China as part of the broader question of how to win the Cold War against Communism. The tragedy of the thirteen men was inseparable from "this struggle we are now in, [that] we call the cold war. The great hope of mankind is that we can find methods and means of progressing a little bit, even if by little steps, toward a true or real peace, and that we do not go progressively toward war."[59]

Speaking like a realist, in line with the strategy of Kennan and the philosophy of Niebuhr, Eisenhower explained that America's challenge was to stand up against totalitarianism without either sacrificing its own principles or stumbling into World War III. Ike argued that the spy trial in Beijing was one element of a grand Communist design: "To fit this incident into the global picture, let me remind you these prisoners have been held by the Chinese for 2 years, so their selection of a time of announcement was, of course, a deliberate act. In fact, we find little evidence in all of the actions of the Communist States that indicates any haphazard actions on their part. Everything they do is deliberate and well thought out." And the intent was precisely to provoke Americans to act on an impulse "to lash out." But war (as Eisenhower was uniquely qualified to say) is a horrible thing. So "we owe it to ourselves and to the world to explore every possible peaceable means of settling difference before we even think of such a thing as war." Eisenhower therefore rejected the calls for a blockade and passed the buck to the United Nations, on whose behalf "at least 11 of these soldiers" were fighting as uniformed troops under United Nations Command as part of the struggle in Korea.[60] It was an impressive performance of manipulating the press and, by extension, the American public, guiding the people toward a realistic course of action—without acknowledging the lie upon which this realism was predicated.

One astute reporter, John M. Hightower of the Associated Press, tried to dig on the distinction between the Arnold crew and Downey/Fecteau, asking the president if he could add anything "about the status of the other two men, in addition to the 11 men who were in uniform?" Eisenhower parried the question, saying, "Well, it is cloudy, and I couldn't discuss it in detail."[61] He took one more question, on an unrelated subject, and the conference wrapped up.

While stopping well short of an admission, the president's description of Downey and Fecteau's case as "cloudy" was hardly a ringing affirmation of their innocence. British diplomats picked up on the signal. The head of the Far Eastern Department at the Foreign Office, C. T. Crowe, was on board with using British influence to help the Americans repatriate the Arnold Eleven. But when it came to Downey and Fecteau, "as President Eisenhower has said, the question of their status is 'cloudy.'"[62]

Having survived the initial press conferences, the interagency working group deliberated on how to handle the diplomatic and public relations dilemma presented by the captive spies. The State Department's lead official was Director of the Office of Chinese Affairs Walter McConaughy, brought back in 1951 from his posting as consul general in Hong Kong. In consultation with his CIA and Defense counterparts, McConaughy rationalized why the public should be kept in the dark about the Downey/Fecteau affair. "Any comprehensive revelation of the precise nature of the mission of Downey and Fecteau, although that mission was legitimate and necessary, would be highly questionable." In the near term, disclosure could jeopardize efforts to get the Arnold Eleven released. "Something of a shadow would be cast over that [Arnold] case which is now absolutely clear. It is believed that the excellent position we are now in as to the 11 airmen would be compromised to some extent." As to the two spies, revealing the facts of their mission would likely prejudice world opinion *against* pressuring for their release. "Politically our case as to the two would not seem airtight to the world at large if essentially all the facts were known. Even on the legal plane, there would be some unresolved questions of considerable import."[63]

McConaughy further asserted that the American public would be outraged if the government "outed" its own agents. In other words, telling the public the truth would be a betrayal of their trust. Then there was the problem of having to contradict earlier statements, which "would seriously weaken our stance." Beijing would score points. "They might actually argue with some plausibility that the sentences are lighter than are customary in such cases in wartime." Finally, there was the need to uphold inherently deceitful traditions of international espionage. To be honest about the case would undermine international norms! "An official and circumstantial revelation of the nature of the mission of these two would be counter to long-established usage of all countries. It is simply not customary for Governments to make any official disclosures regarding these operations, although they are carried on by all Governments in wartime. It is contrary to the practice of nations from time immemorial. It would be a breach of the tradition of official silence on these matters. As one member said 'it is not the form—no country ever does it.'"[64]

On behalf of the CIA, Frank Wisner added a note to the file to clarify that the Downey/Fecteau mission was not some rogue operation by the OPC. He documented the fact that planning and execution for supporting counterrevolutionaries took place in accordance with national security directives from the State Department and on the basis of military orders approved by the Department of Defense.

> It is most significant that the very activities in which these civilians were engaged, had been requested by the Joint Chiefs of Staff and had been approved as to policy by the State Department. Shortly after the outbreak of the Korean war, and on or about 10 July 1950, CIA was officially advised that the JCS had recommended to the Secretary of Defense that CIA be authorized to exploit guerrilla potential *on the Chinese Mainland to accomplish the objective of reducing the Chinese Communist capabilities to reinforce North Korean forces.* On 20 July 1950, the State Department approved a CIA dispatch . . . authorizing the initiation of operations with this identical objective. From time to time thereafter during the course of the Korean hostilities, authorized spokesmen of the Department of Defense, the Joint Chiefs of Staff and the Department of State affirmed and reiterated their support of CIA guerrilla and resistance operations on the Chinese Mainland. In October 1951 the National Security Council, by its Directive 10/5, authorized the conduct of expanded guerrilla activities within China.[65]

A week later, Wisner talked to McConaughy and submitted another memo for the Downey/Fecteau file. He added more details tightening the link between the Third Force project and the Korean War effort, which defined the mission objective in tactical military terms rather than strategic or political ones.

> I should have included in the earlier information at this point the additional information that we were advised in writing by a memorandum dated 15 October 1951 that the JCS had approved and that the Secretary of Defense had concurred in supporting CIA * * * in the development of

> its programs which are designed to support anti-Communist Chinese groups in China (and that) the objectives of these programs are to support US policy in Asia by *interfering mainly through the disruption of communications, with the Communist Chinese capability of reinforcing its effort in North Korea.*[66]

To strengthen the linkage to the United Nations Command in Korea, Wisner also noted the CAT exfiltration flight was approved by the UNC chief of staff.[67]

According to the CIA's in-house study, Wisner and others in the Agency opposed making a distinction between the Arnold Eleven and Downey/Fecteau, causing "serious differences" with Defense and State. "The separation led to great personal bitterness on the part of the Downey family who felt, rightly or wrongly, that it cost their son his freedom, a sentiment that was shared by many people in the Agency."[68]

As the administration did its best to keep the public ignorant of the truth of the Downey/Fecteau case while at the same time taming passions in Congress for retaliation, Eisenhower and Dulles took the final step in a momentous strategic decision that would shape America's role in the Far East for decades to come.

Chiang Kai-shek had been lobbying to join the top tier of US defense treaty allies in Asia, which after the Manila Pact in August 1954 came to include the Kingdom of Thailand and the Republic of Vietnam as part of SEATO, the Southeast Asia Treaty Organization. Mao's provocations in the Taiwan Strait only strengthened John Foster Dulles's resolve to give Chiang a treaty—one that could be used to deter Mao, but also, as necessary, to restrain Chiang. US-ROC treaty negotiations began in November after a major PLA attack on Dachen Island in the Taiwan Strait. The draft language for the treaty to defend Taiwan—as well as a secret bilateral note to constrain Chiang by requiring US approval before the use of force—was finalized on November 23, 1954, the same day that Beijing broke the news of the spy trial.[69] A couple days before Secretary Dulles and ROC Minister of Foreign Affairs George Yeh signed the treaty, PRC media warned the public it was imminent.[70]

The US-ROC defense pact provided Chiang's island state with a formal guarantee of regime safety and national security underwritten by the world's strongest superpower. Despite Premier Zhou's impressive performance in Geneva, Chiang managed to hang on to the China seat at the United Nations and its coveted status as a permanent, veto-wielding member of the Security Council. The US-ROC treaty drove the final nail in the coffin of Third Force visions, dashing Carsun Chang's hopes of US support. But Eisenhower's embrace of Chiang came with strings attached: the new strategy, approved at the National Security Council in December, set aside the goal of counterrevolutionary rollback in favor of a more modest objective of simply keeping the CCP off-balance and defending non-Communist regimes from "subversion."[71] The days of making counterrevolution, for now, were over.

Subversion on Exhibition

With Washington having formalized its commitment to Taipei, Beijing presented evidence of American perfidy in a steady stream of news reports and commentaries on subversive activities, some of which made it into the international press. To educate the masses on the evil designs of the American imperialists, the PRC government organized public exhibitions, a favorite weapon of East and West in the early Cold War battle for hearts and minds. The US Information Agency, for example, produced exhibitions around the world for the Atoms for Peace Campaign, attracting hundreds of thousands of visitors at events staged from Ghana to Kyoto. Western media provided glowing coverage of the exhibitions, which was the by-product of what the historian Kenneth Osgood describes as the Eisenhower administration's "sophisticated strategy of camouflaging propaganda messages by embedding them in news stories and private initiatives."[72]

The Chinese and Soviets were equally sophisticated, and they collaborated on socialist bloc exhibition diplomacy. The British chargé Trevelyan described how in the early 1950s "Russians were at this time swarming over China. . . . They organized vast exhibitions in Peking, Shanghai and Canton, and presented the buildings and exhibits to the Chinese."[73] Major exhibitions could be seen in Shanghai on the evils of Catholicism, featuring a doctored photograph of a Belgian priest cavorting with a local woman; in Wuhan, on the suffering of peasants and their liberation thanks to the land reform movement; in Shenyang, on spies and subversives, organized as part of the Campaign to Suppress Counterrevolutionaries.[74] Beijing's best-known international exhibition was launched in the spring of 1952; it was a traveling exhibit of evidence of alleged germ warfare attacks by the US during the Korean War. It was the centerpiece in a nationwide campaign built around Premier Zhou Enlai's claims that the US Air Force dropped millions of infected animals into Manchuria as biological weapons.[75] Raja Hutheesing was taken to the Korean War exhibition in May 1952: "Every photograph or poster in the exhibition bore captions in three languages, Chinese, Russian and English. The Indian Delegation was conducted through every detail of the exhibition and guides read out each caption. It took more than three hours to go round and Mme. Pandit had to listen to each and every explanation patiently. The Chinese were obviously anxious that she should miss no detail."[76]

Two weeks after the sentencing of Downey and Fecteau, the government staged the Exhibition of Evidence of US Paratrooper Special Agents. Close to one hundred thousand visitors—party cadres, PLA soldiers, students, urban residents, farmers from surrounding areas, and people from around the country—made their way through the Soviet Exhibit Hall at the Working People's Palace of Culture in Beijing. Foreigners were invited, too—embassy staff, journalists, exchange students, Soviet and Hungarian experts, a writer from India. Three to four thousand visitors each day gazed at the displays of wireless transmitters and portable generators, secret codebooks and maps, and every kind of weapon from revolvers to submachine guns. Radio batteries marked "Willard Storage Battery Company, Cleveland, Ohio" proved the American provenance of the secret agents. A photograph of Downey and Fecteau near their burning aircraft, snapped at the moment of their capture by Chinese security forces, was mounted for viewing, along with seven maps of Manchuria that they carried on them—the one labeled "distributed by U.S.A.F. Aeronautical Chart and Information Service" had pencil markings of a line drawn from Tianchi on Changbai Mountain to Laoling, where liaison Li Junying was to be for his pickup. In total there were ten thousand "objects captured from the air-dropped spies"—everything from forged papers to ammunition rounds.[77]

Official news reports praised the Special Agents Exhibition for educating the public and inspiring the masses to greater vigilance in combating subversive threats.

> Tens of thousands of people in the past seven days have seen the exhibition on US spying in China. Among them were visitors from embassies and legations in Peking and many foreign correspondents. Hundreds of visitors since the exhibition opened on 6th December have written in the visitors' books of their indignation at American espionage activities direct against their country. Workers, peasants and armymen have pledged greater vigilance to protect China against those who would attempt to destroy her achievements.[78]

Xinhua News Agency highlighted the visit of a Tibetan dignitary, the tenth panchen lama Panchen Ngoerhtehni, then serving as vice chairman of the National Committee of the Chinese People's Political Consultative Conference—a hint, perhaps, to the Dalai Lama and his brothers.[79]

The party used the exhibition to monitor public opinion. A surveillance report in *Internal Reference* (*Neibu cankao*) offered a fine-grained portrait of exhibit-goers' reactions. Many people were observed taking notes—asked why, an elderly lady responded, "Seeing how bad American agents destroyed our things, I am very angry. I'm writing it down so as never to forget their crimes."

Another woman looked at the photograph of Colonel Arnold and said, "Just look at his face and you can see he's a special agent." Inspecting spy equipment, one kid said, "They brought so much stuff on them; only thing they forgot was a coffin." An ethnic Mongolian looking at Downey's Mandarin phrasebook, open to a page with the sentence "I am a friend of China," said mockingly, "You are a special agent bastard." A Northeast China Party School group member commented that before seeing this exhibit, the damage done by US special agents' was just an abstraction, but now it could be felt deeply. A visitor wrote in the guestbook—prophetically, as it turned out—that the UN secretary general should come see this exhibit for himself. A Public Security Bureau cadre wrote, "In order to do public security work well, we must rely on the masses." Others expressed appreciation of the important work done by the PSB.

In addition to socialist bloc embassies, Finland, India, and Indonesia sent diplomatic staff to view the exhibition, as did the United Kingdom. The party surveillance report quoted the reactions of numerous foreigners—a Czech journalist, a Vietnamese overseas student. One foreigner pointed out that the Japanese ought to know about the secret training camp in Atsugi. The Indian ambassador wrote, "Seeing this exhibit today leaves me feeling deeply moved." One "capitalist" said as he walked out, "Truly scary"—but he left before his name or home country could be determined. Two of the celebrated "turncoats"—the twenty-one US soldiers who chose to stay in China rather be repatriated after the Korean War Armistice Agreement—wrote approving comments in the visitor book. But not all the reactions were entirely positive. Some visitors seemed to complain that the captured foreigners were getting off too easy. An All-China United Workers Association member, for example, wrote that Arnold should be put to death.[80]

The Special Agents Exhibition traveled from Beijing to other Chinese cities as a roadshow. The French journalist Robert Guillain was on a two-month reporting visit in the fall of 1955 and described his visit to the Exhibition in the hinterland city of Hankow.

> People were flocking to it; a visit was compulsory. . . . We were shown photos of American aircraft which had been shot down, photos of the airmen who had been taken prisoner (the famous airmen about whose release so much was written), and an enormous quantity of American military equipment, ranging from tin foods to a rubber dinghy. . . . A group arrived; it was immediately handed over to a guide who, while speaking his piece and pointing out the objects with a long bamboo cane, led his visitors past fifty yards of charts. There he handed his group over to a new "barker" who would conduct them another fifty yards while the first man returned to base and then set out with another group.

Guillain wondered to himself whether the masses were really buying it. "Among these blue processions of civilians in uniform, who would be rash enough to evince some doubt, to preserve his critical faulty, or to try to check the official truths offered to his credulous masses?"[81] A similar question could have been asked of American consumers of the official version of the Downey and Fecteau story they were hearing from elected officials and reading in their free press.

The Dulles brothers received their own internal report on the Special Agents Exhibition, thanks to the UK diplomats on the scene in Beijing.[82] Trevelyan sent a staff member four days in a row to view the scene, taking special interest in Arnold's confession. The Brits confirmed that "Exhibit well attended with long organized queues of government officials, students and workers awaiting entry." "Section on Downey-Fecteau case includes wreckage of C-47 aircraft without identification marks, map of section of Kirin, instructions and equipment for retrieving agent from ground, homing devices for friendly aircraft, implements for making fake passports, etc." The British report added laconically, "Little evidence of obvious faking of exhibits."[83]

From the evidence put on display at the exhibition, combined with what he could glean from the cable traffic, Trevelyan's own inference was that the Chinese were exploiting the obvious guilt of Downey and Fecteau in order to implicate the Arnold Eleven as well, substantiating a broader claim of being under sustained subversive attack from the American imperialists. "What the C47 had been used for was clear enough. The Chinese had put it and its civilian crew in with the others in order to confuse the issue and suggest by the association that the eleven had been on the same sort of business."[84]

As for the American captives, their prison conditions improved now that the attention of the world was suddenly on their case. The Arnold Eleven were transferred to joint cells with looser strictures and better grub. Wallace Brown remembered Christmas dinner 1954 as a special privilege, even though the food tasted awful. The crew was let outdoors. "In spite of the severe cold that winter, we were often taken outside to a courtyard for exercise. The guards even gave us a volleyball and net, which we strung up between two trees that stood about fifteen feet apart. We tried to organize a few games, but usually we just passed the ball around."[85] Downey and Fecteau, too, could now send and receive mail. Jack sent his first letter to his mother Mary, brother Billie, and sister Joan, telling them how much he loved them. "Remember me nightly in your prayers as I do you nightly," he wrote.[86]

13

IMPLAUSIBLE DENIAL

Eisenhower's decision to handle the case of the American prisoners in China via the United Nations internationalized the underlying problem of US-China relations, creating openings for third parties, including the UN secretary general himself, to attempt mediation between hostile governments in Washington and Beijing. Zhou Enlai seized the diplomatic initiative on the world stage, and ironically, it was the issue of detainees that brought the US and PRC to the table in formal bilateral talks for the first time, with mixed results. Domestically, the tendency toward repression slowed in the United States after the downfall of Senator McCarthy, while in China, Chairman Mao continued to swerve back and forth between harsh control and apparent loosening up.

The Peking Formula

With the Eisenhower administration looking to the United Nations to resolve the prisoner dilemma, allies took on enhanced importance, and none more so than Great Britain. But the Brits were pursuing a very different China policy, seeking normalized relations with the PRC and preferring stability to subversion. The British legation in Beijing had been tracking trials of counterrevolutionaries to determine how much real subversion was taking place in the People's Republic, cabling to London in March 1954, "It is often difficult to distinguish between genuine 'counter-revolutionaries' and ordinary criminals. The Chinese now tend to class any serious disturbers of the peace, particularly those whose crimes in any way effect 'economic construction,' as 'counter-revolutionaries' and to claim that their activities are directed by organisations controlled from Formosa or by the United States."[1] The best thing for British interests, which centered on Hong Kong, would be less subversion and less repression.

Most cases of detained British citizens had been resolved; even Robert Ford, given a ten-year sentence a week after Downey, Fecteau and the Arnold Eleven, was slated for early release in May 1955. Pressed by a member of Parliament on the cases of the American prisoners, the British Foreign Office was enthusiastic about helping get the Arnold crew released, but evasive on Downey and Fecteau, except to point out that their confessions proved nothing ("as in the germ-warfare accusations, the Chinese have extorted 'confessions' from the accused to substantiate these claims").[2] The British embassy in Washington wired an update to inform headquarters that "the matter is still under discussion at a high level with the United States government," adding drolly, "presumably still cloudy."[3]

London's larger objective remained trying to establish official relations with the PRC, toward which end Humphrey Trevelyan finally secured a coveted meeting with Zhou Enlai. The premier was in a philosophical mood, explaining Chinese foreign policy in terms of the ancient philosophy of Daoism. Beijing was not seeking to provoke but merely "reacting against Western provocations." Trevelyan applied Zhou's principle to the American prisoner case, inferring that the spy trial was a reaction to John Foster Dulles's recent accusations against the Chinese for engaging in subversive activities and in anticipation of an imminent treaty for Chiang Kai-shek: "They might have let them out if political relations had been better, but decided to convict them without any real evidence and publish general allegations, which I am sure they believe, of Nationalist and American spying, probably because they knew that the Formosan Treaty was going to be signed and in reaction against Mr. Dulles's accusations of their subversion and aggressive intent. . . . This is the kind of statement which can be guaranteed almost always to produce some reaction directed at Western Interests."[4] Given British reservations, the US ambassador to the UN Henry Cabot Lodge advised Secretary Dulles that the UN strategy "should be confined" to the Arnold Eleven.[5]

Focusing on the fliers might also help with another key UN player, India, which served as an honest broker in organizing POW exchanges after the Korean War. But relations between the Eisenhower and Nehru governments were prickly. Indian's top diplomat, Krishna Menon, a trusted confidant of Nehru, requested a meeting with John Foster Dulles to offer his assistance in resolving the spy issue as part of a "comprehensive settlement" between Washington and Beijing. An indignant Dulles retorted that Menon's idea was "totally impossible," warning that "the conviction and imprisonment of these prisoners of war was a blot which, unless they removed it very quickly, would set back the clock very seriously and endanger the whole position in Asia." Menon worried that US retaliation could trigger war. "I said this would be too bad," Dulles wrote in a memo of conversation, "but while we wanted peace, we were not pacifists to a point where we could allow our rights to be trampled upon without any reaction."[6] Menon was an unpopular figure in American diplomatic circles. U. Alexis Johnson called him "that ubiquitous international meddler," and his advice, like India's warnings about China's entry into the Korean War, was easily dismissed.[7]

The United Nations secretary seneral, Swedish diplomat Dag Hammarskjöld, carried more weight in Washington. He, too, was urging Dulles to soften his tone. Given how much "orientals" worry about face, strident condemnation in public view could doom efforts to finesse the prisoners' release, Hammarskjöld reasoned. Dulles replied, "These were not just orientals; they are Communists too."[8]

Ambassador Lodge's efforts succeeded in convincing the UN General Assembly to adopt a resolution on December 10 reiterating the US complaint over the PRC's detention of United Nations Command military personnel in violation of the Korean Armistice Agreement. The resolution gave the secretary general grounds to intercede, and Hammarskjöld promptly sent a cablegram to Beijing proposing a visit. A week later, the reply arrived. "In the interest of peace and relaxation of international tension, I am prepared to receive you in our capital, Peking, to discuss with you pertinent questions. We welcome you to China," Zhou Enlai cabled back.[9]

The Hammarskjöld mission arrived in Beijing on January 5, 1955. The secretary general was focused almost entirely on the Arnold Eleven. His voluminous briefing book said precious little about Downey and Fecteau except that "they were on a confidential mission in support of the United Nations Command."[10]

All thirteen captives benefited from the UN visit in terms of prison life, as they were put together in a shared group cell. Downey remembered "living on the edge of my chair every instant fearing that this was too good to be true."[11] The Arnold crew, reunited with their colonel, were given fresh shaves and new clothes, and had publicity photos taken playing cards. Major Brown recalled meeting Downey and Fecteau: "We were the first Americans they had seen in all this time. It was an incomparable experience for them as well as for Colonel Arnold. The presence of these three made us all the more certain we were being prepared for release."

The group went outside for a photo op playing volleyball, but it was too cold for much of a game. They went back in for "by far the best food we had seen in China. . . . Baked buns, sausages, sliced meats, eggs, butter, and canned foods of all kinds. . . . Good American canned meats!" exclaimed Brown. The prisoners then repaired to a rec room where they were supposed to play ping-pong, checkers, and chess, but the men "were much more interested in talking about our departure theories and in comparing stories with Colonel Arnold and the two civilians." After the party, the prison warden told Brown "that the Chinese government had invited our families to come to China. . . . Later we were told that the U.S. State Department had refused passports to our families and again we were encouraged to write favorably of the proposal. None of us did."[12]

For Premier Zhou, Hammarskjöld's visit was a second diplomatic coup on par with the Geneva Conference, allowing him to play the part of gracious host and tough negotiator with equal aplomb. The Swedish diplomat spent six days on the mission, gently encouraging Zhou to avert what he called a "tragedy of errors"—the misunderstandings between governments having no dialogue with each other, each answering to an emotional public, that could lead to war.[13] Zhou coolly stated the case against the Arnold Eleven as well as Downey and Fecteau, insisting the two missions be seen in tandem. Hammarskjöld argued the view that the Arnold crew was engaged in "innocent" military espionage and psychological warfare (leaflet dropping), not covert subversion. He evaded Zhou's numerous attempts to bring up the salience of Downey and Fecteau.[14]

As a goodwill gesture, Zhou said the Chinese government would welcome the families of the American prisoners to visit them in Beijing. Hammarskjöld returned from his mission with an intuition there was flexibility in Zhou's stance. Although he was not able to resolve the matter, the trip itself established a new precedent for high-level UN mediation between states in the interest of global peace and security—what became known as the Peking formula.

Within a week of Hammarskjöld's return to New York, fighting flared up again in the Taiwan Strait. The PLA occupied the small islet of Yijiangshan on January 18, using it as a forward base to intensify shelling of the larger island of Dachen.[15] As tensions skyrocketed with Washington, putting the new US-ROC defense treaty commitment to the test, the brief spell in purgatory ended abruptly for Downey and Fecteau, who were moved back into separate cells. Arnold crew members volunteered to be sent out of the common cell in their place, but the guards demurred, saying, "Well, we think Downey and Fecteau ought to live together.'" Downey recalled the psychological devastation of removal. "I was practically in tears and my head just dropped to my chest and I knew that was the end of the line, and I foresaw a long haul for us and that these guys (the Arnold crew) were going to get out." It was back to the uninterrupted agony of incarceration alone.

> For once in my life I was pretty accurate in my grasp of things. . . . So Dick and I were taken out and we were put in another corridor in a cell and we were both pretty agitated, at least certainly I was, and we were talking there and saying, "Jesus, thank Christ we are together, at least we got that much, no more solitary"; and the door swings open and [the

> voice saying], "Fecteau, will you step out," and that is the last I saw of him. There I was back in solitary. That was a very miserable day. . . . You always have that wild hope and now!"[16]

In Washington, Premier Zhou's offer of family visits posed legal and political problems for the State Department, which had a policy of banning US citizens from traveling to mainland China. The travel ban was the kind of irony that realists worried about, considering how the US government criticized totalitarian countries for violating the so-called fifth freedom of travel and mobility.

Secretary Dulles ordered that requests from the prisoners' families for passports be rejected.[17] He wrote to Jack's mother, Mary Downey, a few weeks after the Hammarskjöld mission to inform her that the government had decided against allowing families to visit. Privately, Hammarskjöld was dismayed by Dulles's refusal to accept Zhou's goodwill gesture, which he had arranged with the Chinese premier as the next contretemps along a diplomatic path to getting the prisoners released.[18]

The CIA meanwhile created a committee, headed by the Connecticut-born Yale graduate Richard Bissell Jr., to work on the Downey/Fecteau case. Bissell was just about to take the lead on a new spy plane project that would consume his energy and transform the Agency over the years to come; but for the moment, the Bissell group had a lot of scrubbing to do in order to backstop Downey and Fecteau's cover story as civilian employees of the Defense Department. That included convincing their family members to unsee the letters on CIA stationery declaring them presumed deceased.[19] Personnel staff worked through the administrative aspects of managing pay, benefits, and promotions for employees held in prolonged foreign captivity.[20]

There appeared to be little cause to hope for a negotiated release, given how Chairman Mao and President Eisenhower were trading threats as the Taiwan Strait Crisis roiled on. Mao told the newly arrived Finnish ambassador in late January, "The United States cannot annihilate the Chinese nation with its small stack of atom bombs." Mao daydreamed about a Communist-led international order, a "people's united nations," to emerge after America's inevitable defeat in World War III. He also scoffed at the hypocrisy in US accusations against the CCP for subversive activities: "If the warmongers are to make war, then they mustn't blame us for making revolution or engaging in 'subversive activities' as they keep saying all the time. If they desist from war, they can survive a little longer on this earth. But the sooner they make war the sooner they will be wiped from the face of the earth. Then a people's united nations would be set up, maybe in Shanghai, maybe somewhere in Europe, or it might be set up again in New York, provided the U.S. warmongers had been wiped out."[21]

While Chairman Mao used apocalyptic bombast in defiance of the American imperialists, President Eisenhower sounded almost blasé in threatening nuclear war on Red China. In January, Eisenhower received a blank check from Congress in the so-called Formosa Resolution authorizing the use of force to "secure and protect" Taiwan and the Pescadores as well as "related positions and territories of that area."[22] Ike played up his readiness to use massive, even nuclear force. Asked by a reporter whether tactical nukes would be considered in a conflict in the Far East, Eisenhower said flatly, "I see no reason why they shouldn't be used just exactly as you would use a bullet or anything else."[23]

Bandung to Geneva

The sparring in the Taiwan Strait finally began to abate in the spring of 1955 as Zhou Enlai prepared for his third grand performance on the world stage: attendance at the inaugural Asian-African Conference in Bandung, Indonesia. Spearheaded by the host country's leader Sukarno along with Indian prime minister Nehru, the Bandung Conference aspired to bring together a third bloc of postcolonial, developing nations, countries that aligned perfectly with neither Moscow nor Washington. Bandung represented an alternative imagining of the international Third Force, based on solidarity among peoples of color across the global south.

The United States was not officially invited to participate, and John Foster Dulles, watching with suspicion, pretended not to care. The African-American novelist Richard Wright flew from Parisian exile to Bandung and wrote a book about his journey, *The Color Curtain* (1956). Wright was enthralled at the prospect of a postcolonial global gathering, but somewhat disappointed by the dominance of Asia's nationalist leaders over Pan-African voices. According to Wright, the preconference buzz centered around the role that Red China would play and what Zhou Enlai would be like.[24]

Zhou almost didn't make it. Days before the premier's planned departure for Indonesia, the PRC foreign ministry alerted the British legation in Beijing to credible intelligence that Nationalist agents were planning to "make trouble" on Zhou's flight via Hong Kong. The British relayed the warning to Hong Kong colonial authorities to increase security on his transfer. Sure enough, the chartered Air India plane that Zhou was originally scheduled to fly crash-landed at sea after a midair explosion. Most of those on board were killed, but not Zhou, who had changed his itinerary at the last moment.

Within hours of the crash, Beijing demanded an investigation by the British into what they alleged was an attempted assassination. Trevelyan later wrote that he suspected the whole thing was a ruse and that Beijing mercilessly sacrificed a decoy team, bombing the plane themselves, to exploit the incident for political purposes at Bandung.[25] But the official British inquiry determined that Nationalist agents in Hong Kong were indeed involved in planting a bomb on the plane. Before the suspect could be detained for questioning, he smuggled his way to safety as a stowaway on a CAT plane to Taiwan—implicating the CIA, at least in flying the getaway vehicle.[26]

Beijing used the incident to renew pressure on the British to crack down on espionage in Hong Kong, as the *People's Daily* decried "special service organisations" in the colony run by the CIA and US military intelligence. The pressure would keep up for months, with the British China mission cabling to London, "Articles have said that the large number of special agents gathered in Hong Kong has been for a long time a serious threat to the security of China and that this is a position which the Chinese people cannot tolerate."[27]

In the end, Zhou not only arrived safely in Bandung, he turned the conference into another diplomatic triumph for the New China. Richard Wright described how Zhou, "clad in a pale tunic, moved among the delegates with the utmost friendliness and reserve, listening to all arguments with patience, and turning the other cheek when receiving ideological slaps."[28] The foreign affairs commentator William Worthy Jr. was another one of the small group of US citizens to attend the gathering, and he reported for the *Afro-American* that Zhou "emerged as the biggest man in Asia while carefully sidestepping the popularity contest with Nehru which American editorial writers had neatly planned for him."[29]

The twenty-nine nations assembled at Bandung affirmed the Five Principles of Peaceful Coexistence, codified by Zhou and Nehru in the Sino-Indian Panchsheel Agreement signed the previous year. In his speech to the conference, Zhou underscored the point that the group's solidarity was rooted in the fact that "the overwhelming majority of the Asian and African countries and peoples have suffered and are still suffering from the calamities of colonialism." Despite differing ideologies, social systems, and religious beliefs, pan–Afro-Asian unity was possible because of the shared fight against the legacies of colonialism. Zhou linked the anti-imperialist struggle to a "key question" of "so-called subversive activities." Denying charges of using overseas Chinese as a fifth column, Zhou asserted that Chiang Kai-shek was the one carrying out subversive operations—on behalf of American imperialism, no less. Zhou pointed to the example of General Li Mi's army in Burma (a co-host of the conference): "The problem at present is not that we are carrying out subversive activities against the governments of other countries, but that there are people who are establishing bases around China in order to carry out subversive activities against the Chinese government. For instance, on the border between China and Burma, there are in fact remnant armed elements of the Chiang Kai-shek clique who are carrying out destructive activities against both China and Burma."[30]

Even as Zhou appealed to postcolonial solidarity, his message was not one of unmitigated hostility to the West. On the contrary, he put out feelers at Bandung for engaging the United States.[31] The premier outstretched a hand, promising that "the Chinese government is willing to sit down and enter into negotiations with the United States government to discuss the question of relaxing tension in the Far East and especially the question of relaxing tension in the Taiwan area."[32] Zhou reaffirmed the public offer in private discussions with intermediaries to the Americans—Krishna Menon and Humphrey Trevelyan—held in the month after Bandung.[33]

Zhou Enlai's peace offensive had a trickle down effect on the Arnold Eleven, who were given privileges like moving freely through their new cellblock during the day and decorating their walls with photos and magazines from home. Wallace Brown thought that the pictures of automobiles "probably did more to damage their [the jailors] faith in Communism than anything else we could do." The airmen had to attend political study sessions and obligatory propaganda readings, but the guards did not seem to be making a serious effort at thought reform, and English and American novels were made available.[34] Then, at the end of May, Beijing released a separate group of four US jet fighter pilots downed during the Korean War who had been charged with the lesser crime of violating PRC airspace. Nehru and Hammarskjöld got credit for helping to secure their release.[35]

Three months after the third world gathering in Bandung, the "Big Four" met for rare summit talks in Geneva. When Eisenhower sat down with his counterparts from the USSR, UK, and France in July, he was focused on stability in Europe and preventing nuclear war. But Moscow, London, and Paris were united in supporting détente between Washington and Beijing. Premier Zhou was determined to relax tensions. Eisenhower and Dulles capitulated to pressure, agreeing to open ambassador-level talks with the PRC in Geneva starting in August.[36]

Repatriating Overseas Chinese, Eliminating Counterrevolutionaries

On the eve of the first session of the Sino-American Ambassadorial Talks, Zhou Enlai ordered the release of Colonel Arnold and his crew. The gesture was calculated to incur goodwill going into the Geneva talks, helping the US delegation with their top agenda item of repatriating Americans. Zhou made sure to give and gain credit with the United Nations by saying the release was timed to Dag Hammarskjöld's fiftieth birthday, in recognition of his mediation efforts. The Arnold men lumbered south by train on a three-day journey to the last stop at Kowloon station. Hearing their names called one by one, each man walked briskly across Lo Wu Bridge to freedom on the Hong Kong side of the border.[37]

When Jack Downey's mother heard the news back in Connecticut, she was incensed, and took it out on her congressman, Thomas Dodd. Dodd wrote to Allen Dulles: "Mrs. Downey came to my house in a very upset condition to find out the reason for this distinction between her son and the boys who are in uniform."[38]

Mary Downey was not the only one who was unhappy. In the view of the lead negotiator at Geneva, Ambassador U. Alexis Johnson, Zhou's goodwill gesture of releasing the Arnold Eleven backfired in terms of public impact. Rather than expressing gratitude for the humanitarian release, the US press coverage painted a dark picture of the airmen's treatment in captivity. The negative reaction, in turn, soured Beijing's view on the benefits of showing lenience.[39]

Ambassador Johnson felt that the two sides stared at one another across "a chasm of ignorance and hostility."[40] Premier Zhou wanted an "expansive" agenda in Geneva that would address opening bilateral trade and people-to-people exchanges. Zhou also hoped to elevate the discussions to the cabinet level. Secretary Dulles gave Johnson strict instructions to cleave to a narrow agenda of repatriating the forty-one US citizens still detained in Red China.[41] Johnson's counterpart, as before, was Wang Bingnan, now the PRC ambassador to Poland. Wang brought his own list of 105 Chinese nationals being detained against their will in the United States, including a professor of aerodynamics at the California Institute of Technology named Qian Xuesen.[42] Ambassador Wang further claimed that five thousand overseas students and other Chinese in the US were being prevented from returning to their motherland. As the talks continued, Johnson added a list of 450 missing in action cases of lost American servicemen, which he transmitted with faint hope for success.[43]

After grueling negotiations, the two sides finally arrived at a plan for mutual return of civilians known as the Agreed Announcement of the Ambassadors, dated September 10, 1955. Implementation proved uneven and contentious on both sides. About half of the Americans held in China received exit permits soon after the announcement.[44] Allyn Rickett, for example, was summoned to hear a reading of the official charges against him at the Superior Municipal Court of Peking the very next day. He was found guilty, sentenced to six years, and then informed his sentence had been commuted to immediate release. Reading about his release on the front page of the newspaper alongside a report on the talks in

Geneva, Rickett "felt a little perturbed." "Had my trial and subsequent release by the parole board been nothing but a sham?" he asked with the outraged naïveté of a graduate student.[45]

Other cases went less smoothly. The Jesuit Father John W. Clifford had been arrested on espionage charges a month before the end of the Korean War and held in Shanghai jails ever since. He was transferred to a new prison in mid-September after the Agreed Announcement and subjected to intensified interrogation, including threats of the death penalty, which were aimed at coercing him into signing a confession of guilt. He refused, and spent another nine months in prison. Finally, Father Clifford was released. He later wrote a book about his experiences, intended to help Americans survive "brainwashing" if taken captive in Vietnam.[46]

The problem of repatriation was even more daunting on the US side, as there were far more individuals involved. Though Chinese in the United States had not been rounded up and put into camps like Japanese Americans had been just a decade earlier during WWII, some were subjected to "departure controls" after China's entry into the Korean War.[47] Based on the Agreed Announcement, the US government lifted all travel restrictions on Chinese nationals and launched a public information campaign to inform Chinese residents in the US that they were free to return to the People's Republic if they so desired.

Among those who returned was Chen Nengkuan, who had received a PhD in metallurgy from Yale in 1950 and worked for Johns Hopkins University and then Westinghouse. Chen would become a researcher in the PRC nuclear weapons program, which had been approved by the Politburo in January 1955, soon after Chiang Kai-shek got his defense treaty.[48]

The best-known returnee was Cal Tech professor Qian Xuesen, who had been arrested in Los Angeles on September 7, 1950, as he prepared to return to China. Qian was kept under FBI surveillance and house arrest for years based on allegations that he was working for the Communist Party. He was finally granted legal permission to exit the US on August 4, 1955, three days after the release of the Arnold crew.[49] Qian was deported in September and returned to mainland China, where he began his second career as the father of the Chinese missile program. Zhou Enlai would remark a few years later that the Ambassadorial Talks were justified if only for bringing this one man back to China.[50]

Ironically, while Premier Zhou was using the Sino-US Ambassadorial Talks to bring back scientists and students who could help build the New China, Chairman Mao was unleashing a new wave of repression against intellectuals already there. Since the tapering off of the Campaign to Suppress Counterrevolutionaries, Mao had restricted himself to isolated attacks on prominent intellectuals, like the denunciations of Liang Shuming, a stalwart of the Third Force.[51] But the comparative relaxation began to tighten when attacks mounted on the well-known writer Hu Feng, who dared to rebut Chairman Mao's authoritative "Lectures on Art and Literature at the Yan'an Forum" with a kind of countermanifesto submitted to the CCP Central Committee in July 1954. By the spring of 1955, Hu Feng was featured as the villain in "an intensive, nationwide ideological remolding campaign on a scale unprecedented in Communist China," in the words of the historian Merle Goldman.[52]

Mao warned ominously in his speech to the CCP National Conference in March 1955 that the imperialists were planning a surprise attack to trigger World War III. Their accomplices, the enemies of the revolution, were operating furtively within the People's Republic. "The remaining counter-revolutionary forces inside the country are still very active, and, basing ourselves on the facts, we must deal them more blows in a planned and discriminating way so as to further weaken these hidden counter-revolutionaries and ensure the safety of our socialist construction," he intoned.[53] Mao spoke at length in his closing speech to the conference about the "anti-Party alliance" led by senior cadres Gao Gang and Rao Shushi, who were implicated in a plot foiled in early 1954. The Gao-Rao conspiracy rendered the threat of US-Nationalist counterrevolution all the more palpable. The party could not relax its vigilance.[54] Gao committed suicide in August 1954, but Rao was not arrested until April 1955.

The budding campaign against "hidden counter-revolutionaries" turned against the party's own intelligence apparatus when Public Security Minister Luo Ruiqing arrested a top intelligence official, Pan Hannian. Pan was a hero of the 1920s Communist underground who, among other things, assisted Third Force figures in traveling safely from Hong Kong to CCP areas during the Civil War. Pan's arrest was the beginning of a purge of as many as one thousand intelligence and public security officials who were "demoted, transferred, or arrested" in the summer of 1955.[55]

Mao sharpened the attack on Hu Feng, denouncing intellectuals who existed "outside the ranks of the people" and should be made subject to methods of "dictatorship."[56] Hu Feng, under a barrage of criticism from fellow literati since the start of the year, was arrested that summer for attempting to subvert the Communist system.[57] The arrests of the writer Hu Feng and the agent Pan Hannian heralded a new campaign, designed to wipe out a threat that was "by no means confined to the men of the Hu Feng clique, many other secret agents and bad elements have also sneaked in."[58] Having "suppressed" (*zhenya*) counterrevolutionary elements during the Korean War, Mao now launched a movement to eliminate or "purge" (*suqing*) them entirely.

One American who was in the rare position to watch the Campaign to Eliminate Counterrevolutionaries unfold was Sidney Rittenberg. Rittenberg counted himself among the tiny number of Americans who freely chose to settle in Communist China—although his loyalty could not save him from spending the first five years of the PRC imprisoned on suspicion of espionage.

Released in April 1955, Rittenberg joined the translation office in the propaganda department and described the rollout of the new Campaign to Eliminate Counterrevolutionaries. "The party had successfully cleaned out the most obvious of spies, KMT sympathizers, and secret agents. Now the time had come to look for the harder cases, the counterrevolutionaries who had burrowed deep into their organizations and were secretly waiting for a chance to strike back," Rittenberg's work unit was told.[59] The historian Merle Goldman described how the campaign spun out of control "from an orderly instrument of the party into a reign of terror," which was similar to Yang Kuisong's judgment of the previous Campaign to Suppress Counterrevolutionaries as having gone "too far" in Mao's eyes. But the repeated pattern suggests a method in the madness, a purposeful spinning out of control in line with Julia Strauss's theory of the party's "paternalist terror" model of governance.[60]

The wave of repression generated by the Campaign to Eliminate Counterrevolutionaries put Beijing out of step with Moscow, where Nikita Khrushchev was easing pressure on independent voices. Having executed Stalin's feared security chief Lavrenti Beria, Khrushchev had consolidated primacy within the Communist Party of the Soviet Union by 1955. He was reducing the scale of the gulags and introducing what would come to be known as de-Stalinization. Khrushchev was also tentatively probing for ways to lower tensions with the United States and lighten the load of defense spending, and his thaw was having ripple effects in Eastern Europe, where reformist voices were tenuously gaining ground.

Eisenhower was seeking to lower the temperature as well, both in terms of hostility with Moscow as well as the post-McCarthy atmosphere in the United States. The "tendency toward repression" was on the wane since the Senate censured McCarthy on the same day John Foster Dulles signed the treaty for Chiang Kai-shek, the coup de grace in the senator's swift and humiliating fall from power and influence. Eisenhower disliked McCarthy intensely but had waffled over how to neutralize McCarthyism without hurting his party and presidency; the president was relieved by the senator's downfall. The worst seemed to be over. The sociologist Edward Shils wrote of 1954 as the peak of paranoia, and in *The Torment of Secrecy: The Background and Consequences of American Security Policy* (1956) encouraged his readers to ask themselves, "Why have so many of our citizens been so preoccupied with thoughts of subversion, spying and secrecy?"[61]

Quiet Forest

Jack Downey and Dick Fecteau had no way to know about the vicissitudes in Sino-American diplomacy or shifting subversion-repression dynamics of the Cold War. Just weeks after the Agreed Announcement in September 1955, Beijing claimed that the agreement did not apply to prisoners in jail for committing crimes, which the American negotiator, Ambassador Johnson, claimed was news to him. That left about a dozen US citizens, including Downey and Fecteau, without an exit.[62] They were, at least, allowed to receive mail from their families—a care package of not more than eleven pounds, delivered by the American Red Cross via Hong Kong, twice monthly.[63]

Downey was also finally permitted to request a consular visit from the British legation at the end of October 1955.[64] Trevelyan's replacement as chargé d'affaires, Con O'Neill, responded cautiously, cabling for instruction from the State Department.[65] On November 15, O'Neill sent his deputy, A. H. Campbell, to visit Downey in his first friendly official contact since capture. Campbell described the prisoner as cautious and stoical.

> Chinese made no difficulties either over arrangements or during interview, Downey's manner was normal apart from nervousness in presence of English speaking prison attendants. He probably feared lest any imprudent remarks might prejudice chances of his return to United States. For this reason he kept conversation to non-controversial topics and declined offer of further visit though he enquired about his prospects of returning home. He was invited to write again to United Kingdom representative if he required any assistance.[66]

As Downey and Fecteau languished in their cells, a new kind of tradecraft was transforming the CIA. Hi-tech methods being devised to peer behind the Iron and Bamboo Curtains made airborne infiltrations seem quaint by comparison. The CIA image analyst Dino Brugioni described 1955 as "a year of transition to technology."[67] The key figure leading the CIA into a brave new world of electronic espionage and technological collection was Richard Bissell. Bissell's signature project, a top-secret program to develop a high-altitude surveillance plane, started in December 1954 (the same month he was put in charge of the Downey/Fecteau group). The U-2 spy plane made its maiden flight over the USSR on July 4, 1956.[68] U-2 photography gave President Eisenhower hard evidence that Soviet long-range bombers were less of a threat than US Air Force commanders were telling him, which strengthened his case for curtailing defense spending.[69]

Ike was cautious about overusing the so-called Black Lady, fearing the diplomatic blowback of peeking into the neighbors' yards. So Bissell worked out arrangements with the British allowing the Royal Air Force to borrow U-2s for their overflights and then share the intelligence they had gathered. Allies offered operating bases so the planes could fly out of West Germany, Turkey, and Pakistan. Bissell got to work on a higher, faster successor plane as well as a spy satellite program.[70]

The turn from subversion to surveillance could be felt in the Far East. Instead of infiltrating commandos onto mainland China, the CIA was keen to support Chiang Kai-shek's aerial reconnaissance capabilities, testing PRC air defenses as a supplement to the US military's own coastal surveillance. The surveillance missions were not without risks. In August 1956, a US Navy plane collecting electronic intelligence outside Shanghai was shot down, and suspicions lingered, based on spotty information, that there may have been survivors taken captive.[71]

While Chiang Kai-shek and his protégé Chiang Ching-kuo were happy to receive US assistance, the father and son were increasingly focused on governing Taiwan itself. The fight for reunification was becoming more rhetoric than reality. Psywar continued, but the audience for the campaign to reclaim the mainland was primarily on the island of Taiwan. Occasionally, the Nationalist forces pulled off spectacular missions, like a leaflet-dropping mission over Changsha in January 1957 that flew back to Taiwan on a course over Beijing. Chiang Kai-shek personally met the crew on their return and made sure local papers trumpeted the feat. That same month, a Taiwanese B-26 littered Shanghai with reunification leaflets, narrowly escaping chase by a MiG jet, and Guangzhou was plastered with one hundred thousand anti-Communist posters in June.[72] The psywar uptick surely aggravated Beijing. But the annoyance of propaganda material for Chiang to play up back in Taiwan was manageable, a different beast than the threat of paramilitary activities on the mainland.

As subversive activities by the US and Taiwan subsided, repressive tendencies on the mainland entered a phase of relaxation from mid-1956. Chairman Mao reined in the Campaign to Eliminate Counterrevolutionaries and relieved pressure on independent voices, bringing the PRC into alignment with the trend across socialist Eurasia ushered in by Khrushchev's tirade against the excesses of Stalinism in his secret speech, delivered in February 1956.[73] Mao wrestled with the implications of Khrushchev's message in a talk, "On Ten Great Relationships," given in April. The chairman acknowledged that "democratic party personages," a euphemism for Third Force liberals, felt "reservations about the suppression of counter-revolutionaries." De-Stalinization emboldened their critique: "Now that some people have heard that Stalin wrongly put a number of people to death, they jump to the conclusion that we too were wrong in putting those counter-revolutionaries to death." Mao defended the campaigns to suppress and eliminate counterrevolutionaries, citing the Hu Feng case as proof there were still "hidden" subversives carrying out sabotage and psywar from within. But he now conceded they were few in number.[74]

Addressing remnant Third Force elements, Mao affirmed the need for "long-term coexistence and mutual supervision" with non-Communist parties. A "multi-party system" would remain the foreseeable future, he promised.[75] Mao started using a colorful expression, echoed by senior party leaders, to communicate his desire for greater openness: it was time to "let a hundred thoughts contend and a hundred flowers bloom."[76]

The lightened mood could be felt in a new counterespionage film, *Quiet Forest* (1957). Set in Shenyang, the script was inspired by the true story of a couple in Hong Kong who tried to organize an anti-CCP spy ring in the northeast.[77] To spice up the plot, the filmmakers also drew on elements of the Downey/Fecteau case. An American military officer based in Hong Kong named Presley is tricked by a double agent from the mainland into accompanying a plane full of counterrevolutionary paratroopers on a mission into the northeast provinces. In the finale, Presley is frog-marched out of a captured US military plane on a snow-covered Manchurian field. With all the anti-Communist paratroopers killed or captured, a member of the public security team jokes, "Who is going to tell Dulles about this?" Having built up tension from the first scene, using film noir devices, the anxiety over subversive forces is released in the final image of smiling counterespionage agents.

Mao's impulse to relax controls in 1956 may have been encouraged, at least indirectly, by the lull in subversive pressures from the bandit Chiang and the American imperialists. He had reason to feel less paranoid and even somewhat confident as the country enjoyed success in economic construction under the first Five-Year Plan. Downey and Fecteau benefited from the looser atmosphere and were given a six-week break from prison to travel around the country bearing witness to the success of the New China. Downey was left "terribly impressed with all the new developments taking place. . . . For the first time I realized the importance of land reform and the significance of collective farms," or so he would tell a group of visiting American students the following year.[78]

Like the imprisoned American spy, Chinese intellectuals were initially wary of saying anything negative about party rule, despite Mao's invitation for critique. A few well-established iconoclasts like the poet Ai Qing began to speak up. Then in the fall of 1956, two younger intellectuals named Liu Binyan and Wang Meng published breakout writings of sociopolitical critique using an innovative long-form style known as literary reportage.[79] These works of criticism appeared at the same time that Eastern European workers and students took to the streets in resistance against communist rule and Soviet influence, with stunning protests in the industrial Polish city of Poznan and an uprising in Budapest in October. Having

FIGURE 9. Catching spies on film: *Quiet Forest* (1957). Beijing Classic Film Arts.

supported Khrushchev's initial restraint in dealing with the Polish protests, Mao approved of the Soviet leader's decision in October to order a full-scale Soviet invasion of Hungary to crush dissent; indeed, Zhou criticized Khrushchev for considering pulling troops out of Budapest too soon.[80] The dramatic events in Eastern Europe ended up being deeply discouraging for the CIA. After raising the hopes of the protestors with psywar broadcasts via Radio Free Europe, Frank Wisner and his operatives in the OPC found themselves powerless to respond when an actual uprising took place. Wisner took the failure to act in Hungary especially hard; it accelerated a descent into mental illness that would force him to leave the Agency and eventually to take his own life.

Hungary and Poland showed there were risks to relaxation *and* repression. Mao criticized Eastern European communist parties for having "left so many counter-revolutionaries at large."[81] He thought the party should err on the side of boldness and that the real danger was in taking half measures. Yet, the chairman seemed unsure of how to handle his own domestic situation. He fretted at a national conference in January 1957 that the Hundred Flowers Campaign might have opened a Pandora's box. Loyal criticism was veering into subversive territory. Mao was getting word of "queer talk among some professors too, such as that the Communist Party should be done away with, the Communist Party cannot lead them, socialism is no good, and so on and so forth. Before, they kept these ideas to themselves, but since the policy of letting a hundred schools of thought contend gave them an opportunity to speak up, these remarks have come tumbling out."[82] Party leaders warned about the dangers of allowing intellectuals to speak their minds.[83] But Mao decided to push ahead with his invitation for criticism in a February 1957 speech, "On the Correct Handling of Contradictions among the People." Over the reservations of more cautious senior leaders, Mao officially launched an "open-door rectification campaign" in May against party cadres who were inhibiting the Hundred Flowers from blossoming, explicitly encouraging Third Force types to speak up.[84]

At last, the critics stopped holding back. For a little over a month, Chinese intellectuals tasted an exhilarating rush of openness; the pall of repression over free thought and political criticism seemed to have lifted.[85] Third Force voices came out of the woodwork to speak out against the CCP monopoly and abuses of power. In a first, as Merle Goldman explained, "it was the non-Communist intellectuals, particularly the leaders of the CDL, who led the attack on the party."[86] Among the most prominent voices calling for political reform were liberal intellectuals like Chu Anping, who started to run the China Democratic League mouthpiece, *Enlightenment Daily*, like an independent journal.[87]

Chairman Mao wanted the Hundred Flowers Campaign to vent pent-up resentments, channel public opinion, and mobilize the talents of nonparty intellectuals and bourgeoisie. But as educated Chinese—journalists, academics, researchers, artists, students—belatedly answered the chairman's call to speak openly, Mao found himself a target of their criticism. As the historian Andrew Walder observed, Mao "underestimated the resentment that the repressions of the 1950s had created, especially among educated Chinese. He had assumed incorrectly that the relative quiet in China throughout 1956 had meant that there was firm popular trust in the regime."[88]

After a little more than a month of the hundred schools of thought contending and hundred flowers blooming, the lawnmower of repression came out of the shed. A sharp editorial in the *People's Daily* and the publication of an altered version of Mao's February speech "On Handling Contradictions" appeared, ominous warnings of imminent crackdown.[89] The so-called Anti-Rightist Campaign was launched in July. The first targets were the Third Force figures Chu Anping, Luo Longji, and Zhang Bojun, who were denounced as members of an "anti-party plot."[90] Although their punishments were comparatively light, the message to liberals, nonparty elites, and intellectuals generally was clear. The philosopher Zhang Dongsun, the sociologist Fei Xiaotong, and other prominent academics quickly released humiliating self-criticisms in order to pre-empt the coming rectification, as supervision of the China Democratic League was tightened.[91] Liu Binyan was expelled from the CCP. Wang Meng was branded a rightist. The acclaimed novelist Ding Ling, winner of the 1951 Stalin Prize for literature, was struggled against for months on end, excommunicated from the party, and sent to a reform through labor camp.[92] The brutality of the Anti-Rightist Campaign swept away the last, smoldering embers of liberal political ideals and independent intellectual life in 1950s China. Third Force figures who had gone north to join Mao during the Civil War now had to confront the fact that he was as intolerant of dissenting views as Chiang Kai-shek, if not more so. By early 1958, the campaign had labeled over half a million individuals as rightists and enemies of the people.[93]

As countless individuals—starting with Third Force figures—were forced to submit to thought reform once again, Jack Downey fully overcame his own fears of brainwashing. Although his jailors made him read Stalin, they also allowed him to peruse the *New Yorker* and *Yale Alumni Magazine*, sent from his mother via Hong Kong. His guards, it turned out, were not devious masters of mind control like Dr. No, the James Bond villain who would make his debut in Ian Fleming's 1958 novel. As the years passed, Downey gained confidence in his longer-term psychic defenses against thought reform: "One of the things that relaxed me was the eventual discovery that you cannot really be brainwashed. . . . There are some things they can't change [and] basically I came out about the same as I went in. . . . They could scare you into saying just about anything, maybe scare me, I should say, but actually believing it is a much more difficult proposition."[94]

Part IV
RESCUE FROM WITHOUT

14

PRISONERS OF THE PAST

During the relaxation of 1956, Premier Zhou Enlai invited American journalists to come see the New China with their own eyes, waiving the entry ban by sending out invitations to media organizations for extended reporting trips.[1] But Secretary Dulles wouldn't let the press go. The State Department reasserted its travel ban prohibiting US citizens from visiting Red China, linking it to the issue of American captives.

> The United States welcomes the free exchange of information between different countries irrespective of political and social differences. But the Chinese Communist regime has created a special impediment. It adopted the practice of taking American citizens into captivity and holding them in effect as political hostages. . . . So long as these conditions continue it is not considered to be in the best interests of the United States that Americans should accept the Chinese Communist invitation to travel in Communist China.[2]

Chairman Mao Zedong mocked the Dulles travel ban in a speech leading up to the CCP's Eighth Congress. "By prohibiting American journalists from coming to China, Eisenhower and Dulles have now in fact admitted that it does have good points," he said teasingly. "What they dread most is that the articles might include not only invective but a good word here and there, and that would be awkward for them."[3]

The travel ban ensured that virtually the only point of contact between Americans and Chinese was their negotiating teams in Geneva, where the Sino-American

Ambassadorial Talks trudged miserably on, exactly according to Dulles's plan when he agreed to them in the first place. Recognizing that the talks were "dragging on indefinitely with the same tired points being reworked ad infinitum and ad nauseam at every meeting," Dulles "smilingly" commended his exasperated negotiator, Ambassador U. Alexis Johnson, who was reminded that "the talks are precisely fulfilling the primary purpose envisaged by the secretary in 1955."[4] The talks, in other words, were built to fail, but not collapse. Premier Zhou's negotiator, Ambassador Wang Bingnan, proposed people-to-people exchanges to include members of the press in order to break the logjam, but Dulles would not budge.[5]

Pressmen and Spy Moms

Not every American journalist was willing to heed Dulles's writ. William Worthy Jr., a writer for the *Afro-American* and a Nieman Fellow at Harvard, defied the State Department ban to become the first US journalist to visit the People's Republic of China, entering at Hong Kong on January 5, 1957. Worthy, who had been a war correspondent in Korea, interviewed the former Korean War POW and "turncoat" William C. White, whom Worthy described as "having sought racial asylum" in Communist China.[6] Worthy also sat down to interview Premier Zhou, who "demanded—not begged—that Secretary of State Dulles meet him on a basis of equality."[7] Worthy's reports from China, published in the *Afro-American*, demonstrated remarkable balance, calling out the hypocrisy in US policy without glossing over repression in the PRC, which Worthy characterized as a "police state" built on an ideology of dictatorship.[8]

A day after Worthy's unapproved entry, the correspondent Edmund Stevens and the photographer Philip Harrington also defied the ban by entering the PRC from the Soviet Union on an assignment for *Look* magazine. The press corps was emboldened by the defiance of the three newsmen and unhappy with the State Department, which was threatening the men with punitive measures. Facing pressure from unhappy reporters in Washington, John Foster Dulles tried to shift the blame to Beijing, denouncing the Chinese government for suggesting a swap—inviting US journalists for releasing US prisoners.

By the beginning of 1957, the list of American captives in China had been whittled down to nine: four spies and five priests. In addition to Downey, Fecteau, and Redmond, Robert McCann was serving a fifteen-year sentence for espionage, as belatedly revealed to his wife in May 1956.[9] The Catholic priests were serving out four- and five-year sentences either in Ward Road Prison (where Redmond was imprisoned) or under house arrest in Shanghai. Franciscan Fulgence Gross had been arrested in March 1951 in Qingdao during the Campaign to Suppress Counterrevolutionaries. Fathers Joseph McCarthy, Joseph Patrick McCormick, John Paul Wagner, and John Houle had been arrested on June 15, 1953, just before the Korean War Armistice.[10]

Dulles accused Zhou of using the nine prisoners as "blackmail," while the secretary used their incarceration to justify his refusal to allow members of the press to report in the PRC. "I don't believe that the bodies of American citizens ought to be made a subject for that kind of barter," Dulles declared indignantly to the press.[11] When asked about Dulles's statement rejecting a trade of prisoners for journalists, Eisenhower was shifty: "This is a new thought that has come in, a quid pro quo arrangement, and we have tried to keep this thing on the basic principle that people carried out their promises first, before you did anything else, had any further relations. But I will talk to him about it and see exactly what it is he is speaking of."[12] Asked a month later if there had been progress on the issue of allowing newsmen to visit China (with no reference to the tit-for-tat involving the prisoners), Eisenhower was again evasive: "We have studied this very earnestly to see how we could secure from China more news without appearing to be accepting Red China on the same cultural basis that we do other nations, and it is one we are still studying. I can't offer at this moment any change in policy. I merely say we keep examining it."[13] The State Department backed off its threat to apply sanctions on the journalists Worthy, Stevens, and Harrington, after national press organizations brought the issue before the Senate.[14]

As Zhou probed for an opening to the United States and Dulles finagled to keep channels closed, holes were being punched in the plausibility of the ongoing US government denial of guilt regarding Downey and Fecteau. A former US Information Agency employee, Charles Edmundson, appeared on the TV talk show *College Press Conference* and stated that the two men were in fact spies.[15] Later in the year, the *Nation* ran an article by Edmundson, "The Dulles Brothers in Diplomania," as the lead story, with a sinister image of a cloak, dagger, and fedora hat on the cover. Edmundson lambasted the Dulles brothers for running a foreign policy built on deception, and he called for congressional and media oversight of the CIA. He disclosed in print that Downey and Fecteau were CIA agents and called out Secretary Dulles for using imprisoned Americans to justify the ban on journalists visiting China. It was a textbook case, Edmundson argued, of how "public opinion is made the servant rather than the master of foreign policy."[16]

Mary Downey, having endured two years of mourning her son and two more years in limbo after discovering he was alive, was determined to see her boy. The CIA personnel officer Ben DeFelice conferred by phone with her on a regular basis. While recognizing that she was "profoundly distrustful of the CIA," DeFelice praised her as "an absolute, dynamic, and powerful woman determined to do everything possible to secure the release of her son and to allow no one or nothing to get in her way."[17] It was his job of course to "win her confidence." "Security risks both to the government and to the men made it imperative that there be no breach between the families and the Agency; an emotional explosion could negate the cover story and other arrangements and had to be avoided at all costs."[18] Many within the Agency sympathized with Mrs. Downey's desire for greater flexibility on the part of the White House and State Department, which recoiled at any whiff of making a "political concession" to Beijing.[19] Officials at State were less generous in their view of Mrs. Downey, regarding her as an "aggressive old bag," according to one British liaison officer.[20]

In early 1957, Mary secured a meeting with United Nations Secretary General Dag Hammarskjöld, who apologized for the fact that he had not been authorized to lobby Zhou Enlai two years earlier on behalf of her son since Downey and Fecteau were not covered under the definition of UN Command military personnel. To take up the case now, he would need a formal request from the US government, especially since bilateral ambassadorial talks were underway in Geneva.[21]

Mrs. Downey made her way in April to the State Department, where she met with the top East Asia diplomats, Walter S. Robertson (assistant secretary for Far Eastern affairs) and Walter McConaughy (director of Chinese affairs). She pressed the two Walters on reports of a swap that would allow her son to be released in return for some kind of concession. Robertson categorically denied such "rumors," assuring her that absolutely everything "humanly and officially" was being done, and he rejected Mrs. Downey's request of a meeting with President Eisenhower as unnecessary. The assistant secretary subjected Downey to a summary of negotiations over American detainees (ignoring the fact that her son was guilty as charged). He showed her the text of the Agreed Announcement of 1955, insisting that it covered her son and therefore the real problem was the inveterate bad faith of the Communists. They were "ruthless, unprincipled and dishonest," said Robertson, a diehard anti-Communist.

Mary Downey pushed back: What excuse do the Chinese give? Robertson replied, "The only excuse they had offered was the false allegation that we were holding Chinese in this country."[22] Mary was accompanied by Elizabeth Cusack, a diplomat at the UN, who asked if the State Department would help pay Mary's way to Geneva, where she could ask Ambassador Wang Bingnan in person for clemency in her son's case. Robertson demurred, instructing Mary, if she were ever to meet with Ambassador Wang, to make clear that hers was a personal mission and to be sure to chastise the Chinese for failing to live up to the Agreed Announcement.[23]

Not long after the meeting, McConaughy promised to "lend all appropriate assistance to Mrs. Downey if she decides to make the trip to Geneva."[24] But tensions continued to play out between the spy moms and the State Department. John Foster Dulles met with Hugh Redmond's mother in May to tell her that she was prohibited by the Trading with the Enemy Act from visiting her son.[25] When Elizabeth Cusack wrote to the White House requesting a face-to-face meeting between her friend Mary Downey and President Eisenhower, the State Department weighed in against the idea. The president had already met with the stepmother of an imprisoned priest (Father Harold Rigney), thereby demonstrating his concern over the dwindling group of Americans stuck in Red China. He did not meet Hugh Redmond's mother, and there was no reason to meet now with Mrs. Downey. If refused, Downey "is not inclined to be insistent."

Incredibly, the memorandum from the State Department to the president's chief of staff on the question of a meeting with Mary Downey recited the exfiltration cover story as if it were factually true, explaining, "Mr. Downey, a Department of Army civilian, was abroad [*sic*] a plane which disappeared on November 29, 1952 in flight from Korea to Japan."[26] As internal memos and public statements accumulated, officials risked hiding the truth not only from an unsuspecting public, but from the government itself—an example of the state behaving like what Hannah Arendt would later describe as the "self-deceived deceiver."

The State Department was wrong about one thing, at least: Mary Downey would prove to be quite insistent. Unable to get a meeting at the White House or a trip to Geneva, she settled for the time being on a meeting with Ambassador Johnson at Idlewild Airport, Long Island, on July 3, 1957. Two priests had just been released from Chinese custody, giving some cause for hope. The State Department also belatedly loosened the ban preventing journalists from reporting in China. In a perverse irony, however, rather than using the measure as leverage in getting American prisoners released, the department released a combative statement conveying its hope that journalists "may be able to report on the Americans illegally held in Chinese prisons as to whose fate there is deep concern on the part of the American nation."[27] At the ambassadorial talks in Geneva, now it was Johnson who put forward a proposal for an exchange of correspondents, only for Wang Bingnan to shoot it down, reflecting perhaps the repressive atmosphere back home by the autumn of 1957 with the Anti-Rightist Campaign in full steam.[28] The Geneva talks continued to achieve the goal set out by John Foster Dulles: absolutely nothing.

Despite the standoff between the two governments, the American journalist Robert Carl Cohen of NBC News took advantage of the relaxation of travel restrictions to make a reporting trip to China. Cohen accompanied an American student delegation stopping over in China on its way home from the Moscow World Youth

Festival. The students' itinerary in Beijing, with Cohen tagging along, included a meeting with Downey and Fecteau, who openly acknowledged being guilty as charged.[29] Downey appeared suntanned, his hair cut short. The men were being held in twelve-by-fifteen-foot cells and were allowed an hour of exercise daily. Fecteau told the students that he had received 680 letters and spent most of his time reading everything from *Sports Illustrated* to Stalin to Cervantes.[30]

Visiting Shanghai, Robert Cohen was allowed to film inside Ward Prison, where he was told the total number of political prisoners nationwide was six hundred thousand. Brought to see a commune outside Canton, Cohen filmed a community bulletin board with mug shots of eight agents of subversion sent by Chiang Kai-shek, along with photos of their US-made weaponry. All eight special agents faced execution.[31]

With the uptick in press attention to Downey and Fecteau, the State Department ceded to Mary Downey's wishes and requested the intercession of UN Secretary General Dag Hammarskjöld. But they supplied him with the same talking points, reiterating the false cover story, and nothing came of it.[32] Mary contacted the State Department again in November, demanding a passport and permission to go see her son in prison in Beijing as the five-year anniversary of his capture approached. With Kafkaesque warmth, Assistant Secretary Robertson wrote to inform her that her request was "receiving our serious consideration although I wish to warn you that there is not the slightest indication that your trip to China could affect the release of your son. There are many complicated questions involved but I expect that we shall be able to give you a definite decision within the next few days."[33] Mary fired back with reference to a recent court case won by a lawyer in Los Angeles, A. L. Wirin, requesting a passport in order to do legal research in the PRC to help defend his clients John and Sylvia Powell, who were charged by the US government with sedition for having published "pro-Chinese" materials on the controversy over US germ warfare during the Korean War. "It is my belief," Mary wrote, "that my reasons for going to China are of greater import than those the courts thought sufficient to justify Mr. Wirin's journey."[34]

The telephone rang two weeks later at Mary Downey's home in Connecticut to let her know the families of American captives would be allowed to visit China. She was further informed that "the people concerned" would be in touch about providing financial assistance.[35] The PRC government swiftly approved visa applications received via cablegram from the families of Downey, Fecteau, and Redmond. At the same time that the ambassadorial talks in Geneva were being downgraded to a lower rank, family visits for the US prisoners in China were at last moving ahead.[36]

FIGURE 10. Spy moms head to Red China (1958). Getty Images/ New York Daily News.

Scratches on Their Minds

When the spy moms set off in January 1958, they represented the first delegation of private citizens to visit the People's Republic of China with the approval of the US government since the country's founding in 1949. Ironically, it was a CIA-funded operation—the Agency budgeted $14,000 to cover the families' travel expenses, while fretting over what they might learn in discussions with Chinese officials.[37]

The journey of the three mothers, accompanied by Jack's brother William, was duly reported in the press, but without a great deal of fanfare. The *New York Times* ran a one-column curtain-raiser on January 6, followed sporadically by terse wire updates as the visit unfolded. Only once did the historic trip make the front page, with a photo of Mrs. Redmond embracing her son Hugh on January 12.

The Chinese authorities granted the mothers a weeklong extension to their stay, allowing them a total of seven prison visits of two hours each. Jack marveled at how his little brother's voice had deepened. William had followed in his footsteps to Yale. The two talked sports as Mary took the measure of her Jack—he looked thinner but not by much; his spirits were good, no sign of depression.[38] At the end of the month, a grainy picture of the mothers and William walking back to the Free World at the border in Hong Kong appeared on page three of the *New York Times*.[39] Despite the drama of three ordinary mothers traveling halfway around the world to see their captive sons in an exotic, forbidden enemy country, coverage was sparse.

The muted public interest in the spy moms' journey reflected the widespread negativity toward Korean War POWs in the years after the armistice. The *New Yorker* editor and writer Eugene Kinkead had just published a long piece in the October 1957 issue arguing that the postwar generation had failed to beat the ChiComs in Korea because they were deficient in masculinity and Americanness. Kinkead contrasted them with the Greatest Generation, as they would be known, who had defeated Germany and Japan in WWII. Korean War POWs were symbols of a lost American manhood; they let themselves be caught rather than fight to the death, broke easily under interrogation, betrayed fellow captives in the camps, and—in the case of the twenty-one turncoats—even defected to the other side.[40]

Reinforcing these sour views of Korean War POWs, US public attitudes toward Communist China remained stuck in a rut of deep ambivalence, curtailing interest in the spy moms. An incisive study of the psychology of the relationship was published by the journalist Harold Isaacs, *Scratches on Our Minds: American Images of India and China* (1958). "Our emotions about the Chinese have ranged between sympathy and rejection, parental benevolence and parental exasperation, affection and hostility, love and a fear close to hate," Isaacs observed. "Today these contending views and emotions jostle each other at close quarters, for we are in the midst of a great passage from one set to the other."[41] Isaacs charted the history of this "great passage" in American perceptions of China: from the image of a downtrodden, virtuous China, seen in Pearl Buck novels and WWII propaganda—the age of benevolence (1905–37) and admiration (1937–44)—to the image of a corrupt, villainous China ruled by the dictators Chiang and Mao—the eras of disenchantment (1944–49) and hostility (1949–58).[42] The Korean War's "staggeringly new spectacle of Americans suffering defeats at Chinese hands" made the great passage that much harder to bear. McCarthyite hysteria over who lost China may have ebbed from its most intense phase, but "the argument was not ended; it simply came to an exhausted halt." Isaacs's public opinion surveys indicated that a significant number of Americans still harbored a paternalistic love of China but now felt betrayed and held the view that Chinese people were "in short, ungrateful wretches." In the absence of direct contact and exchange, an older sediment of stereotypes rose to the surface of American perceptions: China as a land of cruel, cunning, sadistic Orientals.[43]

If the general public was apathetic to the spy moms' journey to China, there was at least one person in the United States who was paying close attention to the case of the two American captives. Colonel Rudolf Ivanovich Abel was a Soviet operative arrested for espionage in New York City in June 1957. While conferring with his lawyer James Donovan in September—around the time NBC aired footage of Downey and Fecteau in their cells in Beijing—Colonel Abel raised the idea of a spy trade. The problem, as Abel explained it to his lawyer, was that there was no one of his rank in Soviet hands.[44] After Abel's conviction in October, Donovan continued to visit him in prison. During a prison chat on February 12, 1958—a couple weeks after the spy moms had returned from their trip—Abel suggested to Donovan that he go see Allen Dulles. Donovan recalled that Abel "asked that I broach the subject of a possible trade with the CIA chief. He seemed to think that India or another neutral country might be willing, in the interest of lessening world tension, to mediate his exchange for Americans imprisoned in Red China."[45] In other words, Abel wanted his lawyer to suggest to the CIA director a trade—him for Downey and Fecteau.

Days after Colonel Abel floated his idea for a spy swap, Allen Dulles met with Mary Downey to hear about her visit to China and to convey the Agency's concern over her son's ordeal. A couple of weeks later, Dulles sat down with Donovan to hear out the idea of a trade. "I wish, Dulles said, puffing at his pipe, 'we had three or four just like him [Abel] inside Moscow, right now.'" But Dulles pointed out there were no captured agents in Russia for whom to trade. Donovan recalls, "I then advanced the Colonel's proposal that I might trade with Russia for Americans held captive in China—through a neutral third nation like India acting as intermediary." India could offer "political asylum" both to Abel, who would not be acknowledged by Moscow, and to the Americans, who would not be acknowledged by Washington. Allen Dulles was "intrigued" by the Abel proposal and promised Donovan that he would check with his brother. John Foster's answer arrived a few weeks later: a swap could be considered on only one condition—if Moscow acknowledged Abel's guilt.[46] It was an ironic precondition given the US government's refusal to acknowledge the guilt of their own operatives in the PRC.

In the summer of 1958, fighting erupted for a second time in the Taiwan Strait. After shelling by Communist forces in August, the Nationalists stepped up penetration operations, with little success to show for it.[47] The columnist Stewart Alsop detected in John Foster Dulles's handling of the crisis the culmination of a quiet process of "re-leashing" Chiang Kai-shek.[48] Aerial combat between PRC and ROC planes continued into the fall, by which point the second Taiwan Strait Crisis settled into a kabuki pattern of alternating days between bombardments of artillery shells and propaganda leaflets.

Anxiety generated by the second Strait Crisis spurred Eisenhower to sign off on U-2 surveillance flights over mainland China, monitoring for signs of preparation for a full-scale invasion of Taiwan as well as checking on nuclear and missile program development sites.[49] Station Chief Ray Cline began lobbying headquarters to allow the sale of a pair of U-2s for Chiang Kai-shek's use.[50] After the mastermind of the U-2 program, Richard Bissell, officially replaced Frank Wisner as deputy director of plans, he called station chiefs from across Asia for a regional meeting in Manila in January 1959. The CIA station in Taipei remained unenthusiastic about infiltrating agents of subversion. As Station Chief Ray Cline wrote in his memoirs:

> The survivability of these agents was limited and we gradually turned to other intelligence techniques: the occasional traveler, the foreign diplomat, and, above all, the electronic and photographic collection platforms. It is a very stressful experience to sit in a radio shack perched out on high ground above Taipei, listening for clandestine radio signals from teams in Sinkiang; it was heartbreaking when after a time they came through with the prearranged coded signal that indicated the radio operator had been captured. Occasionally a useful item of information would get back from these sources, but they were usually low-level operations and scarcely cost-effective efforts.[51]

The Hong Kong station chief Peter Sichel agreed with Cline about the futility of parachute operations, comparing them to sending "boy scouts into China to blow up railway cars."[52]

Sherman Kent also paid a visit to the Far East that year, including a stop in Taipei, where Chiang Kai-shek's son, Chiang Ching-kuo, presented him with a gift: an inscribed Chinese translation of *Strategic Intelligence for American World Policy*.[53] Around the time of Bissell's Manila conference, Kent heard from a fellow Yale man and friend of the Downey family, Chester Bowles, that Mary Downey was desperate enough to contemplate moving to Beijing to be near her son.[54] Bowles was a prominent Democrat, newly elected to Congress representing Downey's district in Connecticut. A decade earlier, Bowles had served as Truman's ambassador to India, where he developed a close relationship with Prime Minister Nehru. He tried using his Delhi connections to help get Downey and Fecteau released—as imagined in Colonel Abel's spy trade proposal. During the second Taiwan Strait Crisis, Bowles pushed the State Department to make the prisoners the top negotiating priority at the Geneva talks, and received a somewhat dismissive reply from Secretary Dulles.[55]

John Foster Dulles died in office in the spring of 1959, marking the end of an era in American Cold War diplomacy. Mary Downey was more confrontational with the new secretary, Christian Herter, jabbing her finger in his face during their first meeting that year.[56] William Downey made a solo visit to Beijing to see his brother in July, and solicited the help of a lawyer in Hong Kong to submit an amnesty appeal, but it went nowhere.[57] Mary made a second visit, unaccompanied, to visit Jack in August 1960. A heavy storm delayed her entry at Hong Kong by a day, and when she finally arrived in Canton, all flights north were cancelled. The widowed elementary school teacher had no choice but take a forty-four-hour train ride and pray for as many visits with her son as the authorities would allow.[58]

Mary returned to Caolanzi Hutong Prison. Jack looked about the same in body and spirit. He had two cellmates, a Chinese and a Russian, and he asked his mom to mail him a Russian grammar book. Jack would later remember the visits as not entirely pleasant, finding it "somewhat degrading for my mother, for her to have to go over and beg these bastards for her son." His treatment did improve around the time of the visits, and he got a "temporary boost" in morale. But it was a constant emotional whiplash. "Sometimes I thought it is better not even to come in contact with the outside world and home. You have made your peace with the present situation, it can be painful to open the door and see the sunlight, better stay back in your hole."[59] It was a door that, once closed, left searing pain on both sides. When the end of the final visit came, Mary Downey turned back one last time to kiss her boy, not knowing when she would see him again, if he would ever be released. "I couldn't bring myself to leave. Finally, I pulled myself together and forced myself to go out the door and close it. Then I cried."[60]

Counterrevolution in Tibet

As the Yale graduate John Thomas Downey rotted in his Beijing prison cell for having tried and failed to foment counterrevolution, the Yale professor David Nelson Rowe argued in his new book, *Modern China: A Brief History* (1959), that counterrevolutionary victory was just around the corner. In the absence of visible signs of resistance to CCP rule, Rowe posited that Mao faced "internal dissidence so massive that the mere slowness of its development may deceive us into unawareness of it."[61]

Still litigating the loss of China, Rowe blamed the Truman administration for a missed opportunity of epic proportions by failing to intervene in the Chinese Civil War. "When we could have contained Chinese Communism . . . and eventually assisted in its destruction by military force, we refused to do so." He considered the PRC to be "a third-rate power militarily and a vast poorhouse as to economics," which existed only because Moscow propped it up. Yet, contradictorily, Rowe also warned that China—acting as a tool of Soviet aggression—threatened "the takeover by threat of force or actual force" of South Korea, South Vietnam, Taiwan, Malaya, and Thailand.[62]

Invoking the ominous specter of a geopolitical domino effect across Asia, just as General Claire Chennault had a decade earlier, Rowe also offered much the same solution as Chennault had. In order to contain Chinese Communist aggression, Rowe advised providing covert assistance to the latent forces of counterrevolution. "It is the task of a sophisticated economic and political warfare, backed up by constant military readiness, to aid and abet the development of massive dissidence among the suffering Chinese people."[63]

As it turns out, at the time Rowe's book came out, the CIA was resurrecting its former role as patron of anti-Communist subversion in China. But this time around, the covert action was taking place not on the streets of Hong Kong or in the forests of Manchuria but high up on the Tibetan plateau.

The CIA had been trying for years to find a conduit to the Tibetan people's religious and political leader, the fourteenth Dalai Lama, first through his eldest brother Thubten Norbu, who ended up in Washington, and then through his brother Gyalo Thondup, who lived in exile in the Indian hill station of Kalimpong. Arriving in Kalimpong in June 1952, Gyalo missed the chance to run into Carsun Chang, who had left India six months earlier.[64] When the CIA officer John Hoskins landed in Calcutta in September 1956, the Agency's outreach "became more concrete," as Gyalo put it.[65]

There was a flurry of diplomatic and intelligence activity in anticipation of the Dalai Lama's planned visit to India to celebrate the Jayanti—the 2,500th anniversary of the birth of the Buddha. In Beijing, the party leadership hotly debated whether it was prudent to let the Dalai Lama cross the border, but Mao came down on the side of letting him go. "We advised him to go by air, but he refused, preferring to travel by car via Kalimpong, where there are spies from various countries as well as Kuomintang secret agents," Mao told the Central Committee. Mao dared the young lama to go into exile if he wished; after all, "he can't do more than curse us. Our Communist Party has been cursed for thirty-five years."[66] The Dalai Lama was in fact tempted to remain in India, but both Prime Minister Nehru—who was keen on amiable relations with Beijing—and Premier Zhou Enlai—who timed an overlapping visit to Delhi—urged him to go back to his homeland.

The Dalai Lama ultimately agreed to return to Tibet, where the situation continued to deteriorate as Khampa tribesmen on the southeastern edge of the plateau rose up in armed rebellion against CCP rule.[67] The repressive wave of the Anti-Rightist Campaign reached Lhasa, where the party tightened its grip. CCP officials accused exiled Tibetans, including the Dalai Lama's brothers, of working with "the imperialists," a claim the Dalai Lama strenuously denied.[68]

Gyalo Thondup—without his brother's knowledge—did in fact help Hoskins, the CIA's man in Calcutta, recruit a small team of exiles for a reconnaissance mission to assess the counterrevolutionary potential of Tibetan communities in the PRC. Gyalo drove the men across the border from India to East Pakistan, where they were flown to Okinawa to be met by the Dalai Lama's other brother, Thubten Norbu, for transit onward to Saipan—following in the trail of the Third Force agents of subversion.[69]

The training on Saipan would be known as Operation Circus, and by the fall of 1957, the Tibetan agents were ready for Operation Barnum—parachuting into Tibet.[70] A B-17 flown by Polish pilots dropped a two-man team south of Lhasa with a message for the Dalai Lama, hoping to win his blessing for covert action. The response was not encouraging—the Dalai Lama continued to reject violence and rebuffed the CIA offer.[71] But a second team that parachuted into the Kham region of southeastern Tibet quickly linked up with armed resistance.[72] Although the members of the four-man team were killed in fighting, the reports from out of Kham, combined with the debrief from the Lhasa team, indicated that the "internal dissidence" imagined by David Nelson Rowe might actually exist, at least in Tibetan areas.[73]

Back in Washington, there were hopes and fears of a Tibetan version of the Hungarian Uprising. President Eisenhower himself suggested the analogy when asked to explain NATO's failure to respond to the revolt in Budapest, commenting that it would be as hard to move an army into Hungary as it would into Tibet.[74] Despite misgivings, the Agency decided to move ahead with a training program for Tibetan agents of subversion to aid the rebellion in Kham, bringing a second cohort of trainees to Saipan in the summer of 1958.[75] The outbreak of widespread armed rebellion in Tibetan villages and monasteries across Qinghai Province, known to Tibetans as the Amdo region, offered further evidence of ripeness for counterrevolution.[76]

The CIA training program was relocated from Saipan to the mainland United States in the autumn of 1958, starting with ten recruits sent to The Farm in Williamsburg, Virginia.[77] By early 1959, CIA planes were making arms drops on the Tibetan Plateau, and the capital city of Lhasa joined the regions of Kham and Amdo in open insurrection on March 10, 1959.[78] The Dalai Lama escaped in stealth to India, assisted along the way by a Saipan-trained agent.[79]

Operation Circus relocated to a new training facility set up in the Rocky Mountains of Colorado to better approximate conditions in the Himalayas. The Jedburgh model was suddenly making a comeback. A cohort of twenty Tibetan refugees in India were transported via US military airfields in Pakistan, the Philippines, and Okinawa onward to Camp Hale, Colorado.[80] They were the first of several hundred Tibetans to go through Rocky Mountain paramilitary and intelligence training in the coming years.[81] After training, teams would be infiltrated via parachute into Tibetan areas to coordinate supply drops of communications equipment and weaponry, flown by CAT pilots based out of Taiwan.[82]

The maritime archipelago of subversion now extended its reach up to the highest altitudes on the surface of the earth. U-2 planes were involved as well, flying reconnaissance missions over the drop zones for surveillance and allowing CIA analysts to "remap Tibet," as the image analyst Dino Brugioni put it.[83] On at least one occasion, paramilitary training took place on Taiwan, for a small team of Hui Muslims who parachuted into the Amdo region. Those agents of subversion were swiftly captured, and a follow-on supply drop probably went straight into enemy hands.[84]

The Tibetan counterrevolution did not last long. Chinese troops organized a major counterinsurgency campaign in 1960 that decimated rebel holdouts.[85] According to the Dalai Lama's brother Gyalo, CIA assistance for armed resistance was severely curtailed in the final year of the Eisenhower era. Support for Tibetan operations shifted to something called the Mustang Project, equipping an espionage base in the remote Nepalese border town of Mustang, with high-altitude access to western Tibet.[86]

The shift from subversion to surveillance left Gyalo deeply cynical about US motivations for political warfare in his homeland. "The CIA's goal was never independence for Tibet. In fact, I do not think that the Americans ever really even wanted to help. They just wanted to stir up trouble," Gyalo told the China scholar Anne Thurston. Gyalo remained confident that the counterrevolution could have succeeded in military and political terms. "I still believe that if the CIA had given us enough weapons, the resistance would have had a chance. Had I understood how paltry the CIA's support would be, I would never have sent those young men for training. Mao was not the only one to cheat the Tibetans. The CIA did, too."[87]

As Mao Zedong sought to pacify Tibetan areas and the Dalai Lama created a government-in-exile at the Indian border town of Dharamsala, Chiang Kai-shek reopened the Burmese wound in early 1960 by sending troops from Taiwan to reinforce General Li Mi's Yunnan Anti-Communist National Salvation Army. Eisenhower was not happy, but went ahead with his planned visit to Taiwan in June 1960, the first in US history to Chinese territory by a sitting president.

Spy Swaps

By the time Eisenhower landed in Taipei, the grand foreign policy initiative for his final year in office was in tatters. He had been hoping for a breakthrough in relations with Moscow, but his dream of détente imploded in midair with a botched covert operation and a captured spy.

On May Day 1960, Soviet air defenses finally shot down one of Richard Bissell's U-2 planes as it transited the USSR snapping photos from seventy thousand feet. Russian experts recognized the wreckage from photographs of a mystery plane that had made an emergency landing in Yokohama, Japan, the year before, having taken off from its nearby base at the CIA facility in Atsugi.[88] In a replay of the Downey/Fecteau incident, the Eisenhower administration put out a cover story about a disappeared weather monitoring aircraft, walking straight into the trap set by Khrushchev, who produced the plane and its pilot, Francis Gary Powers. Plausible deniability had reached its breaking point. As Eisenhower's press secretary James Hagerty put it to a group of reporters, "If you gentlemen are spies and I am the government and you get caught, I can say I never heard of you or saw you before. But if you strap a U-2 to your back, it is a little more difficult, to say the least, not to admit and assume responsibility."[89]

Just as Beijing had done after the Downey, Fecteau and Arnold Crew trial in December 1954, the Soviet government staged an elaborate exhibition in Moscow's Gorky Park, where massive crowds came to witness the wreckage of the U-2.[90] The incident derailed the upcoming Four Powers Summit in Paris, where the US and Soviet leaders were set to have their first chance to meet in the flesh since the Geneva Summit of 1955. Eisenhower's ambitious dream of inviting Khrushchev to the United States dissolved in acrimony, as the tail of espionage and surveillance wagged the dog of peace and security. In the wake of the U-2 incident, Khrushchev essentially gave up on dealing with Eisenhower in his lame duck year, and Gary Powers—convicted of espionage and put in prison—was held back in reserve.

Moscow lucked upon another pair of useful cards on July 1, 1960, when two US Air Force pilots, Captains Freeman D. Olmstead and John R. McKone, survived the downing of their RB-47 reconnaissance plane as it traversed the Barents Sea (four crewmates died). As a "good-will gesture to the new administration," in the words of lawyer James Donovan, Khrushchev handed over the two servicemen in time for the new president, Jack Kennedy, to proudly announce their homecoming at his inaugural press conference on January 25, 1961.[91] Kennedy waxed hopeful about the larger meaning of the release, signaling his own interest in a thaw by publicly thanking Khrushchev: "The United States Government is gratified by this decision of the Soviet Union and considers that this action of the Soviet Government removes a serious obstacle to improvement of Soviet-American relations."[92] Hoping to reciprocate the goodwill gesture from Moscow, Jack's brother Robert, in his role as attorney general, dropped the case against a pair of alleged Russian spies, an American arrested by the FBI in October 1960 for espionage and a Soviet UN diplomat, Igor Melekh (who was ordered to leave the country by mid-April).[93]

As Khrushchev and Kennedy danced around the possibilities of détente, their intelligence services explored the idea of a spy trade: Colonel Abel for Captain Powers. Using the subterfuge of letters sent between Abel's "wife" in Moscow and his lawyer Donovan in Brooklyn, American and Soviet authorities worked out arrangements for a swap along the lines Abel had proposed back in 1958, but using Powers in place of Downey and Fecteau. Donovan received authorization on January 11, 1962, to orchestrate the trade in Berlin, freeing Abel in return for Powers along with two American graduate students arrested by East German authorities on espionage charges (one of them, Frederic Pryor, was studying economics at Yale).[94]

In his memoir *Craft of Intelligence*, published the following year, Allen Dulles criticized the practice of spy swaps. In principle, making a concession for a spy went against the national interest. As a practical matter, Dulles presumed the Soviets had far more agents in the West than vice versa, thus bartering with the enemy was inherently disadvantageous. And yet, he defended the Abel-Powers exchange, "under the particular circumstances of this rather unusual case." With the advent of U-2 planes and satellites, Dulles wrote wistfully, "Intelligence has come a long way since the good old days when everything could be shoved under the rug of silence."[95]

Like Khrushchev, Mao may have at least toyed with the possibility of improving relations with the next administration in Washington. By 1960, the party could have used a breakthrough. Conditions were desperate in large parts of the country, which was reeling from the disastrous effects of the communization/industrialization movement called the Great Leap Forward, launched with irrational exuberance by Mao in late 1957 and early 1958. Famine gripped cities and countryside alike, eventually taking tens of millions of lives.[96] When General Peng Dehuai, the great hero of the Korean War, gently questioned the wisdom of the campaign in the summer of 1959, Mao orchestrated a merciless purge, sending a warning to others who might dare oppose him. But the catastrophic failure of Mao's program to accelerate "economic construction" damaged the chairman's aura of omniscience. In the same years, Mao antagonized Khrushchev in a contest for primacy in the socialist camp, offending Moscow to the point that Soviet advisers were ordered home from China in the summer of 1960.[97]

Zhou Enlai's vehicle to use in testing out friendly signals toward Washington was the sympathetic American journalist Edgar Snow, famous for his interview with a young Mao and Zhou and the resulting book, *Red Star over China* (1937). Invited back a quarter century later, Snow was given long sessions to chat with Zhou. The premier drew attention to the issue of American prisoners. He reminded Snow that Beijing released so-called prisoners of war back in 1955 in order "to create a favorable atmosphere for the ambassadorial talks at Geneva." After the Agreed Announcement, twenty-five more Americans, even ones who had broken Chinese laws, were released. Zhou then brought up the Downey/Fecteau case in considerable detail:

> There are two United States nationals in Chinese prisons of another category—a very special one. They are air-borne secret agents sent by the United States to China, namely, the very famous Downey and Fecteau. Allen Dulles of the United States Central Intelligence Agency could give you all the details, but perhaps he wouldn't want to give the information in such detail as we would. In early 1955, when Hammarskjöld came to Peking to discuss the question of the United States nationals in Chinese prisons, even he found it inconvenient to bring up their case for discussion. These two were in no way related to the Korean War, but were on a mission of pure espionage and secret-agent activity. If you are interested, I could show you some portions of the notes of my talks with Hammarskjöld for your reference. The notes have never been published.[98]

Edgar Snow had another source on the Downey/Fecteau case, as Mary Downey happened to be in Beijing for her second visit to see Jack, and like Snow, she was staying at the Xinqiao Hotel, not too far from Tiananmen Square.[99] Edgar and Mary often shared meals together, leading Mrs. Downey's State Department minders in Hong Kong to worry that Snow's sympathetic views might be wearing off and that Mary had come to admire the progress of China under Communist rule.[100] Although there was a famine induced by the Great Leap Forward campaign of forced industrialization of the countryside and collectivization of agricultural production, Mary remarked on the "remarkable progress" of Beijing as compared with her previous trip in 1958. She was relieved to see her son had put on weight and seemed to be returning to his old self.

Mrs. Downey was in China for one reason alone: her son—to give him succor and lobby for his release. She had every reason to try to placate the Chinese authorities with kind words about their country to help earn clemency. By contrast, Snow was there to understand conditions in the country and was able to travel widely, albeit chaperoned. He, too, was oblivious to the extent of the extreme deprivation inflicted by Mao and the CCP leadership's unrealistic and callous revolutionary enthusiasm.

Snow's interview with Premier Zhou did not appear in print until the month of Kennedy's inauguration, running as the controversial cover story of *Look* magazine for January 1961. By then, Snow had already briefed Kennedy's nominee for secretary of state, Dean Rusk, with whom he had met almost immediately on arrival in New York from his five-month stay in China. Rusk ostentatiously displayed zero interest in what Snow had to say.[101]

Premier Zhou may have been floating another olive branch across the Pacific in April, when Beijing followed Moscow's lead in releasing an imprisoned spy. Robert McCann, ten years into his fifteen-year sentence, was released early on humanitarian grounds. The humanitarian gesture, sadly, was not a subterfuge. McCann was gravely ill at the time of release. He only made it as far as Clark Air Force Base in the Philippines, where after a month of medical treatment he died before being able return to his native soil.[102] It was hardly the kind of gesture the new Kennedy administration could make much of, especially to the public.

Covert Camelot

As it was, China was not high on the list of national security priorities for Kennedy and his brain trust of Harvard men like Special Assistant Arthur Schlesinger Jr., Secretary of Defense Robert McNamara, National Security Advisor McGeorge Bundy, and Attorney General Robert Kennedy. There was less turnover in security and intelligence—J. Edgar Hoover remained in charge of the FBI and Allen Dulles kept his position as CIA director. They had a far more urgent and sensitive topic than China to discuss with JFK in the early weeks and months of his presidency: a covert plot to overthrow Fidel Castro's two-year-old revolutionary government in Cuba.

With planning well underway, JFK decided to go through with the scheme to help an exile army invade the island and subvert Castro—something roughly along the lines of the Guatemala coup of 1954. But when the counterrevolutionary band landed in the Bay of Pigs in mid-April, fiasco ensued. Members of the invasion force were rapidly captured or killed and Castro made the United States into a laughingstock for its role in the bungled coup plot. The Bay of Pigs would bring an end not only to Allen Dulles's directorship (though Kennedy let him linger on for six more months), but also to the CIA's 1950s image as omnipresent and omnipotent. As William Colby remembered it, "Suddenly the Agency appeared to be, not an elite corps of slick, daring James Bond operatives, but rather a collection of bunglers, launching harebrained escapades and leading men uselessly to their death."[103]

The young charismatic president gave voice to the national mood of revulsion at the basic notion of covert foreign policy. Returning to the discourse of America's liberal "traditions" in the mode of Whit Griswold, Kennedy told a conference of members of the press: "The very word 'secrecy' is repugnant in a free and open republic and we are as a people inherently and historically opposed to secret societies, to secret oaths and to secret proceedings. We decided long ago that the dangers of excessive and unwarranted concealment of pertinent facts far outweighed the dangers which are cited to justify it. Even today, there is little value in ensuring the survival of our nation if our traditions do not survive with it."[104] But of course, Kennedy himself had approved the Cuban operation, and would sign off on more efforts to subvert the Castro regime, including through assassination. Even as JFK publicly repudiated secrecy, he authorized psywar, paramilitary activities, and invasive surveillance around the world—including China's frontiers of subversion.

Kennedy was briefed early on about covert intelligence-gathering operations in Tibet, and the first CIA-trained team parachuted into Tibet on his authority in March, a month before the Bay of Pigs. They were wiped out within weeks.[105] Kennedy's ambassador to India, the Harvard economist John Kenneth Galbraith, lobbied to stop the Tibet covert operations, but was overruled by White House advisers.[106] The Mustang Project justified its existence with an intelligence bonanza in October, when a Tibetan reconnaissance team ambushed a PLA unit and captured a cache of military publications. The seized materials eventually reached the desks of Sherman Kent's analysts in Washington, shedding light on the calamity of the Great Leap Forward and its detrimental impact on Chinese military readiness.[107]

Eisenhower had warned Kennedy during their awkward transition meeting that the most important national security threat might well be a country many Americans would not have even heard of—tiny Laos, a poor, landlocked nation that shared a border with China and both Vietnams.[108] Initially, one covert initiative that the new administration did *not* look on favorably was Chiang Kai-shek's small but meddlesome satellite army along the Burma-Laos border. When the Burmese military shot down one of Chiang's planes en route from Taiwan with supplies, an embarrassed White House stepped up pressure on Taipei to complete the evacuation of four thousand Nationalist troops in Burma that spring.[109]

Despite shutting down Taiwan's army in Burma, it wasn't long before Kennedy was authorizing dramatic increases in covert assistance and special forces in Laos, Cambodia, and Vietnam. A leading role was played by the CIA front company Air America, as CAT was now known. Six months after repudiating secret foreign policy in the wake of the Bay of Pigs, JFK struck a very different tone on a visit to the CIA's brand-new headquarters, the campus at Langley, Virginia. "Your successes are unheralded—your failures are trumpeted," he told the nation's top spies, analysts, and agents. "I sometimes have that feeling myself [laughter]. But I'm sure you realize how . . . in the long sweep of history how significant your efforts will be judged."[110]

As Southeast Asia absorbed increasing attention and resources, it was natural to be tempted to apply pressure on North Vietnam's ally. In the spring of 1962, the CIA and Chiang Kai-shek indulged the fantasy that the refugee crisis in Hong Kong might be the long-awaited opportunity to reignite counterrevolution in the mainland, which was still reeling from years of economic dislocation and famine. James Lilley recalled, "The question then came up of whether the U.S. and Taiwan could exploit this situation by air-dropping 150-man armed teams into China to organize an opposition force. My experience in the 1950s in Hong Kong, Taiwan, and Korea told me this would not work. Sure enough, the few exploratory operations run from Taiwan were quickly captured and 'neutralized.'"[111] The historian John Garver documented a spike in US-sponsored "unconventional warfare exercises" by Nationalist forces starting in mid-1962 that continued for the next three years.[112] Taiwan also emerged as a key base in the Far East for U-2 surveillance flights, with Nationalist pilots adding a layer of plausible deniability for the Americans.[113] Beijing downed one of Chiang's U-2s on September 9, 1962, protesting vehemently about the standing pattern of aggressive surveillance.[114]

There was little public scrutiny of the covert assistance to the Nationalists in Taiwan or Tibetans in Nepal. The high drama of Cold War tension remained focused on the struggle with the Soviet Union, which came close to blows in Europe during the Berlin Crisis of 1961 and to the brink of nuclear war in October 1962 during the Cuban Missile Crisis. Postfamine China, with its backward economy and Maoist ideology, was threatening, but in an esoteric and remote way. China remained a scratch on the American mind during the Kennedy years.

Orientalist fears and fantasies of Chinese subversion would pop up, like in the edgy noir film *The Manchurian Candidate* (1962), staring Frank Sinatra, based on the Richard Condon novel about a returned Korean War POW brainwashed into becoming an unwitting agent-assassin. The villain of *The Manchurian Candidate*, Dr. Yen Lo, played off classic tropes in anti-Asian prejudices. The same year marked the arrival on screen of the stoical British secret agent James Bond, played to perfection by Sean Connery. Connery's Bond may have been gorgeous on the surface, but he had an instinctive brutality about him, that absence of conscience examined by Arendt in *The Origins of Totalitarianism*. In the Fleming novels, Bond's adversary was the Soviet counterintelligence organization SMERSH. But for the films, the enemy was changed to a sinister global syndicate of criminals, anarchists, and sociopaths known as SPECTRE. SPECTRE represented yet another variation on the idea of a Third Force, a symbol of neither European socialist solidarity or Afro-Asian postcolonial solidarity, but rather of criminality and villainy.

Strategy of Subversion

While Anglo-American fears of subversion—communist or criminal—were becoming the stuff of 1960s pop culture iconography, a former psychological warfare specialist named Paul Blackstock was working on a pioneering academic study of covert foreign policy, eventually published as *The Strategy of Subversion: Manipulating the Politics of Other Nations* (1964). Retired from US military intelligence and teaching at the University of South Carolina, Blackstock deconstructed the US government's reliance on subversion as a tool of statecraft and analyzed the subversion-repression dynamic at work in the Cold War with a detachment reminiscent of the early Cold War realists.

Covert subversion, Blackstock asserted, was an understudied hallmark of modern international relations. "For centuries the Great Powers have used aggressive, clandestine intervention, i.e., covert operations, as an instrument of statecraft, as an ally of diplomacy in peacetime, and as a valuable auxiliary to military force in time of war," he wrote. Yet, by not really studying it, scholars had essentially adopted the fiction of states that covert action does not really exist.[115] His book sought to dredge it to the surface.

Although Blackstock did not cite Arendt, there were echoes of *The Origins of Totalitarianism* in his method of tracing contemporary subversion back to the age of European imperialism. Documenting how the Bolsheviks and the Nazis used covert subversion as a primary instrument of foreign policy, Blackstock argued that US policymakers were unwittingly following that Bolshevik-Nazi model in the name of Allen Dulles's "Cold War mission." As a result, fears of subversion were running in every direction. "In a totalitarian atmosphere of mutual suspicion, fear, and denunciation, this nightmare fantasy of universal subversion can lead to such mad excesses as the Great Purges in the U.S.S.R. or the less spectacular but no less malevolent persecution of millions of innocent victims by the Nazi Secret Police. In the U.S., the effects of McCarthyism are well known."[116]

Blackstock rejected the premise that covert action was an effective means of waging cold war. The historical success rate for foreign subversion, low throughout the eighteenth and nineteenth centuries, was no better since 1947. In Europe, for example, CIA efforts came to naught despite uprisings in East Germany, Poland, and Hungary, whereas countries that resisted Moscow like Yugoslavia and Albania did so of their own accord.[117] In other key arenas for covert competition like Southeast Asia and sub-Saharan Africa, Blackstock saw little moral or even ideological difference between the Americans and the Soviets. Instead, both sides intervened with a basic *purposelessness* to their secret playing of a Cold War Great Game. Blackstock wrote:

> On the highest level, political warfare for both the U.S. and the U.S.S.R. means "cooperating with our friends abroad" or "giving them moral and ideological support." On the operational level, it means airlifting military advisers and equipment and setting up the intelligence networks on which they rely for vital information. On the lowest level, in the rice paddies of Southeast Asia or in the African bush, it means a struggle without quarter where "counter-insurgency" forces are pitted against "national liberation movements" which employ all the techniques of guerrilla warfare, including espionage, terror, and assassination.[118]

Blackstock developed a model for studying how subversive efforts proceeded along four stages: penetration/infiltration; forced disintegration/atomization; subversion; and defection.[119] In practice, the stages of subversion rarely ended well. Despite Blackstock's pessimistic findings, the former intelligence officer in him could not resist offering some practical advice for how to increase the odds of succeeding in a subversive campaign. The key was that "covert operations aimed at seizure of power must build up a counter-elite which can establish the permanency and legitimacy of the new regime."[120] Although China was not a focal point of his study, the key lesson applied well to the failure of the Third Force initiative.

The Strategy of Subversion was not a handbook for regime change—far from it. Blackstock's main purpose was to point out that the most serious risk inherent in clandestine activities is the danger not to the adversary, but to oneself. "Once a secret intelligence and/or covert operational agency is permitted to operate under the protective mantle of the highest security classification, it is capable of directly shaping foreign policy by operations which structure the course of historical events . . . in other words, covert operational agencies can create situations of fact to which national policy—regardless of what it might have been—must later be adjusted."[121] His warning would prove prophetic.

The Strategy of Subversion was a demanding read, designed for an audience of academics and garnering positive reviews from the likes of Harold Lasswell, who was still teaching at Yale. Blackstock's historical and theoretical points about the moral ambiguity at the heart of the Cold War and the perils to liberal democracy inherent in covert foreign policy found a larger audience in fictional form. A British MI-6 junior officer-turned-novelist, David Cornwell, using the pseudonym John le Carré, published *The Spy Who Came in From the Cold*. Set during the Berlin Crisis, it was a dark take on the covert side of the Cold War that became the best-selling book in the United States for most of 1964.

Along with le Carré and Blackstock, another individual who had become deeply concerned about the role of the CIA was the man who created it. Harry

Truman interrupted his taciturn postpresidency in December 1963 to make a rare intervention in the political realm. Truman warned in a *Washington Post* op ed that the Agency had exceeded the boundaries of its original mandate, with dangerous consequences. "This quiet intelligence arm of the President has been so removed from its intended role that it is being interpreted as a symbol of sinister and mysterious foreign intrigue—and a subject for cold war enemy propaganda," Truman lamented.[122]

As living embodiments of America's failed strategy of covert subversion against Mao's China, Jack Downey and Dick Fecteau quietly passed the grim anniversary of a decade in foreign captivity on JFK's watch, with scant diplomatic prospect for release and anemic public interest in their case. Mary Downey made return trips to China in May 1962 and November 1964, generating a spurt of news articles but no more than that. William Downey continued to explore legal stratagems to appeal for his brother's release, to no effect. There were other random efforts at mediation, like that by a colorful figure named Morris "Two Gun" Cohen, a bodyguard for the Nationalist Party founder Sun Yat-sen who had been arrested by the Japanese and released in a prisoner exchange in 1943. Cohen wrote to Zhou Enlai in 1962, encouraging him to release the prisoners.[123] Nothing came of it. Downey and Fecteau had come to embody the state of US-China relations as a whole: prisoners of the past, a lost cause.

15

WAR AND REVOLUTION

With US-China relations trapped in the inertia of mutual hostility and misunderstanding, each country entered into its own vortex of tumult and transformation in the mid-1960s. After the collective trauma of the Kennedy assassination on November 22, 1963, Americans tried to rally behind President Lyndon B. Johnson and his healing, utopian vision of a Great Society, as the Reverend Martin Luther King Jr. carried on the crusade against racial injustice. But LBJ's liberal domestic agenda of advancing civil rights, eradicating poverty, and ensuring healthcare for all became imperiled by his foreign policy instincts in Asia. The loss of China haunted LBJ like a bad ghost, and his doctrine for Asia boiled down to the dictum, "I'm not going to let Vietnam go the way of China."[1] Johnson's escalation spurred the early Cold War realists to come out of the woodwork to object to the Vietnam War, and the old China Hands did the same, calling for a radical shift in China policy. But Mao Zedong was distracted by fomenting a new, massive wave of revolt, chaos, and repression—the Great Proletarian Cultural Revolution—which among other things reinvigorated the spirit of antagonism against imperialist America.

The Loss of Vietnam

The American public had been but dimly aware of the steady increase in security commitment to South Vietnam under JFK, who sent roughly fifteen thousand US military and intelligence advisers to Saigon. The public knew nothing of their government's complicity in a coup d'état against the unpopular South Vietnamese president Ngo Dinh Diem that left him dead and put another unpopular regime in his place just weeks before Kennedy's own death.[2] And Americans were largely in the dark about the extent of US clandestine operations, including infiltrating Vietnamese Jedburghs by air and sea into North Vietnam to carry out paramilitary assignments.[3] These covert activities would pave the way for full-scale US participation in Vietnam's civil war.

No matter how many quiet Americans Washington sent to Saigon, South Vietnam's authoritarian regime struggled to win over its own people—dramatized in the Buddhist crisis of 1963—while North Vietnam and its insurgency in the South, the Viet Cong, were, if nothing else, unified in their determination to expel the Americans and reunify the country. Desperate not to be the man who lost 'Nam, LBJ approved an invigorated campaign of covert operations, known as Oplan-34A, in January 1964. Secret infiltration ops formed the backdrop to an incident off the North Vietnam coast in August involving US Navy surveillance ships in the Gulf of Tonkin. Assuming the ships to be part of an ongoing clandestine penetration, Communist Vietnamese patrols fired on them. The shots missed, but Johnson and his generals interpreted the incident as a brazen, unprovoked attack. A second attack initially reported by the vessels turned out not to have happened at all. But by then, LBJ had his causus belli, and he used the Tonkin incident to get a congressional blessing for the use of military force.

Planned by the administration long in advance, the Tonkin Resolution was consciously modeled on the Formosa Resolution that Eisenhower and Dulles got through Congress at the height of the first Taiwan Strait Crisis in January 1955.[4] With permission from the legislative branch, Johnson ordered the first overt bombing missions by US planes against targets in North Vietnam, resulting in the first US POWs captured by Hanoi. He tried nonetheless to keep Vietnam out of the public eye, focusing on domestic priorities as the platform for his election campaign. It was only after victory at the polls in November 1964 that LBJ, backed by a wide consensus in policy and defense circles, geared up for overt military intervention in Vietnam.[5] His national security advisor McGeorge Bundy and defense secretary Robert McNamara—carry-overs from the Kennedy administration whom Johnson insecurely referred to as "the Harvards"—were confident they could avoid a repeat of the loss of China.[6]

With minimal public debate, Johnson led the nation across the Rubicon in early 1965 when he ordered a large-scale bombing campaign against targets in North Vietnam (Operation Rolling Thunder) and deployment of US combat troops to the South. The two Marine battalions that landed on China Beach at the coastal city of Danang were ostensibly sent to provide security for the airfield, which was destined to become the busiest in the world as the hub for bombing missions.[7] Typical of LBJ's "penchant for deception and secrecy," in the words of his biographer Robert Caro, the president deliberately avoided alerting the American public to the dramatic shift in policy.[8] But the escalation was obvious enough to skeptics in the media, on Capitol Hill, and in allied capitals.

To head off incipient criticism, Johnson gave a televised policy speech at Johns Hopkins University, with former president Dwight Eisenhower in the front row. He explained why the US had no choice but to fight this "dirty and brutal and difficult" war in Vietnam. In making his pitch to the nation, Johnson played up the China angle, calling on his fellow Americans to resist not only the attempt at "total conquest" by North Vietnam but also the "new face of an old enemy . . . another reality: the deepening shadow of Communist China."[9] The president's speech was initially well received by the foreign policy establishment. "The best and the brightest," in journalist David Halberstam's ironic phrase, fell in line to support fighting a land war in Asia.

One prominent academic who remained unconvinced by the president's reasoning for war was Hans Morgenthau, who was still teaching at the University of Chicago. Morgenthau had been dubious of the regime in South Vietnam ever since meeting President Diem on a visit to Saigon back in 1955 (the same year Graham Greene's *The Quiet American* came out). He wrote op eds on a regular basis opposing the deepening US entanglement. Not long after Johnson's speech at Hopkins, Morgenthau published a long rebuttal in the *New York Times* under the devastating title "We Are Deluding Ourselves in Vietnam." The "deepening shadows," as LBJ called them, were to be found in Washington, not Hanoi and Beijing. "We are under a psychological compulsion to continue our military presence in South Vietnam as part of the peripheral military containment of China"—a strategy, Morgenthau explained, that was doomed to failure.[10]

As an embryonic antiwar movement emerged in 1965 on college campuses and at folk music festivals, Morgenthau embraced his unlikely role as a gadfly in a tweed coat. He traveled to Washington, D.C., to participate in a national teach-in, debated against McGeorge Bundy on network television, and published a blandly titled, harshly critical collection of essays, *Vietnam and the United States* (1965).[11]

From his perch at Princeton's Institute for Advanced Study, George Kennan, less openly oppositional than Morgenthau, also called on the administration to reduce, not increase, its footprint in Vietnam. Kennan told a home-court audience at Princeton that the US needed to learn "not to worry so much about these remote countries scattered across the southern crescent, to let them go their own way."[12] The White House was not listening, and the Pentagon barreled ahead, ordering over forty battalions deployed to South Vietnam in July, as the mission objective drifted effortlessly and tragically from security to victory. By

Christmas 1965, 180,000 American soldiers were fighting communism in Vietnam, supplemented by a massive contingent of South Korean allies who were in the war at America's request and expense.[13]

Remaking Revolution

As Lyndon Johnson sunk his country into the quagmire of a faraway war, Mao Zedong whipped his people into a renewed frenzy of making revolution at home.

The Tonkin Resolution, in fact, was a trigger for renewed policy radicalism by Mao, who launched a massive industrial effort in the interior provinces in anticipation of large-scale war with the United States along the seaboard and/or with the Soviet Union on the vast northern border. The Third Front Campaign was "the most expensive industrialization campaign of the Mao era," in the words of the historian Covell Meyskens, yet even that was dwarfed in significance by the chairman's next project.[14] By the time Johnson had ordered combat troops deployed to Danang, Mao was plotting the Great Proletarian Cultural Revolution, an extreme form of mass mobilization orchestrated to allow the aging chairman to reassert total political dominance, purging near equals in the party and military and replacing them with his devotees.

One of the first senior figures to be overthrown was the former minister of public security Luo Ruiqing, who had been in charge of public security and counterintelligence throughout the 1950s. General Luo had returned to People's Liberation Army duties in 1959 and was serving as PLA chief of staff when he was denounced by his comrade, Marshall Lin Biao. Luo was stripped of office and struggled against, and he leapt from a building in early 1966 in a suicidal effort to end his persecution. General Luo survived, severely injured, only to be struggled against further.[15]

Encouraged by Mao, Lin Biao stoked the fires of the revolutionary upsurge, colluding with Mao's wife, Jiang Qing, in the name of a new party organization, the Central Cultural Revolution Group, created in May 1966. A troika materialized with the re-emergence of the counterintelligence and security henchman Kang Sheng, who was instrumental in assisting Mao with the first major purge of senior cadres.[16] To encourage student radicalism, Kang sent his wife on a covert mission to incite the first outburst of cultural revolutionary violence at Peking University.[17] Before long, college campuses and secondary schools became hotbeds of Maoist fervor and political violence. Ardent youth spontaneously formed shock troops known as the Red Guards, professing quasi-religious devotion to their elderly hero Chairman Mao, who egged them on with calls to "bombard the headquarters."

The Great Proletarian Cultural Revolution hit full stride in August 1966 when upward of a million Red Guards filled the cavernous Tiananmen Square to hail Comrade Mao in a series of mass rallies. President Liu Shaoqi was denounced as capitalist roader number one, stripped of office, and brutalized in huge criticism sessions. He would eventually die from the physical abuse and denial of medical attention. Deng Xiaoping, a perpetual candidate for successor to Mao and, like Liu, something of a moderate, was purged from office. Spared the physical torment experienced by Liu Shaoqi and Luo Ruiqing, Deng was sent into internal exile to do menial labor at a tractor factory far from the capital. Of the highest-ranking moderates, only Zhou Enlai retained his post; he was left in place by Mao to counterbalance the radical faction around Lin Biao, Jiang Qing, and Kang Sheng.

The Cultural Revolution destabilized life for party cadres and common people alike. It was simultaneously a struggle within the power elite and an eruption of what the historians Jeremy Brown and Matt Johnson call "Maoism at the grassroots."[18] In contrast to the geographical remoteness of the Vietnam War to most Americans, the Cultural Revolution was an intimate and inescapable reality for everyone living in China in the late 1960s. The chaos it unleashed tore down and reshaped virtually all institutions and structures of society—home and neighborhood, farm and factory, school and hospital, army barracks and party cells.

This included, naturally, prisons. Detention centers and labor camps overflowed once again with an influx of alleged spies, subversives, and enemies of the people, as during the campaigns of the 1950s. But this time, the power structure of the prison itself was a target of the revolution. Jack Downey and Dick Fecteau noticed the changing of the guard within their jail: "All of the honchos of the prison staff were overthrown," Downey recalled of the situation in 1966. "Some of them were thrown out of their administrative posts and made to carry night soil. The food really became crude, and all the amenities were curtailed."[19] The overcrowding translated into less time alone, as Fecteau began sharing his cell with a Chinese prisoner known as Maha. Cultural Revolutionary ideological fervor also meant prisoners had to participate more actively in group study sessions. Most mornings at ten, Fecteau and Maha would be joined by Downey for obligatory recitations of the Maoist script.

One day in 1966, a new prisoner joined Downey's and Fecteau's group study session—a third American. US Air Force Major Philip E. Smith had been shot down on September 20, 1965, flying his F-104 near Hainan Island during a combat mission in Vietnam. After four months of interrogation in Guangzhou, Smith was transferred to a facility in Beijing and then into the same prison as Downey and Fecteau. The major was astonished to meet the two Korean War prisoners, so unlike in personality ("Downey was much more extroverted, talkative, and ready to laugh than the more serious and subdued Fecteau"), yet equally stoical.[20] Smith forgave their willingness to comply with the warden's demands to write up reports on Mao's latest speech, whereas he refused to participate in study sessions, adhering to the Military Code of Conduct. Smith made distracting noises during Radio Peking listening hour and actively resisted going through the motions of thought reform, causing him to lose privileges like time with Downey and Fecteau. The men created a dead-drop communication system at the latrine, passing messages on scraps of paper.

A second downed pilot from the Vietnam War, US Navy Lieutenant Robert Flynn, joined their cellblock after being shot down over southern China in August 1967. According to Smith, a fifth American inmate would appear in their cellblock the following year: Hugh Redmond, transferred from Shanghai's Ward Prison. Smith caught a fleeting glimpse of Redmond, "gaunt, threadbare, and haunted-looking, a death's head," and overheard him arguing in Chinese with the guards. Redmond scribbled a note on toilet paper with the straw of a broom and managed to get it to Downey, who passed the message on to Smith. Redmond warned that he expected his sentence to be increased, that his health was not good, that he did not anticipate making it out alive.[21]

Return of the Realists and China Hands

As the American captives watched China vault headlong into the Cultural Revolution from the confinement of their cells, gnawing doubts grew back home in the United States about the country's proper role in Asia.

A culture of dissent was calling into question the assumption, forged on the anvil of the loss of China, the Korean War, and McCarthyism, that subverting Communist China was a sensible policy objective. Criticism of the war in Vietnam was getting louder and sharper. Worryingly for President Johnson, grumbling in the Senate was no longer coming just from irascible doves like Wayne Morse of Oregon, a Democrat who had abandoned the Republican Party in 1952 over its capitulation to McCarthy, and one of the only two senators to vote against the Tonkin Resolution. Skepticism had spread to heartland liberals like Senate Majority Leader Mike Mansfield of Montana, who had taught Far Eastern history before entering politics, and South Dakota's George McGovern, whose views of Asia had been shaped as a doctoral candidate in history reading Fairbank and Lattimore.[22]

The pivotal figure in the Senate was Arkansas Democrat J. William Fulbright, a champion of liberal internationalism abroad—and racial segregation at home—from the day he entered Congress in 1942. Fulbright sponsored a historic bill after WWII to fund international exchange for students and scholars that created what became known as Fulbright Program grants, the kind that had enabled Allyn and Adele Rickett to go to China in 1948.[23] Appointed the youngest chairman of the Senate Foreign Relations Committee in 1959, Fulbright was an ally and friend of Lyndon Johnson and played a key role in helping LBJ get the Tonkin Resolution passed. On civil rights, however, Fulbright broke from the president, opposing the Civil Rights Act in 1964 and the Voting Rights Act in 1965. As Fulbright watched the escalation in Vietnam unfold over the course of that year, he came to bitterly regret his complicity in giving the White House a blank check for war. Channeling Reinhold Niebuhr, the Arkansas senator worried that the country was falling victim to "the arrogance of power, the tendency of great nations to equate power with virtue and major responsibilities with a universal mission."[24] Determined to draw the public's attention to a war being fought without genuine congressional approval, a war he thought was not in the national interest, Fulbright convened "educational" hearings in early 1966 on two underdebated foreign relations topics: Vietnam and China.

The Fulbright Hearings were a surprise television hit, evoking memories of the dramatic confrontation between Alger Hiss and Whittaker Chambers that helped launched Richard Nixon's national career in 1948, and the Army-McCarthy hearings that proved to be Joe McCarthy's undoing in 1954. At the heart of the committee-room drama was the return to the limelight of the early Cold War realists George Kennan and Hans Morgenthau, as well as the rival China Hands John King Fairbank and David Nelson Rowe.

Kennan was the opening star witness called by Fulbright, speaking to a crowded committee room and transfixing millions of viewers who watched on their televisions.[25] Sophisticated but direct, Kennan gave a master class in how the nation's leaders had gotten the country stuck in the wrong war in the wrong place at the wrong time. Not only did Vietnam lack geostrategic significance, the Johnson escalation also represented a drain on scarce resources and a distraction from graver perils. The entire domino theory on which defending South Vietnam was predicated was a myth—Southeast Asia was hardly on the brink of falling wholesale to Communism.

Kennan distanced himself from his own legendary *Foreign Affairs* article and the doctrine of containment that it spawned, regretting that he had not been more precise back in 1947 about the need to limit the places where the US would commit to taking a stand. He also regretted failing to stress the importance of *non*-military forms of containment. In any case, the situation had changed—Communism really had been a monolith in the late 1940s, whereas now, with the Sino-Soviet split in full view, there were two popes in the socialist camp. Communist Vietnam could be expected to act in its national interests and push away from China once the matter of its own territorial integrity and security was settled. Kennan—the original architect of containment—quoted John Quincy Adams's famous injunction not to go out searching for monsters to destroy, and confessed he was becoming something of a "neo-isolationist" in his later years.[26] He coolly explained that it would be madness to continue with military escalation in Vietnam and that the administration's promises of victory rang hollow. "The Vietcong will go on controlling at night the villages we control during the daytime," Kennan predicted, sounding like Thomas Fowler from *The Quiet American*.[27] He cautioned against a sudden withdrawal, advising instead that US forces hold a strictly defensive posture in preparation for coming home soon. Speaking as a diplomatic historian, Kennan noted that "counsels of patience and restraint have been more effective, as a general rule, than the counsels of violence and particularly the unleashing of unlimited violence."[28]

Kennan's participation in the hearings reflected how far he had traveled since 1948, when he was instrumental in promoting political warfare in Italy and setting up the OPC in the CIA. Almost two decades later, Kennan now supported Senator Fulbright's mission of going directly to the American public, laying out complicated foreign policy questions, and offering nuanced, unpleasant assessments. Prompted by Fulbright to respond to criticism of the hearings, Kennan replied, "It is essential, indispensable in fact, to the workings of our democratic system that there be this sort of a discussion, and that the people listen in and draw their own conclusions."[29]

Having garnered national attention by challenging the wisdom of the war in Vietnam, the Fulbright Hearings shifted to the China question for the month of March. The overall framework was provided by the first expert witness, Doak Barnett, who was based in Asia throughout much of the 1950s and was now a professor at Columbia University. He told the committee that what was needed was "creative and imaginative thinking" about "how to reestablish a reasonable basis for contact and discourse between the United States and China."[30] Barnett advised a policy of "containment without isolation," a paradigm that made front-page news in the *New York Times*, setting the stage for the return to Senate chambers of the country's pre-eminent China scholar, John King Fairbank.[31]

Fairbank had not testified to Congress since the Lattimore inquisition, after which his frequent contributions to current affairs publications slowed to a trickle. Distilling the essential insights from his decade of academic work away from the national stage, Fairbank provided the senators with a panoramic view of China's relations with the West since the nineteenth century, putting the United States' violent intervention in Vietnam and inveterate hostility toward China in a broader context. "History helps in getting a sense of reality," he said.[32]

As Fairbank professorially explained China's unhappy historical experience of modernization at the mercy of stronger imperial powers, he drew a moral for current US policy toward Asia. Rather than Communist aggression and subversion, "one of the most important problems we have right now is how we control ourselves and the control of American power," as he put it to Senator Albert Gore Sr.[33] Fairbank challenged the self-righteous premise that rationalized the administration's drift into Vietnam, puncturing the myth of American exceptionalism by noting unflattering parallels to nineteenth-century European imperial powers: "Stuck in a dirty war today, we would do well to lower our self-esteem, be not so proud, acknowledge our Western inheritance of both good and evil, and see ourselves as hardly more noble and not much smarter than the British and French in their day. We must be steadfast and restrained. We cannot take East Asia or ourselves out of power politics."[34]

Fairbank inserted a simple ethical core in his policy advice. "The real test, I repeat, is whether we can be more constructive than destructive in areas of Vietnam we can influence." America's problem in Vietnam consisted precisely in the reliance on the power of destruction. America's problem with respect to China was the lack of doing anything constructive. The two problems were interrelated—an end to the fighting in Vietnam presupposed figuring out "how you get China in the international order."[35]

Fairbank compared US-China rapprochement to therapy, arguing that the behavior of revolutionary China could be moderated as the country was socialized into the international order. Inverting the meaning of psywar, Fairbank offered Cold Warriors a new mission of "gradually manipulating Peking into an acceptance of the international world, as an alternative to trying to subvert it." A China that was no longer subject to American efforts of subversion was a China that might be coaxed and tamed into a less subversive role in the world for itself. "My whole point this morning has been that in the end, if you want the Chinese Communists to stop trying to stir up the undeveloped world as their main claim to fame, your real alternative is to get them into international contact."[36]

The *New York Times* ran a report of Fairbank's testimony on page one with a picture of his face above the fold, accompanied by a news analysis piece arguing that although the Fulbright Hearings seemed unlikely to deter the Johnson administration, they were making a dent on public opinion.[37] Among the millions of Americans following the hearings was the revered theologian of international affairs, Reinhold Niebuhr. Now in his mid-seventies and suffering ill health, Niebuhr had recently stepped down from the journal he founded in 1941, *Christianity and Crisis*. He was moved by the Fulbright Hearings to pen a letter to the editor of the *New York Times* on the subject of American "fears of China." Niebuhr praised the Senate committee's "exercises in political sanity." "Let us hope this process of enlightenment continues. For we are in a neurotic darkness about China. Our neurosis manifests itself in alternate moods of pretending that China does not exist and terrible fears of Chinese power and malice."[38]

Defenders of the "neurotic darkness" had a chance to make their case in the hearing room a week later, when the Republican minority called its expert witnesses. Included on the list of speakers was Fairbank's old nemesis, David Nelson Rowe of Yale. Addressing the committee after a weekend of antiwar marches in cities across the country, Rowe criticized the Kennedy and Johnson administrations for escalating the war too *slowly* and for bombing North Vietnam too sparingly. These "military inhibitions" were the principal impediments to victory.[39] Behind Vietnam stood the menacing image of Red China, a monster of both strength and weakness, that was doomed to "weakness and mediocrity and complete totalitarianism and military adventurism."[40] Rowe lambasted Barnett's paradigm of "containment without isolation" as a contradiction in terms; there was no way to recognize Beijing without abandoning Taiwan, which, he warned, was tantamount to "political suicide."[41] Still a staunch supporter of Chiang Kai-shek's regime in Taiwan, Rowe boasted of the ease with which Nationalist guerrillas landed secretly on the China coast, enjoyed a "hospitable" reception, and slipped back to Taiwan. He cited evidence of numerous penetration operations staged over the last four years.[42]

Rowe became most animated when he began questioning the motives of his opponents, Americans who promoted détente with Beijing. He referred to "pro-Communist-China and anti-anti-Communist elements" that sought to convince the US government to soften its policy in line with Beijing's desire to buy time and gain breathing room. Rowe's testimony dripped with scorn for Fairbank and Barnett. "Are they merely stupid? Or hypocritical? Or are they trying to be 'smart'?"[43] Rowe alleged that the main professional association of Asia experts, the Association of Asian Studies, was a pro-Communist organization, heir to the subversive Institute of Pacific Relations, against which he had testified to the Senate back in 1952.[44]

Rowe's allegations of ulterior motives were not limited to his academic rivals. His written statement accused the Senate Foreign Relations Committee itself of designing the hearings so as to promote the line of "civilian propagandists," creating an illusion of divisions in public opinion which did not exist. Senator George Aiken of Vermont may have been getting flashbacks to 1950, when he was among the minority of Republican senators who openly denounced Senator McCarthy's methods. During questioning, Aiken observed that Rowe had left the accusations against the committee out of his oral presentation, and pushed him to deny the implicit charge that Chairman Fulbright was working against the interests of the United States. Fulbright later took up the issue, querying Rowe on who exactly were the "anti-anti-Communists" who, Rowe previously had stated, were more dangerous than the Viet Cong. Rowe cited an interview in *Look* magazine with the Korean War POW defector Morris Willis, who named converts to the CCP among the handful of American expatriates residing in China. Fulbright turned the conversation on its head, asking Rowe if he knew the names of any Americans who had been to the PRC recently. "In fact, we had been looking for someone who had some firsthand information about China," Fulbright said wryly.[45] Pressed further by the senator to articulate his own paradigm for US-China policy, Professor Rowe summed up his position as "hostility matched by containment."[46]

The *New York Times* allotted a front-page story to Rowe and fellow witnesses called by the Republican minority, quoting chunks of Rowe's testimony—including his accusations against the *Times* for propagandistic journalism in its coverage of the hearings.[47] In the column next to Rowe's photo, the paper ran an article on a recent speech by another old China Hand, delivered at a Harvard conference hosted by Professor Fairbank. The speaker was Owen Lattimore, visiting from self-imposed exile in England, where he was professor of Chinese studies at the University of Leeds. The voice of yet another ghost of the early Cold War moment became audible again (Lattimore's prolific output for US publications had largely dried up since his trials).[48] Now Lattimore was back with a vengeance. In the Harvard talk, he called Johnson's Asia policy "an increasingly disastrous failure," one that dealt in "the shadow of facts, rather than the facts as they are."[49] In a subsequent lecture at Brown University, Lattimore skewered the administration for making a "mess" in Vietnam based on irrational fears of China as a "hidden menace." Even the Barnett-Fairbank paradigm of "containment without isolation" did not really get at the heart of the problem. Lattimore quipped that "perhaps what the world needs is a policy that will control expansion of the United States in the sixties without returning to the isolation of the thirties."[50]

The closing session of the Fulbright Hearings saw the return of the other giant of realism, as Hans Morgenthau was called to testify. The Morgenthau finale was a bookend to Kennan's opening session two months prior, symbolizing the arc of critique of US grand strategy since "Sources of Soviet Conduct" and *Politics among Nations* came out in 1947 and 1948. Morgenthau weighed into the debate by arguing that the PRC should be understood as a rival advancing its perceived national interests as an aspiring great power, rather than a subversive rogue regime acting for the sake of communist ideology. He further posited that China's territorial ambitions could be expected to extend no further than the borders of its traditional empire, one of the few matters on which Mao Zedong in Beijing and Chiang Kai-shek on Taiwan agreed.[51]

Morgenthau challenged the Barnett-Fairbank thesis of "containment without isolation" from a different direction, arguing that while the policy of isolation—

designed to deny legitimacy and ultimately bring down the PRC government—was a total failure, the real problem was the underlying strategy of "peripheral military containment." China was destined to resume its status as the dominant power on the Asian continent; indeed, it was well on its way to restoring that position of centrality. Borrowing from the work of Fairbank and others on Chinese imperial precedents, Morgenthau anticipated that the PRC was likely to exert hegemony in cultural and political forms, rather than in outright military expansion (except with Taiwan, which by definition was an "internal" matter). Preventing Chinese dominance in Asia would require nothing less than full-scale war and destruction of the Chinese state. The lesson was simple, if sobering. "If we do not want to set ourselves goals which cannot be obtained with the means we are willing to employ, we must learn to accommodate ourselves to the political and cultural predominance of China on the Asian mainland."[52]

Sparring with fellow expert witness, Professor Robert Scalapino of the University of California, Morgenthau would not budge from his central contention that merely trying to improve "social relations" with the PRC was insufficient and indeed hypocritical, given the underlying policy of military containment. "If we are convinced that it serves our vital national interest to leave the Seventh Fleet in the Strait of Taiwan and to surround the periphery of China with a number of isolated military strongholds, then we must face not only the possibility but the likelihood of war with China."[53] Morgenthau also took aim at the analytical failure to recognize how far global communist solidarity had disintegrated, with socialist bloc nations pursuing "separate and sometimes antagonistic political interests in spite of their Communist ideology. In our relations with China we are still obsessed with the conspiratorial concept of Communism."[54]

Pressed by the senators on how he would propose to fight communism, Morgenthau shifted seamlessly from Great Power realism to progressive liberalism. The US should compete for the loyalty of the disgruntled masses by standing on the side of radical but noncommunist social revolution, pointing to the model of the Catholic Church in Latin America.[55] Since it was too late for China, all the US could do was seek nonviolent means to limit its influence, competing in the political, economic, and cultural spheres rather than preparing to fight on the battlefield. Once again, the *New York Times* put the Fulbright Hearings on the front page.[56]

Surreptitious Totalitarianism

Although Morgenthau's testimony to the Fulbright Committee was limited to the topics at hand (China and Vietnam), his writings by the mid-1960s reflected the interests of an international relations thinker who had become preoccupied by the *domestic* problems of his adoptive country. In a collection of essays, *Truth and Power*, Morgenthau would enumerate the challenges facing the United States: "the militarization of American life, the Vietnam War, race conflicts, poverty, the decay of the cities, the destruction of the natural environment."[57] He was also increasingly disconcerted over "the tendency of the government to discredit and stifle dissent."[58] Morgenthau complained of being the target of a White House campaign to discredit him, blaming President Johnson's intolerance of loyal opposition: "He [Johnson] must either silence and corrupt the intellectuals by making them into his agents, or he must discredit those who cannot be silenced and corrupted."[59] LBJ, with his propensity to "personalize all forms of dissent" (in the words of the historian Fredrik Logevall), in fact ordered FBI surveillance of Senator Fulbright after the hearings, casting about for evidence that he might be acting as an agent for communist interests.[60]

Fresh revelations about the role of the CIA intensified Morgenthau's fears of "surreptitious totalitarianism" in the United States. Like many intellectuals, he was outraged at the extensive Agency funding of private foundations and civic organizations in the US, which was exposed in March 1967 by *Ramparts*, an innovative journal linked to the New Left movement. The chickens of psywar were coming home to roost. One anonymous foundation head interviewed by *Ramparts* recounted being approached by a pair of CIA officials eager to provide funding for donor recipients. In a scene reminiscent of James McClure Henry approaching Zhang Fakui in Hong Kong in 1950, the CIA men told the foundation director, "We are trying to pose an alternative to communism and want to back third-force programs, which we could not do if it was known that this support comes from a government source."[61] Morgenthau published a commentary on the *Ramparts* bombshell with the blunt title, "How Totalitarianism Starts: The Domestic Involvement of the CIA."[62]

Morgenthau's dear friend Hannah Arendt was worried too. Attuned to the dangerous allure of the secret agent, she had been rattled by what she read in one of the early critical exposes of CIA activities, *Invisible Government* (1964), by journalists David Wise and Thomas Ross. In the preface to the 1967 edition of *The Origins of Totalitarianism*, Arendt warned of "the rise of an 'invisible government' by secret services, whose reach into domestic affairs, the cultural, educational, and economic sectors of our life, has only recently been revealed." The overreach of the CIA, like the quagmire in Vietnam, had less to do with opposing Communist totalitarianism than with "American ascendancy to world power," as the US fell prey to the temptation to employ secret agents in a neo-imperial Great Game.[63]

Searing in their critique of American exceptionalism and bracing in their dissent against America's imperialist and totalitarian tendencies, the early Cold

War realists Arendt, Morgenthau, Kennan, and Niebuhr would appear conservative by the standards of the late 1960s. In terms of political thought, however, they remained classical liberals who recognized the harsh realities of international politics while seeing through the hubris in American hegemony. As radical protest gained ground on the left, mainstream nationalist liberals in the foreign policy establishment and within government hesitated to speak out in public against Johnson or Vietnam. But quietly, even men like Bob McNamara, a prime architect of the war, began to suffer doubts about the strategy by the summer of 1967. In strict secrecy, McNamara tasked a research group to compile an in-house study into how the United States had become entangled in Vietnam, tracing the history of covert involvement back to the Truman years. The journalist David Halberstam would describe McNamara's classified in-house history as "a covering White Paper along the lines of the China White Paper."[64]

By the start of 1968, half a million US soldiers were fighting in Vietnam. A million and a half tons of explosives, including napalm and defoliants, had rained down from American aircraft.[65] The secret war in neighboring Laos—managed by the CIA with help from its proprietary airline Air America (the rebranded CAT)—had escalated into a sustained air war.[66] Despite this massive commitment of men and materiel, the Communist army in the North and the Viet Cong insurgency in the South were resilient, while the military government in South Vietnam remained unstable, unpopular, and corrupt.

Over the lunar new year in late January, known to Vietnamese as Tet, VC commandos staged attacks throughout the South, including on the US embassy in Saigon. A large Communist force stunned the Americans by seizing control of the former imperial capital of Hue, forcing US Marines and South Vietnamese troops to engage in weeks of street fighting to reclaim the city. Even though Hue was recaptured and the Tet Offensive was repelled, it dealt a crushing psychological blow to US public support for the war, forcing Johnson to announce he would not run for re-election.[67]

The violence roiling Southeast Asia seemed to wash back across the Pacific and seep across America over the course of 1968, a tragic year in the country's political history. Reverend King was slain on April 4—one year to the day that he gave his first antiwar speech, "Beyond Vietnam." King's assassination triggered nationwide mourning and violent protest in major cities across the country; the rage and sorrow could be felt among Black soldiers even in faraway Danang.[68] Liberals then lost the hope of the Democratic Party, Bobby Kennedy, shot dead in Los Angeles as he campaigned for the presidency. The Democratic Party convention in Chicago that summer was marred by violence and police brutality against protestors, as millions of viewers watched the clashes on TV seeing either mob violence or police-state brutality, depending on their political affiliation.

Hannah Arendt despaired over the uninspiring choice between a lackluster Democratic nominee, Hubert Humphrey, and the scheming Republican candidate Richard Nixon, whom she was old enough to remember from his early days as a prophet of McCarthyism. Arendt summed up her diagnosis of America's problem in the title of her new book, *On Violence* (1970).[69]

Her friend Hans Morgenthau was no fan of Humphrey or Nixon, either. But Morgenthau was far more disturbed by the third-party option on the ballot: former Alabama governor George Wallace, a white supremacist candidate mobilizing what Morgenthau called the "fascist vote."[70] The Third Force option for American voters in 1968 was the antithesis of Schlesinger's Vital Center—it was Wallace's promise to "stand up for America." Morgenthau thought Humphrey stood no chance to win, and thus saw in Nixon the sole virtue of being able to absorb right-wing fascism back into the mainstream conservative Republican Party. It was a triage situation. For the sake of the republic, the most urgent priority was to make Wallace disappear. Morgenthau compared Nixon's role to that of Charles de Gaulle, whose return to power in France in 1958 dissipated the surging right-wing populist movement of Pierre Poujade. "In America, nothing is determined once and for all, and anything is possible, the worst and the best," Morgenthau warned. "Wallace may rise to become the American Hitler, or he may fade away as the American Poujade."[71]

Nixon defeated Humphrey and Wallace in November 1968. As the realists agonized over what Arendt would call the "crises of the republic," Fairbank and the China Hands offered their best advice to the president-elect. A small group of Asia experts, mostly Harvard colleagues, drafted a confidential memorandum to the incoming administration outlining their vision for "relaxation of tensions between China and the United States, and the eventual achievement of reconciliation."[72] The informal study group was chaired by the Harvard professor of law Jerome Alan Cohen, who, as luck would have it, happened to be a classmate of Jack Downey's from the Yale class of 1951. The experts passed their memo to Cohen's colleague in the Harvard Government Department, Henry Kissinger, who was unexpectedly tapped by Nixon to join the administration as national security advisor.[73]

Fairbank did not take a leading role in the memo. But he remained in the public eye during the presidential transition, condemning the war in Vietnam and enmity toward China. "The greatest menace to mankind may well be the American tendency to over-respond to heathen evils abroad, either by attacking them or by condemning them to outer darkness," Fairbank warned.[74]

16

RELEASE

The end of the Cold War between the United States and China can be read between the lines of the transcript of conversations between two men, Zhou Enlai and Henry Kissinger. Their dialogue in the summer of 1971 was cloaked in secrecy, a cardinal virtue in Kissinger's philosophy of foreign relations and the organizing principle of Richard Nixon's approach to presidential power. The secret dialogue moved swiftly out into the open as a shocking détente between the two countries, ending two decades of antagonism when Nixon met Mao in Beijing. US-China rapprochement also helped Nixon and Kissinger have the courage to, at long last, end the tragic war in Vietnam. Yet the White House's obsession with secrecy, its paranoia over subversion, and its tendency toward repression were hurtling the country towards a political travesty that would dwarf the significance of these foreign policy breakthroughs. At least, in the ebbing of the hostility between the United States and China and just before the tidal wave of Watergate hit, first Dick Fecteau and then, finally, Jack Downey were free to go home.

The Realism of Kissinger and Nixon

Like Hans Morgenthau and Hannah Arendt, Henry Kissinger had endured the harrowing personal experience of being Jewish in Nazi Germany. He was a boy when the Weimar Republic collapsed into Hitler's Reich, and at age fifteen, in 1938, he managed to flee with his parents to safety in the United States.[1] Halfway through his undergraduate education as an accounting major at the City

College of New York, Kissinger joined the US Army in 1943. He fought in the war and after V-Day was stationed in occupied Germany, where he used his local knowledge and language skills in the Counter Intelligence Corps.

On returning to the United States, Kissinger transferred to Harvard University in 1947—the same year that Downey started Yale. His senior thesis, "The Meaning of History: Reflections on Spengler, Toynbee and Kant" (1950), was an early exercise in the realist philosophy of international relations. Bearing the marks of the French existentialist writers Jean-Paul Sartre and Albert Camus, Kissinger's thesis offered a rudimentary form of "imperial existentialism," in the phrase of the historian Greg Grandin.[2]

Staying on at Harvard for graduate studies, Kissinger did what Third Force intellectuals were doing half a world away in Hong Kong—he started a journal. *Confluence*, published from 1952 to 1958, was also similar to the journals of Carsun Chang and his Third Force friends in that it received indirect, covert assistance from the CIA.[3] As the ambitious editor of *Confluence*, Kissinger coaxed contributions out of Harvard mentors like Arthur Schlesinger and an A-list of 1950s intellectuals, including Arendt, Morgenthau, and Niebuhr. Kissinger received a submission from William F. Buckley Jr. in defense of McCarthyism but turned it down for being too contentious. When Senator McCarthy took on the Army, the institution that confirmed Kissinger's new identity as an American, Kissinger suffered nightmares of Weimar, writing to Schlesinger, "We are witnessing, it seems to me, something that far transcends McCarthy, the emergence of totalitarian democracy."[4]

It was Schlesinger who helped Kissinger secure a coveted entrée into the power elite, recommending him to the Council on Foreign Relations in New York, a club for the foreign policy establishment, and the publisher of *Foreign Affairs*. The editor Hamilton Fish Armstrong, who launched Kennan's career as a public intellectual with the "X" article, steered Kissinger's first article into print in the spring of 1955. Whereas Kennan had recoiled awkwardly from government service and preferred to influence policy discussions from the distance of academe (teaching at his alma mater, Princeton), Kissinger seemed to be on a perpetual quest for political appointment, even after he secured a tenured post at Harvard.

Kissinger's political ambitions were stymied for years by betting on the wrong patron. He became consigliere to the perennial Republican Party hopeful Nelson Rockefeller, who failed to win the party nomination in 1960. Again with the help of Schlesinger, Kissinger jumped at a consultancy in the Kennedy National Security Council in 1961, but he lasted less than a year.[5] After Rockefeller tried and failed to get the party nomination again in 1964, Kissinger tested the waters with LBJ, taking a sabbatical from Harvard to travel to Saigon as a State Department consultant in 1965 and using a contact in Paris to help the administration open a back-channel negotiation with Hanoi in 1967.[6] For the third time in a row, Rockefeller failed to get the nomination in 1968, but Kissinger finally realized his ambition when he was tapped by Nixon to serve as national security advisor. The two men did not know each other well. It was a match was encouraged by William F. Buckley Jr., a powerful voice on the right, and blessed by Arthur Schlesinger Jr., who was still hoping that by some miracle the country could find its vital center.[7]

Prior to joining the Nixon administration, Henry Kissinger had not systematically studied or written about China. His books and articles dealt with European diplomatic history, nuclear strategy, and the transatlantic alliance, and apart from an early research project in Korea in 1951 and trips to South Vietnam, his time spent in Asia was limited. His new boss was a different matter.

As Eisenhower's vice president, Nixon had made a six-week fact-finding tour across Asia after the Korean War Armistice, and he kept up the portfolio. His first article for *Foreign Affairs,* calculated to show off his foreign policy chops in the run-up to his presidential campaign, was titled "Asia after Viet Nam." The tone of Nixon's *Foreign Affairs* piece was far removed from the commie-hunter rhetoric of his early days in Congress—Nixon sounded more like John King Fairbank and other critics of the policy of isolation, writing suggestively, "We simply cannot afford to leave China forever outside the family of nations, there to nurture its fantasies, cherish its hates and threaten its neighbors."[8] Nixon campaigned on a promise to end the unpopular war in Vietnam by winning "an honorable peace," echoing Eisenhower's campaign promises regarding the unpopular war in Korea. As with Eisenhower's in November 1952, so Nixon's message resonated well at the ballot box in November 1968.

Once he was in power, Nixon's strategy for the Vietnam War was to ramp up pressure on the enemy in order to get concessions at the negotiating table.[9] Again, there were echoes of Eisenhower, who wanted to generate military pressure on the enemy without triggering a domestic backlash. Rather than reverse the "bombing halt" declared by LBJ just before the November 1968 election, Nixon and Kissinger instead initiated a secretive bombing campaign, code-named Operation Menu, against suspected communist targets in the neutral nation of Cambodia, along with stepped-up special forces covert action.[10] The administration also took steps to make South Vietnam—and allies in Asia—sacrifice more of their own blood and treasure, rather than depend on the United States, a plan known as "Vietnamization."

Nixon explained his strategy, without mentioning the secret bombing, during a stopover on Guam, the island in the old archipelago of subversion, on his inaugural overseas trip in July 1969. Journalists dubbed it the Guam Doctrine. Rapprochement with Beijing fit neatly into the logic of Nixon's strategy for Asia, since neutralizing the threat from China would put added diplomatic pressure on North Vietnam to agree to peace terms and give the United States cover for disengagement from South Vietnam. There was obvious value to a thaw in relations with Beijing at the global level of geopolitical calculation as well. Given the ferocity of the Sino-Soviet split, détente with Beijing could create room for Nixon and Kissinger to practice triangular diplomacy, playing the two communist giants off each other. But would China, still in the throes of the Cultural Revolution, be willing to play the triangular game? And how to open a channel to the leadership in Beijing—ultimately, to Chairman Mao? The task fell to Kissinger.

Secret Wars, Secret Talks

In pursuing détente with China, Kissinger was obsessed with secrecy to a degree matched only by his boss. Kissinger credited the president's obsession with secrecy as an essential asset in opening the channel to China—Nixon's "administrative style lent itself to the secretive, solitary tactics the policy required."[11] But it was not just in regards to China. The two men ran US foreign policy like a covert operation that had to be hidden from adversaries, allies, and, most importantly, their own "bureaucracy"—a four-letter word in the Kissingerian lexicon. While the realists and the China Hands were out in the public square trying to persuade their fellow citizens that the time had come to stop subverting the Chinese government, Kissinger treated establishing relations like a clandestine mission.

From very early on, Downey and Fecteau popped up on Kissinger's radar as necessary elements in the process of improving relations. The imprisoned spies were a thorn in the flesh that would have to be removed as part of a breakthrough. Kissinger explained in a memo less than a month after inauguration, "The problem of the incarceration of Jack Downey and other Americans in Communist China has been a tough and longstanding one. This was the earliest and it has been the most persistent topic of negotiations between ourselves and the Communists since the mid-50s."[12] In his memoirs, Kissinger described the problem of American prisoners more poetically as one of "the hoary standbys of bilateral perplexity."[13] He did not want to get stuck in perplexity like the unimaginative bureaucrats at the State Department. The Sino-American Ambassadorial Talks, in fact, were still lumbering away in Geneva, not having generated a single deal since the Agreed Announcement on repatriating nationals back in 1955. They were precisely what Kissinger wished to avoid.

Unfortunately for Kissinger, the administration made very little progress during its first year and a half in office toward either of the key objectives in its strategy for Asia—ending the war in Vietnam and breaking the deadlock with China. Their one tangible achievement was to begin bringing troops home from Vietnam, based on a two-year timetable to reduce the force in half and continue down from there. Nixon's offset for the troop reduction was to step up the secret war in Cambodia, which did little to weaken Hanoi's will to fight.

Instead, the principal effect of the secret war was to aggravate paranoia in an innately suspicious White House. When the *New York Times* reported leaked details on the secret bombing of Cambodia in May 1969, Nixon and Kissinger went to J. Edgar Hoover—still FBI director after forty-five years—and asked him to wiretap journalists and officials.[14] The White House was becoming a microcosm of the ways in which fear of subversion accelerated tendencies toward repression.

Another unintended consequence of the secret war was to endanger the fragile equilibrium in Cambodia, where a military coup against the neutralist leader Prince Norodom Sihanouk in the spring of 1970 unleashed savage attacks against Cambodia's sizeable ethnic Vietnamese population. Hanoi sent troops across the border to support the indigenous Cambodian Communist guerrillas, known as the Khmer Rouge.[15] Nixon used North Vietnam's move to bring what had been a secret air war into the open as a new American ground war, announcing that US forces would assist in a "Cambodian incursion." He justified the attack in expansive, nationalistic language that would have given the early Cold War realists pause: "If, when the chips are down, the world's most powerful nation, the United States of America, acts like a pitiful helpless giant, the forces of totalitarianism and anarchy will threaten free nations and free institutions throughout the world."[16]

Protest erupted on college campuses against the perverse logic of starting a new war in Cambodia to end the despised one in Vietnam. Yale had emerged as a lightning rod for protest at the gates of the power elite, with the local trials of the New Haven Black Panther Party members adding racial controversy to antiwar sentiment. Violence was averted at a huge May Day protest in the New Haven Green on the steps of campus, thanks in part to the pacifist presence of Chaplain William Sloane Coffin Jr., the Yale class of 1949 CIA agent–turned–civil rights activist.[17] Days later, however, National Guardsmen in Ohio dispatched for crowd control at Kent State University shot and killed four protestors, horrifying the nation. A week later at Jackson State in Mississippi, police opened fire on Black students protesting militarism abroad and racism at home, killing two and injuring a dozen more. "The incompetence and pathology is really shocking," Morgenthau wrote in a letter to Niebuhr.[18]

By May 1970, Kissinger had managed to open secret talks in Paris with his North Vietnamese counterparts, but he still lacked a reliable communication channel to Beijing. Deciphering China was no easy task, as the country remained in the throes of Cultural Revolution ferment yet seemed adrift in terms of domestic policy and foreign relations.

The cult of Mao pervaded daily life, and media organs spouted out endless ideological sloganeering. Schools were closed and youths wandered the country making revolution, or hiding from its torments. Ongoing elite power struggles around Mao were mirrored at the grassroots level in Red Guard factionalism, as the competition to prove ultimate loyalty to Mao degenerated in many places to the point of low-grade civil war. Mao had to reimpose a semblance of order by dispatching PLA units to select cities and, in a strange parallel to Nixon's emphasis on law and order, the chairman launched a "strike hard" campaign against counterrevolutionaries in 1970 that resulted in hundreds of thousands arrested.

Years of Maoist radicalism left the PRC isolated in the socialist bloc and resented by postcolonial Afro-Asian leaders. The foreign relations outlook became dire with armed clashes against Soviet troops along the Sino-Russian border, raising the prospect of nuclear war with its communist neighbor. This bleak situation gave Zhou Enlai an opening to try to develop a less militant and autarkic foreign policy.[19] And there was one way to cut the Gordian knot of China's antagonism with the world—détente with the imperialist superpower, the United States.

In a replay of 1955, Premier Zhou used the prisoner issue to hint at the possibility of improving relations with a new administration in Washington. At least that was how Kissinger interpreted the release of the Maryknoll priest James Edward Walsh, who was set free from Shanghai's Ward Prison on July 10, 1970. Ordained a bishop in southern China as a missionary in the 1920s, Walsh was detained on espionage charges in 1951 but released, only to be re-arrested in 1958 and given a twenty-year sentence for spying.[20] Tragically, Bishop Walsh walked to freedom across Lo Wu Bridge in Hong Kong carrying an urn with the ashes of Hugh Redmond. Chinese authorities claimed that Redmond committed suicide in April. The CIA doubted that Redmond would have endured nineteen years of incarceration, only to take his own life.[21]

Zhou Enlai sent another positive signal later in the year—this time, not by releasing an American but by inviting one to come visit. In another echo of past probes, Zhou invited Edgar Snow to make an extended trip to China, as he had during the Eisenhower-Kennedy transition in 1960 and once again in late 1964 as Lyndon Johnson prepared for his second term.[22] Snow and his wife featured prominently as props during a mass rally to commemorate the founding of the PRC on October 1, 1970, standing in the ultimate place of honor on either side of Chairman Mao, up on the balustrade overlooking Tiananmen Square. Kissinger missed the signal in the noise. He later acknowledged, "We had missed the point when it mattered. Excessive subtlety had produced a failure of communication."[23]

Mao gave Snow a sit-down interview in December in which he explicitly indicated his willingness to meet with Nixon. But Snow was not, as Mao apparently thought, a conduit to the CIA.[24] Quite the contrary, he lived in a kind of self-imposed exile in Geneva. Although Snow was debriefed in Switzerland by a CIA official, he neglected to pass on Mao's invitation for a visit.[25] As Kissinger recollected, Mao and Zhou "once again overestimated our subtlety and our intelligence capabilities."[26]

Snow's account of his interview with Mao was not published until late April 1971, running as *Life* magazine's cover story, "Inside China." By then, Zhou and Kissinger had found alternate means to pry open a secret channel.[27]

Nixon had been sending friendly signals of his own by lifting the remaining restrictions on US citizen travel to mainland China and talking in public about his desire to make the trip himself. The public signaling of interest in a thaw got a major boost in early April thanks to a serendipitous encounter at the world ping-pong championships in Nagoya, Japan, where Glenn Cowan—an American player born in the same year that Downey and Fecteau were captured—accidentally boarded the PRC team bus and made a Chinese friend. In short order, the US team was invited to visit China after the tournament. Premier Zhou welcomed them in person and congratulated the group on opening a "new chapter" in US-China relations.

Zhou must have appreciated the irony of the ping-pong players, including long-haired Cowan, nicknamed the Hippie, representing the first private delegation of Americans to visit Communist China with their government's approval since the spy moms back in 1958. The *New York Times* coverage of the ping-pong delegation, which included three American newsmen—another first—was ebullient. John King Fairbank surmised that the fury of the initial phase of the Cultural Revolution had cooled off enough to create an opening for dialogue. He wrote that the time was ripe to bring the era of Sino-American hostility and isolation to an end.[28]

Fairbank was right. Behind the scenes, Nixon leaned on a trusted ally, Pakistani president General Yahya Khan, to open a back channel to Zhou. In an exchange of letters, the two sides agreed in early June on plans for Kissinger to make a secret trip to Beijing a month hence.[29] Fearing criticism from allies in Asia, Republicans in Congress, and colleagues in the Department of State and Defense, Kissinger, who reveled in "sub-rosa diplomacy," approached his trip like a covert operation.[30]

As Kissinger prepped for his journey, the culture of secrecy at the White House plunged to new depths of paranoia when the *New York Times* began publishing excerpts of the in-house history on Vietnam policy compiled on the order of then-defense secretary McNamara in 1967. Documents in the anthology had been leaked by Daniel Ellsberg, a defense researcher who knew Kissinger from graduate studies at Harvard and had served under CIA psywar hero Colonel Lansdale in Vietnam, where he became convinced of the folly of the Vietnam War and outraged at the deception of the public.[31] The leaked documents initially were called the Vietnam Archive, but another name quickly caught on, a name that bore the scars of Whittaker Chambers's Pumpkin Papers and Dean Acheson's China White Paper. The so-called Pentagon Papers not only documented the failure of one administration after another in Vietnam, but also—and more damningly—they exposed the government's long-running deceit of the American public. Hannah Arendt described the depressing impact of reading the Pentagon Papers: "The quicksand of lying statements of all sorts, deceptions as well as self-deceptions, is apt to engulf any reader who wishes to probe this material, which, unhappily, he must recognize as the infrastructure of nearly a decade of United States foreign and domestic policy."[32]

Richard Nixon had the opposite takeaway. In his mind, the Pentagon Papers reinforced the political imperative of enforcing absolute secrecy. Nixon ordered the Justice Department to issue an injunction to force the *New York Times* to cease publication. "I don't give a goddamn about repression, do you?" Nixon asked Kissinger. "No," his national security advisor answered gruffly.[33] But the Supreme Court did give a goddamn, rejecting the Justice Department's injunction on the grounds that newspapers were guaranteed the freedom to publish the Pentagon Papers in the public interest.

So the White House turned to covert methods, setting up a Special Investigations Unit tasked with silencing subversive critics of the president like Daniel Ellsberg. The "nonlegal" unit included the former FBI agent G. Gordon Liddy and the former CIA agent Howard Hunt, who had learned the tricks of the trade with the OSS in China and the OPC in Japan. "They were tough and experienced agents ready to operate clandestinely on behalf of the President and his re-election," in the words of the investigative journalist Seymour Hersh.[34] It was as if the archetypal agent of subversion—the handmaiden of empire examined by Arendt in *The Origins of Totalitarianism*, Graham Greene in *The Quiet American*, and Paul Blackstock in *The Strategy of Subversion*—had made the long journey home from the front lines of the Cold War to the seat of democracy in the White House. The former agents Liddy and Hunt gave their five-man unit a disarmingly American name, "the Plumbers," which was nefarious in its political subtext. The American Jedburghs had landed.

Fulbright Redux

The Plumbers got to work on covert ops, starting with a break-in of Ellsberg's psychiatrist's office in Los Angeles in search of incriminating personal material. President Nixon ordered yet another military campaign in Southeast Asia, sponsoring a South Vietnamese invasion of Laos with US air support. Senator Fulbright once again had had enough, and he organized a round of hearings to revisit the topics broached five years earlier: getting out of Vietnam and into mainland China.

The Fulbright Committee's Vietnam hearings ran for over a month, punctuated by dramatic testimony from a young veteran named John Kerry, who had joined the Navy after graduation from Yale in 1966 and rose to the rank of lieutenant, commanding a Swift Boat in Vietnam. Appearing before the committee in late April to speak on behalf of Vietnam Veterans against the War, Kerry eloquently denounced the atrocities being committed by the US military against the Vietnamese people and the moral corruption of young Americans drafted into an unjust and unpopular war. "How do you ask a man to be the last man to die for a mistake?" Kerry famously asked, days after a crowd of two hundred thousand antiwar protestors filled the Washington Mall.[35]

As in 1966, the committee followed up the Vietnam deliberations with sessions on the China question. In a sign of how attitudes had changed, this time, the senators themselves led off, presenting various resolutions in support of normalizing ties and bringing the PRC into the United Nations. Fulbright then called in three experts. The Pulitzer prize–winning historian Barbara Tuchman blasted the policy of nonrecognition, drawing on research from her new book, *Stillwell and the American Experience in China, 1911–1945.* The Yale professor Arthur Galston—a plant physiologist rather than a China Hand—shared impressions from a recent two-week visit to the PRC that included a meeting with Zhou Enlai. Finally, the Harvard law professor Jerome Cohen testified on the legal complexities involved in normalizing US-PRC relations.

As the day of testimony was coming to a close, Professor Cohen asked Chairman Fulbright if he could make one final point, a "final fling," as he called it. Cohen proceeded to summarize the case of American prisoners in China, focusing attention on the plight of his "acquaintance and college classmate" Jack Downey. Alluding to the release of the Arnold Eleven just prior to the Geneva talks in 1955, Cohen encouraged Beijing to make an "important gesture" by releasing the prisoners. But he acknowledged that Downey was not easily pardoned. In a back-and-forth, Cohen and Fulbright all but read Downey and Fecteau's guilt into the *Congressional Record.*

THE CHAIRMAN: What was his [Downey's] alleged crime?

MR. COHEN: He was alleged, with Mr. Fecteau, to have committed acts of espionage and subversion against China in the employ of the Central Intelligence Agency.

THE CHAIRMAN: Was he a pilot in a plane?

MR. COHEN: They were, the Chinese say specifically, on board a plane that was landing Chinese Nationalist agents in China during the Korean War.

THE CHAIRMAN: He was a spy.

MR. COHEN: Exactly.

THE CHAIRMAN: He was a spy, I see.

MR. COHEN: Exactly.[36]

Cohen noted that the American public had been fed a false cover story by John Foster Dulles, which even the *New York Times* reported essentially as fact. "The *Times* sang a very different tune then, one should point out," Cohen observed.

Cohen proposed to the committee that the US government conduct an official inquiry, in the expectation that the facts would substantiate Beijing's version of what happened in 1952. On the basis of an official admission that Beijing had been telling the truth of the matter and "expression of U.S. regret for the whole incident," Cohen thought it might be feasible to ask for Downey and Fecteau's release. Cohen faulted the government for refusing to acknowledge the facts, turning an Orientalist cliché on its head by remarking how "we Americans have this unusual concern for 'face.'"[37] Although the *New York Times* included a brief report on the session, no mention was made of Cohen's contention that the government had been lying about Downey and Fecteau.[38]

As the hearings neared an end, the committee heard from an opponent of rapprochement, Senator Peter Dominick (R-Colorado), who had studied at Yale in the 1930s and flew missions over the Himalayas to supply Chiang Kai-shek's troops during WWII.[39] Dominick pushed back against the "onslaught of optimism" over granting United Nations membership to Communist China, "a regime that practices tyranny at home and encourages revolution and warfare around the world."[40] As his expert consultant, Senator Dominick brought along none other than David Nelson Rowe.

Professor Rowe offered a legalistic argument that the UN seat should continue to be held by the Nationalist government in Taiwan, which was still run by the eighty-four-year-old Chiang Kai-shek, who for decades had groomed his son to inherit paramount leadership. Rowe's written statement concluded, "If and when Red China changes its international objectives and removes itself as a source of international criminality, we can deal with the new objective situation thus created when the time comes. In the meantime, President Nixon's minimal avowed objectives of not allowing Peking 'to dictate to the world the terms of its participation' in the United Nations should receive the wholesale and enthusiastic support of all Americans without reference to party loyalties or affiliations."[41]

Rowe's testimony seemed to have little effect. The *New York Times* covered the hearings but barely mentioned Rowe's name, focusing instead on calls by other China experts for the government to release an in-house China Study commissioned in 1953. Senator Fulbright linked the China Study to the Pentagon Papers as additional evidence of systematic efforts by the executive branch—across Democratic and Republican administrations—to keep the public and Congress in the dark on critical foreign policy matters.[42]

Nixon's Secret Agent

While William Fulbright invited experts to air their views before the public on what to do about relations with China, Henry Kissinger was preparing furiously for Operation Polo, as his secret mission to Beijing was nicknamed.[43]

In a pre-trip memo to Nixon, Kissinger laid out the principal topics for discussion, a short list of problems—mostly defined as places—where US and Chinese positions clashed but where "national interests" might be reconciled, starting with Vietnam, Taiwan, the USSR, and South Asia. Kissinger's draft also addressed that "hoary standby of bilateral perplexity," the four imprisoned Americans. Reminding Nixon that Downey and Fecteau were in fact guilty as charged, Kissinger did *not* contemplate making a public acknowledgment or apology. Instead, he framed the issue as a problem for China—how to release the men without losing face. Kissinger explained: "Downey and Fecteau are accused (legitimately) of being intelligence agents. . . . Being strong on principle, the Chinese may find it difficult to release Downey and Fecteau at all (or in the case of Fecteau, until his 20 year sentence is up). . . . Nevertheless, they may be willing to act favorably in the interests of improving their image before the American people if a formula can be found in which they are not put on the spot and principle will be served." Kissinger did not want to recycle old "clichés" in raising the matter with Zhou. He would ask if there was any action the PRC wanted of the US. He would reaffirm that Nixon's goal was "to disassemble on our side the barriers which have been erected between us for so many years" and to resolve issues pragmatically going forward.[44]

Reviewing Kissinger's proposed talking points at a White House meeting the week before the secret trip, Nixon found the negotiation positions too soft and "forthcoming." He wanted Kissinger to harden the posture by building on three fears: of US aggression to end the stalemate in Vietnam, of a "resurgent and militaristic Japan," and of the Soviet threat on their northern border. Nixon did not say much about the detained Americans except that he expected "the release of all U.S. POWs held in China" should be accomplished prior to a summit.[45]

Kissinger had wondered whether Zhou would have seen Professor Cohen's testimony to the Fulbright Committee.[46] As it turned out, while Kissinger was in Pakistan preparing for his covert flight to Beijing, Cohen drew wider public attention to Downey's case with an op ed to the *New York Times* titled "Will Jack Make His 25th Reunion?"[47]

Kissinger must have had a lot on his mind as he sat down with Premier Zhou on July 9, 1971, for the first-ever direct talks between senior officials of the governments of the PRC and the US. Almost immediately, he raised what would be a central preoccupation throughout the dialogue to come—the need for secrecy. Opacity was required, Kissinger averred, "so we can meet unencumbered by bureaucracy, free of the past, and with the greatest possible latitude."[48]

Zhou was also preoccupied with secrecy, but in a different sense. He brought up the CIA numerous times, complaining to Kissinger about US covert assistance to a dissident group called the Taiwanese Independence Movement. Kissinger's response was to mock the Agency: "There is an exaggerated opinion in the minds of people in many parts of the world about the abilities of the CIA."[49] Kissinger wriggled out of the topic of covert subversion and returned to his main agenda item, Vietnam. Kissinger offered a sweeping indictment of US foreign policy since the end of WWII, describing the degeneration of a liberal superpower that found itself an unwitting hegemon, failing in its global role in economic and military terms.[50] President Nixon was facing up to these realities and trying to extricate the US from Vietnam in the process, Kissinger explained.

On day two of his visit, Kissinger was treated to a two-and-a-half-hour "secret tour" of the Forbidden City, conjuring visions of "the living quarters of past emperors." Marathon talks resumed, covering the items on Kissinger's list and those added by Zhou—Korea and Japan, among others. All told, the two men spent seventeen hours in dialogue that ranged from the philosophy of international relations to the specifics of a presidential visit.

Just before heading to the airport to catch his flight back to Pakistan, Kissinger slipped "one final point" into his last conversation with Zhou: "The President asked me to raise this as a matter of personal kindness. We are aware of four Americans sentenced to prison in China. While we are not disputing the circumstances, we would consider it as an act of mercy if the People's Republic of China could pardon all or some of them whenever, in its judgment, it felt that conditions were right. This is not a request. I'm asking it as a favor."[51] Zhou's answer was noncommittal but hinted at some flexibility. There was a legal process for shortening their sentences based on good behavior, he said, adding, "We will continue to study this matter."[52] By keeping the issue off the main agenda, Kissinger underscored the personal nature of the appeal from Nixon. He also avoided what might have turned into a long digression on the decades-old problem of captive citizens, not to mention the risk of reopening the issue of covert efforts to subvert the PRC government and lying about these activities to its own public and the international community.

Kissinger departed Beijing in a kind of diplomat's ecstasy. His memo to Nixon, "My Talks with Chou Enlai," invites comparison with George Kennan's Long Telegram as a seminal document in Cold War grand strategy. Whereas Kennan sent his telegram from Moscow through State Department channels, Kissinger's memo was for the president's eyes only (as Kissinger wrote to his deputy, Al Haig, "a leak or even a hint is likely to blow everything").[53] Kennan excused the excessive length of his telegram due to the urgency of the issue of Soviet intentions, "questions so intricate, so delicate, so strange . . . so important" that they required an exposition to answer. Kissinger's memo overflows with a different kind of self-importance, starting with the title, "*My* Talks with Chou Enlai," and captured in the opening sentence: "My two-day visit to Peking resulted in the most searching, sweeping and significant discussions I have ever had in government." (Kissinger had only been in government for two and a half years; one wonders how Zhou appraised the quality of discussion based on his two decades as premier and half-century career in intelligence.)

Kissinger felt that his talks with Zhou teeing up Nixon's visit "may well have marked a new departure in international relations," with the potential to "transform the very framework of global relationships." Sounding a bit like Edgar Snow after his 1936 stay in Yan'an, Kissinger wrote in awe of the "tough, idealistic, fanatical, single-minded and remarkable people" he had met on his journey. It was almost too marvelous to put into words; he feared his account "would do violence" to the meaning of "Chinese behavior, so dependent on nuances and style."[54]

Nixon was in equal parts thrilled at the success of the trip and jealous of his adviser's claim on credit for the historic breakthrough. The president quickly went on live television to reveal the secret trip and announce his plans to go to meet Mao for himself. Conservative critics, William F. Buckley Jr. among them, pounced, and Kissinger was dispatched to convince them of the wisdom in talking to Beijing.[55] Overall, however, there was broad public support for Nixon's gambit, which released pent-up curiosity among Americans in how China had changed during the preceding twenty years of alienation.

Kissinger made a follow-on preparatory trip, called Polo Two, in October 1971 to make concrete preparations for the summit and a joint communiqué. Before leaving for Beijing, Kissinger heard from Richard Helms, appointed CIA director by LBJ in 1966. Director Helms affirmed that as far as the matter of Downey and Fecteau's guilt was concerned, the Agency had no objection to making an exception to the rule of deniability. "If it would help secure the release of these officers, an admission to the Chinese of their affiliation with the Agency and the fact that they were on an intelligence mission at the time of their capture would not now present serious security problems," Kissinger was informed.[56]

Although Kissinger's party could travel in the open this time, they detected much greater tension on the part of their hosts on their arrival in Shanghai, the epicenter of Cultural Revolution radicalism. It was a stressful time, just weeks after a shocking turn of events in elite party politics when Marshal Lin Biao, Mao's heir apparent, died in a plane crash as he fled the country with his wife and son, ostensibly after a failed coup attempt against the chairman. Lin's downfall dealt a blow to the radical faction, creating room for Premier Zhou to pursue a moderate course.

The atmosphere improved for the Americans when they arrived in Beijing, where the premier enjoyed home-court advantage. Breaking the ice at the outset of talks, Zhou showed off his cultural sophistication by making the ultimate in-joke to Kissinger at the expense of their aides, Yale-educated Winston Lord and Harvard-educated translator Ji Chaozhu. Zhou asked playfully:

> ZHOU: I have a lot of schoolmates probably in Harvard. In the United States, which is first, Harvard or Yale? Maybe Yale isn't so well known?
>
> KISSINGER: You are absolutely right, Mr. Prime Minister.
>
> CHOU: In the . . . in 1910 when I was in middle school, I knew more about Yale than Harvard. At that time more people were praising Yale than Harvard. I don't know the reason.
>
> KISSINGER: Because Harvard people are so retiring. Mr. Lord is from Yale.[57]

During a long morning session, Zhou was in a less playful mood. He raised the topic of covert US support in Taiwan, again singling out the Taiwanese Independence Movement. Seeking to establish Taiwan as an independent democratic state, the group was in a certain sense a new iteration of the Third Force, opposed as much by Chiang Kai-shek as by Mao Zedong. Kissinger again played down the CIA. "As I told the Prime Minister the last time, he vastly overestimates the competence of the CIA." With gentle prodding from Zhou, Kissinger gave a crash course in the organization of US intelligence, including the roles of the National Security Council and the Pentagon. "I am being candid—this is not information we generally tell other governments," Kissinger said, candidly.[58]

Zhou refused to let Kissinger brush off the CIA, lecturing him on the Agency's decades of meddling around the world: "After the Second World War you appeared to be very powerful both militarily and in the matter of economic aid. So the CIA thought they had the right to look into everything. The result of this is causing disharmony in the world." Even in China, Zhou added, CIA activities might have decreased but they were "perhaps not nonexistent." Kissinger again tried to laugh off Zhou's talk of agents of subversion, saying how CIA officials "write long, incomprehensible reports and don't make revolution." Zhou would not relent, responding cryptically, "We reserve our judgment on this." Kissinger fell back on Harvard-Yale jokes, saying dismissively of the CIA, "They are mostly from Yale," and Zhou temporarily played along, pointing to Winston Lord for comic relief, "He is from Yale." Kissinger quipped, "Does he look like a revolutionary?"[59]

But Zhou was not done. He turned serious again. "Those reports you referred to are intelligence," he said. "While you use the word revolution, we say subversion."

Kissinger dropped the ironic humor; changing tack, he gave assurances to Zhou. "I understand. We are conscious of what is at stake in our relationship, and we will not let one organization carry out petty operations that could hinder this course." After promising to review "all those activities" once again, Kissinger asked Zhou to alert him about "measures that affect you directly, either in respect to the Taiwan Independence Movement or others." Sensing the gravity of Zhou's charge about subversion, Kissinger declared point-blank, "It's not our policy to subvert the government of the People's Republic of China or its policy."

Zhou veered off into an extended discussion of how the CCP, unlike the CIA, did not interfere in other countries' affairs, using the example of the deposed Cambodian prince Sihanouk, who lived at liberty in exile in China. Speaking of the dangers facing Sihanouk if he were to travel abroad, Zhou brought up his own near-death flying experience traveling to the Bandung Conference in April 1955—tactfully leaving the matter of CIA complicitly unmentioned. While insisting that China did not fear the CIA, Zhou warned Kissinger to take the Agency more seriously. "There are often some organizations that even though you are their chairman the more they seal you off. Chairman Mao has a thesis: those who hail you are not the ones who support you," Zhou said, presumably with Marshall Lin Biao on his mind. Nixon might have agreed with the sentiment. Kissinger again promised, "We will not let officials subvert the trend we have started." The meaning of subversion in US-China relations had come full circle.

Returning to a substantive negotiation about how to reconcile positions on the most sensitive issue between them—the status of Taiwan—Kissinger admitted the obvious fact that many domestic forces in the United States would oppose détente with Beijing in loyalty to Taipei. Kissinger confessed he would not be able to control even his own bureaucracy, and that Zhou should be prepared to hear mixed signals. Zhou warned Kissinger, "It's not possible to go out in all four directions. Then you will be like Don Quixote."[60]

That evening, after more Harvard-Yale jokes, Zhou Enlai shared intelligence about a US reconnaissance flight that neared the PRC's southern border.[61] Kissinger promised to make inquiries, suggesting that the US military might be attempting to sabotage their meeting: "This was not a flight that was authorized from Washington. Perhaps Admiral McCain is not as harmless as I said yesterday."[62] Reciprocating Zhou's gesture of intelligence sharing, Kissinger informed Zhou that Chiang Kai-shek's General Staff was contemplating a reconnaissance overflight to disrupt their talks. As the session ended, Kissinger shared one more piece of intel, giving Zhou a heads-up that the US would be staging an underground nuclear test soon on the Aleutian Island of Amchitka in Alaska. "These are much too expensive things," Zhou observed wearily.[63]

Kissinger's stay in Beijing dragged on longer than planned as the State Department insisted that he delay his return to avoid coinciding with a vote in the United Nations, where the majority of states in the General Assembly now wanted to switch the China seat from Taipei to Beijing. On his last evening in Beijing after marathon negotiations with Zhou over the key aspects of their "diplomatic revolution," Kissinger finally raised the question of the four prisoners—the two Korean War spies and two Vietnam War pilots. Feigning ignorance, Kissinger told Zhou, "I have now inquired, and I find that Fecteau and Downey did engage in activities that would be considered illegal by any country."

"That's right," replied Zhou.

Kissinger then asked "as an act of clemency" to release them for the "very good impression" it would make on the American public. Zhou indicated that their sentences might be shortened by year end, before Nixon's visit. The Vietnam War fliers could not be released until the US signed a peace agreement with Hanoi, but "it might be possible that we could release the spies earlier, although their crimes were heavier." "It would mean a great deal to the American people," Kissinger said.[64]

Zhou's attitude left Kissinger optimistic that Fecteau would get out soon, that Downey's sentence would be shortened, and that the pilots Flynn and Smith were certain to be released along with the other Vietnam POWs once peace negotiations were concluded with Hanoi. "All of this may be possible without our having to make any public statements about the activities of our men," Kissinger reported happily to Nixon. There would be no need for a public act of contrition over the decades of lying about spying, no moment of what Reinhold Niebuhr called the "abatement of pretensions." On the contrary, the logic of secrecy applied to the resolution of the spy case just as it did to its origins. Kissinger added in his note to the president, "It is absolutely essential to keep this information secret, for any public disclosure of Chinese intentions would almost certainly wreck our chances for early releases."[65]

Not long after Kissinger's departure from Beijing, Mary Downey returned to the city accompanied by her son and daughter-in-law for the usual two-week stay and eight visits to see Jack in prison. Seventy-year-old Mary picked up positive signals from Jack, which she shared with the press afterward. "At the end of our visit, Jack told us that he had been informed by the prison authorities that his case was being reviewed to determine whether, under the policy of leniency, he might be released rather than serve out his life sentence."[66]

Right on Zhou's schedule, good news came through the secret US-China channel in Paris in December 1971 that—after nineteen years in captivity—Dick Fecteau would be released at Hong Kong in three days' time. He was to be accompanied by another American, Maryann Harbert, who had disappeared three years earlier after departing Hong Kong on a private yacht for a pleasure cruise. But once again, as with the release of Hugh Redmond's ashes and a dying Robert McCann, bad news came along with the good: Harbert's boating companion, Gerald Ross McLaughlin, was reported to have resisted interrogation, behaved badly, and committed suicide in detention in March 1969.

As for Jack Downey, his life sentence was reduced to five years starting from December 13, 1971, as Kissinger predicted.[67]

The release of Fecteau and Harbert made front-page news, but readers were reminded that Downey still remained behind bars. The White House communications staff made sure to get a follow-up story giving the president credit for persuading Zhou to show mercy. In the absence of a presidential admission of guilt, Professor Jerome Cohen used another op ed to semi-officially acknowledge Downey and Fecteau's status by citing confirmation from anonymous officials at the State Department.[68]

"So Many Snowflakes"

After all the buildup—the decades of enmity—it was perhaps inevitable that there was something anticlimactic in the conversation between Mao Zedong and Richard Nixon when they met in person on the afternoon of February 21, 1972. Nixon was stilted and formulaic, leading Mao cuttingly to suggest to the president that he "could do a little less briefing."[69] The chairman seemed more interested in talking to Dr. Kissinger than President Nixon. "You have been famous about your trips to China," Mao said slyly, pressing a wound of jealousy between the two men, perhaps.

Time magazine had just put Kissinger on the cover with the headline, "Nixon's Secret Agent," printing a dime-story account of his dozen secret visits to Paris over the past thirty months of (fruitless) negotiations with his North Vietnamese counterparts, prompting Nixon to joke to Mao, "He doesn't look like a secret agent." The dialogue degenerated into macho innuendo as Nixon praised Kissinger's ability to "use pretty girls as a cover." Mao asked Nixon if he often made use of girls. "It would get me into great trouble if I used girls as a cover," replied Nixon. Zhou joked, "Especially during elections."[70]

After the hour-long talk with Mao, Nixon spent most of the rest of the week doing glorified sightseeing, as Kissinger handled the heavy lifting of negotiating the final language on the Shanghai Communiqué. At his departure toast, Nixon hailed the visit as a "week that changed the world," which it certainly was.[71] Not much changed for Downey, however, who was allowed to watch television coverage of the historic moment of Sino-US reconciliation.[72] His president had been a stone's throw from his Beijing prison, but Downey would have to hold on until his shortened term finished in 1976, it seemed.

Though China Hands like John Fairbank had been calling for an end to the policy of isolation since at least the Fulbright Hearings of 1966, the secret mission by Kissinger and the presidential trip by Nixon came as a shock to the public. Nixon's credentials as a staunch anti-Communist inoculated him against criticism from the right, giving birth to the maxim of international relations pundits that only Nixon could go to China. The drama of the trip gave Nixon a foreign policy triumph to carry into his re-election campaign; even the legendary jazz musician Miles Davis was moved in March 1972 to compose an ode to the visit, which he called "Red China Blues."[73]

The American public approved of US-China rapprochement, but allies in Asia—Japan, South Korea, South Vietnam, but above all, Taiwan—did not. Meanwhile, the fighting in Vietnam was far from over. Hanoi staged a large-scale spring offensive in 1972, and Nixon ordered a bombing campaign against targets in North Vietnam, code-named Operation Linebacker.[74] The American electorate was pleased to see the number of soldiers stationed in Vietnam steadily dwindling, and even the bombing polled well.[75] Nixon's public disclosure that Kissinger had been engaged in secret negotiations with North Vietnamese counterparts in Paris since August 1969 blunted the criticism of his antiwar Democratic opponent, Senator George McGovern. Nixon defeated McGovern in November 1972 by one of the biggest margins in electoral college history.

Flush from victory and frustrated by the lack of progress at the Paris talks, Nixon ordered another bombing campaign against North Vietnam. B-52s dropped their bombs on Hanoi for the first time in a late December campaign known as Operation Linebacker II. Although the so-called Christmas bombing inflamed the peace movement and engendered international criticism, *Time* named Nixon Man of the Year for a second time in a row—this time around, however, he had to share the glory. The two faces of American realpolitik, President Nixon and Dr. Kissinger, appeared on the January 1, 1973, cover of *Time*, carved into a chunk of pink marble in an ironic nod to Mount Rushmore.

Nixon's second inaugural address proclaimed "a new era of peace in the world," and the following week, America's unpopular, undeclared war in Vietnam finally ended with the stroke of Henry Kissinger's pen. The Paris Peace Accords established a sixty-day period within which the United States would withdraw its remaining forces from South Vietnam and the Communist side would release 591 American POWs. As the historian George Herring noted, "The 'peace' agreements of January 1973 merely established a framework for continuing the war without direct American participation."[76]

Days after the Paris Peace Accords, Nixon held a press conference to take a victory lap, offering details about the release of Vietnam War POWs. The final question raised the issue of the three American prisoners in China. Nixon expressed confidence in the release of the two pilots, Flynn and Smith. "Downey, also?" the reporter asked. Nixon's reply was the first explicit comment on the case by a president since Eisenhower's terse statement that the matter was "cloudy." Never before had the commander in chief spoken Downey's name in public. Nixon answered:

> Downey is a different case, as you know. Downey involves a CIA agent. His sentence of 30 years has been, I think, commuted to 5 years, and we have also discussed that with Premier Chou En-lai. I would have to be quite candid: We have no assurance that any change of action, other than the commutation of the sentence, will take place, but we have, of course, informed the People's Republic through our private channels that we feel that would be a very salutary action on his part. But that is a matter where they must act on their own initiative, and it is not one where any public pressures or bellicose statements from here will be helpful in getting his release.[77]

Nixon's reply was a rather abrupt and incomplete way to blow a twenty-year cover story and, by default, acknowledge that the enemy had been telling the truth the whole time. Even this long-awaited moment of public admission seemed designed to avoid contrition. Nixon was responding to a reporter's question rather than making a prepared statement; he got an essential fact wrong (Downey had been sentenced to life, not thirty years); he falsely implicated the press in colluding to hide the truth ("as you know"); and even the choice of verb ("involves") was a kind of dodge, avoiding an unvarnished admission that Jack Downey *was* an agent of subversion. The *New York Times* clarified things somewhat the next day with an article headlined "Nixon Acknowledges American Jailed in China Is C.I.A. Agent," although it did not make the cut for front page news.[78]

While Nixon sought credit for ending the Vietnam War, Kissinger was off on a fifth voyage to Beijing. As part of the preparations, he was informed that Mary Downey's health was declining. The China expert on the National Security Council recommended that he raise the release with Zhou as a "humanitarian action" that would help normalize relations.[79]

As talks unfolded in mid-February 1973, this time it was Zhou Enlai who brought up the prisoners. Prompted by Kissinger's mention of how the US public would reject giving economic aid to North Vietnam until and unless all POWs were released, Zhou interjected ("before I forget it") that Flynn and Smith would be released within the sixty-day implementation period set out in the Paris Peace Accords. As to Downey, Zhou explained that his release would have to wait "until the latter part of this year. You can tell his mother he is in excellent health."

Kissinger seized the opening to let Zhou know that Mrs. Downey was "quite ill." Zhou and Kissinger could not resist the chance for ironic banter:

> CHOU EN-LAI: Yes. If her situation becomes critical, you can tell us through your liaison officer, Ambassador Huang Hua. His [Downey's] behavior has been very good. It seems to be too good.
>
> DR. KISSINGER: We have no means of communicating with him so we can't tell him to become a little worse.
>
> CHOU EN-LAI: [Laughs] But perhaps when he goes back he won't behave exactly the same as he does. It won't be too much in his interest to do so.

Reverting to sincerity, Kissinger stressed the importance of these gestures "to the American public." "He was correctly charged . . . and the President has said so publicly," Kissinger added, referring to Nixon's January press conference.[80]

Late that night, after midnight, Kissinger was summoned for an audience with Mao. Congratulating each other for having transformed US-China relations from enemies to friends, Kissinger pointed to intelligence sharing as proof of friendship. "We speak to no other country as frankly and as openly as we do to you," Kissinger told Mao.[81]

The chairman was happy to dwell on one of his favorite topics—intelligence. Zhou laughed as Mao spoke, uncomfortably perhaps, given his historical role as architect of the party's intelligence apparatus and his recent struggles over internal security against Kang Sheng. Mao switched back and forth effortlessly between apparent sincerity and biting irony: "But let us not speak false words or engage in trickery. We don't steal your documents. You can deliberately leave them somewhere and try us out. Nor do we engage in eavesdropping and bugging. There is no use in those small tricks. And some of the big maneuvering, there is no use to them too. I said that to your correspondent, Mr. Edgar Snow. I said that your CIA is no good for major events." Mao went on mocking the CIA—as Kissinger had done on his previous visits—for writing intelligence reports that "come as so many snowflakes." But Mao was not gloating; his own intelligence service was no better—"It is the same with them. They do not work well." Zhou laughed when Mao cited the treachery of his successor Lin Biao as an example. "For instance, they didn't know about Lin Biao." Mao added, deviously, "Then again, they didn't know you wanted to come."[82]

The visit of February 1973 rekindled a bit of the enthusiasm Kissinger had felt on the original Operation Polo. "We are now in the extraordinary situation that, with the exception of the United Kingdom, *the PRC might well be closest to us in its global perceptions*," he reported to Nixon. "No other world leaders have the sweep and imagination of Mao and Chou nor the capacity and will to pursue a long range policy."[83]

FIGURE 11. Mao, Zhou, and Kissinger (1973). Wikimedia Commons.

FIGURE 12. The moment of release (1973). Getty Images/Bettmann.

A Mother's Love

Back in Washington in time for the one-year anniversary of the president's visit to China, Kissinger conferred with Nixon about how to take the next step down the path of détente—opening a Liaison Office in Beijing. They agreed that the crucial thing was to have *their* man running the office. A career man—a foreign service official in the State Department—wouldn't understand "the game," as Nixon put it.

> KISSINGER: But that really has to be done by you and me.
> NIXON: Alone!
> KISSINGER: Alone.
> NIXON: Alone. Alone.
> KISSINGER: This is too dangerous.
> NIXON: You know I was thinking that—.[84]

Their discussion turned to the Downey case. Nixon wondered if he should call Jack's brother William. Kissinger agreed it would be appropriate and vouched for the brother.

Once William Downey was on the line, Nixon code-switched to his sonorous presidential-sounding voice, as he explained the welcome news that Zhou Enlai "indicated to Dr. Kissinger a positive action will be taken" by releasing his brother toward the end of the year. "We wish we could have done it sooner but you know we worked hard on it. We pressed it and in this case the diplomacy might have paid off."

Nixon passed the line to Kissinger who filled in the details, explaining that Mary Downey's ill health would serve as the subterfuge to trigger release. The president would pass a message in July about her health condition so that Zhou could initiate a legal process, and Jack should be out in the fall—it was as good as a "practical guarantee," Kissinger assured William. As a parting line, Kissinger swore Downey to secrecy. "You'll keep that as you have kept everything else secret. I mean of course you'll tell your mother."

The moment after they hung up the call, Nixon without skipping a beat shifted to a perennial obsession—"that god-damned Kennedy," as he called Senator Ted Kennedy, the younger brother of Jack and Bobby. Securing Downey's release was just another example of how Nixon *did* what the Kennedys only talked about. In full Iago mode, Kissinger stroked Nixon's insatiable ego, marveling at the "revolutionary impact on American consciousness" that the president had initiated.[85] Kissinger held a lengthy press conference the following day, where he informed the world that the two fliers, Flynn and Smith, would be released soon, and Jack Downey was expected to be released later in the year.[86]

Things went too much according to plan. Two weeks after the call, Mary Downey's health really did take a turn for the worse. She suffered a stroke and had to be hospitalized in New Britain, Connecticut. The Republican governor, Thomas Meskill, happened to be a boyhood friend of Jack's, and he relayed the news immediately to the White House.

As instructed by Zhou, Kissinger sent word to Beijing. The plan for Downey's release was accelerated—Zhou Enlai ordered Jack Downey freed in three days' time.

"Isn't that great about Downey?" Nixon enthused to his press secretary as they polished the wording of the press release, carefully crediting the president with catalyzing the release of the last American prisoner in Red China.

"We did it, Henry!" Nixon enthused as Kissinger entered the Oval Office.[87]

"Marvelous, marvelous," Nixon repeated half to himself, musing aloud how it must have been even worse to be imprisoned in China than in Vietnam, as he prepared to board his helicopter for the weekend at Camp David.[88] The *New York Times* put the announcement of the imminent release of "Downey of the CIA" on the front page with a family photo of Mary and her two sons during their most recent visit to see Jack in prison.[89]

Downey walked across Lo Wu Bridge into the freedom of Hong Kong on March 12, 1973, "clearing the slate at last of the human legacies of the period of hostility," as Kissinger put it.[90] Downey would later recall the joy he felt at being saluted by British colonial authorities, knowing he was among friends.[91] He changed out of prison garb into a suit and was flown via Clark Air Base in the Philippines all the way to Bradley Airport in Hartford, Connecticut, where a police escort rushed him by car to the New Britain hospital.

The Downey family waited until the last minute to tell Mary. She had mourned her son as dead, only to learn he was alive but imprisoned for life in a forbidden country. She had quietly, stubbornly fought her own government to let her at least visit him, and then patiently, persistently appealed to the enemy regime to let him out.[92] In the final end, it was a mother's love that freed Jack Downey.

He entered the hospital room and clasped her frail hand in his. Their road of trials was completed. Speaking later to media assembled at the hospital, Downey expressed no ill will toward either his captors or his own government. He made no effort to cast himself as a hero. "I thought the 20 years were to a large extent wasted," he observed, with the detachment of Marcus Aurelius.[93]

"We got a good play out of this Downey thing," Kissinger remarked to Nixon in the Oval Office the day Jack walked across Lo Wu Bridge.[94]

EPILOGUE

By the time Richard Nixon spoke to the press a mere three days after Downey's release, it was as if the twenty-year saga of the American agent of subversion imprisoned in Red China had already played out. The tale was so fantastic—a graduate of Yale in the prime of his youth, serving his country on a secret mission into enemy territory, miraculously survives his plane being shot down, held incognito for two years, sentenced to life in prison, rotting in a Peking prison cell for decades as his own government gaslights the public into thinking him innocent, finally liberated so he could be by his mother's side as she lay dying. Why did the Downey affair not resonate more powerfully with the American public at the time of his release?

A glimpse of the answer can be had by looking at the questions journalists prepared for President Nixon at that press conference on March 15, 1973. It is as if one can see the tsunami forming on the horizon, making it easy to overlook the fate of John T. Downey as a mere wave breaking on the shore. The White House press corps was in no mood to congratulate the administration on securing the release of a captive American, let alone to listen dutifully to Nixon's details about the planned Liaison Office in Beijing. Instead, they wanted to hear more about the once-obscure story of a break-in at the Democratic National Committee Headquarters in the Watergate apartment complex that had taken place eight months prior.[1]

A pair of investigative journalists at the *Washington Post*, Carl Bernstein and Bob Woodward (who graduated from Yale in 1965, a year ahead of John Kerry) had been doggedly chasing Watergate, which at first blush seemed to be a local burglary story for the metro section. Digging by Bernstein, Woodward, and others unearthed a bizarre cast of former US intelligence officers and Cuban exile agents whose involvement raised disturbing questions about White House complicity in "intelligence operations" directed against the political opposition, as well as illegal and unethical efforts to cover up the wrongdoing. The trial of the Watergate burglars, including ex-CIA officers Howard Hunt and James McCord, drew more attention to the case in January, as did disconcerting admissions to the Senate Judiciary Committee by L. Patrick Gray, Nixon's nominee for FBI director after the death of J. Edgar Hoover. By the time of Downey's release, "Watergate was going to burst," as Bernstein and Woodward put it.[2] In his self-exculpatory and self-pitying *Memoirs*, Nixon recalled the press conference on the ides of March as the moment when he came to grips with the magnitude of the scandal that would engulf and destroy his presidency. "It was during this conference that for the first time I began to realize the dimensions of the problem we were facing with the media and with Congress regarding Watergate: *Vietnam had found its successor.*"[3]

Nixon was right, if for the wrong reasons. The weight of deception amassed over a quarter century of covert foreign policy had been brought to a breaking point by Nixon's paranoia. The pathologies of secrecy, like the violence of war, could not be contained overseas forever. The government's exercise of clandestine powers concentrated in the hands of the president and the CIA was a cancer that had spread from the extremities of foreign policy to the heart of the body politic. The culture of insecurity and brutishness in the Nixon White House allowed the cancer to metastasize in the form of secret recordings, wiretaps, break-ins, and cover-ups. As Hannah Arendt wrote, "In the realm of politics . . . self-deception is the danger par excellence; the self-deceived deceiver loses all contact with not only his audience, but also the real world, which still will catch up with him, because he can remove his mind from it but not his body."[4] Facing a hostile press days after Jack Downey's release, Richard Nixon could feel the real world catching up with him.

It took more than a year of political evasion, press scrutiny, and public dismay before Watergate became too much even for the machinations of Tricky Dick. The American people's faith in government had been shaken by the tumult of the 1960s; when Nixon finally resigned on August 9, 1974, he left the public trust in ruins. More revelations of illicit CIA activities, including domestic surveillance on US citizens, came to light at the end of the year in reporting by Seymour Hersh for the *New York Times*.[5] Among the reforms enacted in the wake of Watergate was a sweeping inquiry by the Senate into intelligence activities and clandestine operations. Thanks to the work of the committee led by Senator Frank Church (D-Idaho), 1975 became known as the Year of Intelligence. Information provided to the Church Committee by CIA director Bill Colby made the Bay of Pigs fiasco and the *Ramparts* exposé look like child's play by comparison. In the disenchantment of the post-Watergate moment, the CIA was stripped of whatever was left of the 1950s aura of unseen omniscience and quiet omnipotence.

The turn against intelligence could be felt on college campuses, where Agency recruiters could no longer expect to be welcomed by administration, faculty, and students, like in the good old days of the early Cold War. Not only had the CIA been severely discredited, university culture was changing—even in the traditionalist Ivy League. Yale finally began admitting women undergraduates, for example, in 1969. If William F. Buckley Jr. was, in his contrarian and ultraconservative way, the iconic early Cold War Yalie, the equivalent sensation of the Watergate era was arguably Garry Trudeau, class of 1970. Trudeau began his satirical and subversive political cartooning in the *Yale Daily News* and launched the revolutionary comic strip *Doonesbury* as a master's student in fine arts. The ironic sensibility of *Doonesbury*, a liberalism that could laugh at the world and at itself, was hardly a student culture conducive to recruiting agents of subversion who would surrender their authenticity and risk their lives to become secret Cold Warriors. Glimpses of the so-called family jewels of covert activities by the CIA only confirmed the skepticism of the Doonesbury generation.

The vast deception that erupted to the surface of American politics in the volcano of Watergate also spewed up the ashes of a failed China policy. The reckoning was a long time coming, originating in the promise made by the Truman Doctrine to stop the spread of communism followed a year and half later by the loss of China, America's first great defeat in the Cold War. There was neither political will nor public support to wage overt war against either the People's Republic of China or the Soviet Union, so in the gap between means and ends, a covert policy of aiding the forces of counterrevolution and subversion took shape. The US military campaigns in Korea and Vietnam, fought despite public misgivings and without a declaration of war from Congress, added rationale and resources for maintaining the secret policy of subversion against the PRC. But China remained lost to the United States.

Nixon changed that, and China would be the one thing he was seen to have gotten right. After two decades of covert aggression, the sudden reversal in US-China relations was orchestrated, ironically, in the mode of a clandestine operation by "Nixon's secret agent," Henry Kissinger. In a further irony, public disgust with government secrecy post-Watergate did not undermine the influence of Kissinger, who stayed on as national security advisor and secretary of state under Nixon's successor, Gerald Ford. Kissinger's secretive and amoral brand of realpolitik, treating diplomacy as a game of power balancing based on security interests and political wins, came to overshadow and eclipse the early Cold War philosophy of a realism grounded in self-restraint, humility, and even love. The strategic realism of Kennan and political realism of Morgenthau, let alone the existentialist realism of Arendt and Christian realism of Niebuhr, became relics of an earlier time, lost traditions of American diplomacy to be rediscovered by future generations.

But credit must be given where credit is due. The Cold War between China and the United States did end thanks to the diplomatic minuet performed by those two odd couples, the consiglieres Kissinger and Zhou, and their princes, Nixon and Mao. As a result of their machinations, the relationship between the American and Chinese people could begin to come out of the shadows and move away from hostility. This process was helped by the death of Mao in the autumn of 1976, coming after the death of Zhou that spring. The abnormality—the monstrosity, really—of Maoism finally abated as post-Mao leaders declared the end of the Cultural Revolution. Alas, China after Mao would not escape the predicament of fearing subversion and relying on repression, just as the United States would continue to struggle against its own tendencies toward repression, albeit with greater institutional capacity to resist the danger of what Hans Morgenthau called "surreptitious totalitarianism."

Those struggles are ongoing today, as is the challenge of navigating US-China relations in a realistic, principled and—dare one say—loving way. The temptation of reverting to Cold War patterns of covert subversion—playing out not only on land, sea, and air, but also in unseen domains from outer space to cyberspace—should give us pause in light of the history of how that went the first time it was tried. One hopes that, in the words of Jonathan Spence, "at least—if each partner in the equation has attained a new level of self-awareness—there is a chance that the old misconceptions will not be repeated." In confronting the past, we find clues to a better future together.

Acknowledgments

This book came to be thanks to two amazing editors and the team at Cornell University Press. Emily Andrew saw the promise in the proposal and pointed my ship in the right direction. She found a pair of anonymous readers whose interventions spurred major improvements to the initial draft; I am in their debt. Before her departure, Emily handed me off to Michael McGandy, whose perfect sense of structure and flow guided the book into port. The Cornell team has been a delight to work with—my thanks to Clare Jones for directing production and Sarah Noell for driving publicity.

Yonsei University was an idyllic academic base for the years devoted to this project. Supportive colleagues in the Graduate School of International Studies, stellar historians at Underwood International College, and thoughtful students who took Modern Chinese History and US-China Relations—every one of you added a brick to the making of this book; thank you. With support from the University of Sydney–Yonsei University Joint International Program Development Fund, I was able to spend the winter of 2018 in Australia, benefiting from long conversations with China scholars including Amy King, Richard McGregor, and Frederick Teiwes. Vietnam welcomed our family the following winter just before the world walled up, and I am thankful for the hospitality and insights of Uyen T. Nguyen, my student when she was an undergrad at Yonsei UIC who became my teacher on Vietnamese history as she pursues her doctorate.

I am grateful to colleagues who were gracious or foolish enough to agree to look at chunks of the manuscript, including David Atwill, Bob Carlin, Chen Changwei, Annping Chin, Tom Gold, Phil Pan, Orville Schell, and Susan Shirk. Jerry Cohen, doyen of Chinese legal studies, is a longtime mentor and encouraged me in this project, for which I am deeply thankful. Special thanks are due to Chen Changwei at Peking University, an old friend and brilliant scholar who helped me from the hopeful beginning to the bitter end. Zhao Ma at Washington University tirelessly responded to my pleas for help and, more importantly, provided a model of what cutting-edge PRC history can look like; the same goes for Brian DeMare, Benno Weiner, and Covell Meyskens, who proffered tips on finding 1950s photographs in my hour of need. I am indebted to Shen Zhihua, a pioneer of Cold War history research in China, for enlightening conversations in Shanghai and Seoul. An ongoing catalyst to my own efforts was simply keeping up with the burgeoning field of global Cold War history, including stimulating work by Paul Chamberlain, Lorenz Luthi, Masuda Hajimu, Lien-Hang T. Nguyen, and Odd Arne Westad, and sources from the Wilson Center's Cold War International History Project and George Washington University's National Security Archive.

Reading widely in the history of intelligence (and the occasional spy novel) was another of the obligatory joys of this project. Special acknowledgment is owed to Nicholas Dujmovic, former deputy chief historian at the CIA, director of the Intelligence Studies Program at Catholic University of America, and Downey/Fecteau guru, who schooled me on the ABCs of doing CIA history over lunch in the Catholic University cafeteria; I'm grateful for his guidance. In addition to Nick's superb article for *Studies in Intelligence*, my book builds on the work of generations of researchers who dug into different aspects of the Downey/Fecteau saga, including Ted Gup, Roger Jeans, William Leary, Evan Thomas, Daniel Aaron Rubin, Xue Gongtian and Lou Ruixi, and Zhang Guolu. I am lucky to have gotten to know the legendary CIA officer Don Gregg, who played a part in some of these events and from whom I've learned much over the years. Lastly, my thanks to Bob Carlin, one of the great intelligence writers of his generation, for passing on so much wisdom. My own grasp of what strategic intelligence means owes a great deal to martinis with Bob in Beijing, Busan, Washington, and Helsinki.

Librarians and archivists make historians possible. First thanks go to the Universities Service Centre for China Studies at the Chinese University of Hong Kong—this book would not have worked without the unfettered access to their rare sources. I also wish to thank helpful staff at the Hoover Institution Library and Archives at Stanford University, the US National Archives and Records Administration, Peking University Library, Shanghai Library, and the Yale University Manuscripts and Archives. The USMC commandant's chair, retired Colonel Philip M. Pastino, kindly tracked down records of a Sherman Kent lecture given at the National War College. Towson University librarian Rick Davis went beyond the call of duty helping me find articles published in the *Baltimore Afro-American* by William Worthy Jr. Thank you to the digital librarians who made the CIA's CREST archive content available online, though I will miss the old days of colored paper printouts from the two designated computers. Same thanks goes to the digital stewards of *Foreign Relations of the United States* and the UK National Archives Foreign Office Files. My research bore out the aphorism that journalists write the first draft of history, and thanks are due to the *New York Times* for intrepid reporting made easily available via the TimesMachine archive. Last but certainly not least, my thanks to the indefatigable librarians at Yonsei University for many years of help hunting materials.

A succession of talented and resourceful research assistants came to my salvation at key junctures. Julie Zhu scanned reams of Yale history with a keen eye to relevance. Kyu Eun Kim scoured the National Archives and CIA records. Gene Kim carved out time from his PhD studies to chase down elusive sources. Kathy Son made more calls to the library checking on ILL requests than she would probably care to remember. Digital wizard Gaby Magnuson graciously helped with image research.

This project was fortunate to receive indirect support from some phenomenal nongovernment organizations. The National Committee on US-China Relations accepted me into its Public Intellectuals Program, where my thinking was reshaped by conversations within the cohort, emails across the community, and wisdom from our Elders—John Berninghausen, Jan Berris, Tom Gold, Mike Lampton, Terry Lautz, Anne Thurston, and above all, the dearly-missed Ezra Vogel. Comrades Orville Schell, Susie Jakes, and many friends at the Asia Society let me road test ideas for the book as part of their innovative programming. The National Committee on American Foreign Policy invited me to share thoughts on its founder, Hans Morgenthau, and the ensuing dialogue with the brilliant Nick Thompson of the *Atlantic* helped sharpen my understanding of the realists. Becoming part of the Pacific Century Institute and the lively network around Spencer Kim opened doors and offered support that enriched this book immensely. In Seoul, friends at the East Asia Foundation and *Global Asia* editorial group, starting with my Yonsei colleague emeritus Chung-in Moon, have been an enduring source of stimulation and succor.

One of the best ways to see the holes in one's argument is being forced to explain it to an audience of experts. I am grateful to Michael Szonyi and Dan Murphy for giving me the floor at the Harvard Fairbank Center for Chinese Studies, to Alex Wang for the invitation to present at UCLA's Asia Pacific Center, and to Jeff Wasserstrom for hosting me at UC Irvine. Jeff's intellectual generosity is a model for us all, and I've been fortunate to see it up close on panels from Osaka to Los Angeles as well as in the daily flow of smart tweets. Speaking of Twitter and being forced to explain one's argument (or not), I'm grateful for that worldwide web of curious minds and informed observers. Despite its obvious flaws, I learned a great deal out there that shaped this research, especially from those I follow. So thanks, Jack.

Still, nothing substitutes for talking through complex ideas with lifelong friends. Bottomless wells of conversation with Jonathan Ansfield, Gady Epstein, Woo Lee, and Evan Osnos informed this project in ways seen and unseen, as did those with Steve Platt, Tobie Meyer-Fong, Josh Chin, Paul Tonks, Dan Levine, Phil Tinari, June Shee, Jinn Su, Eddan Katz, Ethan Leib, Aaron Matz, David Ponet, Eric Ballbach, Antoine Bondaz, John Nilsson-Wright, and Ramon Pacheco Pardo. Another chronic interlocutor, Ed Wong, merits special mention for biking the streets of Xicheng with me in search of Caolanzi Hutong and sharing the photograph. And thanks to Tian Feiyu for making the trip, albeit in vain, to the Military Museum looking for the wreckage.

How does a middle-aged author adequately express the debt incurred to one's family? The truth is, everyone is mostly just glad it's over, and words fall short. Thank you, above all, to my beloved Jeong-eun, for never giving up on my finishing this thing and for infusing our life together with the spirit of adventure every step along the way. To our little ones, Senna, Sean, and Hannah, thank you for giving me something infinitely more interesting than writing a book; being your dad and watching you grow up is the best thing in life. Mom, the first and last reader of everything we write and the editor in chief of our best selves, how can I possibly acknowledge your contribution? I just hope you and Vince, Uncle Pat and Aunt Mimi, Megan and Keith, Margot and Rose, all like it. Jane, if the craft holds up, it's because a little of your and Don's magic rubbed off. Thank you to the Park family for weekend writing sessions and to Yunsun for joining me in the perfect cure for writer's block, the waves at Woljeong. To the one who is always invisibly by my side, thank you Dad, hope you like it too.

My greatest debt as a historian will always be owed to Jonathan Spence. I only wish I could have finished this book before he passed from our midst.

Notes

PROLOGUE

1. Steven Lee Myers, "An Alliance of Autocracies? China Wants to Lead a New World Order," *New York Times*, March 30, 2021; Chris Buckley and Keith Bradsher, "Marking Party's Centennial, Xi Warns That China Will Not Be Bullied," *New York Times*, July 1, 2021; "Speech by Xi Jinping at a Ceremony Marking the Centenary of the CPC," Xinhua, July 1, 2021.

1. THE LOSS OF CHINA

1. Winston Churchill, *Closing the Ring* (Boston: Houghton Mifflin, 1951), 328; Herbert Feis, *The China Tangle: The American Effort in China from Pearl Harbor to the Marshall Mission* (Princeton, NJ: Princeton University Press, 1953), 105; Tang Tsou, *America's Failure in China, 1941–1950* (Chicago: University of Chicago Press, 1964), 42; Rana Mitter, *Forgotten Ally: China's World War II, 1937–1945* (Boston: Houghton Mifflin Harcourt, 2013).

2. On troop numbers, see Tsou, *America's Failure*, 341; on racism, see Harold R. Isaacs, *No Peace for Asia* (New York: Macmillan, 1947), 214–15. Generally, see Gordon H. Chang, *Fateful Ties: A History of America's Preoccupation with China* (Cambridge, MA: Harvard University Press, 2015).

3. Tsou, *America's Failure*, 123–24.

4. Tsou, 195–201.

5. US Department of State, *The China White Paper: August 1949*, ed. Lyman P. Van Slyke (Stanford, CA: Stanford University Press, 1967), 1:87–92.

6. Hans Morgenthau, *Politics among Nations: The Struggle for Power and Peace* (New York: Knopf, 1948), 429.

7. Feis, *China Tangle*, 422–23.

8. Richard Bernstein, *China 1945: Mao's Revolution and America's Fateful Choice* (New York: Vintage, 2014).

9. Daniel Kurtz-Phelan, *The China Mission: George C. Marshall's Unfinished War, 1945–1947* (New York: W. W. Norton, 2018).

10. Simei Qing, *From Allies to Enemies: Visions of Modernity, Identity, and U.S.-China Diplomacy, 1945–1960* (Cambridge, MA: Harvard University Press, 2007), 58–62.

11. John King Fairbank, *China Perceived: Images and Policies in Chinese-American Relations* (New York: Knopf, 1974), 15.

12. Qing, *Allies to Enemies*, 83; Zhongyun Zi, *No Exit? The Origin and Evolution of U.S. Policy toward China, 1945–1950* (Norwalk, CT: EastBridge, 2003), xvi.

13. Kenneth Scott Latourette, *The United States Moves across the Pacific: The A.B.C.'s of the American Problem in the Western Pacific and the Far East* (New York: Harper & Brothers, 1946), viii, 81.

14. Latourette, 126, 134–35, 139.

15. Fairbank, "Our Chances in China," September 1946, in *China Perceived*, 4.

16. John King Fairbank, *The United States and China* (Cambridge, MA: Harvard University Press, 1948), 331, 330.

17. Harry S. Truman, "Address of the President to Congress, Recommending Assistance to Greece and Turkey," March 12, 1947, Harry S. Truman Library and Museum,

https://www.trumanlibrary.gov/library/research-files/address-president-congress-recommending-assistance-greece-and-turkey?documentid=NA&pagenumber=1.

18. John Leighton Stuart, *Fifty Years in China: The Memoirs of John Leighton Stuart, Missionary and Ambassador* (New York: Random House, 1954), 183.

19. Tsou, *America's Failure*, 451; Odd Arne Westad, *Decisive Encounters: The Chinese Civil War, 1946–1950* (Stanford, CA: Stanford University Press, 2003), 168–72.

20. John Paton Davies, *China Hand: An Autobiography* (Philadelphia: University of Pennsylvania Press, 2011); Paul J. Heer, *Mr. X and the Pacific: George F. Kennan and American Policy in East Asia* (Ithaca, NY: Cornell University Press, 2018).

21. John Lewis Gaddis, *George F. Kennan: An American Life* (New York: Penguin, 2012), 298.

22. Quoted in John Lewis Gaddis, "'Defensive Perimeter' Concept," in *Uncertain Years: Chinese-American Relations, 1947–1950*, ed. Dorothy Borg and Waldo H. Heinrichs (New York: Columbia University Press, 1980), 62–63.

23. Westad, *Decisive Encounters*, 192–95; Harold Miles Tanner, *Where Chiang Kai-shek Lost China: The Liao-Shen Campaign, 1948* (Bloomington: Indiana University Press, 2015).

24. "To Review and Define United States Policy toward China," PPS/39, September 7, 1948, in *Foreign Relations of the United States* (hereafter *FRUS*) *1948*, 8:122.

25. On Kennan's reliance on Davies, see Gaddis, *Kennan*, 358–59; Davies, *China Hand*, 302–5.

26. Quoted in Ross Y. Koen, *The China Lobby in American Politics* (New York: Harper & Row, 1974), 92.

27. Dean Acheson, *Present at the Creation: My Years in the State Department* (New York: Norton, 1969), 257; CIA-ORE Far East / Pacific Branch, "Intelligence Highlights No. 36, Jan 12–19, 1949."

28. Tsung-jen Li, *The Memoirs of Li Tsung-jen* (Boulder, CO: Westview Press, 1979), 484, 491.

29. Qing, *Allies to Enemies*, 99.

30. Zi, *No Exit*, 136–37.

31. John F. Kennedy, "Remarks of Representative John F. Kennedy," January 30, 1949, John F. Kennedy Presidential Library and Museum, https://www.jfklibrary.org/archives/other-resources/john-f-kennedy-speeches/salem-ma-19490130. On the barbed private correspondence between Kennedy and Fairbank that summer, see Paul M. Evans, *John Fairbank and the American Understanding of Modern China* (New York: Basil Blackwell, 1988), 125.

32. Dean Acheson, "Letter of Transmittal," in US Department of State, *China White Paper*, xvi.

33. John King Fairbank, "Toward a Dynamic Far Eastern Policy," *Far Eastern Survey*, September 7, 1949, 209–12; Zi, *No Exit*, 169–70.

34. Zi, *No Exit*, 174.

35. Walter Lippman, "The White Paper: The Chiang Stranglehold," September 12, 1949, in *Commentaries on American Far Eastern Policy* (New York: American Institute of Pacific Relations, 1950), 6.

36. Zi, *No Exit*, 171.

37. Mao Zedong, "Cast Away Illusions, Prepare for Struggle," August 14, 1949, in *Selected Works of Mao Tse-Tung* (Peking: Foreign Languages Press, 1967), 4:426.

38. Mao, "Why It Is Necessary to Discuss the White Paper," August 28, 1949, in *Selected Works*, 4:442.

39. Mao, "Cast Away Illusions," 4:427.

40. Mao, 4:430.

41. “The Position of the United States with Respect to Asia,” NSC 48/2, December 30, 1949, in *FRUS: 1949*, 7.2:387.

42. Harry S. Truman, “The President’s News Conference,” January 5, 1950, Harry S. Truman Library and Museum, https://www.trumanlibrary.gov/library/public-papers/3/presidents-news-conference.

43. Dean Acheson, speech to the National Press Club, January 12, 1950, *Department of State Bulletin*, January 23, 1950, 111–18.

44. Kenneth Scott Latourette, *The American Record in the Far East, 1941–1951* (New York: Macmillan, 1952), 89.

45. John Foster Dulles, *War or Peace* (New York: Macmillan, 1950), 245.

46. Harold R. Isaacs, *Scratches on Our Minds: American Images of China and India* (New York: John Day, 1958), 192.

47. Eric Frederick Goldman, *The Crucial Decade: America, 1945–1955* (New York: Knopf, 1956), 112–13.

48. Jonathan Spence, *To Change China: Western Advisors in China, 1620–1960* (New York: Penguin, 1980).

49. James Lilley, with Jeffrey Lilley, *China Hands: Nine Decades of Adventure, Espionage, and Diplomacy in Asia* (New York: Public Affairs, 2004), 46; Brooks Mather Kelley, *Yale: A History* (New Haven, CT: Yale University Press, 1999), 396–97.

50. Kelley, *Yale*, 397.

51. Kelley, 401.

52. George A. Kennedy, *ZH Guide: An Introduction to Sinology* (New Haven, CT: Far Eastern Publications, 1953), viii.

53. Latourette, *The Development of China* (New York: Houghton Mifflin, 1946), 174, x–xi, 307.

54. Rebecca S. Lowen, *Creating the Cold War University: The Transformation of Stanford* (Berkeley: University of California Press, 1997); Bruce Cumings, “Boundary Displacement: Area Studies and International Studies during and after the Cold War,” *Bulletin of Concerned Asian Scholars* 29, no. 1 (1997): 6–26.

55. Justin Zaremby, *Directed Studies and the Evolution of American Education* (New Haven, CT: Whitney Humanities Center, 2006).

56. Peter Grose, *Gentleman Spy: The Life of Allen Dulles* (Amherst: University of Massachusetts Press, 1994), 51.

57. Charles Seymour, February 6, 1948, *Vital Speeches of the Day* (1948), 282–83.

58. Charles Seymour, “To Listen and to Inquire,” June 20, 1948, *Vital Speeches of the Day* (1948), 624–25.

59. Seymour, 624.

60. Charles Seymour, June 1949, *Vital Speeches of the Day* (1949), 637.

61. Kelley, *Yale*, 410.

62. John King Fairbank, *Chinabound: A Fifty-Year Memoir* (New York: Harper & Row, 1982), 326.

63. Lilley, *China Hands*, 65.

64. Jerome Karabel, *The Chosen: The Hidden History of Admission and Exclusion at Harvard, Yale and Princeton* (New York: Houghton Mifflin, 2005), 213–14.

65. Kelley, *Yale*, 406.

66. Alfred Whitney Griswold, “Report to the Alumni, 1951–52,” December 1952, in *Essays on Education* (New Haven, CT: Yale University Press, 1954), 110; cf. Karabel, *Chosen*, 202, 219–21.

67. *The Yale Banner 1951: With a Summary of 250 Years of Yale*, ed. Paul Drummond Rust III, John Chaloner Borden Jr., and John L. Geismar (New Haven, CT: Yale Banner Publications, 1951), 285.

68. *Yale Banner*, 83.
69. *Yale Banner*; Karabel, *Chosen*, 211.

2. REALISM AND RESTRAINT

1. George F. Kennan, *Memoirs, 1925–1950* (Boston: Little, Brown, 1967), 355–56.
2. [George F. Kennan], "The Sources of Soviet Conduct," *Foreign Affairs*, July 1947, 861, 867.
3. [Kennan], "Sources," 867.
4. George F. Kennan, "Comments on the Problem of National Security," March 28, 1947, in *Measures Short of War: The George F. Kennan Lectures at the National War College, 1946–1947*, ed. Giles D. Harlow and George C. Maerz (Washington, DC: National Defense University Press, 1991), 168.
5. Walter Lippmann, *The Cold War: A Study in U.S. Foreign Policy* (New York: Harper & Brothers, 1947), 18.
6. Lippmann, 21, 44, 53–54.
7. Gaddis, *Kennan*, 255.
8. Kennan, *Memoirs*, 500.
9. Gaddis, *Kennan*, 360.
10. George F. Kennan, *American Diplomacy, 1900–1950* (New York: New American Library, 1951), 3.
11. Kennan, 103.
12. Kennan, 52.
13. Kennan, 50.
14. Kennan, 53–54.
15. Daniel Rice, "Reinhold Niebuhr and Hans Morgenthau: A Friendship with Contrasting Shades of Realism," *Journal of American Studies* 42, no. 2 (August 2008): 262; Paulo Jorge Batista Ramos, "The Role of the Yale Institute of International Studies in the Construction of the United States National Security Ideology, 1935–1951" (PhD diss., University of Manchester, 2003), 323–31.
16. Hayden V. White, *Metahistory: The Historical Imagination in Nineteenth-Century Europe* (Baltimore: Johns Hopkins University Press, 1973), 55. Gaddis, *Kennan*, points out Kennan's obsession with Gibbon.
17. Reinhold Niebuhr, *The Irony of American History* (Chicago: University of Chicago Press, 2008), xxiv.
18. Niebuhr, 41, 125.
19. Niebuhr, 39, xxiv, 169, 133, 155.
20. Niebuhr, 134.
21. Fairbank, "Our Chances in China," 19.
22. Latourette, *American Record*, 203.
23. Goldman, *Crucial Decade*, 115.
24. Niebuhr, *Irony*, 147.
25. Kennan, *American Diplomacy*, 103.
26. Niebuhr, *Irony*, 148.
27. Reinhold Niebuhr, *Christian Realism and Political Problems* (New York: Scribner, 1953), 135.
28. Hans J. Morgenthau, "Fragment of an Intellectual Autobiography: 1904–1932," in *Truth and Tragedy: Tribute to Hans J. Morgenthau*, ed. Kenneth W. Thompson and Robert J. Myers (New Brunswick, NJ: Transaction Books, 1984).
29. Daniel F. Rice, *Niebuhr and His Circle of Influence* (Cambridge: Cambridge University Press, 2013), 147.

30. Christoph Frei, "Politics among Nations: A Book for America," in *Hans Morgenthau and the American Experience*, ed. Cornelia Navari (Cham, Switzerland: Palgrave Macmillan, 2018), 55–74.

31. Morgenthau, *Politics among Nations*, 8, 74–75.

32. Morgenthau, 195–96.

33. Hans J. Morgenthau, *In Defense of the National Interest: A Critical Examination of American Foreign Policy* (New York: Knopf, 1951), 208.

34. Morgenthau, 40. For context, see Cornelia Navari, "The National Interest and the 'Great Debate,'" in *Morgenthau and the American Experience*, 75–93.

35. Morgenthau, *National Interest*, 58.

36. Morgenthau, 7.

37. Morgenthau, 40.

38. Morgenthau, 89, 131, 207, 201.

39. Hannah Arendt, *The Origins of Totalitarianism* (New York: Harcourt, Brace, 1951), viii.

40. Arendt, vii, 378.

41. Arendt, viii–ix.

42. Gaddis, *Kennan*, 243.

43. Robin W. Winks, *Cloak and Gown: Scholars in the Secret War, 1939–1961* (New York: Quill, 1987), 41–43; Bruce Kuklick, *Blind Oracles: Intellectuals and War from Kennan to Kissinger* (Princeton, NJ: Princeton University Press, 2007), 84.

44. Nicholas J. Spykman, *America's Strategy in World Politics* (New York: Harcourt, Brace, 1942), 165.

45. Spykman, 472.

46. Spykman, 457.

47. Spykman, 90.

48. Spykman, 469–70.

49. Nicholas J. Spykman, *The Geography of the Peace*, ed. Helen R. Nicholl (New York: Harcourt, Brace, 1944), 45.

50. Spykman, 57.

51. William T. R. Fox, *The Super-Powers: The United States, Britain, and the Soviet Union—Their Responsibility for Peace* (New York: Harcourt, Brace, 1944), 4, 9, 11.

52. Fox, 19, 84, 162.

53. Frederick Sherwood Dunn, "The Common Problem," in *The Absolute Weapon: Atomic Power and World Order*, ed. Frederick Sherwood Dunn and Bernard Brodie (New York: Harcourt, Brace, 1946), 16.

54. Arnold Wolfers, "The United States in Search of a Peace Policy," *International Affairs* 23, no. 1 (January 1947): 22.

55. Arnold Wolfers, "Statesmanship and Moral Choice," *World Politics* 1, no. 2 (January 1949): 195.

56. Ramos, "Yale Institute of International Studies," 166–67.

57. On the rise of the term "national security" in the 1940s, see Daniel Yergin, *Shattered Peace: The Origins of the Cold War and the National Security State* (New York: Houghton Mifflin, 1977), 193–220.

58. Harold Lasswell, *National Security and Individual Freedom* (New York: McGraw-Hill, 1950), 89–90.

59. Griswold, *Essays on Education*, viii.

60. Griswold, 48, 45.

61. Griswold, "Inaugural Address" (October 6, 1950), in *Essays on Education*, 1–8.

62. Griswold.

63. Griswold.
64. Arnold Wolfers, "National Security as an Ambiguous Symbol," *Political Science Quarterly* 67, no. 4 (December 1952): 486.
65. Wolfers, 492.
66. Wolfers, 494.
67. Wolfers, 498.

3. SUBVERSION AND REPRESSION

1. David M. Oshinsky, *A Conspiracy So Immense: The World of Joe McCarthy* (New York: Oxford University Press, 1983), 108.
2. Robert P. Newman, *Owen Lattimore and the "Loss" of China* (Berkeley: University of California Press, 1992), 56–58.
3. Claire Lee Chennault, *Way of a Fighter: The Memoirs of Claire Lee Chennault* (New York: Putnam, 1949), 104.
4. Newman, *Lattimore*, 65–66.
5. Owen Lattimore, *China Memoirs: Chiang Kai-shek and the War against Japan*, comp. Fujiko Isono (Tokyo: University of Tokyo Press, 1990), 143.
6. Fairbank, *Chinabound*, 185.
7. Maochun Yu, *OSS in China: Prelude to Cold War* (Annapolis, MD: Naval Institute Press, 2011), 15.
8. US Senate, *Institute of Pacific Relations: Report of the Committee on the Judiciary*, 82nd Cong., 3967 (1952) (hereafter *IPR Report*).
9. David Nelson Rowe, *Modern China: A Brief History* (Princeton, NJ: Van Nostrand, 1959), 65.
10. Fairbank, *Chinabound*, 174.
11. Fairbank, 44–45.
12. Fairbank, 185–86.
13. Fairbank, 218; Yu, *OSS in China*, 87.
14. Fairbank, *Chinabound*, 285.
15. David Nelson Rowe, *China among the Powers* (New York: Harcourt, Brace, 1945), 3, 20, 135.
16. Rowe, 145, 52.
17. Rowe, 158, 150.
18. Evans, *John Fairbank and the American Understanding of Modern China*, 98–99.
19. Fairbank, *United States and China*, 4–5.
20. Fairbank, 201.
21. Fairbank, 259–60.
22. Fairbank, 266.
23. Fairbank, 295.
24. Newman, *Lattimore*, 95.
25. Newman, 135–36.
26. Newman, 194.
27. Owen Lattimore, *The Situation in Asia* (New York: Greenwood Press, 1949), 3.
28. Lattimore, 43.
29. Lattimore, 53.
30. Lattimore, 58.
31. Lattimore, 143–53.
32. Lattimore, 176.
33. Owen Lattimore, *Ordeal by Slander* (Boston: Little, Brown, 1950), 88, 90.
34. Lattimore, *Situation in Asia*, 177.
35. Fairbank, *Chinabound*, 344–48.

36. John King Fairbank and Têng Ssu-yu, *China's Response to the West: A Documentary Survey, 1839–1923* (Cambridge, MA: Harvard University Press, 1954), 276.
37. Fairbank and Têng, 2.
38. Fairbank and Têng, 2–3.
39. Conrad Brandt, John King Fairbank, and Benjamin Schwartz, *A Documentary History of Chinese Communism* (Cambridge, MA: Harvard University Press, 1952), 11.
40. David Nelson Rowe Papers (hereafter Rowe Papers), Hoover Institution Archives, Stanford University.
41. Lilley, *China Hands*, 68.
42. Rowe Papers; Raymond L. Garthoff, *A Journey through the Cold War: A Memoir of Containment and Coexistence* (Washington, DC: Brookings Institution Press, 2001), 5.
43. Rowe Papers.
44. Jay Walz, "Lattimore Named as 'Top Soviet Spy' Cited by McCarthy," *New York Times*, March 27, 1950, 1, 9.
45. "*Amerasia* Affair, China, and Postwar Anti-Communist Fervor," Federal Bureau of Investigation Library, 1945–1973, Archives Unbound, Gale.
46. Newman, *Lattimore*, 32.
47. Newman, 131; Koen, *China Lobby*, 122; Joyce Mao, *Asia First: China and the Making of Modern American Conservatism* (Chicago: University of Chicago Press, 2015), 66.
48. Gary May, *China Scapegoat: The Diplomatic Ordeal of John Carter Vincent* (Prospect Heights, IL: Waveland Press, 1982), 160–67.
49. Christopher M. Elias, *Gossip Men: J. Edgar Hoover, Joe McCarthy, Roy Cohn, and the Politics of Insinuation* (Chicago: University of Chicago Press, 2021), 71.
50. Newman, *Lattimore*, 161.
51. Quoted in Tsou, *America's Failure*, 466.
52. John A. Farrell, *Richard Nixon: The Life* (New York: Doubleday, 2017), 93–128; Irwin F. Gellman, *The Contender: Richard Nixon, the Congress Years, 1946–1952* (New Haven, CT: Yale University Press, 2017).
53. Goldman, *Crucial Decade*, 111.
54. Newman, *Lattimore*, 189.
55. Goldman, *Crucial Decade*, 136.
56. Newman, *Lattimore*, 227–48.
57. Goldman, *Crucial Decade*, 141.
58. Elias, *Gossip Men*.
59. William S. White, "F.B.I. Shows Data on Alleged Top Spy to Senate Inquiry," *New York Times*, March 25, 1950, 1; Walz, "Lattimore Named," 1.
60. Lattimore, *Ordeal by Slander*, 1.
61. John King Fairbank, "A Personal Letter to Various Friends and Colleagues in Far Eastern Studies," March 27, 1950, Rowe Papers.
62. Lattimore, *Ordeal by Slander*, 223.
63. Rowe to Fairbank, April 19, 1952, Rowe Papers; Lattimore, *Ordeal by Slander*, 222.
64. Lattimore, 14, 91, 15, 245.
65. Lattimore, 114.
66. Masuda Hajimu, *Cold War Crucible: The Korean Conflict and the Postwar World* (Cambridge, MA: Harvard University Press, 2015), 56.
67. *IPR Report*, 2.
68. May, *China Scapegoat*, 190.
69. Fairbank, *Chinabound*, 339.
70. *IPR Report*, 3773.
71. "Yale Expert Advocates War on China Unless Red Soldiers Leave Korea," *New Haven Register*, December 17, 1950.

72. Rowe to Penniman, December 4, 1950, Rowe Papers.
73. C. Darwin Stolzenbach and Henry Kissinger, *Civil Affairs in Korea, 1950–1951* (Chevy Chase, MD: Operations Research Office, May 12, 1952); Niall Ferguson, *Kissinger: 1923–1968 The Idealist* (New York: Penguin, 2015), 266–72.
74. David Nelson Rowe and Willmoore Kendall, eds., *China: An Area Manual* (Chevy Chase, MD: Operations Research Office, 1953).
75. "Lattimore Called Stalinism Agent by Yale Prof.," Associated Press, March 27, 1952; *IPR Report*, July 2, 1952, 2050, 4.
76. *IPR Report*, 3980.
77. "Fairbank Hits Rowe of Yale for Charges," *Harvard Crimson*, March 29, 1952; "Fairbank and Friend," *Boston Herald*, April 2, 1952.
78. Fairbank to Rowe, April 7, 1952, Rowe Papers.
79. Fairbank, "Our Chances in China," 16.
80. Rowe to Fairbank, April 28, 1952, Rowe Papers.
81. Quoted in May, *China Scapegoat*, 236.
82. *IPR Report*, 218.
83. May, *China Scapegoat*, 197, 259–60. Service was dismissed in December 1951, Vincent in December 1952, Davies in November 1954.
84. James C. Thompson Jr., Peter W. Stanley, and John Curtis Perry, *Sentimental Imperialists: The American Experience in East Asia* (New York: Harper & Row, 1981), 233.
85. Newman, *Lattimore*, 413.
86. Judd to Rowe, November 12, 1952, Rowe Papers.
87. Judd to Rowe, February 16, 1953, Rowe Papers; Newman, *Lattimore*, 422.
88. Judd to Rover, February 16, 1953, Rowe Papers.
89. Newman, *Lattimore*, 423–24, 435.
90. Rover to Rowe, July 3, 1953, Rowe Papers.
91. Rowe to Rover, July 8, 1953, Rowe Papers.
92. Newman, *Lattimore*, 466.
93. Newman, 458.
94. Sipes to Rowe, June 7, 1954, Rowe Papers.
95. Sipes to Rowe, June 11, 1954, Rowe Papers.
96. Newman, *Lattimore*, 462–64.
97. Newman, 466–71.
98. Davies, *China Hand*, 1–7.
99. William F. Buckley Jr. and L. Brent Bozell, *McCarthy and His Enemies: The Record and Its Meaning* (Chicago: H. Regnery, 1954), 245.
100. Buckley and Bozell, 311.
101. Buckley and Bozell, 159.
102. Buckley and Bozell, 157.
103. William F. Buckley Jr., *God and Man at Yale: The Superstitions of "Academic Freedom"* (Chicago: H. Regnery, 1951), 106.
104. Buckley, 177.
105. Buckley, 101.
106. Seymour to Woods, September 8, 1949, Seymour Papers, Yale Manuscripts and Archives.
107. Michael Holzman, "The Ideological Origins of American Studies at Yale," *American Studies* 40, no. 2 (1999): 71–99.
108. "Report of the President's Advisory Committee," February 9, 1952, Griswold Papers, Yale Manuscripts and Archives.
109. Gaddis, *Kennan*, 394.
110. Kelley, *Yale*, 435.

111. Griswold, "Alumni Day Address," February 22, 1952, in *Essays on Education*, 81.
112. Griswold, "Letter to Irving S. Gold," April 19, 1951, Griswold Papers, Yale.
113. Jeremi Suri, *Henry Kissinger and the American Century* (Cambridge, MA: Harvard University Press, 2007), 94.
114. Xiaobing Li, *China's Battle for Korea: The 1951 Spring Offensive* (Bloomington: Indiana University Press, 2014).
115. *Yale Banner*, 303.
116. *Yale Banner*, 29.
117. Lilley, *China Hands*, 68.
118. Griswold, "Survival Is Not Enough," *Atlantic Monthly*, April 1951, in *Essays on Education*, 11.
119. Griswold, 12.
120. Griswold, "Report to Alumni, 1950–51," in *Essays on Education*, 64.
121. Benjamin Fine, "Task of Educators Cited by Dewey," *New York Times*, June 12, 1951, 24.
122. "Griswold Urges Yale Seniors to Be Individuals," *New York Herald Tribune*, June 11, 1951.
123. Griswold, "Baccalaureate Address," June 10, 1951, in *Essays on Education*, 27.
124. Griswold, 27–28.
125. Griswold, 31–32.
126. George Wilson Pierson, *Yale College: An Educational History, 1871–1921* (New Haven, CT: Yale University Press, 1952), x.

4. INTELLIGENCE OR PSYWAR

1. Jeffrey T. Richelson, *A Century of Spies: Intelligence in the Twentieth Century* (New York: Oxford University Press, 1997), 77.
2. Christopher Andrew, *The Secret World: A History of Intelligence* (New Haven, CT: Yale University Press, 2019).
3. Richard Dunlop, *Donovan: America's Master Spy* (New York: Skyhorse, 2014), 284–91.
4. Roberta Wohlstetter, *Pearl Harbor: Warning and Decision* (Stanford, CA: Stanford University Press, 1962).
5. Dunlop, *Donovan*, 333–34.
6. Arthur B. Darling, *The Central Intelligence Agency: An Instrument of Government, to 1950* (University Park: Pennsylvania State University Press, 1990), 43. Darling taught US history and foreign policy at Yale from 1922 to 1933; he completed his authorized CIA history in December 1953.
7. Stewart Alsop and Thomas Wardell Braden, *Sub Rosa: The O.S.S. and American Espionage* (New York: Reynal & Hitchcock, 1946), 136–84.
8. Curt Gentry, *J. Edgar Hoover: The Man and the Secrets* (New York: Norton, 2001).
9. William Donovan, "Memorandum for the President," November 18, 1944, in *The Central Intelligence Agency: History and Documents*, ed. William M. Leary (Tuscaloosa: University of Alabama Press, 1984), 124.
10. Sarah-Jane Corke, *US Covert Operations and Cold War Strategy: Truman, Secret Warfare and the CIA, 1945–1953* (New York: Routledge, 2014), 16.
11. Theodore H. White and Annalee Jacoby, *Thunder Out of China* (New York: William Sloane Associates, 1946), 161.
12. Yu, *OSS in China*, 209.
13. Darling, *Central Intelligence Agency*, 38–39.
14. Corke, *Covert Operations*, 16–23.
15. Melvyn P. Leffler, *A Preponderance of Power: National Security, the Truman Administration, and the Cold War* (Stanford, CA: Stanford University Press, 1992), 44–49.

16. Anne Karalekas, "History of the Central Intelligence Agency," in Leary, *CIA: History and Documents*, 24. Karalekas drafted the history of covert action activities since the creation of the CIA for the US Senate's Church Committee investigation in 1975.

17. Darling, *Central Intelligence Agency*, 76, 94–95.

18. Darling, 119–20, 151.

19. Karalekas, "History of the CIA," 26.

20. Darling, *Central Intelligence Agency*, 151–53.

21. William Colby, *Honorable Men: My Life in the CIA* (New York: Simon & Schuster, 1978), 71.

22. On the crafting of the National Security Act, see Clark M. Clifford, with Richard C. Holbrooke, *Counsel to President: A Memoir*, (New York: Anchor Books, 1991), 146–71. The loophole was a carry-over from Truman's original order in January 1946 creating the Central Intelligence Group (Leary, *CIA: History and Documents*, 126–27).

23. Kaeten Mistry, *The United States, Italy, and the Origins of the Cold War* (New York: Cambridge University Press, 2014); Gaddis, *Kennan*, 294–95.

24. Kennan, *Memoirs, 1925–1950*, 143.

25. Darling, *Central Intelligence Agency*, 104.

26. Darling, 248–49.

27. Darling, 246.

28. "NSC Directive to the Director of Central Intelligence," NSC 4-A, December 17, 1947, in *The CIA under Harry Truman: CIA Cold War Records*, ed. Michael Warner (Washington, DC: Central Intelligence Agency, 1994), 173–75.

29. Karalekas, "History of CIA," 40.

30. Darling, *Central Intelligence Agency*, 262–65.

31. See Josef Korbel, *The Communist Subversion of Czechoslovakia 1938–1948: The Failure of Coexistence* (Princeton, NJ: Princeton University Press, 1959).

32. Karalekas, "History of CIA," 40.

33. Corke, *Covert Operations*, 50; Stephen Kinzer, *The Brothers: John Foster Dulles, Allen Dulles, and Their Secret World War* (New York: St. Martin's Griffin, 2013), 89.

34. William Colby, who arrived in Italy in the fall of 1953, described it as "by far the CIA's largest covert political-action program undertaken until then or, indeed, since" (Colby, *Honorable Men*, 109).

35. Darling, *Central Intelligence Agency*, 266; Gaddis, *Kennan*, 316. Corke surmises John Paton Davies may have written the original draft of what became PPS/9 (Corke, *Covert Operations*, 53–54).

36. "Policy Planning Memorandum Staff," May 4, 1948, in *FRUS: Establishing the Intelligence Community, 1945–1950*, 269.

37. "NSC Directive on Office of Special Projects," NSC 10/2, June 18, 1948, in Warner, *CIA under Truman*, 214.

38. NSC 10/2, 216.

39. NSC 10/2, 215–16.

40. Gaddis, *Kennan*, 317–19.

41. Darling, *Central Intelligence Agency*, 277–78; Karalekas, "History of CIA," 46; Corke, *Covert Operations*, 61–63.

42. Joseph Burkholder Smith, *Portrait of a Cold Warrior* (New York: Putnam, 1976), 74.

43. Darling, *Central Intelligence Agency*, 166–92.

44. John Prados, *Presidents' Secret Wars: CIA and Pentagon Covert Operations from World War II through the Persian Gulf War* (Chicago: Elephant Paperbacks, 1986), 37–44.

45. Richard J. Aldrich, *The Hidden Hand: Britain, America, and Cold War Secret Intelligence* (London: John Murray, 2002), 160–65; Harry Rositzke, *CIA's Secret Operations: Espionage, Counterespionage, and Covert Action* (New York: Reader's Digest, 1977), 172.

46. Corke, *Covert Operations*, 98–99; Scott Anderson, *The Quiet Americans: Four CIA Spies at the Dawn of the Cold War—a Tragedy in Three Acts* (New York: Random House, 2020).

47. Corke, *Covert Operations*, 111.

48. Rositzke, *Secret Operations*, 18.

49. John K. Singlaub, with Malcolm McConnell, *Hazardous Duty: An American Soldier in the Twentieth Century* (New York: Summit Books, 1991), 119.

50. John K. Singlaub, interview, in William B. Breuer, *Shadow Warriors: The Covert War in Korea* (New York: Wiley, 1996), 23.

51. Singlaub, *Hazardous Duty*, 143–44.

52. Matthew Aid, "US Humint and Comint in the Korean War: From the Approach of the War to the Chinese Intervention," in *The Clandestine Cold War in Asia, 1945–65: Western Intelligence, Propaganda and Special Operations*, ed. Richard J. Aldrich, Gary D. Rawnsley, and Ming-Yeh T. Rawnsley (London: Frank Cass, 2000), 22.

53. Rositzke, *Secret Operations*, 52.

54. Ted Gup, *The Book of Honor: The Secret Lives and Deaths of CIA Operatives* (New York: Anchor Books, 2001), 9–42; Justin M. Jacobs, *Xinjiang and the Modern Chinese State* (Seattle: University of Washington Press, 2016), 199–200.

55. Walter Bedell Smith, *My Three Years in Moscow* (Philadelphia: Lippincott, 1950), 86.

56. Ludwell Lee Montague, *General Walter Bedell Smith as Director of Central Intelligence, October 1950–February 1953* (University Park: Pennsylvania State University Press, 1992), 204; "Staff Conference," October 22, 1951, in Warner, *CIA under Truman*, 436.

57. Sherman Kent, *Reminiscences of a Varied Life: An Autobiography* (Washington, DC: E. G. Kent, 1991), 227.

58. Kent, 228–29.

59. Montague, *Smith*, 131; Kent, *Reminiscences*, 233–34.

60. Kennan, *Memoirs*, 307, 354–55.

61. Harlow and Maerz, *Measures Short of War*, 100–105.

62. Sherman Kent, "Strategic Intelligence," January 6, 1947, National War College Archives.

63. Kent, *Reminiscences*, 241; Whittaker Chambers, "Faith for a Lenten Age," *Time*, March 8, 1948.

64. Darling, *Central Intelligence Agency*, 301–2.

65. Hans Morgenthau, "Review of *Strategic Intelligence for American World Policy*," *American Political Science Review* 43, no. 5 (October 1949), 1046–47.

66. Darling, *Central Intelligence Agency*, 154.

67. "Remarks of Sherman Kent, World Situation Demands Better Strategic Intelligence for America," *Yale Interprets the News*, June 5, 1949.

68. "Remarks of Sherman Kent."

69. Sherman Kent, *Strategic Intelligence for American World Policy* (Princeton, NJ: Princeton University Press, 1949), 205.

70. Kent, 182.

71. Kent, 180.

72. Kent, *Reminiscences*, 263–64.

73. Kent, *Strategic Intelligence*, 3–4.

74. Grose, *Gentleman Spy*, 275.

75. Jack Davis, "The Kent-Kendall Debate of 1949," *Studies in Intelligence* 35, no. 2 (Summer 1991): 37–50.

76. Willmoore Kendall, "The Function of Intelligence," *World Politics* 1, no. 4 (July 1949): 550.

77. Charles R. Shrader, *History of Operations Research in the US Army* (Washington, DC: US Government Printing Office, 2006), 67.

78. Anthony Olcott, "Revisiting the Legacy: Sherman Kent, Willmoore Kendall, and George Pettee—Strategic Intelligence in the Digital Age," *Studies in Intelligence* 53, no. 2 (June 2009).

79. Kent, *Reminiscences*, 244.

80. Montague, *Smith*, 55–56. The Senate confirmed Smith as director on August 28, 1950, and he started official duties on October 7—the delay was due to recovering from ulcer surgery. Karalekas, "History of the CIA," 29; Kent, *Reminiscences*, 244–45.

81. Donald P. Steury, ed., *Sherman Kent and the Board of National Estimates* (Washington, DC: Central Intelligence Agency, 1994), 155.

82. Montague, *Smith*, 134.

83. Grose, *Gentleman Spy*, 18.

84. Grose, 51.

85. Deidre Bair, *Jung: A Biography* (Boston: Little, Brown, 2003), 481–95.

86. Allen Welsh Dulles, *Germany's Underground* (New York: Macmillan, 1947), xiii.

87. Allen W. Dulles, William H. Jackson, and Mathias F. Correa, "The Central Intelligence Agency and National Organization for Intelligence," January 1, 1949, 131, https://www.cia.gov/readingroom/docs/CIA-RDP86B00269R000500040001-1.pdf.

88. Dulles, Jackson, and Correa, 107.

89. Kent, *Strategic Intelligence*, 3–4.

90. Montague, *Smith*, 14.

91. Kent, *Reminiscences*, 273.

92. Grose, *Gentleman Spy*, 318.

93. "Memorandum from the Director of Central Intelligence (Smith) to the National Security Council," May 8, 1951, in *FRUS: The Intelligence Community, 1950–1955*, 68.

94. Darling, *Central Intelligence Agency*, 411.

95. Director's Log [OPC], September 13, 1951, 27, http://www.foia.cia.gov/sites/default/files/document_conversions/1700319/1951-09-01.pdf.

96. Director's Log [OSO], September 27, 1951, 63.

97. Rositzke, *Secret Operations*, 168.

98. Director's Log [OPC], September 17, 1951, 36.

99. Director's Log [OPC], October 29, 1951, 116.

100. Kim Philby, *My Silent War* (London: Panther, 1980), 143–44.

101. Director's Log [OSO], September 25, 1951, 53.

102. Rositzke, *Secret Operations*, 28.

103. Rositzke, 36.

104. Rositzke, 171–72; Evan Thomas, *The Very Best Men: The Daring Early Years of the CIA* (New York: Simon & Schuster, 2006), 67.

105. Beetle met daily with deputies and other senior staff for a "Director's Meeting" until June 6, 1952, and hired an executive assistant tasked with "a daily log listing all important incoming and outgoing communications, meetings, and conversations" (Montague, *Smith*, 82, 95).

106. Director's Log, September 5, 14, 25, 1951.

107. Director's Log [OSO], September 13, 1951.

108. Director's Log, September 11–13, 1951.

109. Director's Log, October 15, 1951.

110. Director's Log [OPC], September 4, 1951, 4; cf. Blaine Harden, *King of Spies: The Dark Rein of America's Spymaster in Korea* (New York: Viking, 2017).

111. Karalekas, "History of the CIA," 43.

112. Karalekas, 48.

113. Karalekas, 53.

114. Thomas, *Very Best Men*, 37–38; Corke, *Covert Operations*, 2.

115. Montague, *Smith*, 92.

116. Corke, *Covert Operations*, 135.

117. Grose, *Gentleman Spy*, 371.

118. Mark Joseph Gasiorowski and Malcolm Byrne, eds., *Mohammad Mosaddeq and the 1953 Coup in Iran* (Syracuse, NY: Syracuse University Press, 2004).

119. Aldrich, *Hidden Hand*, 174–79.

120. Corke, *Covert Operations*, 5.

121. "Report by the Director of Central Intelligence," April 23, 1952, in Warner, *CIA under Truman*, 460.

122. Karalekas, "History of the CIA," 50–51.

123. "Remarks of Sherman Kent," June 5, 1949.

124. Richard Harkness and Gladys Harkness, "The Mysterious Doings of the CIA," *Saturday Evening Post*, November 6, 1954, 64.

125. Director's Log [Training], December 8, 1951, 198.

126. Winks, *Cloak and Gown*, 54.

127. Winks, *Cloak and Gown*, 247–321; cf. Holzman, "Ideological Origins of American Studies at Yale," on Pearson as a key figure in on-campus CIA recruitment.

128. Lilley, *China Hands*, 69.

129. Lilley, 70.

130. Simon Willmetts, *In Secrecy's Shadow: The OSS and CIA in Hollywood Cinema, 1941–1979* (Edinburgh: Edinburgh University Press, 2016).

131. William Sloane Coffin, *Once to Every Man: A Memoir* (New York: Atheneum, 1977), 90–91.

132. Arendt, *Origins of Totalitarianism*, 220.

133. Arendt, 221.

134. Montague, *Smith*, 97–99.

135. Donald P. Gregg, *Pot Shards: Fragments of a Life Lived in CIA, the White House, and the Two Koreas* (Washington, DC: New Academia Publishing, 2014), 21; Colby, *Honorable Men*, 85; Lilley, *China Hands*, 73–75.

136. Smith, *Cold Warrior*, 123–24.

137. Smith, 128.

138. Gregg, *Pot Shards*, 22.

139. Gregg, 21.

140. Thomas, *Very Best Men*, 50; Gregg, *Pot Shards*, 22.

141. Wilbur Schramm, ed., *The Nature of Psychological Warfare* (Chevy Chase, MD: Operations Research Office, 1953), 288.

142. Paul Myron Anthony Linebarger, *Psychological Warfare* (New York: Duell, Sloan & Pearce, 1954), 44.

143. Smith, *Cold Warrior*, 85–99.

144. Anderson, *Quiet Americans*, 371; Larry Berman, *Perfect Spy: The Incredible Double Life of Pham Xuan An* (New York: Smithsonian Books, 2008), 136.

145. Rositzke, *Secret Operations*, 156.

146. Linebarger, *Psychological Warfare*, 268.

147. Linebarger, 281.

5. AT WAR IN KOREA

1. James F. Schnabel, *The United States Army in the Korean War: Policy and Direction, the First Year* (Washington, DC: Army Center of Military History, 1992), 64.

2. Steven Casey, *Selling the Korean War: Propaganda, Politics, and Public Opinion in the United States, 1950–1953* (New York: Oxford University Press, 2008), 30.

3. "Statement Issued by the President," June 27, 1950, in *FRUS: 1950*, 7:119.

4. Shu Guang Zhang, *Mao's Military Romanticism: China and the Korean War, 1950–1953* (Lawrence: University Press of Kansas, 1995), 72.

5. Robert Accinelli, *Crisis to Commitment: US Policy toward Taiwan, 1950–1955* (Chapel Hill: University of North Carolina Press, 1996), 65–66.

6. Allen W. Dulles, *The Craft of Intelligence* (New York: Harper & Row, 1963), 155.

7. Shen Zhihua, *Mao, Stalin and the Korean War: Trilateral Communist Relations in the 1950s*, trans. Neil E. Silver (New York: Routledge, 2012), 125–29.

8. Allen S. Whiting, *China Crosses the Yalu: The Decision to Enter the Korean War* (Stanford, CA: Stanford University Press, 1960), 23; William Stueck, *Rethinking the Korean War: A New Diplomatic and Strategic History* (Princeton, NJ: Princeton University Press, 2002), 104.

9. Whiting, *China Crosses the Yalu*, 64–65; Charles A. Willoughby and John Chamberlain, *MacArthur, 1941–1951* (New York: McGraw-Hill, 1954), 382–87.

10. Joseph C. Goulden, *Korea: The Untold Story of the War* (New York: McGraw-Hill, 1983), 235.

11. Stueck, *Rethinking the Korean War*, 89.

12. Schnabel, *Army in Korea*, 199.

13. Masuda, *Cold War Crucible*, 110–12.

14. Roy Edgar Appleman, *South to the Naktong, North to the Yalu* (Washington, DC: Army Center of Military History, 1961), 607–8.

15. Schnabel, *Army in Korea*, 194.

16. "Chou Says Peking Won't Stand Aside," *New York Times*, October 2, 1950, 3.

17. Appleman, *South to the Naktong*, 608.

18. Chen Jian, *China's Road to the Korean War: The Making of the Sino-American Confrontation* (New York: Columbia University Press, 1994), 171–86; Shen, *Mao, Stalin*, 149–56.

19. Qing, *Allies to Enemies*, 160.

20. Xiaobing Li, Allan R. Millett, and Bin Yu, eds., *Mao's Generals Remember Korea* (Lawrence: University of Kansas Press, 2001), 31.

21. K. M. Panikkar, *In Two Chinas: Memoirs of a Diplomat* (London: George Allen & Unwin, 1955), 108.

22. Panikkar, 110.

23. Breuer, *Shadow Warriors*, 89.

24. U. Alexis Johnson, with Jef Olivarius McAllister, *The Right Hand of Power: The Memoirs of an American Diplomat* (Englewood Cliffs, NJ: Prentice-Hall, 1984), 105.

25. Johnson, 101.

26. Whiting, *China Crosses the Yalu*, 114.

27. Montague, *Smith*, 65.

28. Warner, *CIA under Truman*, 349–72.

29. CIA, "Critical Situations in the Far East," ORE 58–50, October 12, 1950, https://www.cia.gov/readingroom/docs/DOC_0001166750.pdf.

30. Omar Bradley, "Substance of Statements Made at Wake Island Conference, October 15, 1950," Truman Library and Museum, https://www.trumanlibrary.gov/library/research-files/substance-statements-made-wake-island-conference?documentid=NA&pagenumber=12; Richard H. Rovere and Arthur M. Schlesinger Jr., *The General and the President, and the Future of American Foreign Policy* (New York: Farrar, Straus and Young, 1951).

31. Breuer, *Shadow Warriors*, 92.

32. CIA, "Review of the World Situation," CIA 10-15, October 18, 1950, http://www.foia.cia.gov/sites/default/files/document_conversions/5829/CIA-RDP86B00269R000300040007-7.pdf.

33. Appleman, *South to the Naktong*, 761.

34. Appleman, 669.

35. "Memorandum by the Director of the Central Intelligence Agency (Smith) to the President," November 1, 1950, *FRUS: 1950*, 7:731.

36. Max Hastings, *The Korean War* (New York: Simon & Schuster, 1987), 130.

37. Appleman, *South to the Naktong*, 755.

38. Zhang Xingxing, ed., *Kangmei yuanchao: 60 nian de huimou* (Beijing: Dangdai Zhongguo chubanshe, 2011), 31.

39. Schnabel, *Army in Korea*, 246.

40. Truman, "The President's News Conference," November 16, 1950, Truman Library and Museum, https://www.trumanlibrary.gov/library/public-papers/287/presidents-news-conference.

41. Kent, *Reminiscences*, 244–45.

42. Hastings, *Korean War*, 154.

43. "The Commander in Chief, Far East (MacArthur) to the Joint Chiefs of Staff," November 28, 1950, in *FRUS: 1950*, 7:888.

44. Hastings, *Korean War*, 183.

45. Xiaobing Li, *Attack at Chosin: The Second Chinese Offensive in Korea* (Norman: University of Oklahoma Press, 2020), 128–29.

46. Kent, *Strategic Intelligence*, 74.

47. Kent, 64.

48. Karalekas, "History of the CIA," 33.

49. Colby, *Honorable Men*, 103–4.

50. Robert F. Futrell, *The United States Air Force in Korea 1950–1953* (Washington, DC: Office of Air Force History, 1991), 516–18.

51. Malcolm A. Cagle and Frank A. Manson, *The Sea War in Korea* (Annapolis, MD: Naval Institute Press, 1957).

52. US Congress, *Military Situation in the Far East* (Washington, DC: US Government Printing Office, 1951), 1:731–32.

53. Aid, "Humint and Comint," 37–42.

54. Central Intelligence Agency, *Clandestine Services History: The Secret War in Korea, June 1950–June 1952* (CS Historical Paper no. 52, July 17, 1968), 20.

55. Ed Evanhoe, *Darkmoon: Eighth Army Special Operations in the Korean War* (Annapolis, MD: Naval Institute Press, 1995), 36–38.

56. Evanhoe, 54.

57. John W. Thornton, *Believed to Be Alive* (Middlebury, VT: P. S. Eriksson, 1981).

58. Evanhoe, *Darkmoon*, 115–17.

59. Evanhoe, 142.

60. Evanhoe, 90.

61. David Cheng Chang, *The Hijacked War: The Story of Chinese POWs in the Korean War* (Stanford, CA: Stanford University Press, 2020), 340.

62. Central Intelligence Agency, *Secret War in Korea*, 19.

63. Goulden, *Korea*, 466.

64. See William M. Leary, *Perilous Missions: Civil Air Transport and CIA Covert Operations in Asia* (Washington, DC: Smithsonian Institution Press, 2002), 124–25; Prados, *Presidents' Secret Wars*, 68–69.

65. Goulden, *Korea*, 469–71.

66. "Scope and Pace of Covert Operations," NSC 10/5, October 23, 1951, in Warner, *CIA under Truman*, 438.

67. Corke, *Covert Operations*, 118.

68. Breuer, *Shadow Warriors*, 172–75.

69. Director's Log [OPC], September 14, 1951, 29; September 25, 1951, 56; October 5, 1951, 76; September 25, 1951, 56; October 12, 1951, 89; October 19, 1951, 100.

70. Director's Log [OPC], September 14, 1951, 29.

71. Aid, "Humint and Comint," 23.

72. Director's Log [OSO], November 30, 1951, 178.

73. Michael E. Haas, *In the Devil's Shadow: UN Special Operations during the Korean War* (Annapolis, MD: Naval Institute Press, 2000), 41–42.

74. Central Intelligence Agency, *Secret War in Korea*, 76.

75. Director's Log [OPC], October 19, 1951, 100.

76. Director's Log [OPC], December 5, 1951, 190.

77. Central Intelligence Agency, *Secret War in Korea*, 10.

78. Central Intelligence Agency, 6.

79. Central Intelligence Agency, 19.

80. Haas, *Devil's Shadow*, 201–2.

81. Haas, 203.

82. Evanhoe, *Darkmoon*, 124–60.

83. Frederick Cleaver et al., eds., *UN Partisan Warfare in Korea, 1951–1954* (Chevy Chase, MD: Operations Research Office, 1956), 94.

84. Singlaub, *Hazardous Duty*, 183.

85. Central Intelligence Agency, *Secret War in Korea*, 8–9.

86. Lindesay Parrott, "Red China Charges 'Provocation' by U.S. Navy in Formosa Strait," *New York Times*, July 29, 1952, 1, 2.

87. *Kangmei yuanchao zhanzheng shi* (Beijing: Junshi kexue chubanshe, 2011), 2:409.

88. Westad, *Decisive Encounters*, 237.

89. Chen Jian, "The Ward Case and Emergence of Sino-American Confrontation, 1948–1950," *Australian Journal of Chinese Affairs* 30 (July 1993): 163–64.

90. Jan Kiely, *The Compelling Ideal: Thought Reform and the Prison in China, 1901–1956* (New Haven, CT: Yale University Press, 2014), 272.

91. Frederic Wakeman, *Spymaster: Dai Li and the Chinese Secret Service* (Berkeley: University of California Press, 2003), 147.

92. Qing, *Allies to Enemies*, 134.

93. Mao Zedong, "Report to 3rd Plenary Session of 7th Central Committee," June 6, 1950, in *Selected Works* (1977), 5:27–29.

94. Mao, 5:27.

95. Mao, 5:31.

96. Julia Strauss, "Paternalist Terror: The Campaign to Suppress Counterrevolutionaries and Regime Consolidation in the People's Republic of China, 1950–1953," *Comparative Studies in Society and History* 44, no. 1 (2002): 80–105.

97. Mao Zedong, "CCP Central Committee Directives," December 19, 1950, in *Selected Works*, 5:53.

98. Frank Dikötter, *The Tragedy of Liberation: A History of the Chinese Revolution, 1945–1957* (New York: Bloomsbury, 2013), 137–38; Masuda, *Cold War Crucible*, 183–84; Westad, *Decisive Encounters*, 324.

99. Jerome Alan Cohen, *The Criminal Process in the People's Republic of China, 1949–1963* (Cambridge, MA: Harvard University Press, 1968), 299.

100. Mao Zedong, "The Party's Mass Line Must Be Followed in Suppressing Counter-revolutionaries," May 1951, in *Selected Works*, 5:51; Andrew Walder, *China under Mao: A Revolution Derailed* (Cambridge, MA: Harvard University Press, 2015), 65–66.

101. Mao, *Selected Works*, 5:51.

102. Mao Zedong, "Directives," May 8, 1951, in *Selected Works*, 5:55–56.

103. Dikötter, *Tragedy of Liberation*, 142–43.

104. Masuda, *Cold War Crucible*, 192.

105. Masuda, 121–29.

106. Jeremy Brown, "From Resisting Communists to Resisting America: Civil War and Korean War in Southwest China, 1950–1951," in *Dilemmas of Victory: The Early Years of the People's Republic of China*, ed. Jeremy Brown and Paul Pickowicz (Cambridge, MA: Harvard University Press, 2010), 105–29.

107. Dikötter, *Tragedy of Liberation*, 85–86.

108. Yang Kuisong, "Reconsidering the Campaign to Suppress Counterrevolutionaries," *China Quarterly* 193 (March 2008): 120; Mao Zedong, "On the Correct Handling of Contradictions among the People," February 27, 1957, in *The Secret Speeches of Chairman Mao: From the Hundred Flowers to the Great Leap Forward*, ed. Timothy Cheek, Merle Goldman, and Roderick MacFarquhar (Cambridge, MA: Harvard University Press, 1989), 142.

109. Michael Dutton, *Policing Chinese Politics: A History* (Durham, NC: Duke University Press, 2005), 167.

110. Kiely, *Compelling Ideal*, 277.

111. Raja Hutheesing, *Great Peace: An Asian's Candid Report on Red China* (New York: Harper & Brothers, 1953), 188.

112. Hutheesing, 189.

113. Dikötter, *Tragedy of Liberation*, 116–20; Raymond Kerrison, *Bishop Walsh of Maryknoll: Prisoner of Red China* (New York: Lancer Books, 1963), 22.

114. W. Allyn Rickett and Adele Rickett, *Prisoners of Liberation* (Garden City, NJ: Anchor, 1973), 11.

115. Rickett and Rickett, 18.

116. Rickett and Rickett, 44–46; Zhao Ma, "Urban Space and Illegal Narcotics: Korean Drug Dealers in Wartime Beijing," *Zhongyang yanjiuyuan jindaishi yanjiusuo jikan* 111 (June 2021): 113–55.

117. Rickett and Rickett, 49.

118. Rickett and Rickett, 127.

119. Rickett and Rickett, 64.

120. Rickett and Rickett, 211, 231.

121. Director's Log [OSO], November 21, 1951, 162.

6. THE THIRD FORCE

1. Graham Greene, *Ways of Escape* (New York: Washington Square Press, 1980), 145.

2. Pyle was often mistakenly thought to be based on Edward Lansdale. Norman Sherry, *The Life of Graham Greene*, vol. 2: *1939–1955* (London: Penguin Books, 2004), 417. Few have cared to figure out the inspiration for York Harding.

3. Graham Greene, *The Quiet American* (New York: Penguin Books, 2004), 17.

4. Greene, 17.

5. Greene, 136.

6. CIA, "Current Intelligence Bulletin," February 16, 1952, CIA-RDP79T00975A000500550001-5, 5; Fredrik Logevall, *Embers of War: The Fall of an Empire and the Making of America's Vietnam* (New York: Random House, 2012), 300.

7. Pierre Birnbaum, *Léon Blum: Prime Minister, Socialist, Zionist*, trans. Arthur Goldhammer (New Haven, CT: Yale University Press, 2015).

8. Carlo Sforza, "Italy, the Marshall Plan, and the 'Third Force,'" *Foreign Affairs* 26, no. 3 (April 1948): 450–56.

9. Léon Blum, "Troisième Force européenne," *Le Populaire*, June 1, 1948; CIA, "The Current Situation in France," ORE 85–49, November 14, 1949, CIA-RDP78-01617A003700130003-4; Charles A. Micaud, "The Third Force Today," in *Modern France: Problems of the Third and Fourth Republics*, ed. Edward Meade Earle (Princeton, NJ: Princeton University Press, 1951), 137–52. "The year 1947 was the year of Blum's 'Third Force.'" Joel Colton, *Léon Blum: Humanist in Politics* (New York: Knopf, 1966), 466.

10. Isser Woloch, *The Postwar Moment: Progressive Forces in Britain, France, and the United States after World War II* (New Haven, CT: Yale University Press, 2019).

11. Arthur M. Schlesinger Jr., "Not Right, Not Left, But a Vital Center," *New York Times*, April 4, 1948, 6.

12. Arthur M. Schlesinger Jr., *The Vital Center: The Politics of Freedom* (Boston: Houghton Mifflin, 1949), 167.

13. Schlesinger, 167–68.

14. Prados, *Presidents' Secret Wars*, 35; Ray S. Cline, *Secrets, Spies, and Scholars* (Washington, DC: Acropolis Books, 1976), 63, 129.

15. Schlesinger, *Vital Center*, 238.

16. Schlesinger, 223.

17. Schlesinger, "Not Right, Not Left."

18. Carsun Chang, *The Third Force in China* (New York: Bookman Associates, 1952), 45

19. See Roger B. Jeans, ed., *Roads Not Taken: The Struggle of Opposition Parties in Twentieth-Century China* (Boulder, CO: Westview, 1992).

20. Roger B. Jeans, *Democracy and Socialism in Republican China: The Politics of Zhang Junmai (Carsun Chang), 1906–1941* (Lanham, MD: Rowman & Littlefield, 1997), 203; Edmund S. K. Fung, *In Search of Chinese Democracy: Civil Opposition in Nationalist China, 1929–1949* (Cambridge: Cambridge University Press, 2000), 132.

21. Lloyd Eastman, "China's Democratic Parties," in Jeans, *Roads Not Taken*, 191; Fung, *Chinese Democracy*, 148.

22. Chang, *Third Force*, 114.

23. Israel Epstein, *The Unfinished Revolution in China* (Boston: Little, Brown, 1947), 152–53; Fung, *Chinese Democracy*, 231.

24. White and Jacoby, *Thunder Out of China*, 276–77.

25. Fairbank, *Chinabound*, 241–64.

26. Lyman P. Van Slyke, *Enemies and Friends: The United Front in Chinese Communist History* (Stanford, CA: Stanford University Press, 1967), 169; Qing, *Allies to Enemies*, 68–69.

27. Chang, *Third Force*, 28.

28. Charlotte Brooks, "The Chinese Third Force in the United States: Political Alternatives in Cold War Chinese America," *Journal of American Ethnic History* 34, no. 1 (Fall 2014): 53–85; Charlotte Brooks, *Between Mao and McCarthy: Chinese American Politics in the Cold War Years* (Chicago: University of Chicago Press, 2015).

29. Howard L. Boorman, ed., *Biographical Dictionary of Republican China* (New York: Columbia University Press, 1970), 3:435–36; Eastman, "China's Democratic Parties," 192.

30. Eastman, "China's Democratic Parties," 194.

31. Stuart, *Fifty Years in China*, 188.

32. Stuart, 184–85.

33. Wakeman, *Spymaster*, 344–45.

34. Fairbank, *United States and China*, 287.

35. White and Jacoby, *Thunder Out of China*, 295–96.
36. White and Jacoby, 313.
37. White and Jacoby, 313.
38. Sun Yuemei, "The Third Force and the Marshall Mission" (MA thesis, University of Georgia, 2000), 75–77.
39. "Personal Statement by the Special Representative of the President," January 7, 1947, in US Department of State, *China White Paper*, 2:688.
40. "Minutes of Meeting of the Secretaries of State, War, and Navy," February 12, 1947, *FRUS: 1947*, 7:621.
41. "Memorandum Prepared in the Embassy in China for the Minister-Counselor of Embassy (Butterworth)," July 5, 1947, *FRUS: 1947*, 7:185.
42. "Memorandum by General Wedemeyer to the Secretary of State," July 2, 1947, *FRUS: 1947*, 7:533.
43. Van Slyke, *Enemies and Friends*, 199.
44. Qing, *Allies to Enemies*, 92.
45. Kiely, *Compelling Ideal*, 261.
46. Van Slyke, *Enemies and Friends*, 207.
47. Fairbank, *Chinabound*, 317.
48. John King Fairbank, "China's Prospects and U.S. Policy," *Far Eastern Survey* 16, no. 13 (July 2, 1947): 145, 148.
49. Fairbank, 286, 287.
50. John King Fairbank, "Can We Compete in China?," *Far Eastern Survey* 17, no. 10 (May 19, 1948): 117.
51. Brandt, Fairbank, and Schwartz, *Documentary History*, 475.
52. Brandt, Fairbank, and Schwartz, 479.
53. Lattimore, *Situation in Asia*, 221; Alessandro Brogi, *Confronting America: The Cold War between the United States and the Communists in France and Italy* (Chapel Hill: University of North Carolina Press, 2011).
54. Lattimore, *Situation in Asia*, 50–51.
55. Lattimore, 177.
56. Lattimore, 177.
57. Rickett and Rickett, *Prisoners of Liberation*, 32.
58. Chang, *Third Force*, 280.
59. Panikkar, *In Two Chinas*, 59.
60. Chang, *Third Force*, 280.
61. Peter Ivanov, "Miscellany of China's Political Spectrum, 1945–1950," in Jeans, *Roads Not Taken*, 177.
62. Qing, *Allies to Enemies*, 116–17.
63. A. Doak Barnett, *Communist China: The Early Years, 1949–1955* (New York: Frederick A. Praeger, 1964), 11–12.
64. Boorman, *Biographical Dictionary*, 1:34.
65. Roger B. Jeans, *The CIA and Third Force Movements in China during the Early Cold War: The Great American Dream* (Lanham, MD: Lexington Books, 2017), 51; Li Guizhong, *Zhang Junmai nianpu changbian* (Beijing: Zhongguo shehui kexue chubanshe, 2016), 269.
66. Zheng Dahua, *Zhang Junmai zhuan* (Beijing: Shangwu yinshu guan, 2012), 404–5.
67. Zhang Fakui, *Zhang Fakui koushu zizhuan: Guomindang lujun zongsiling huiyi lu* (Beijing: Dangdai Zhongguo chubanshe, 2012), 386–87; Jeans, *CIA and Third Force*, 51.
68. Chang, *Third Force*, 307.
69. Chang, 6, 238, 95.
70. Chang, 109.

71. Chang, 318, 308.
72. Chang, *Third Force*, 12–13.
73. Chang, 307. Chang insisted that 90 percent of Chinese were anti-Communist (30).
74. Chang, 307.
75. Chang, 23, 311–12.
76. Chang, *Third Force*, 314.
77. Chang, 315.
78. Chang, 316.
79. Chang, 13.
80. Chang, 14.
81. Hsiang-kuang Chou, *Political Thought of China* (Delhi: S. Chand, 1954), 200–204.

7. MAKING COUNTERREVOLUTION

1. Oliver J. Caldwell, *A Secret War: Americans in China, 1944–1945* (Carbondale: Southern Illinois University Press, 1972), 26.
2. Caldwell, *Secret War*, 93–95.
3. Caldwell, 179–80.
4. Lilley, *China Hands*, 50.
5. Singlaub, *Hazardous Duty*, 153, 154.
6. Singlaub, 154.
7. Singlaub, 155.
8. Qing, *Allies to Enemies*, 97.
9. Dikötter, *Tragedy of Liberation*, 23.
10. Westad, *Decisive Encounters*, 197
11. Chang, *Third Force*, 236.
12. Boorman, *Biographical Dictionary*, 3:406.
13. Xiaobing Li and Hongshan Li, eds., *China and the United States: A New Cold War History* (Lanham, MD: University Press of America, 1997), 274.
14. H. Bradford Westerfield, *Foreign Policy and Party Politics* (New Haven, CT: Yale University Press, 1955), 350.
15. "Transcript of Conversation," May 11, 1949, in *FRUS: 1949*, 9:550.
16. Chennault, *Way of a Fighter*, vii, viii–ix, x, xvii.
17. Westerfield, *Foreign Policy*, 350.
18. "The Ambassador in China (Stuart) to the Secretary of State," May 30, 1949; "The Minister-Counselor of Embassy in China (Clark) to the Secretary of State," June 6, 1949, in *FRUS: 1949*, 9:553–54.
19. "Probable Developments in China," ORE 45–49, June 16, 1949, https://catalog.archives.gov/id/6924348.
20. Mao Zedong, "Address to the Preparatory Meeting of the New Political Consultative Conference," June 15, 1949, in *Selected Works*, 4:406.
21. Congressional Record, 81st Cong. (July 6, 1949), 97.7:8921–24.
22. "The Chinese Ambassador (Koo) to the Secretary of State," August 15, 1949, in *FRUS: 1949*, 9:655.
23. "Memorandum by the Executive Secretary of the National Security Council (Souers) to the Council," October 19, 1949, in *FRUS: 1949*, 9:572; "Survival Potential of Residual Non-Communist Regimes in China," ORE 76–49, October 19, 1949, https://catalog.archives.gov/id/6924359.
24. "Memorandum by the Assistant Secretary of State for Far Eastern Affairs (Butterworth) to the Secretary of State," October 21, 1949, in *FRUS: 1949*, 9:575.
25. Leary, *Perilous Missions*, 67–83.

26. "Memorandum of Conversation, by the Secretary of State," December 29, 1949, in *FRUS: 1949*, 9:490.

27. "Memorandum of Conversation."

28. Felix Smith, *China Pilot: Flying for Chiang and Chennault* (Washington, DC: Brassey's, 1995), 193.

29. Alfred T. Cox, *Civil Air Transport (CAT): A Proprietary Airline*, vol. 1, *The History of Civil Air Transport 1946–1955* (Washington, DC: Central Intelligence Agency, 1969), 62.

30. Ronald L. McGlothlen, *Controlling the Waves: Dean Acheson and U.S. Foreign Policy in Asia* (New York: Norton, 1993), 123–24; Accinelli, *Crisis to Commitment*, 44–49; Hsiao-ting Lin, *Accidental State: Chiang Kai-shek, the United States, and the Making of Taiwan* (Cambridge, MA: Harvard University Press, 2016), 159–161.

31. "Memorandum on JCS Requirements" in "McConaughy to Robertson," December 9, 1954, NARA 611.95A251/12-954, RG 59, North Korea Files 1950–1954, Box 2887 [dated "on or about July 10, 1950"].

32. "Memorandum on JCS Requirements."

33. Montague, *Smith*, 195.

34. Mao, *Asia First*, 31–32.

35. Secretary of Defense, "Courses of Action Relative to Communist China and Korea," NSC 101 (January 12, 1951), *Truman Library*, https://www.trumanlibrary.gov/library/research-files/courses-action-relative-communist-china-and-korea-national-security-council?documentid=NA&pagenumber=4.

36. CIA, "Communist China," NIE-10 (January 17, 1951), 1, https://www.cia.gov/readingroom/docs/DOC_0001084983.pdf; cf. Montague, *Smith*, 140–41.

37. CIA, 2–3.

38. CIA, 3.

39. Leary, *Perilous Missions*, 132–33.

40. Prados, *Presidents' Secret Wars*, 70–71.

41. CIA, "Director's Staff Meeting," March 23, 1951, http://www.foia.cia.gov/sites/default/files/document_conversions/1700319/1951-03-23a.pdf.

42. Goulden, *Korea*, 477.

43. Rovere and Schlesinger, *General and the President*, 5.

44. Walter S. Poole, *The History of the Joint Chiefs of Staff: The Joint Chiefs of Staff and National Policy* (Washington, DC: Office of Joint History, 1980), 4:207.

45. "Report to the National Security Council by the Executive Secretary (Lay)," NSC 48/5, May 17, 1951, in *FRUS: 1951*, 6.1:12.

46. "Memorandum from Robert P. Joyce of the Policy Planning Staff to the Director of the Policy Planning Staff (Nitze)," June 21, 1951, in *FRUS: Intelligence Community, 1950–1955*, 75.

47. "Memorandum from Robert P. Joyce."

48. CIA, "Director's Meeting," July 25, 1951, http://www.foia.cia.gov/sites/default/files/document_conversions/1700319/1951-07-25a.pdf.

49. CIA, "Information Report: Chinese Communist and Chinese Nationalist Attempts to Disrupt Third Force Activities in Hong Kong," December 1, 1951, CIA-RDP82-00457R009400370010-1.

50. CIA, "Current Intelligence Bulletin," July 25, 1951, CIA-RDP79T00975A00030023001-2.

51. CIA, "Information Report: Struggle for Power between Political Department and Pao Mi Chu," October 6, 1951, CIA-RDP82-00457R008900090010-8.

52. "Scope and Pace of Covert Operations," NSC 10/5, October 23, 1951, in Warner, *CIA under Truman*, 438.

53. Lilley, *China Hands*, 78.
54. Cited in Leary, *Perilous Missions*, 142.
55. Thomas, *Very Best Men*, 52–53.
56. CIA, "Information Report: Political Unrest in Kwangsi Province," December 6, 1951, CIA-RDP82-00457R00940030005-4.
57. Chennault, *Way of a Fighter*, 361.
58. Prados, *Presidents' Secret Wars*, 64; Benno Weiner, *Chinese Revolution on the Tibetan Frontier* (Ithaca, NY: Cornell University Press, 2020), 44.
59. Frank Holober, *Raiders of the China Coast: CIA Covert Operations during the Korean War* (Annapolis, MD: Naval Institute Press, 1999), 178–94.
60. Chris Pocock and Clarence Fu Jing Ping, *The Black Bats: CIA Spy Flights over China from Taiwan, 1951–1969* (Atglen, PA: Schiffer, 2010), 14.
61. Melvyn C. Goldstein, *A History of Modern Tibet, 1913–1951* (Berkeley: University of California Press, 1989), 607–10.
62. Gyalo Thondup and Anne F. Thurston, *The Noodle Maker of Kalimpong: The Untold Story of My Struggle for Tibet* (New York: Public Affairs, 2015), 89–93.
63. Goldstein, *Modern Tibet*, 792–98.
64. Director's Log [OPC], October 1, 1951, 67.
65. Weiner, *Tibetan Frontier*, 57.
66. Richard Michael Gibson with Wen H. Chen, *The Secret Army: Chiang Kai-shek and the Drug Lords of the Golden Triangle* (Singapore: John Wiley and Sons, 2011), 18–40; John Prados, *The Ghosts of Langley: Into the CIA's Heart of Darkness* (New York: New Press, 2017), 86; Thomas, *Very Best Men*, 54; Karalekas, "History of the CIA," 49.
67. Leary, *Perilous Missions*, 129; Gibson, *Secret Army*, 60.
68. Leary, *Perilous Missions*, 129–30.
69. Gibson, *Secret Army*, 75.
70. Smith, *Cold Warrior*, 78.
71. Bertil Lintner, *Burma in Revolt: Opium and Insurgency since 1948* (Chiang Mai: Silkworm Books, 1999), 101–2.
72. Director's Log [OPC], September 4, 1951, 3.
73. Director's Log, September 4, 1951, 3–4.
74. Gibson, *Secret Army*, 104; Thomas, *Very Best Men*, 56.
75. "Statement by the President," June 27, 1950, *Wilson Center*, http://digitalarchive.wilsoncenter.org/document/116192.
76. Karl Lott Rankin, *China Assignment* (Seattle: University of Washington Press, 1964), 69.
77. Smith, *Cold Warrior*, 77; Joe F. Leeker, "CAT, Air Asia, Air America—the Company on Taiwan III: Work for the US Government," in *The History of Air America*, University of Texas at Dallas Library e-book (August 24, 2015), 2.
78. Lilley, *China Hands*, 79.
79. Matthew Aid and Jeffrey T. Richelson, "U.S. Intelligence and China: Collection, Analysis, and Covert Action," May 27, 2011, National Security Archive, 11–12.
80. Director's Log [OPC], October 2, 1951, 70.
81. Thomas, *Very Best Men*, 51.
82. Director's Log [OPC], September 18, 1951, 37.
83. Director's Log [OPC], October 2, 1951, 70.
84. Director's Log [OPC], September 11, 1951, 18; September 14, 1951, 30.
85. Director's Log [OPC], November 26, 1951, 169.
86. *Neibu cankao*, October 28, 1952, 348–49.
87. *Neibu cankao*, November 17, 1950, 75.

88. *Neibu cankao*, February 12, 1954, 121–24. The report identified Ed Hamilton, the chief of CIA guerrilla training on Jinmen, by name; Cf. Holober, *Raiders*, 28.
89. Director's Log [OPC], September 13, 1951, 26.
90. Director's Log [OPC], September 25, 1951, 57.
91. Director's Log [OPC], September 18, 1951, 38.
92. Director's Log [OPC], November 19, 1951, 156; October 22, 1951, 103.
93. Director's Log [OPC], October 19, 1951, 100; October 22, 1951, 103; November 19, 1951, 156.
94. Director's Log [OPC], December 12, 1951, 206; Holober, *Raiders*, 51–54.
95. Lin, *Accidental State*, 206.
96. Accinelli, *Crisis to Commitment*, 101.
97. Holober, *Raiders*, 57–58.
98. *Neibu cankao*, October 28, 1952, 348–49.
99. "Memorandum by the Assistant Secretary of State for Far Eastern Affairs (Allison) to John Foster Dulles," in *FRUS: 1952–1954*, 14.1:63.

8. HONG KONG FIGHT LEAGUE

1. Philby, *My Silent War*, 142.
2. Feis, *China Tangle*, 284.
3. Humphrey Trevelyan, *Living with the Communists: China 1953–5, Soviet Union 1962–5* (Boston: Gambit, 1971), 71.
4. Aldrich, *Hidden Hand*, 293.
5. Cline, *Secrets, Spies, and Scholars*, 124.
6. Director's Log [OSO], September 11, 1951, 17.
7. Dulles, *Craft of Intelligence*, 18.
8. Trevelyan, *Living with the Communists*, 60.
9. Chi-Kwan Mark, *Hong Kong and the Cold War: Anglo-American Relations 1949–1957* (New York: Oxford University Press, 2004), 184.
10. Johannes R. Lombardo, "A Mission of Espionage, Intelligence and Psychological Operations: The American Consulate in Hong Kong, 1949–1964," in Aldrich, Rawnsley, and Rawnsley, *Clandestine Cold War in Asia*, 66.
11. Mark, *Hong Kong*, 189; Lombardo, "Mission of Espionage," 67.
12. Director's Log [OSO], November 1, 1951, 121–22.
13. Quoted in Mark, *Hong Kong*, 192.
14. Epstein, *Unfinished Revolution*, 147.
15. Rositzke, *Secret Operations*, 27.
16. Dikötter, *Tragedy of Liberation*, 44.
17. Cheng Siyuan, *Zhenghai mixin* (Harbin: Beifang wenyi chuban, 2011), 240.
18. Prados, *Presidents' Secret Wars*, 65.
19. Li, *Memoirs*, 554–55.
20. Jeans, *CIA and Third Force*, 20, 34–38.
21. Boorman, *Biographical Dictionary*, 3:58–59.
22. Philip Snow, *The Fall of Hong Kong: Britain, China, and the Japanese Occupation* (New Haven, CT: Yale University Press, 2003), 206–60; Boorman, *Biographical Dictionary*, 3:61.
23. Li, *Memoirs*, 535.
24. Jeans, *CIA and Third Force*, 38.
25. Zhang, *Koushu zizhuan*, 370.
26. Mark, *Hong Kong*, 189.
27. CIA, "Information Report: Hsu Chung-chih and Third Force Elements," May 7, 1951.

28. Zhang, *Koushu zizhuan*, 370–71; Cheng, *Zhenghai mixin*, 241; Mark, *Hong Kong*, 190. Jeans identified him as the OPC agent Ake Hartmann, who came to Hong Kong from the Philippines (Jeans, *CIA and Third Force*, 60).

29. Zhang, *Koushu zizhuan*, 370–72.

30. Chen Zhengmao, *Wuling niandai Xianggang disanshili yundong shiliao soumi* (Taipei: Xiuwei zixun keji chuban, 2011), 53.

31. Zhang, *Koushu zizhuan*, 372–73.

32. Mark, *Hong Kong*, 189; Li Zongren to Harry Truman, May 14, 1951, National Archives and Records Administration 746G.00/5-1451 (hereafter NARA); Li to Acheson, May 16, 1951, NARA 746G.00/5-1651.

33. Zhang, *Koushu zizhuan*, 376–79.

34. Zhang, 378.

35. Zhang, 388.

36. Zhang, 375. The release of the Fight League Manifesto was delayed until October 10, 1952—coinciding with the Nationalist Party Congress in Taipei (Chen, *Wuling niandai Xianggang*, iii).

37. Zhang, *Koushu zizhuan*, 379.

38. Zhang, 380.

39. Richard Helms with William Hood, *A Look over My Shoulder: A Life in the Central Intelligence Agency* (New York: Ballantine Books, 2003), 93.

40. Zhang, *Koushu zizhuan*, 380.

41. On Cai, see Jeans, *CIA and Third Force*, 12–20.

42. Jeans, *CIA and Third Force*, 116.

43. Zhang, *Koushu zizhuan*, 381.

44. Zhang, 389.

45. Zhang, 381.

46. Zhang, 383–84.

47. Zhang, 386.

48. Zhang, 392.

49. Office of Current Intelligence [CIA], "Current Intelligence Digest," May 12, 1952, 4.

50. Mark, *Hong Kong*, 188; Yang Tianshi, "The Third Force," in Jeans, *Roads Not Taken*, 272.

51. *Neibu cankao*, March 27, 1951, 105–6.

52. *Neibu cankao*, 106.

53. *Neibu cankao*, 107–8.

54. Lattimore, *Situation in Asia*, 153.

55. "Staff Conference" (October 27, 1952), in Warner, *CIA under Truman*, 470.

56. Warner, *CIA under Truman*, 460.

57. Montague, *Smith*, 213–14.

58. "Remarks of the President," November 21, 1952, in Warner, *CIA under Truman*, 472.

9. MANCHURIAN MANHUNT

1. E. J. Kahn Jr., *A Reporter in Micronesia* (New York: Norton, 1966), 31–33, 39.

2. Daniel Immerwahr, *How to Hide an Empire: A History of the Greater United States* (New York: Farrar, Straus and Giroux, 2019).

3. Walter Pincus, *Blown to Hell: America's Deadly Betrayal of the Marshall Islanders* (New York: Diversion Books, 2021).

4. Smith, *China Pilot*, 215–16.

5. Zhang, *Koushu zizhuan*, 371.

6. Jeans, *CIA and Third Force*, 128.

7. Smith, *China Pilot*, 216.

8. Zhang, 395.
9. Victor Marchetti and John D. Marks, *The CIA and the Cult of Intelligence* (New York: Knopf, 1974), 110.
10. Director's Log, September 5, 1951, 6.
11. Director's Log [OPC], November 9, 1951, 137.
12. Director's Log [OPC], September 10, 1951, 18.
13. Director's Log [OSO], September 10, 1951, 16.
14. Smith, *China Pilot*, 216.
15. Smith, 216.
16. Director's Log [OPC], November 26, 1951, 169.
17. Xue Gongtian and Lou Ruixi, "Jianmie Antu xian jingnei Meiguo dongjiang tewu jishi," in *Zhiyuan kangmei yuanchao jishi*, ed. National People's Consultative Conference Documents and Historical Materials Standing Committee (Beijing: Zhongguo wenshi chubanshe, 2000), 774. Xue and Lou's chapter is a local history sponsored by the Jilin Province Chinese People's Political Consultative Conference.
18. Ralph W. McGehee, *Deadly Deceits: My 25 Years in the CIA* (New York: Sheridan Square, 1983), 21.
19. Zhang, *Koushu zizhuan*, 371. According to Jeans, training shifted from Chigasaki to Okinawa and Saipan (for Manchurian teams) in 1952, with the Okinawa program discontinued due to US Army objections (Jeans, *CIA and the Third Force*, 123–28).
20. Sara Mansfield Taber, *Born under an Assumed Name: The Memoir of a Cold War Spy's Daughter* (Washington, DC: Potomac Books, 2012), 346.
21. Director's Log [DD/A], September 14, 1951, 30.
22. Director's Log [OPC], September 20, 1951, 45.
23. Koen, *China Lobby*, 43–5; Lin, *Accidental State*, 166–69.
24. Rumors mentioned in Smith, *China Pilot*, 216. Li Zongren alleged that on the day Chiang resigned the presidency (in January 1949), he directed Mow to withdraw $10 million and disperse it across his own personal accounts (Li, *Memoirs*, 507).
25. Director's Log, September 4, 1951, 3.
26. Director's Log, September 20, 1951, 43; Lilley, *China Hands*, 80.
27. Leary, *Perilous Missions*, 138.
28. Quoted in Leary, 138.
29. Nicholas Dujmovic, "Extraordinary Fidelity: Two CIA Prisoners in China, 1952–73," *Studies in Intelligence* 50, no. 4 (2006): 2.
30. Cited in Joe F. Leeker, "CAT, Air America and Japan," in *History of Air America*, 51.
31. *Jilin sheng biannian jishi*, Jilin Provincial Library e-book (2003), 1005, https://www.jlplib.com.cn/szzy/jlsbnjs/201101/P020110118730834159523.pdf
32. James J. White, *Missing in Action: People and Policies* (Washington, DC: Central Intelligence Agency, 1974), 9; Xue and Lou, "Jianmie," 775–76; Dujmovic, "Extraordinary Fidelity," 2. ST was the digraph for Far East Division/China Branch operations. See Kenneth Conboy and James Morrison, *The CIA's Secret War in Tibet* (Lawrence: University Press of Kansas, 2002), 55.
33. Xue and Lou, "Jianmie," 776–77.
34. Colby, *Honorable Men*, 36.
35. Ellery Anderson, *Banner over Pusan* (London: Brown Watson, 1961), 157.
36. Xue and Lou, "Jianmie," 777.
37. White, *Missing in Action*, 12.
38. Xue and Lou, "Jianmie," 777.
39. Xue and Lou, 778.
40. Xue and Lou, 775.
41. Xue and Lou, 778–79.

42. Ewen Montagu, *The Man Who Never Was* (New York: Oxford University Press, 1996).
43. Donald Downes, *The Scarlet Thread: Adventures in Wartime Espionage* (London: Derek Verschoyle, 1953), 81.
44. Xue and Lou, "Jianmie," 779.
45. James C. Scott, *Seeing Like a State: How Certain Schemes to Improve the Human Condition Have Failed* (New Haven, CT: Yale University Press, 1998).
46. Frederic Wakeman, "'Cleanup': The New Order in Shanghai," in Brown and Pickowicz, *Dilemmas of Victory*, 43.
47. Dikötter, *Tragedy of Liberation*, 224.
48. Wakeman, "Cleanup," 44.
49. Barnett, "Social Controls," April 1953, in *Communist China*, 45, 51.
50. Xue and Lou, "Jianmie," 780.
51. Xue and Lou, "Jianmie," 780-81; on the First Bureau, see Michael Schoenhals, *Spying for the People: Mao's Secret Agents, 1949–1967* (New York: Cambridge University Press, 2013), 30–33.
52. *Jilin sheng biannian jishi*, 1009.
53. Xue and Lou, "Jianmie," 782.
54. Zhang Guolu, "1952: Sante kongjiang Changbaishan," Jilin sheng gongan ting, May 16, 2012, http://gat.jl.gov.cn/jyfc/gash/201205/t20120516_1207954.html (accessed April 22, 2016). Zhang Guolu was a retired Jilin Province public security officer.
55. Xue and Lou, "Jianmie," 783.
56. Xue and Lou, 784. On Man Zhihui, see Zhang, "1952."
57. Xue and Lou, "Jianmie," 785–86.
58. Dujmovic, "Extraordinary Fidelity," 2.
59. Xue and Lou, "Jianmie," 787.
60. Xue and Lou, 788. According to Zhang Guolu's account, Liu Haichun was shot in the leg before they were able to subdue the intruder (Zhang, "1952").
61. *Jilin sheng biannian jishi*, 1009.
62. Xue and Lou, "Jianmie," 775.
63. Xue and Lou, 789–91.
64. Zhang, "1952."
65. *Jilin sheng biannian jishi*, 1009.
66. Lilley, *China Hands*, 80.
67. Thomas, *Very Best Men*, 52–53.
68. "230 American Airdropped Agents Captured or Killed," New China News Agency, November 24, 1954.
69. *Jilin sheng biannian jishi*, 1011.
70. David Wise, *Tiger Trap: America's Secret Spy War with China* (New York: Houghton Mifflin Harcourt, 2011), 203.
71. *Kangmei yuanchao zhanzheng shi*, 2:332.
72. Walter G. Hermes, *Truce Tent and Fighting Front: United States Army in the Korean War* (Honolulu: University of Hawai'i Press, 1966), 314; Isaacs, *Scratches on Our Minds*, 233.
73. Hermes, 318.
74. Casey, *Selling the Korean War*, 344–45.
75. "Address by Dwight D. Eisenhower," October 25, 1952, 1, *Eisenhower Library*, https://www.eisenhowerlibrary.gov/sites/default/files/research/online-documents/korean-war/i-shall-go-to-korea-1952-10-24.pdf.
76. "Address by Eisenhower," 5.
77. "Text of Gen. Eisenhower's Foreign Policy Speech in San Francisco," *New York Times*, October 9, 1952, 24; Kenneth Alan Osgood, *Total Cold War: Eisenhower's Secret Propaganda Battle at Home and Abroad* (Lawrence: University of Kansas Press, 2006), 46.

78. Matthew M. Aid, *The Secret Sentry: The Untold Story of the National Security Agency* (New York: Bloomsbury, 2009), 43–44.

79. Smith, *Cold Warrior*, 102.

10. EXFILTRATION

1. D. K. R. Crosswell, *Beetle: The Life of General Walter Bedell Smith* (Lexington: University Press of Kentucky, 2010), 44.

2. Montague, *Smith*, 263.

3. William I. Hitchcock, *The Age of Eisenhower: America and the World in the 1950s* (New York: Simon & Schuster, 2018), 91; Casey, *Selling the Korean War*, 337.

4. Chennault, *Way of a Fighter*, xvii.

5. Casey, *Selling the Korean War*, 336.

6. David P. Fields, *Foreign Friends: Syngman Rhee, American Exceptionalism, and the Division of Korea* (Lexington: University Press of Kentucky, 2019).

7. Dwight D. Eisenhower, *Mandate for Change: The White House Years, 1953–1956* (New York: New American Library, 1965), 133.

8. Hermes, *Truce Tent*, 366–67; Eisenhower, *Mandate*, 130–34.

9. Casey, *Selling the Korean War*, 337.

10. Eisenhower, *Mandate*, 131.

11. Grose, *Gentleman Spy*, 333.

12. Hastings, *Korean War*, 317.

13. White, *Missing in Action*, 10.

14. Dujmovic, "Extraordinary Fidelity," 2.

15. Gregg, *Pot Shards*, 38–39.

16. Zhang, "1952."

17. Dujmovic, "Extraordinary Fidelity," 3.

18. Crosswell, *Beetle*, 43–44.

19. Crosswell, 44.

20. Warner, *CIA under Truman*, xxvi; Montague, *Smith*, 218; E. Howard Hunt, *Undercover: Memoirs of an American Secret Agent* (New York: Putnam, 1974), 103.

21. Smith, *Cold Warrior*, 104; Thomas, *Very Best Men*, 59; Colby, *Honorable Men*, 147–58.

22. Allen W. Dulles, *The Secret Surrender* (New York: Harper & Row, 1966), 87.

23. Aid and Richelson, "U.S. Intelligence and China," 4. On the senior representative position, see Montague, *Smith*, 219, 227. Howard Hunt joined North Asia Command in June 1954 and gave a damning portrayal of Admiral Overesch as a buffoon (Hunt, *Undercover*, 113).

24. Wisner to McConaughy, "American Prisoners Held by the Chinese Communists," December 14, 1954, NARA 611.95a.251/12-1454.

25. White, *Missing in Action*, 36.

26. Smith, *China Pilot*, 204.

27. William M. Leary, "Robert Fulton's Skyhook and Operation Coldfeet," *Studies in Intelligence* 38, no. 5 (1995): 99–109; Haas, *Devil's Shadow*, 103–4.

28. Cox, *Civil Air Transport*, 3:Tab J, 3.

29. White, *Missing in Action*, 12.

30. Bina Cady Kiyonaga, *My Spy: Memoir of a CIA Wife* (New York: Perennial, 2001), 113.

31. Smith, *China Pilot*, 218.

32. Cox, *Civil Air Transport*, 3:Tab J, 10.

33. "Staff Conference," October 27, 1952, in Warner, *CIA under Truman*, 470.

34. Smith, *Cold Warrior*, 132.

35. Dulles, *Craft of Intelligence*, 91.

36. Director's Log [OPC], October 11, 1951, 86; October 17, 1951, 95.

37. Haas, *Devil's Shadow*, 99.

38. Haas, 111–12.

39. Gregg, *Pot Shards*, 38–39.

40. Schoenhals, *Spying*, 20–23.

41. *Jianguo yilai Liu Shaoqi wengao* (Beijing: Zhongyang wenxian chubanshe, 1998), 4:324–27.

42. Frederick Teiwes, "Establishment and Consolidation of the New Regime," in *The Cambridge History of China*, ed. John King Fairbank and Roderick MacFarquhar (Cambridge: Cambridge University Press, 1987), 14:82–88.

43. Quoted in Schoenhals, *Spying*, 21.

44. Dikötter, *Tragedy of Liberation*, 234.

45. Xue and Lou, "Jianmie," 792.

46. Zhang, "1952."

47. Xue and Lou, "Jianmie," 792.

48. Downey and Fecteau interviews in CIA-produced film, *Extraordinary Fidelity* (Center for the Study of Intelligence, 2011), https://www.youtube.com/watch?v=M5wJw3MvwaY; Dujmovic, "Extraordinary Fidelity," 3–4; Leary, *Perilous Missions*, 139; Colby, *Honorable Men*, 45.

49. Smith, *Cold Warrior*, 134.

50. Xue and Lou, "Jianmie," 793–94.

51. Zhang, "1952."

52. Downey and Fecteau in *Extraordinary Fidelity*.

53. Xue and Lou, "Jianmie," 794–95.

54. Hsiao-ting Lin, *Modern China's Ethnic Frontiers: A Journey to the West* (New York: Routledge, 2011), xxii.

55. Mao Zedong, *Jianguo yilai Mao Zedong junshi wengao* (Beijing: Junshi kexue chubanshe, 2010), 2:83–84.

56. Mao, 2:83–84.

57. Luo Ruiqing, *Luo Ruiqing lun renmin gong'an gongzuo* (Beijing: Qunzhong chubanshe, 1993), 165.

58. Luo, 165.

59. Mao, *Junshi wengao*, 2:128.

60. Mao, 2:128–29.

61. Dujmovic, "Extraordinary Fidelity," 6–8.

62. Hutheesing, *Great Peace*, 230.

63. Downey in *Extraordinary Fidelity*.

64. Fecteau in *Extraordinary Fidelity*.

65. Rickett and Rickett, *Prisoners of Liberation*, 95.

66. Downey in *Extraordinary Fidelity*.

67. Dujmovic, "Extraordinary Fidelity," 7.

68. Quoted in Nicholas Daniloff, *Of Spies and Spokesmen: My Life as a Cold War Correspondent* (Columbia: University of Missouri Press, 2008), 196.

69. Edward Hunter, *Brain-Washing in Red China: The Calculated Destruction of Men's Minds* (Tokyo: Charles E. Tuttle, 1951), 12.

70. Charles S. Young, *Name, Rank, and Serial Number: Exploiting Korean War POWs at Home and Abroad* (New York: Oxford University Press, 2014); Susan L. Carruthers, *Cold War Captives: Imprisonment, Escape, and Brainwashing* (Berkeley: University of California Press, 2009).

71. Stephen Kinzer, *Poisoner in Chief: Sidney Gottlieb and the CIA Search for Mind Control* (New York: Griffin, 2019), 54.

72. Monica Kim, *The Interrogation Rooms of the Korean War: The Untold Story* (Princeton, NJ: Princeton University Press, 2019).

73. Downey in *Extraordinary Fidelity.*

74. Gregg, *Pot Shards*, 40.

75. On mourning Stalin, see Steve E. Kiba, *The Flag: My Story, Kidnapped by Red China* (Bloomington, IN: 1st Books, 2002), 51; Robert Ford, *Captured in Tibet* (London: Harrap, 1957), 224; Peter Lum, *Peking, 1950–1953* (London: Robert Hale, 1958), 164–66.

11. QUIET AMERICANS

1. Haas, *Devil's Shadow*, 193; White, *Missing in Action*, 8.

2. White, *Missing in Action*, 16.

3. White, 13.

4. Montague, *Smith*, 266.

5. Kent, *Strategic Intelligence*, 96–100.

6. Hitchcock, *Age of Eisenhower*, 93.

7. Eisenhower, *Mandate for Change*, 146.

8. Kiba, *Flag*, 217.

9. Wallace L. Brown, *The Endless Hours: My Two and a Half Years as a Prisoner of the Chinese Communists* (New York: Norton, 1961), 44.

10. Bill Baumer, *The Extended Mission of Stardust Four Zero* (N.p.: Closson Press, 1999), 68.

11. Brown, *Endless Hours*, 44, 148.

12. Brown, 152, 161, 181.

13. Kiba, *Flag*, 52.

14. Kiba, 206.

15. Prados, *Presidents' Secret Wars*, 88–89; Robert Burns, "Soldiers' Cold War Ordeal," Associated Press, August 29, 1998; Haas, *Devil's Shadow*, 116; Michael E. Haas, *Apollo's Warriors: US Air Force Special Operations during the Cold War* (Honolulu: University of Hawai'i Press, 2002), 82–83.

16. Hunt, *Undercover*, 104.

17. White, *Missing in Action*, 37.

18. Kiba, *Flag*, 37.

19. Hutheesing, *Great Peace*, 23.

20. Bao Ruo-wang (Jean Pasqualini) and Rudolph Chelminski, *Prisoner of Mao* (New York: Coward, McCann & Geoghegan, 1973), 43.

21. Downey in *Extraordinary Fidelity.*

22. Kiba, *Flag*, 114–16.

23. Kiely, *Thought Reform*, 252.

24. Kiely, 253.

25. Kiely, 245–48.

26. Robert Jay Lifton, *Thought Reform and the Psychology of Totalism: A Study of "Brainwashing" in China* (New York: Norton, 1961). Lifton did his Hong Kong interviews in 1954–55.

27. Arendt, *Origins of Totalitarianism*, 438.

28. Dikötter, *Tragedy of Liberation*, 246.

29. Rickett and Rickett, *Prisoners of Liberation*, 175.

30. Ford, *Captured in Tibet*, 194.

31. Ford, 237.
32. Ford, 231.
33. Rickett and Rickett, *Prisoners of the Liberation*, 224.
34. Barnett, "Prison Indoctrination," March 1955, in *Communist China*, 115.
35. Hastings, *Korean War*, 318–19.
36. "Kwangtung Provincial Government Commends Border Forces for Annihilating Secret Agents Who Illicitly Crossed the Border," *Southern Daily* (Canton), April 28, 1954, British Foreign Office Files (FO_371-110209_FOLDER_1_1954.pdf), 49.
37. *Kangmei yuanchao zhanzheng shi*, 2:410.
38. Eisenhower, *Mandate for Change*, 230.
39. Hitchcock, *Age of Eisenhower*, 104–6.
40. Eisenhower, *Mandate for Change*, 119.
41. Helms, *Look over My Shoulder*, 106.
42. Gasiorowski and Byrne, *Mohammad Mosaddeq*.
43. Anderson, *Quiet Americans*.
44. Nick Cullather, *Secret History: The CIA's Classified Account of Its Operations in Guatemala, 1952–1954* (Stanford, CA: Stanford University Press, 2006).
45. Harkness, "Mysterious Doings," 66.
46. Harkness, 68.
47. Aid, *Secret Sentry*, 47.
48. The CIA took credit at the time for advising the "pro-American Egyptian military junta" and referred to the overthrow of Mossadegh as a "CIA-influenced triumph" (Harkness, "Mysterious Doings," 66).
49. Kent, *Reminiscences*, 293.
50. Peter L. Mattis and Matthew J. Brazil, *Chinese Communist Espionage: An Intelligence Primer* (Annapolis, MD: Naval Institute Press, 2019), 83–88.
51. Trevelyan, *Living with the Communists*, 82–83. Ford had been accused of espionage in December 1950 (Ford, *Captured in Tibet*, 178).
52. Johnson, *Right Hand of Power*, 233.
53. Johnson, 235.
54. Pocock and Fu, *Black Bats*, 20.
55. "Two Missing Airmen Reported Held by Reds," *New York Times*, March 10, 1953, cited in James D. Sanders, Mark A. Sauter, and R. C. Kirkwood, *Soldiers of Misfortune: Washington's Secret Betrayal of American POWs in the Soviet Union* (Washington, DC: National Press Books, 1992), 16.
56. Zhang Baijia and Jia Qinqguo, "Sino-American Ambassadorial Talks," in *Re-examining the Cold War: U.S.-China Diplomacy, 1954–1973*, ed. Robert S. Ross and Changbin Jiang (Cambridge, MA: Harvard University Press, 2001), 178.
57. CIA, "CIA Personnel Missing in Action," December 4, 1953, CIA-RDP84-00499R00010008-5.
58. Nancy Bernkopf Tucker, *The China Threat: Memories, Myths, and Realities in the 1950s* (New York: Columbia University Press, 2012), 64; Accinelli, *Crisis to Commitment*, 144.
59. Tucker, *China Threat*, 63.
60. "2 U.S. Officers Die in Quemoy Attack by Chinese Reds," *New York Times*, September 5, 1954, 1.
61. Yang Huei Pang, *Strait Ritual: China, Taiwan, and the United States in the Taiwan Strait Crises, 1954–1958* (Hong Kong: Hong Kong University Press, 2019).
62. National Security Council, *Current Policies of the Government of the United States of America Relating to the National Security*, vol. 1, pt. 3, Far East–Communist China (November 7, 1952), 3, available in U.S. Declassified Documents Online, October 23, 2016.

63. Zhang, *Koushu zizhuan*, 389.

64. Nicholas Dujmovic, "Review of *Legacy of Ashes: The History of CIA*," *Studies in Intelligence* 51, no. 3 (2007). Cf. Rositzke, *Secret Operations*, 173; Jeans, *CIA and Third Force*, 171.

65. Jeans, *CIA and Third Force*, 193–95.

66. Zhang, *Koushu zizhuan*, 389.

67. "Kwangtung Provincial Government," *Southern Daily*, April 28, 1954.

68. Zhang, *Koushu zizhuan*, 390, 391, 394.

69. "Eisenhower Frees Chiang to Raid Mainland," *New York Times*, February 3, 1953, 1.

70. Eisenhower, *Mandate for Change*, 551; Breuer, *Shadow Warriors*, 220.

71. Pocock and Fu, *Black Bats*, 19–21.

72. *Neibu cankao*, January 28, 1954, 340–41.

73. *Neibu cankao*, 340–41.

74. *Neibu cankao*, 343. The Dongshan raid is described in Holober, *Raiders*, 195–222.

75. Lin, *Accidental State*, 218.

76. *Neibu cankao*, February 12, 1954, 123–24.

77. *Neibu cankao*, November 18, 1954, 231; *Neibu cankao*, December 6, 1954, 83–84.

78. "Fukien People' Court Sentences U.S.-Chiang Agents," Xinhua, November 10, 1954, British Foreign Office Files (FO_371-110209_FOLDER_1_1954.pdf), 57–59.

79. *Neibu cankao*, December 7, 1954, 94–95.

80. Tucker, *China Threat*, 59.

81. Dunlop, *Donovan*, 501–2.

82. David Wise and Thomas B. Ross, *The Invisible Government* (New York: Bantam, 1962), 141–42.

83. *Neibu cankao*, November 19, 1954, 258.

84. *Neibu cankao*, January 28, 1954, 344–45.

85. "Minutes of the First Meeting between Premier Zhou Enlai and Nehru," October 19, 1954, Wilson Center Digital Archive, https://digitalarchive.wilsoncenter.org/document/117825.pdf?v=d2290588815b029b328f929201e0c81c.

86. Ming-Yeh T. Rawnsley, "Taiwan's Propaganda Cold War: The Offshore Islands Crises of 1954 and 1958," in Aldrich, Rawnsley, and Rawnsley, *Clandestine Cold War in Asia*, 92.

87. Thomas, *Very Best Men*, 155.

88. Andrew Tully, *CIA: The Inside Story* (New York: William Morrow, 1962), 202; Holober, *Raiders*, 222.

89. Rositzke, *Secret Operations*, 38.

12. SUBVERSION ON TRIAL

1. Brown, *Endless Hours*, 215–16, 219, 224.

2. Baumer, *Extended Mission*, 100–101.

3. Fecteau in *Extraordinary Fidelity*.

4. Cohen, *Criminal Process*, 299.

5. "U.S. Spies Admit Espionage Training," New China News Agency, November 26, 1954, British Foreign Office Files (FO_371-110209_FOLDER_1.pdf).

6. Downey in *Extraordinary Fidelity*.

7. "U.S. Spies Admit."

8. Baumer, *Extended Mission*, 103.

9. Daniloff, *Spies and Spokesmen*, 197.

10. Dikötter, *Tragedy of Liberation*, 103–4.

11. Director's Log [OSO], September 10, 1951, 15.

12. Director's Log [OSO], 15.

13. Lum, *Peking*, 25–26.
14. Lum, 89.
15. *Neibu cankao*, August 20, 1951, 49–50.
16. "U.S. Spies Sentenced in Shanghai," Xinhua, September 12, 1954, British Foreign Office Files, British Embassy (Peking) to Far Eastern Department, Foreign Office (London), September 23, 1954, S/O No. 460 (1017/29/54), (FO_371-110209_FOLDER_1_1954.pdf), 39.
17. "U.S. Spies Sentenced."
18. Singlaub, *Hazardous Duty*, 157; cf. Gup, *Book of Honor*, 43–66; Maury Allen, *China Spy: The Story of Hugh Francis Redmond* (Yonkers, NY: Gazette Press, 1998).
19. Director's Log, September 7, 1951, 10.
20. "U.S. Spies Sentenced."
21. *Neibu cankao*, December 6, 1954, 84–85.
22. Dulles, *Craft of Intelligence*, 182.
23. Aid, *Secret Sentry*, 13–23.
24. Eisenhower, *Mandate*, 282.
25. Cited in Jerome Alan Cohen and Hungdah Chiu, *People's China and International Law: A Documentary Survey* (Princeton, NJ: Princeton University Press, 1974), 636.
26. Cited in Cohen and Chiu, 638.
27. Johnson, *Right Hand of Power*, 236.
28. White, *Missing in Action*, 25, 42, 24, 12.
29. Lane to Dulles, January 4, 1954, NARA 611.95A241/1-654, 7–10.
30. "Memorandum: Joint State-Defense Department Background on Efforts to Secure the Return of American Prisoners of War Who Might Still Be Held in Communist Custody," February 1, 1954, NARA 611.95a241/2-154, 1-254, 15–18.
31. Lane to Dulles, November 24, 1954, NARA 611.95A251/11-2454 A/53, 1-254, 41.
32. Mao, *Asia First*.
33. Mao, *Asia First*.
34. "Memorandum Prepared in the Department of Defense for the Operations Coordinating Board," November 24, 1954, *FRUS: 1952–52*, 14.1:408.
35. Dulles to Amconsul Geneva and Amembassy London, November 23, 1954, NARA 611.95A241/11-2354 CS/HHH, 37.
36. Dulles to Amconsul Geneva.
37. "Cases of John T. Downey and Richard Fecteau, Civilians Captured by Chinese Communists during the Korean Hostilities," British Foreign Office Files (FO 1955_FO_371-115178 (110706) Release.pdf), 67.
38. Gowan to Secretary of State, November 29, 1954, NARA 611.95A241/11-2954, 58–59.
39. "Arthur R. Ringwalt [American Embassy London] to C. T. Crowe," FC 10116/13, British Foreign Office Files (1954_FO_371-110209_FOLDER_1.pdf), 90–91.
40. "Memorandum by the Deputy Under Secretary of State (Murphy)," November 24, 1954; *Department of State Bulletin*, December 6, 1954, 611.95A241/11-2954, 856–57.
41. Trevelyan, "From Peking to Foreign Office Telegram 972," November 29, 1954, British Foreign Office Files (FO_371-110209_FOLDER_1.pdf), 148.
42. Trevelyan, *Living with the Communists*, 52, 84.
43. Trevelyan, 84.
44. Crowe, "United States Personnel Imprisoned by the Chinese," November 26, 1954, British Foreign Office Files, FC 10116/13B (FO_371-110209_FOLDER_1_1954.pdf), 85–86.
45. "Memorandum by the Deputy Under Secretary of State (Murphy)," November 24, 1954.

46. "Memorandum by the Director of the Policy Planning Staff (Bowie)," November 26, 1954, *FRUS: 1952–54*, 14.1:410.

47. "World Reactions to Certain Possible US Courses of Action against Communist China," NIE 100-6-54, November 28, 1954, *FRUS: 1952–1954*, 14.1:411.

48. "World Reactions."

49. Quoted in White, *Missing in Action*, 34.

50. Saltonstall to Dulles, December 1, 1954, NARA 611.95A241/12-154 A/53, 70.

51. Dodd to Eisenhower, November 30, 1954, NARA 611.95A241/1-3054 A/35, 99–101.

52. Eisenhower, *Mandate*, 556; *New York Times*, November 28, 1954.

53. United Press, November 25, 1954, NARA 611.94A241/12-354 A/38, 104.

54. "Staff Conference," October 27, 1952, in Warner, *CIA under Truman*, 470.

55. "Memorandum of Telephone Conversation," December 1, 1954, in *FRUS: 1952–54*, 14.1:420.

56. "Release of American Citizens," December 1, 1954, NARA 230 Downey, 6.

57. "Memorandum of Telephone Conversation," 422.

58. "Memorandum of Discussion at the 226th Meeting of the National Security Council," December 1, 1954, in *FRUS, 1952–1954*, 14.1:419.

59. *Public Papers of the Presidents of the United States: Dwight D. Eisenhower, 1954* (Washington, DC: Office of the Federal Register, 1960), 2:1074.

60. *Public Papers of Eisenhower*, 1074, 1076, 1077.

61. *Public Papers of Eisenhower*, 1078.

62. C. T. Crowe, "United States Airmen Imprisoned in China," December 8, 1954, British Foreign Office Files, FC 10116/13C (FO_371-110209_FOLDER_1.pdf), 89, 105.

63. "Memorandum by the Director of the Office of Chinese Affairs (McConaughy) to the Assistant Secretary of State for Far Eastern Affairs (Robertson)," December 9, 1954, in *FRUS: 1952–54*, 14.1:435. See analysis in Daniel Aaron Rubin, "Pawns of the Cold War: John Foster Dulles, the PRC, and the Imprisonments of John Downey and Richard Fecteau" (MA thesis, University of Maryland, College Park, 2004).

64. "Memorandum by . . . McConaughy," December 9, 1954.

65. "Memorandum by . . . McConaughy."

66. Wisner, "American Prisoners Held by the Chinese Communists," December 14, 1954, NARA 2887, 611.95a.251/12-1454.

67. Wisner.

68. White, *Missing in Action*, 36, 35.

69. "Report by the Secretary of State to the National Security Council," October 28, 1954, in *FRUS: 1952–1954*, 14.1:365; "Memorandum by the Secretary of State to the President," November 23, 1954, in *FRUS: 1952–1954*, 14.1:403.

70. "US Hurries to Conclude Talks with Bandit Chiang over Military Aggression Treaty," *People's Daily*, November 29, 1954.

71. "Current U.S. Policy toward the Far East," NSC 5429/5, December 22, 1954, in *FRUS: 1952–54*, 12.1:428; cf. Tucker, *China Threat*, 56, 77.

72. Osgood, *Total Cold War*, 178.

73. Trevelyan, *Living with the Communists*, 33.

74. Trevelyan, 64; Brian DeMare, *Land Wars: The Story of China's Agrarian Revolution* (Stanford, CA: Stanford University Press, 2019), 20–21; Strauss, "Paternalist Terror," 96.

75. Ruth Rogaski, *Hygienic Modernity: Meanings of Health and Disease in Treaty-Port China* (Berkeley: University of California Press, 2014), 294.

76. Hutheesing, *Great Peace*, 214.

77. "Exhibition of U.S. Spies' Equipment," New China News Agency, December 6, 1954, British Foreign Office Files (1954_FO_371-110210_FOLDER_2.pdf), 91–93.

78. "Exhibition of U.S. Spies' Equipment," 97.
79. British Foreign Office Files (1955_FO_371-115023 (110706) Policy [1].pdf), 112.
80. *Neibu cankao*, January 7, 1955, 108–12.
81. Robert Guillain, *600 Million Chinese*, trans. Mervyn Savill (New York: Criteri, 1957), 119–20.
82. Rubin, "Pawns of the Cold War," 30.
83. "Butterworth [London] to Secretary of State [telegram]," December 17, 1954, NARA 611.95A241/12-1754, 187.
84. Trevelyan, *Living with the Communists*, 156.
85. Brown, *Endless Hours*, 238.
86. Mary Downey, with J. Robert Moskin, "My Son Is a Prisoner in Red China," *Look* 24, December 6, 1960, 75.

13. IMPLAUSIBLE DENIAL

1. "British Embassy, Peking, to Far Eastern Department," March 24, 1954, British Foreign Office Files (FO_371-110209_FOLDER_1_1954.pdf), 14.
2. Eden, "Draft Reply to Parliament," December 6, 1954, British Foreign Office Files (1954_FO_371-110210_FOLDER_2), 116.
3. Makings, December 7, 1954, British Foreign Offices Files (1954_FO_371-110210_FOLDER_2.pdf), 129.
4. Trevelyan, January 22, 1955, British Foreign Offices Files (FO_371-115038 (110425) Policy.pdf), 108.
5. Lodge to Dulles, December 2, 1954, NARA 611.95A241/12-254, 85–87.
6. Dulles, "Memorandum of Conversation with Krishna Menon," December 3, 1954, NARA 611.95A241/12-354, 105.
7. Johnson, *Right Hand of Power*, 222.
8. Lodge to Dulles, December 4, 1954, NARA 611.95A241/12-454.
9. "American Fliers in Red China," December 17, 1954, NARA 2887, 611.95A3/12-1754; *Zhou Enlai nianpu* (Beijing: Zhongyang wenxian chubanshe, 1997), 1:627.
10. "US Dept of State Briefing Book for UN Jan mission to Beijing," British Foreign Office Files (1955_FO_371-115178 (110706) Release [7].pdf), 67.
11. White, *Missing in Action*, 46.
12. Brown, *Endless Hours*, 239–42.
13. Brian Urquhart, *Hammarskjold* (New York: Norton, 1994), 109–10.
14. "Record of Meetings between UN Secretary-General Dag Hammarskjöld and Zhou Enlai," January 6, 1955, Wilson Center Digital Archive, https://digitalarchive.wilsoncenter.org/document/122619.pdf?v=c8cf40bc96132f7ee6aa568f0f7335e4
15. Gong Li, "Tension across the Taiwan Strait in the 1950s: Chinese Strategy and Tactics," in Ross and Jiang, *Re-examining the Cold War*, 149.
16. White, *Missing in Action*, 47.
17. Rubin, "Pawns of the Cold War," 39–40.
18. Urquhart, *Hammarskjold*, 115–17.
19. White, *Missing in Action*, 26. Allen Dulles assigned the U-2 spy plane project to Bissell on November 26, 1954; see Dino A. Brugioni, *Eyes in the Sky: Eisenhower, the CIA, and Cold War Aerial Espionage* (Annapolis, MD: Naval Institute Press, 2015), 99–101.
20. Dujmovic, "Extraordinary Fidelity," 13–15.
21. Mao Zedong, *Selected Works*, 5:152.
22. "Joint Resolution by the Congress," January 29, 1955, in *FRUS: 1955–57*, 2;56.
23. Dwight Eisenhower, "The President's News Conference," March 16, 1955, http://www.presidency.ucsb.edu/ws/index.php?pid=10434

24. Richard Wright, *The Color Curtain: A Report on the Bandung Conference* (Jackson, MS: Banner Books, 1994), 129.
25. Trevelyan, *Living with the Communists*, 157–60.
26. Steve Tsang, "Target Zhou Enlai: The 'Kashmir Princess' Incident of 1955," *China Quarterly* 139 (September 1994): 766–82.
27. *People's Daily*, April 17, 1955, British Foreign Office Files (1955/6_FO_371-115141_Folder_9 [1].pdf), 50, 49.
28. Wright, *Color Curtain*, 157.
29. William Worthy Jr., "Bandung in Retrospect," *Baltimore Afro-American*, June 11, 1955, 7.
30. Zhou Enlai, "Supplementary Speech of Premier Zhou Enlai at the Plenary Session of the Asian African Conference," April 15, 1955, Wilson Center Digital Archive, https://digitalarchive.wilsoncenter.org/document/114673.
31. Zhang Baijia, "The Changing International Scene and Chinese Policy toward the United States, 1954–1970," in Ross and Jiang, *Re-examining the Cold War*, 51.
32. Zhang and Jia, "Sino-American Ambassadorial Talks," 180.
33. Zhang and Jia, 182.
34. Brown, *Endless Hours*, 244–46.
35. "Four of U.S. Airmen Freed by Chinese Reds after 'Conviction' in Trial," *New York Times*, May 31, 1955, 1.
36. Eisenhower, *Mandate*, 605.
37. Baumer, *Extended Mission*, 127.
38. White, *Missing in Action*, 35.
39. Johnson, *Right Hand of Power*, 255.
40. Johnson, 242.
41. Tucker, *China Threat*, 97–98.
42. Wang Bingnan, *Zhong-Mei huitan jiunian huigu* (Beijing: Shijie jishi, 1985), 49.
43. Johnson, *Right Hand of Power*, 252–53.
44. Johnson, 249.
45. Rickett and Rickett, *Prisoner of Liberation*, 314–19.
46. John W. Clifford, S. J., *In the Presence of My Enemies* (New York: Norton, 1963), 179–89.
47. Meredith Oyen, *The Diplomacy of Migration: Transnational Lives and the Making of U.S.-Chinese Relations in the Cold War* (Ithaca, NY: Cornell University Press, 2015), 191.
48. John Wilson Lewis and Xue Litai, *China Builds the Bomb* (Stanford, CA: Stanford University Press, 1988); Wise, *Tiger Trap*, 157–58.
49. Iris Chang, *Thread of the Silkworm* (New York: Basic Books, 1995), 188–90.
50. Wang, *Zhong-Mei huitan*, 55–56.
51. Mao Zedong, "Criticism of Liang Shu-ming's Reactionary Ideas," September 16–18, 1953, in *Selected Works*, 5:121–29.
52. Merle Goldman, *Literary Dissent in Communist China* (Cambridge, MA: Harvard University Press, 1967), 129.
53. Mao Zedong, "Opening Speech," March 21, 1955, in *Selected Works*, 5:157.
54. Mao Zedong, "Closing Speech," March 31, 1955, in *Selected Works*, 5:161–68.
55. Mattis and Brazil, *Chinese Communist Espionage*, 44, 129–34; Dutton, *Policing Chinese Politics*, 180–85.
56. Mao Zedong, "In Refutation of 'Uniformity of Public Opinion,'" May 24, 1955, in *Selected Works*, 5:173.
57. Goldman, *Literary Dissent*, 150.
58. "Material on the Counter-revolutionary Hu Feng Clique," May/June 1955, in *Selected Works*, 5:180.

59. Sidney Rittenberg and Amanda Bennett, *The Man Who Stayed Behind* (Durham, NC: Duke University Press, 1993), 189–90.

60. Goldman, *Literary Dissent*, 157; Yang, "Reconsidering," 113; Strauss, "Paternalist Terror."

61. Edward Shils, *The Torment of Secrecy: The Background and Consequences of American Security Policy* (Chicago: Ivan R. Dee, 1996), 61.

62. Johnson, *Right Hand of Power*, 256–58.

63. "Memorandum on the Case of John Thomas Downey," July 16, 1957, NARA 230 Downey.

64. British Foreign Office Files (1955_FO_371-115199_FOLDER_1 [5].pdf), 158.

65. British Foreign Office Files (1955_FO_371-115200_FOLDER_2 [8].pdf), 99.

66. British Foreign Office Files, 44.

67. Brugioni, *Eyes in the Sky*, 126.

68. Richard M. Bissell Jr., with Jonathan E. Lewis and Frances T. Pudlo, *Reflections of a Cold Warrior: From Yalta to the Bay of Pigs* (New Haven, CT: Yale University Press, 1996), 92.

69. Bissell, 112–13.

70. Bissell, 131–38.

71. Pocock and Fu, *Black Bats*, 25; Aid and Richelson, "U.S. Intelligence and China," 8; Sanders, Sauter, and Kirkwood, *Soldiers of Misfortune*, 185; Beverly Shaver, "Truth and Lies," *Washington Post*, May 7, 2006.

72. Pocock and Fu, *Black Bats*, 34–35.

73. Walder, *China under Mao*, 130.

74. Mao Zedong, "On the Ten Major Relationships," in *Selected Works*, 5:297–98.

75. Roderick MacFarquhar, *The Origins of the Cultural Revolution*, vol. 1: *Contradictions among the People 1956–1957* (Oxford: Oxford University Press, 1974), 49.

76. MacFarquhar, 51–56.

77. Lu Xiaoning, *Moulding the Socialist Subject: Cinema and Chinese Modernity (1949–1966)* (Boston: Brill, 2020), 1–34.

78. "US Visitors Tell of 2 Held in China," *New York Times*, September 9, 1957.

79. Goldman, *Literary Dissent*, 178–79.

80. Qiang Zhai, "China's Emerging Role on the World Stage," in *The Regional Cold Wars in Europe, East Asia, and the Middle East: Crucial Period and Turning Points*, ed. Lorenz Lüthi (Stanford, CA: Stanford University Press, 2015), 78–81.

81. Mao Zedong, "Speech at Second Session of Eighth Central Committee," November 15, 1956, in *Selected Works*, 5:342.

82. Mao Zedong, "Talks at a Conference of Secretaries of Provincial, Municipal and Autonomous Region Party Committees," January 18, 1957, in *Selected Works*, 5:353.

83. Goldman, *Literary Dissent*, 184–85.

84. Goldman, *Literary Dissent*, 189–90.

85. Walder, *China under Mao*, 137–39.

86. Goldman, *Literary Dissent*, 191; MacFarquhar, *Origins of the Cultural Revolution*, 219.

87. Rittenberg, *Man Who Stayed Behind*, 213; Goldman, *Literary Dissent*, 192.

88. Walder, *China under Mao*, 146.

89. MacFarquhar, *Origins of the Cultural Revolution*, 262–69.

90. Dikötter, *Tragedy of Liberation*, 292.

91. Kiely, *Thought Reform*, 290–91.

92. Goldman, *Literary Dissent*, 223.

93. Walder, *China under Mao*, 150.

94. Dujmovic, "Extraordinary Fidelity," 12.

14. PRISONERS OF THE PAST

1. Anthony Lewis, "Peiping Lifts Ban on U.S. News Men," *New York Times*, August 7, 1956.

2. Quoted in Roderick MacFarquhar, ed., *Sino-American Relations, 1949–1971* (New York: Praeger, 1972), 131.

3. Mao Zedong, "Strengthen Party Unity and Carry Forward Party Traditions," August 30, 1956, in *Selected Works*, 5:313.

4. "McConaughy to Johnson," January 30, 1957, in *FRUS: 1955–57*, 3:231.

5. Wang, *Zhong-Mei huitan*, 62–64.

6. William Worthy Jr., "Inside the Bamboo Curtain: No Romances in Red China Universities," *Baltimore Afro-American*, March 23, 1957, 4.

7. William Worthy Jr., "Racial Arrogance Gave Birth to Red China, Bill Worthy Reports," *Baltimore Afro-American*, February 2, 1957, 1.

8. Worthy, "Racial Arrogance"; Robeson Taj Frazier, *The East Is Black: Cold War China in Black Radical Imagination* (Durham, NC: Duke University Press, 2015), 72–107.

9. "Ex China Captive Is Dead of Cancer," *New York Times*, May 5, 1961.

10. "General Information on American Citizens Imprisoned in Communist China," NARA 230 Downey Extras, 65–74.

11. "Secretary Dulles' News Conference of February 5," *Department of State Bulletin* no. 922 (1957), 302. It remains unclear if the Chinese side made an actual offer, not to mention whether it would include Downey and Fecteau—Wang Bingnan would later insist that a trade was on the table. "Ex-C.I.A. Man Accuses Dulles," *New York Times*, September 6, 1983, 11; Rubin, "Pawns of the Cold War," 56–59.

12. Dwight Eisenhower, "The President's News Conference," February 6, 1957, https://www.presidency.ucsb.edu/node/234089.

13. Dwight Eisenhower, "The President's News Conference," March 6, 1957, https://www.presidency.ucsb.edu/node/233116.

14. US Congress, *Hearings before the Senate Committee on Foreign Affairs on Department of State Passport Policies*, April 11, 1957, 122.

15. "2 Captives of China Called U.S. Agents," *New York Times*, February 25, 1957, 46.

16. Charles Edmundson, "The Dulles Brothers in Diplomania," *The Nation*, November 9, 1957, 317.

17. White, *Missing in Action*, 75.

18. White, 32.

19. White, 52.

20. British Foreign Office Files (FO 21-663 (110427) Sino-US_1970 [4].PDF), 194.

21. "Memorandum of Conversation: Efforts on Behalf of John Downey, American Prisoner of Chinese Communists," April 15, 1957, NARA 230 Downey.

22. "Efforts on Behalf of John Downey."

23. "Efforts on Behalf of John Downey."

24. McConaughy to Cusack, April 25, 1957, NARA 230 Downey.

25. Gup, *Book of Honor*, 99; Allen, *China Spy*.

26. "Memorandum for Brig. Gen. A. J. Goodpaster, The White House: Request of Mrs. William C. Cusack that the President Receive Mrs. Mary Downey," May 24, 1957, NARA 230 Downey.

27. MacFarquhar, *Sino-American Relations*, 143.

28. MacFarquhar, 176–81.

29. Frederic Grab, "Visitors in Peiping Report 2 Americans in Prison Are Well," *New York Times*, September 8, 1957, 12.

30. "U.S. Visitors Tell of 2 Held in China," *New York Times*, September 9, 1957, 7; Wise and Ross, *Invisible Government*, 115.

31. Robert Cohen, "Inside Red China," NBC (1957).

32. Lodge to Hammarskjöld, September 24, 1957, NARA 230 Downey.

33. Robertson to Downey, November 14, 1957, NARA 230 Downey.

34. Downey to Robertson, November 25, 1957, NARA 230 Downey.

35. "Your Telephone Call to Mrs. Downey," December 5, 1957, NARA 230 Downey.

36. Johnson, *Right Hand of Power*, 260; Dana Adams Schmidt, "U.S. Captives' Kin Ask Chinese Visas," *New York Times*, December 17, 1957, 10.

37. White, *Missing in Action*, 70–71.

38. Downey with Moskin, "My Son," 76.

39. Tillman Durdin, "Five U.S. Citizens Enter Red China," *New York Times*, January 7, 1958, 10; "U.S. Mother Asks Chou to Free Son," *New York Times*, January 12, 1958, 1; Tillman Durdin, "Mothers Hopeful of Red Clemency," *New York Times*, January 27, 1958, 3; Drumright to Dulles, January 17, 1958, NARA 611.95A251/1-1758, RG 59, North Korea Files 1955–1959, Box 2587.

40. Carruthers, *Cold War Captives*, 205–13.

41. Isaacs, *Scratches on Our Minds*, 64.

42. Isaacs, 71.

43. Isaacs, 192–93.

44. James Donovan, *Strangers on a Bridge: The Case of Colonel Abel and Gary Francis Powers* (New York: Scribner, 2015), 71.

45. Donovan, 273–74.

46. Donovan, 281, 282; cf. E. H. Cookridge, *Spy Trade* (New York: Walker and Company, 1971), 86.

47. Conboy and Morrison, *Secret War in Tibet*, 101.

48. Stewart Alsop, "The Story behind Quemoy: How We Drifted Close to War," *Saturday Evening Post*, December 13, 1958.

49. Brugioni, *Eyes in the Sky*, 262–66, 305–6; Gregory W. Pedlow and Donald E. Welzenbach, *The Central Intelligence Agency and Overhead Reconnaissance: The U-2 and OXCART Programs* (Washington, DC: CIA History Staff, 1992), 215.

50. Bissell, *Reflections*, 120; Brugioni, *Eyes in the Sky*, 306–7. The request was eventually approved and and they began flying missions out of Taiwan in the summer of 1960.

51. Cline, *Secrets, Spies, and Scholars*, 176–77.

52. Thomas, *Very Best Men*, 187.

53. Kent, *Reminiscences*, 294.

54. CIA, "Deputies' Meeting," January 19, 1959, 5, CIA-RDP80B01676R002400060146-1.

55. CIA, "Letter to Chester Bowles from Allen W. Dulles," October 4, 1958, CIA-RDP80R01731R000400470003-8.

56. White, *Missing in Action*, 72.

57. White, 56–57.

58. Downey with Moskin, "My Son," 77.

59. White, *Missing in Action*, 74.

60. Downey with Moskin, "My Son," 78.

61. Rowe, *Modern China*, 97.

62. Rowe, 99, 83, 77.

63. Rowe, 97.

64. For more on CIA contacts with the brothers, see Conboy and Morrison, *Secret War in Tibet*.

65. Gyalo and Thurston, *Noodle Maker of Kalimpong*, 169.

66. Mao Zedong, "Speech at Second Session of Eighth Central Committee," November 15, 1956, in *Selected Works*, 5:346.

67. Dalai Lama, *My Land and My People: The Original Autobiography of His Holiness the Dalai Lama of Tibet* (New York: Grand Central, 1997), 103–8.

68. Dalai Lama, 132.

69. Conboy and Morrison, *Secret War in Tibet*, 39–46.

70. Carole McGranahan, *Arrested Histories: Tibet, the CIA, and Memories of a Forgotten War* (Durham, NC: Duke University Press, 2010), 95.

71. Conboy and Morrison, *Secret War in Tibet*, 69.

72. John Kenneth Knaus, *Beyond Shangri-La: America and Tibet's Move into the Twenty-First Century* (Durham, NC: Duke University Press, 2012), 116; Conboy and Morrison, *Secret War in Tibet*, 58–65.

73. Conboy and Morrison, *Secret War in Tibet*, 71.

74. Helms, *Look over My Shoulder*, 162.

75. Gyalo and Thurston, *Noodle Maker of Kalimpong*, 177–78; Conboy and Morrison, *Secret War in Tibet*, 74.

76. Weiner, *Chinese Revolution*, 172, 187.

77. Conboy and Morrison, *Secret War in Tibet*, 86–89.

78. Knaus, *Beyond Shangri-La*, 120; Conboy and Morrison, *Secret War in Tibet*, 79.

79. Conboy and Morrison, *Secret War in Tibet*, 91.

80. Conboy and Morrison, 98–99.

81. McGranahan, *Arrested Histories*, 133. Gyalo estimates over 250 agents were trained between 1957 and 1963 (Gyalo and Thurston, *Noodle Maker of Kalimpong*, 201).

82. McGranahan, *Arrested Histories*, 104.

83. Brugioni, *Eyes in the Sky*, 277.

84. Conboy and Morrison, *Secret War in Tibet*, 102–5.

85. Gyalo and Thurston, *Noodle Maker of Kalimpong*, 186–87; Conboy and Morrison, *Secret War in Tibet*, 132–33.

86. Gyalo and Thurston, *Noodle Maker of Kalimpong*, 205–7.

87. Gyalo and Thurston, 296, 202.

88. Francis Gary Powers, with Curt Gentry, *Operation Overflight: A Memoir of the U-2 Incident* (Washington, DC: Brassey's, 2004), 49–56.

89. Tully, *CIA: Inside Story*, 128.

90. Cookridge, *Spy Trade*, 42.

91. Donovan, *Strangers*, 362.

92. John F. Kennedy, "The President's News Conference," January 25, 1961, http://www.presidency.ucsb.edu/ws/index.php?pid=8533.

93. "Release of Melekh," September 1961, John F. Kennedy Library, https://www.jfklibrary.org/asset-viewer/archives/JFKNSF/331/JFKNSF-331-020. Cookridge speculated the spies were traded for Olmstead and McCone (*Spy Trade*, 71–84).

94. Cookridge, *Spy Trade*, 92.

95. Dulles, *Craft of Intelligence*, 114, 184.

96. Yang Jisheng, *Tombstone: The Great Chinese Famine, 1958–1962*, trans. Stacy Mosher and Guo Jian (New York: Farrar, Straus and Giroux, 2012); Zhou Xun, ed., *The Great Famine in China, 1958–1962* (New Haven, CT: Yale University Press, 2012); Frank Dikötter, *Mao's Great Famine* (New York: Walker, 2010).

97. Lorenz M. Lüthi, *The Sino-Soviet Split: Cold War in the Communist World* (Princeton, NJ: Princeton University Press, 2008).

98. Edgar Snow, *The Other Side of the River: Red China Today* (New York: Random House, 1962), 90; Edgar Snow, "Red China's Leaders Talk Peace on Their Terms," *Look* 25 (January 31, 1961).

99. Snow, *Other Side of the River*, 366.

100. "AmConGeneral, Hong Kong to Department of State," September 2, 1960, NARA 293.1111 Downey.

101. John Maxwell Hamilton, *Snow: A Biography* (Baton Rouge: Louisiana State University Press, 2003), 237–38.

102. "Ex China Captive Is Dead of Cancer," *New York Times*, May 5, 1961.

103. Colby, *Honorable Men*, 184.

104. Wise and Ross, *Invisible Government*, 205.

105. Bruce Riedel, *JFK's Forgotten Crisis: Tibet, the CIA, and the Sino-Indian War* (Washington, DC: Brookings Institution Press, 2015), 57–58.

106. Riedel, 60.

107. Conboy and Morrison, *Secret War in Tibet*, 161–63.

108. Joshua Kurlantzick, *A Great Place to Have a War: America in Laos and the Birth of a Military CIA* (New York: Simon & Schuster, 2016).

109. Gibson, *Secret Army*, 191–224.

110. "Remarks upon Presenting the National Security Medal to Allen W. Dulles," November 28, 1961, John F. Kennedy Library, https://www.jfklibrary.org/asset-viewer/archives/JFKWHA/1961/JFKWHA-058-003/JFKWHA-058-003.

111. Lilley, *China Hands*, 100.

112. John W. Garver, *The Sino-American Alliance: Nationalist China and American Cold War Strategy in Asia* (Armonk, NY: M. E. Sharpe, 1997), 103–8.

113. Aid and Richelson, "U.S. Intelligence and China," 14.

114. "Nationalist U-2 Downed by Reds over East China," *New York Times*, September 10, 1962, 1.

115. Paul W. Blackstock, *The Strategy of Subversion: Manipulating the Politics of Other Nations* (Chicago: Quadrangle Books, 1964), 303–4.

116. Blackstock, 321, 40.

117. Blackstock, 305.

118. Blackstock, 33.

119. Blackstock, 43.

120. Blackstock, 310.

121. Blackstock, 190.

122. Harry S. Truman, *Washington Post*, December 22, 1963, quoted in Wise and Ross, *Invisible Government*, 101.

123. British Foreign Office Files (1962_FO 371-164906 (110603) Sino-US [3].pdf).

15. WAR AND REVOLUTION

1. Robert Dallek, *Flawed Giant: Lyndon B. Johnson and His Times, 1961–1973* (New York: Oxford University Press, 1999), 100.

2. Prados, *Presidents' Secret Wars*, 239–55.

3. Thomas L. Ahern Jr., *The Way We Do Things: Black Entry Operations into North Vietnam* (Washington, DC: Center for the Study of Intelligence, 2005).

4. Stanley Karnow, *Vietnam: A History* (New York: Penguin, 1997), 360–61, 372.

5. Fredrik Logevall, *Choosing War: The Lost Chance for Peace and the Escalation of War in Vietnam* (Berkeley: University of California Press, 2001).

6. David Halberstam, *The Best and the Brightest* (New York: Random House, 1992), 408.

7. Halberstam, 547.

8. Robert A. Caro, *The Years of Lyndon Johnson: The Passage of Power* (New York: Knopf, 2013), 530; Halberstam, *Best and the Brightest*, 362.

9. Lyndon B. Johnson, "Address at Johns Hopkins University: Peace without Conquest," April 7, 1965, https://www.presidency.ucsb.edu/node/241950; Dror Yuravlivker,

"'Peace without Conquest': Lyndon Johnson's Speech of April 7, 1965," *Presidential Studies Quarterly* 36, no. 3 (2006): 457–81.

10. Hans Morgenthau, "We Are Deluding Ourselves in Vietnam," *New York Times*, April 18, 1965, E25.

11. Jennifer W. See, "A Prophet without Honor: Hans Morgenthau and the War in Vietnam, 1955–1965," *Pacific Historical Review* 70, no. 3 (2001): 439.

12. "Kennan Bids U.S. Reduce Asia Role," *New York Times*, February 26, 1965, 3; Heer, *Mr. X and the Pacific*, 199–212.

13. Logevall, *Choosing War*, 373; Min Yong Lee, "The Vietnam War: South Korea's Search for National Security," in *The Park Chung Hee Era: The Transformation of South Korea*, ed. Byung-kuk Kim and Ezra Vogel (Cambridge, MA: Harvard University Press, 2011), 403–28.

14. Covell F. Meyskens, *Mao's Third Front: The Militarization of Cold War China* (Cambridge: Cambridge University Press, 2020), 2.

15. Roderick MacFarquhar and Michael Schoenhals, *Mao's Last Revolution* (Cambridge, MA: Harvard University Press, 2006), 20–27.

16. MacFarquhar and Schoenhals, 32–51.

17. John Byron and Robert Pack, *The Claws of the Dragon: Kang Sheng* (New York: Simon & Schuster, 1992), 300–316.

18. Jeremy Brown and Matthew D. Johnson, *Maoism at the Grassroots: Everyday Life in China's Era of High Socialism* (Cambridge, MA: Harvard University Press, 2015); Yang Jisheng, *The World Turned Upside Down: A History of the Cultural Revolution* (New York: Farrar, Straus and Giroux, 2021).

19. Daniloff, *Spies and Spokesmen*, 197–98.

20. Philip E. Smith and Peggy Herz, *Journey into Darkness* (New York: Pocket Book, 1992), 161.

21. Smith and Herz, 173, 192, 192–95.

22. Robert Mann, *A Grand Delusion: America's Descent into Vietnam* (New York: Basic Books, 2002), 293.

23. Alessandro Brogi, Giles Scott-Smith, and David J. Snyder, eds., *The Legacy of J. William Fulbright: Policy, Power, and Ideology* (Lexington: University Press of Kentucky, 2019).

24. J. William Fulbright, *The Arrogance of Power* (New York: Random House, 1966), 8.

25. Kennan's photo was featured on the front page and he was profiled as the Man in the News ("Scholar Diplomat: George Frost Kennan," *New York Times*, February 11, 1966, 1, 2).

26. George F. Kennan, February 10, 1966, in *Supplemental Foreign Assistance, Fiscal Year 1966—Vietnam: Hearings before the Senate Committee on Foreign Relations* (Washington, DC: US Government Printing Office, 1966), 386.

27. Kennan, 354, 422.

28. Kennan, 371.

29. Kennan, 387.

30. A. Doak Barnett, March 8, 1966, in *U.S. Policy with Respect to Mainland China: Hearings before the United States Senate Committee on Foreign Relations* (Washington, DC: Government Printing Office, 1966), 3 (hereafter *China: Hearings*).

31. Barnett, 4; E. W. Kenworthy, "China Expert Urges U.S. to Ease Policy," *New York Times*, March 9, 1966, 1, 7.

32. Fairbank, March 10, 1966, in *China: Hearings*, 166.

33. Fairbank, 146.

34. Fairbank, 106.

35. Fairbank, 144.

36. Fairbank, 123.

37. E. W. Kenworthy, "China Expert Says U.S. Is Overreacting to Peking," *New York Times*, March 11, 1966; Tom Wicker, "The Peking Enigma," *New York Times*, March 11, 1966, 14.

38. Reinhold Niebuhr, "Fears of China," *New York Times*, March 20, 1966, E15. Fulbright read Niebuhr's statement into the record during the hearings (*China: Hearings*, 432).

39. Rowe, March 28, 1966, in *China: Hearings*, 523.

40. Rowe, 497.

41. Rowe, 500.

42. Rowe, 528.

43. Rowe, 500.

44. Rowe, 504.

45. Rowe, 538.

46. Rowe, 541.

47. E. W. Kenworthy, "3 Experts Defend U.S. China Policy," *New York Times*, March 29, 1966, 1, 4.

48. John N. Thomas, *The Institute of Pacific Relations: Asian Scholars and American Politics* (Seattle: University of Washington Press, 1974), 127.

49. John H. Fenton, "Lattimore Calls U.S. Policy in Asia an Increasingly Disastrous Failure," *New York Times*, March 27, 1966, 21.

50. "Lattimore Terms American Policy in Vietnam a 'Mess,'" *New York Times*, March 29, 1966, 4.

51. Morgenthau, March 30, 1966, in *China: Hearings*, 552.

52. Morgenthau, 559.

53. Morgenthau, 587.

54. Morgenthau, 565

55. Morgenthau, 601.

56. E. W. Kenworthy, "U.S. Urged to Seek a Moderate China," *New York Times*, March 31, 1966, 1, 10.

57. Hans J. Morgenthau, *Truth and Power: Essays of A Decade, 1960–70* (New York: Praeger, 1970), 6.

58. Morgenthau, 4.

59. Hans J. Morgenthau, "Truth and Power," November 1966, in *Truth and Power*, 22.

60. Logevall, *Choosing War*, 298; Randall Bennett Woods, *Fulbright: A Biography* (New York: Cambridge University Press, 1995), 407–8.

61. Sol Stern, "A Short Account of International Student Politics and the Cold War with Particular Reference to the NSA and CIA, Etc.," *Ramparts* 5 (March 1967), 31.

62. Hans J. Morgenthau, "How Totalitarianism Starts: The Domestic Involvement of the CIA," March 1967, in *Truth and Power*, 51–55.

63. Hannah Arendt, "Preface to Part Two: Imperialism," June 1967, in *Origins of Totalitarianism*, xx.

64. Halberstam, *Best and the Brightest*, 366.

65. Karnow, *Vietnam*, 512.

66. Kurlantzick, *America in Laos*, 141.

67. Mark Bowden, *Hue 1968: A Turning Point of the American War in Vietnam* (New York: Atlantic Monthly Press, 2018).

68. Martin Luther King Jr., "Beyond Vietnam: A Time to Break Silence," April 4, 1967; Michael Herr, *Dispatches* (New York: Knopf, 1968), 158–59.

69. Elisabeth Young-Bruehl, *Hannah Arendt: For Love of the World* (New Haven, CT: Yale University Press, 2004), 420–21.

70. Hans J. Morgenthau, "Nixon vs. Humphrey," November 1968, in *Truth and Power*, 205.

71. Morgenthau, 206.

72. "Memorandum for President-Elect Nixon on US Relations with China," November 6, 1968, in *Congressional Record: Senate, Extension of Remarks* (Washington, DC: Government Printing Office, 1970), 116.31:41256.

73. Henry Kissinger, *White House Years* (New York: Simon & Schuster, 2011), 165.

74. "U.S. Cautioned on Its China Policy," *New York Times*, December 30, 1968, 20.

16. RELEASE

1. Suri, *Kissinger*, 44.

2. Greg Grandin, *Kissinger's Shadow: The Long Reach of America's Most Controversial Statesman* (New York: Metropolitan Books, 2015), 13.

3. Hugh Wilford, *The Mighty Wurlitzer: How the CIA Played America* (Cambridge, MA: Harvard University Press, 2008), 124–28.

4. Walter Isaacson, *Kissinger: A Biography* (New York: Faber and Faber, 1992), 72–73; Ferguson, *Kissinger*, 285.

5. Shannon E. Mohan, "'Memorandum for Mr. Bundy': Henry Kissinger as Consultant to the Kennedy National Security Council," *Historian* 71, no. 2 (2009): 234–57.

6. Ferguson, *Kissinger*, 623–56, 753–62.

7. Suri, *Kissinger*, 202–3.

8. Richard M. Nixon, "Asia after Viet Nam," *Foreign Affairs* 46, no. 1 (October 1967): 121.

9. Mark Philip Bradley and Mary L. Dudziak, eds., *Making the Forever War: Marilyn B. Young on the Culture and Politics of American Militarism* (Amherst, MA: University of Massachusetts Press, 2021), 150.

10. Ben Kiernan, *How Pol Pot Came to Power: Colonialism, Nationalism, and Communism in Cambodia, 1930–1975* (New Haven, CT: Yale University Press, 2004), 285–88.

11. Kissinger, *White House Years*, 163.

12. Henry Kissinger, "Memorandum for Mr. Price," February 14, 1969, CIA CREST/LOC-HAK-1-1-35-0.

13. Kissinger, *White House Years*, 684.

14. Seymour M. Hersh, *The Price of Power: Kissinger in the Nixon White House* (New York: Summit Books, 1983), 83–97.

15. Kiernan, *Pol Pot*, 297–308.

16. Karnow, *Vietnam*, 609.

17. Geoffrey Kabaservice, *The Guardians: Kingman Brewster, His Circle, and the Rise of the Liberal Establishment* (New York: Henry Holt, 2004).

18. John Bew, *Realpolitik: A History* (New York: Oxford University Press, 2016), 262.

19. MacFarquhar and Schoenhals, *Last Revolution*, 301–7, 345–56.

20. Kerrison, *Bishop Walsh*.

21. Kissinger, *White House Years*, 697; Gup, *Book of Honor*, 216.

22. Hamilton, *Snow*, 254–74.

23. Kissinger, *White House Years*, 699.

24. Li Zhisui, *The Private Life of Chairman Mao: The Memoirs of Mao's Personal Physician Dr. Li Zhisui* (New York: Random House, 1994), 106.

25. Patrick Tyler, *A Great Wall: Six Presidents and China, An Investigative History* (New York: Public Affairs, 2000), 85–86.

26. Kissinger, *White House Years*, 702.

27. Alexander Pantsov and Steven I. Levine, *Mao: The Real Story* (New York: Simon & Schuster, 2012), 557.

28. John King Fairbank, "The Time Is Ripe for China to Shift Outward Again," *New York Times*, April 18, 1971, E1.

29. Gary Bass, *The Blood Telegram: Nixon, Kissinger, and A Forgotten Genocide* (New York: Knopf, 2014).

30. Tyler, *Great Wall*, 78.

31. Janny Scott, "Now It Can Be Told: How Neil Sheehan Got the Pentagon Papers," *New York Times*, January 7, 2021.

32. Hannah Arendt, "Lying in Politics: Reflections on the Pentagon Papers," in *Crises of the Republic* (New York: Harcourt Brace Jovanovich, 1972), 4.

33. Robert Dallek, *Nixon and Kissinger: Partners in Power* (New York: Harper Collins, 2007), 312.

34. Hersh, *Price of Power*, 390–96.

35. George C. Herring, *America's Longest War: The United States and Vietnam, 1950–1975* (New York: Wiley, 1979), 264–67.

36. Jerome A. Cohen, June 25, 1971, in *United States Relations with the People's Republic of China: Hearings before the United States Senate Committee on Foreign Relations* (Washington, DC: Government Printing Office, 1972), 152–53 (hereafter *People's Republic of China: Hearings*).

37. Cohen, 153.

38. Terence Smith, "Specialists Urge Ties with Peking," *New York Times*, June 26, 1971, 9.

39. Alexander S. Dominick, ed., *Flying the Hump: The War Diary of Peter H. Dominick* (Green Bay, WI: M&B Global Solutions, 2018).

40. Peter Dominick, June 28, 1971, in *People's Republic of China: Hearings*, 156, 161.

41. David Nelson Rowe, June 28, 1971, in *People's Republic of China: Hearings*, 175.

42. Terence Smith, "3 Ask to Release China '53 Study," *New York Times*, June 29, 1971, 10.

43. Richard M. Nixon, *RN: The Memoirs of Richard Nixon* (New York: Warner Books, 1979), 553.

44. Henry Kissinger, "Americans Detained in China," June 28, 1971, in CIA CREST LOC-HAK-464-6-1-9.

45. "Memorandum for the President's File," in *FRUS: 1969–1976*, 17:137.

46. Kissinger, "Americans Detained."

47. Jerome Alan Cohen, "Will Jack Make His 25th Reunion," *New York Times*, July 7, 1971, 37.

48. Winston Lord, "Memcon of Your Conversation with Chou En-lai," July 29, 1971, in *The Beijing-Washington Back-Channel and Henry Kissinger's Secret Trip to China*, National Security Archive Electronic Briefing Book No. 66, ed. William Burr (Washington, DC: National Security Archive, 2002), 34:3, https://nsarchive2.gwu.edu/NSAEBB/NSAEBB66/#docs.

49. Lord, 15.

50. Lord, 39–40.

51. Lord, 9.

52. "Memcon, Kissinger and Zhou," July 11, 1971, in Burr, *Beijing-Washington Back-Channel*, 38:10.

53. "Message from Kissinger to Haig," July 11, 1971, in Burr, *Beijing-Washington Back-Channel*, 39:2.

54. Henry Kissinger, "My Talks with Chou En-lai," July 14, 1971, in Burr, *Beijing-Washington Back-Channel*, 40:1.

55. Evelyn Goh, *Constructing the U.S. Rapprochement with China, 1961–1974: From 'Red Menace' to 'Tacit Ally'* (New York: Cambridge University Press, 2005), 216–18.

56. *FRUS: 1969–76*, 17:164n15.

57. "Memoranda of Conversation, Beijing, October 20, 1971, 4:30–4:40 p.m. and 4:40–7:10 p.m.," in *FRUS: 1969–76*, E-13:36.

58. "Memorandum of Conversation, Beijing, October 21, 1971, 10:30 a.m.–1:45 p.m.," in *FRUS: 1969–76*, 17:162.

59. "Memorandum of Conversation, Beijing, October 21, 1971, 10:30 a.m.—1:45 p.m.," in *FRUS: 1969–76*, 17:162.

60. "Memorandum of Conversation, Beijing," in *FRUS: 1969–76*, 17:162.

61. "Memorandum of Conversation, Beijing, October 22, 1971, 4:15–8:28 p.m.," in *FRUS: 1969–76*, E-13:44.

62. "Memorandum of Conversation, Beijing, October 23, 1971, 9:05–10:05 p.m.," in *FRUS: 1969–76*, E-13:48. Admiral John S. McCain was Commander-in-Chief of Pacific Command.

63. "Memorandum of Conversation, Beijing," in *FRUS: 1969–76*, E-13:48.

64. "Memorandum of Conversation, Beijing, October 26, 1971, 5:30–8:10 p.m.," in *FRUS: 1969–76*, E-13:55.

65. "Memorandum from the President's Assistant for National Security Affairs (Kissinger) to President Nixon," November 1971, in *FRUS: 1969–76*, 17:164.

66. "Mother Says Downey Is Hopeful China Will Set Him Free Soon," *New York Times*, November 15, 1971, CIA CREST RRDP83-00764R000300070007-6.

67. "Message from Nancy Oullette to the President's Deputy Assistant for National Security Affairs (Haig), Paris, December 10, 1971," in *FRUS: 1969–76*, E-13:72.

68. "Chinese Release Fecteau But Keep Downey in Prison," *New York Times*, December 13, 1971, 1, 25; "Nixon Made Appeal to China to Release American Captives," *New York Times*, December 14, 1971, 1, 6; Jerome Alan Cohen, "China's Prisoners: Pawns in a Game of Peking Chess," *New York Times*, December 15, 1971, E3.

69. "Memorandum of Conversation," February 21, 1972, in *The Kissinger Transcripts: The Top Secret Talks with Beijing and Moscow*, ed. William Burr (New York: Norton, 1998), 62.

70. "Memorandum of Conversation," 60.

71. Nixon, *RN*, 580.

72. Smith and Herz, *Journey*, 220.

73. Margaret Macmillan, *Nixon and Mao: The Week That Changed the World* (New York: Random House, 2007), 273–75.

74. Lien-Hang T. Nguyen, *Hanoi's War: An International History of the War for Peace in Vietnam* (Chapel Hill, NC: University of North Carolina Press, 2012), 250–51.

75. Karnow, *Vietnam*, 636, 642.

76. Herring, *America's Longest War*, 285.

77. Nixon, "The President's News Conference," January 31, 1973, https://www.presidency.ucsb.edu/documents/the-presidents-news-conference-86.

78. Eric Pace, "Nixon Acknowledges American Jailed in China Is C.I.A. Agent," *New York Times*, February 1, 1973, 17.

79. "Memorandum from John H. Holdridge of the National Security Council Staff to the President's Assistant for National Security Affairs (Kissinger)," January 18, 1973, in *FRUS: 1969–76*, 18:4.

80. "Memorandum of Conversation, Beijing, February 17, 1973, 2:20–6:25 p.m.," in *FRUS: 1969–76*, 18:10.

81. "Memorandum of Conversation," February 17, 1973, in Burr, *Kissinger Transcripts*, 87–88.

82. Burr, *Kissinger Transcripts*, 88.

83. "Memorandum from the President's Assistant for National Security Affairs (Kissinger) to President Nixon," February 27, 1973, in *FRUS: 1969–76*, 18:17.

84. "Conversation between President Nixon and his Assistant for National Security Affairs (Kissinger)," February 21, 1973, in *FRUS: 1969–76*, 18:15.

85. "Conversation No. 859-32," February 21, 1973, *Nixon White House Tapes*, Nixon Presidential Library and Museum, https://web.archive.org/web/20160905062551/https://www.nixonlibrary.gov/forresearchers/find/tapes/tape859/859-032.mp3.

86. R. W. Apple Jr., "U.S. and China Will Soon Set Up Offices in Capitals for Liaison," *New York Times*, February 23, 1973, 1, 15.

87. "Conversation No. 875-2," March 9, 1973, *Nixon White House Tapes*, Nixon Presidential Library and Museum.

88. "Conversation No. 875-4," March 9, 1973, *Nixon White House Tapes*, Nixon Presidential Library and Museum; *Weekly Compilation of Presidential Documents* (1973), 9:245.

89. "China to Free Downey of the C.I.A. Monday," *New York Times*, March 10, 1973, 1.

90. Henry Kissinger, *Years of Upheaval* (Boston: Little, Brown, 1982), 70.

91. Downey in *Extraordinary Fidelity*.

92. "Downey Back Home to Visit His Mother," *New York Times*, March 13, 1973, 1.

93. Lawrence Fellows, "Downey Is Doubtful His Imprisonment 'Benefited Anyone,'" *New York Times*, March 14, 1973, 1, 6.

94. "Conversation between President Nixon and His Assistant for National Security Affairs (Kissinger)," March 12, 1973, in *FRUS: 1969–76*, 18:20.

EPILOGUE

1. Richard Nixon, "The President's News Conference," March 15, 1973, https://www.presidency.ucsb.edu/documents/the-presidents-news-conference-85.

2. Carl Bernstein and Bob Woodward, *All the President's Men* (New York: Simon & Schuster, 1974).

3. Nixon, *RN*, 783.

4. Arendt, "Lying in Politics," 36.

5. Seymour M. Hersh, "Huge C.I.A. Operation Reported in U.S. against Antiwar Forces, Other Dissidents in Nixon Years," *New York Times*, December 22, 1973, 1.

Index

Index note: page locators in *italics* denote a photograph on the page.